The social and political thought
of R.G. Collingwood

The social and political thought of R.G. Collingwood

DAVID BOUCHER

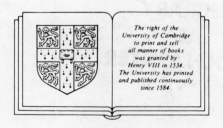

The right of the
University of Cambridge
to print and sell
all manner of books
was granted by
Henry VIII in 1534.
The University has printed
and published continuously
since 1584.

CAMBRIDGE UNIVERSITY PRESS

Cambridge

New York   New Rochelle   Melbourne   Sydney

Published by the Press Syndicate of the University of Cambridge
The Pitt Building, Trumpington Street, Cambridge CB2 1RP
32 East 57th Street, New York, NY 10022, USA
10 Stamford Road, Oakleigh, Melbourne 3166, Australia

© Cambridge University Press 1989

First published 1989

Printed in the United States of America

Library of Congress Cataloging-in-Publication Data
Boucher, David.
The social and political thought of R.G. Collingwood.
Includes index.
1. Collingwood, R.G. (Robin George), 1889–1943 –
Contributions in political science. 2. Collingwood,
R.G. (Robin George), 1889–1943 – Contributions in
sociology. I. Title.
JC257.C6B68   1989   320′.092′4   88 – 28535
ISBN 0-521-36384-5 (hard covers)

British Library Cataloging-in-Publication applied for

To
Clare, Emma, and Lucy,
and my three sisters,
Elaine, Diane, and Hilary

You cannot say, or guess, for you know only
A heap of broken images, where the sun beats,
And the dead tree gives no shelter, the cricket no relief,
And the dry stone no sound of water.

T.S. Eliot

Do not go gentle into that good night,
Old age should burn and rave at close of day;
Rage, rage against the dying of the light.

Dylan Thomas

Contents

Preface

My aim throughout this book has been to construct, with reference to the unpublished and published works of Collingwood, a faithful representation of his social and political thought. I have attempted to articulate a theory that is consistent with his many concerns, and that brings together material from disparate sources in order to present a contingently related whole whose parts serve to illuminate each other. Because such an exercise has not been undertaken previously, the emphasis of this study is upon achieving an understanding of Collingwood's complex concerns rather than upon criticizing his conclusions. Criticism is, of course, wholly legitimate, but I leave that work to others who may wish to explore Collingwood's social and political thought further. I have set myself the strictly limited objective of understanding what Collingwood was trying to do, and this has often entailed understanding what many of his contemporaries were doing.

I say nothing here about my methodological predilections, although I am aware that it has become almost obligatory to do so in recent studies in the history of political thought. For those who are interested in my views on methodology, I refer you to my article 'Conversation and Interpretation' (*New Literary History,* 1986), in which I put forward an essentially constructivist view of history, derived from such theorists as Bradley, Oakeshott, Gadamer, and Ricoeur.

I began the work for this book while still a tutorial fellow in University College, Cardiff. I look back with affection at my former colleagues in the Department of Politics who created a most congenial atmosphere in which to work. I was extremely fortunate, and I owe my good fortune largely to Professor Joan Rydon, to whom I am deeply indebted, in being able to continue my research in La Trobe University, Australia. I hope that Professor Rydon's faith in me will be at least partially rewarded by the publication of this book.

The staff in the reference section of La Trobe University Library and in the Modern Manuscripts Reading Room in the Bodleian Library at Oxford deserve the highest praise for their unfailingly courteous help. The research undertaken in the Bodleian Library was generously funded by the Nuffield Foundation, England, and the School of Social Sciences Research Committee at La Trobe University. I am grateful to Mrs. Teresa Smith, Collingwood's daughter, for consenting to meet me to discuss the project on a number of occasions while I was in Oxford and for granting me permission to quote from the unpublished manuscripts of her father.

Sincere thanks are due to Conal Condren, Andrew Vincent, and James Connelly, who read and commented upon some of the material which forms the chapters of this book. Their suggestions for improvement were invaluable. Tariq Modood has read most of the typescript and discussed many of the ideas with me. To Tariq I owe a considerable debt, both for his critical appraisal of the chapters and, with his wife, Glyn (and daughter Ghiz), for making me thoroughly welcome in Oxford. W.J. van der Dussen and Peter Nicholson considered the arguments with scrupulous care and saved me from some major and minor errors. Rex Martin, the reader for Cambridge University Press, made many invaluable suggestions for improvement, and I am grateful for the very sound advice offered me. I wish the result could better reflect the quality of advice so unselfishly given. All the deficiencies which remain are my sole responsibility.

It was Bernard Bosanquet who felt that his philosophy was the result of the work of a whole generation of thinkers and that he was the vehicle of the thought of his age. Similarly, this study owes much to those Collingwood scholars who have with unrelenting effort gone beyond the published works to discover sources which illuminate and modify the more public sources. W.J. van der Dussen has been important in this respect, but in particular I would like to thank Peter Johnson and James Connelly, both of the University of Southampton, who alerted me to many items of correspondence still extant and generously supplied me with copies of some of these – for example, the Knox correspondence and the Clarendon Press Archive letters.

All the secretaries in the Department of Politics have had a hand in producing the typescript of this book. I am deeply grateful to Liz Byrne for typing, with remarkable efficiency and tireless perseverance, the greatest portion. I would also like to thank Marilu Espacio, Louise Gigliotti, and Mary Zaccari for their similarly efficient contributions to the completion of the typescript. Without secretarial assistance of this quality my task would have been much more burdensome. The index for the book was produced in the History of Ideas Unit, Australian National University.

Finally, Clare, my wife, and Emma, my daughter, have contributed more than they know to the writing of this book, and to them I offer my love and appreciation. I also extend my love to Lucy, who arrived after the book was completed.

David Boucher
La Trobe University, Melbourne
Australian National University, Canberra

1

Collingwood in context

1. Introduction

It has now become commonplace to refer to R. G. Collingwood as an unduly neglected thinker. Agnes Heller, for instance, expressed this view only a few years ago in dedicating her book *A Theory of History*[1] to the memory of Collingwood. Collingwood may still be undervalued among Heller's sociological colleagues, but philosophers of history and historians of ideas have come to acknowledge his significance. However, it is still essentially correct to suggest that aspects of Collingwood's work suffer relative neglect. One such area is his political philosophy. This is all the more surprising when one considers that in the early days of the Second World War Collingwood put aside his lifelong ambition to bring to fruition his mature thoughts on the philosophy of history and instead decided to devote his remaining energies to 'recovering the hard boiled Hobbesian attitude to politics',[2] in an endeavour to make sense of the crisis in twentieth-century European civilization. In a letter to O. G. S. Crawford, Collingwood made it clear that he regarded it as a 'public service' to articulate and publish his thoughts on 'the first principles of politics'.[3] The result was the publication of *The New Leviathan,* which, of all the books published in his own lifetime, received the most favourable and enthusiastic reviews.[4] Very little attention has been given to Collingwood's political philosophy subsequent to the initial responses to the publication of one of the few attempts in the first half of the twentieth century to expound a 'grand theory' of politics. Grand theory is once again becoming a respectable and fashionable intellectual pursuit,[5] which serves to underplay or disguise the distinct novelty of the emergence of a book such as *The New Leviathan* from the walls of the Oxford colleges in the 1940s. Isolated studies of Collingwood's political philosophy have appeared from time to time, and some intrepid Ph.D. students have attempted to unravel the

1

complexities of this aspect of his work,[6] but on the whole scholars tend to be rather dismissive of his political theory. Indeed, in a relatively recent examination of Collingwood's political theory an eminent Conservative intellectual, Maurice Cowling, simply brushed aside *The New Leviathan* as the muddled thoughts of a dying man.[7]

Given the immense reputation in philosophy of history, aesthetics, philosophy of science, and hermeneutic theory that Collingwood has posthumously acquired, the time has come to look once again at his political philosophy. This aspect of his work is not isolated from the others but rests upon and incorporates much of his general philosophical outlook. The aim of this book is to rescue Collingwood's political philosophy from its state of relative neglect and place it in the context of his other philosophical concerns. In order to understand more fully the development of his political and ethical theories, I have made extensive use of Collingwood's unpublished papers. They reveal that *The New Leviathan* was not a hastily conceived and ill-executed treatise, or, as is often claimed, primarily an expedient response to the Second World War, but a work which has firm roots in what Collingwood himself described as the 'many thousand pages of manuscript on every problem of ethics and politics'.[8]

2. Life and career

Collingwood was born 22 February 1889 at Cartmel Fell in Lancashire. His father, W. G. Collingwood, was John Ruskin's secretary and biographer, and an accomplished author, painter, and archaeologist in his own right. Collingwood's father took it upon himself to educate his son at home until he was thirteen, after which Robin Collingwood was sent to grammar school and, a year later, to Rugby. It was during his first thirteen years that the foundations of his various and many talents were laid. Under the tutelage of his father, Collingwood became proficient at reading ancient and modern languages, a talent he put to good use later on in reading German, French, and Italian philosophy, as well as the 'classics' in Latin and Greek; in reading or refereeing manuscripts for the Macmillan Press and Oxford University Press; in translating works of Croce and de Ruggiero; and in facilitating his own archaeological work, not least of which was the continuation of Haverfield's project of collecting and deciphering the Roman inscriptions in Britain. In addition, he was taught to sing, play the piano, draw, and paint. All these skills he also put to good use. The training of his voice he believed to be an essential prerequisite for a professional teacher; as a means of relaxing he composed tunes and played them, although he refrained from this as he got older. Drawing and painting, too, were a form of relaxation and equipped him admirably for his archaeological pursuits. His archaeological publications are beautifully illustrated with diagrams and maps, and the thousands of Roman inscriptions he collected were also drawn by his own hand. The task of completing these inscriptions was entrusted by Collingwood to R. P. Wright in 1938, and the first volume was published in 1965.[9] It is ironic that Collingwood's 'hobby' gained him an international reputation in his own lifetime, something that had eluded him in his philosophical work. On Collingwood's death in 1943, for example, the obituary notice in the *New York Times* referred only to Collingwood's collection of seven thousand inscriptions, and said that he 'probably knew more than any other authority about everyday life in the Britain of the Roman period'.[10]

During his early years Collingwood was also taught the rudiments of sailing by his father, and throughout his life this was a major recreation for him. During periods of recuperation, after bouts of serious illness, he would take a boat out sailing or else go on a long cruise on a cargo boat.[11] After his first serious stroke in 1938, for instance, working on the principle of kill or cure, he embarked upon an abortive four-month cruise in a nineteen-foot sailing yacht called *Zenocrate*. After only a week he encountered a gale on the shoreline between Southend and Plymouth and found himself in difficulties. His yacht had to be towed ashore. This incident was reported in the *London Times,* and Collingwood is claimed to have said that he had believed that 'the yacht would founder at any moment'.[12] Collingwood, however, strongly denied that his predicament was as serious as it had been portrayed in the *Times.* As late as mid-1939 Collingwood joined a crew of young Oxford students on a cruise around the Greek islands. This stimulating experience and the pleasure he gained from the companionship of the young crew inspired him to publish his impressions of the journey.[13]

It was also during his early years at home that Collingwood developed a curiosity about, and a delight in, philosophy and the natural sciences. Collingwood's own account of his induction into these subjects indicates that the curiosity was largely self-motivated.[14] His disappointment at not being able to understand, at the age of eight, 'Kant's Theory of Ethics' is an often-quoted illustration of the precociousness of Collingwood minor. At the same time Collingwood would undoubtedly have been introduced to the work of that great polymath of the nineteenth century, a friend of the family as well as the employer of W. G. Collingwood, John Ruskin. Through his father and elder sisters, Collingwood must have become thoroughly acquainted with Ruskin's work. William M. Johnston makes a great deal of Ruskin's purported influence on Collingwood. He suggests, for example, that

Collingwood did not achieve a vision of the unity of experience by setting out to resurrect Hegel. Indeed the vision came to him not from books at all. Rather it was transmitted to him by his father, who had received it from John Ruskin. If Collingwood reincarnated many of Hegel's achievements and still more of his goals, the capacity to do so came not from Hegel but from Ruskin.[15]

This, I think, overstates the case. It is certainly true that Collingwood admired Ruskin's erudite manner and immense range of interests, but this is hardly sufficient grounds for attributing to Ruskin the inspiration for Collingwood's interest in Hegel. Indeed, in reading Collingwood's lecture on Ruskin one is reminded of Edward Caird's procedure of enquiry. Of Caird it was once said that he 'will show us Comte or Kant as "almost persuaded" to be Hegelians'.[16] The same is true of Collingwood's account of Ruskin. While acknowledging that Ruskin probably never read a word of Hegel, and as likely as not would have had difficulty in understanding him anyway, Collingwood talks of the 'Hegelism of Ruskin' and of Ruskin's 'kinship with Hegel'.[17] Ruskin could not provide a philosophy for Collingwood, but Collingwood could, and did, provide a philosophy, albeit Hegelian, for Ruskin.

The all-round education that Collingwood received at home up until his thirteenth year provided him throughout his life with the exemplar of what a child's education should be. He returned to this topic many times during his life, and the experience of his early years provides the foundation for his view, expressed most explicitly in *The New Leviathan,* that if the values of civilization are to be preserved and passed on to a new generation, then parents have to take the responsibility for educating their own children.

In contrast to the halcyon days of his childhood, Collingwood appears to have been deeply unhappy at Rugby School, disillusioned with what purported to be a formal education. He was later of the view that far from developing the intellect the system served to inhibit natural inquisitiveness and dulled the sensibilities of youth. His hostility to the whole public school system in England stems from his time at Rugby. The living conditions he likened to those of a pigsty; the teaching he found boring because of the poor quality of the teachers; the intellectual worth of the curriculum was less than adequate because the time-tabling militated against continuity and depth. The emphasis upon athletics, he believed, while ostensibly designed to divert youth from thoughts of sex, actually served to provide a necessary release of the energies stifled in the classroom.[18] The reminiscences of one of Collingwood's former students reveal that Collingwood sometimes made disparaging remarks about the British institution he loved to hate. Tom Hopkinson recalls Collingwood saying to him, 'I went to Rugby, where we thought winter a time for playing football – and summer a time for thinking about playing football.'[19]

In 1908, in spite of, rather than because of, his education at Rugby, Collingwood gained a classical scholarship to University College, Oxford, the college from which his father had graduated in 1876, taking a second class degree in Classical Moderations in 1874 and a first in *Literae Humaniores* in 1876. Going up to University College from Rugby, Collingwood maintained, 'was like being let out of prison'.[20] Once given the freedom to indulge his insatiable appetite for learning, Collingwood quickly demonstrated his aptitude for academic pursuits. He took a first in Classical Moderations in 1910 and a first in *Literae Humaniores* in 1912. Prior to the latter result being announced, Collingwood was elected to a philosophy fellowship at Pembroke College. He was to remain on the faculty until 1935, with the exception of the years 1914 to 1918, when he served with his father in the intelligence department of the Admiralty, and of a few months after the autumn of 1918 when he was compelled, because of his marriage, temporarily to vacate his fellowship. Collingwood was, in fact, the first Pembroke tutorial fellow to take advantage of the recently amended statutes concerning marriage. He was also the only tutorial fellow allowed to live outside the college, but was required to reside there three nights a week during term time.[21] From 1924 to 1933 Collingwood was joint editor of the *Transactions of the Cumberland and Westmorland Antiquarian and Archaeological Society,* a position he resigned after a bout of chickenpox which led to serious health complications necessitating a term's leave of absence in 1932.

After 1933 a series of professional distinctions were bestowed upon Collingwood in recognition of his very high achievements in philosophy and archaeology. In 1934 he was elected a fellow of the British Academy. This honour was all the more appreciated because the academy, he felt, provided for him 'a more open-minded audience'[22] than that to which he was accustomed in Oxford. In 1935, after having long expressed the wish to be lightened of his teaching burdens, and having applied unsuccessfully in 1928 for a chair in moral philosophy, Collingwood was appointed Waynflete Professor of Metaphysical Philosophy at Magdalen College. The previous incumbent, J. A. Smith, had personally supported Collingwood's application.[23] In 1938 the University of St. Andrews, in Scotland, undertook to honour Professor Collingwood by conferring upon him the honourary degree of LL.D. No direct evidence exists as to who recommended that Collingwood should be honoured by the university. However, it appears that it was his former pupil, close friend, and later literary executor who made the recommendation, Sir Malcolm Knox, then professor of moral philosophy at (and later the principal of) St. Andrews.[24]

Collingwood was unable to attend the July graduation ceremony, as he had intended, to receive the degree, because he had suffered the first of the series of strokes that eventually led to his early death. He did, however, receive his LL.D. at a small ceremony held in October of 1938. Professor A. Blyth Webster, in introducing Collingwood, referred to his outstanding achievements in philosophy and archaeology, and said that St. Andrews was proud that it was 'still in time to be the first University to give him his honorary degree'.[25] Collingwood resigned his chair in 1941 on the grounds of ill health and died on 9 January 1943 in Coniston, where he had retired to live with his second wife and his daughter.

As a university academic Collingwood undertook his teaching and research duties with the utmost seriousness. He also served for many years as a reader of manuscripts for the Macmillan Press and later became a most valued delegate for Oxford University Press, because of his efficiency and his ability to read a variety of foreign languages, including German, French, and Italian. Teaching and research, for him, were integrally related, and he managed to combine them in a way rarely equalled today. His books, even those posthumously published, were first 'tried out' on students in the form of lectures.[26] Even *The New Leviathan,* with which the present study is principally concerned, had its origin in the lectures on moral philosophy delivered every year, at times with substantial revisions, from 1921 to 1927, and then in 1929, 1930, 1932, 1933, and 1940. During the Michaelmas term of 1940 and the Hilary term of 1941 Collingwood delivered a series of lectures entitled 'Philosophical Theory of Society and Politics', which is no longer extant but is believed to have been the preliminary draft of much of the central parts of *The New Leviathan.*[27]

Collingwood did not believe in an amateur approach to teaching. On becoming a tutor at Pembroke College he took a number of singing lessons in order to polish his lecture presentation and delivery.[28] The combination of his professional delivery and substantive content made Collingwood's lectures highly attractive to eager young undergraduates, who, in his days at Pembroke, turned up in sufficient numbers to necessitate moving to a larger lecture theatre.[29] Many of the students who attended the lectures were not formally enrolled for philosophy but merely went along because of the reputation of Collingwood as a lecturer. Reminiscences of those who attended his lectures certainly indicate that this reputation was not misplaced. In the view of E. W. F. Tomlin, for instance, Collingwood discharged his duties as a lecturer 'with brilliance', and C. V. Wedgwood states that 'trains of thought which are sometimes blurred on the printed page registered with impressive clearness in the lecture-room'.[30] These sentiments were echoed by Richmond, McCallum, Knox, and Bouch in their obituaries and assessments of Collingwood.[31] Richmond, McCallum, and Knox qualify their praise by suggesting that the ease of delivery and the polished structure of the lectures made the more gifted students suspect Collingwood of being sophistic. This was compounded, at least in his philosophical lectures, by the fact that Collingwood's approach to philosophy, relying heavily upon history, was out of keeping with the 'realist' philosophical tendencies of the times. In tutorials, he was noted for his ability to delineate the terms of complex problems with precision and clarity. Indeed, his breadth of knowledge and practical skills enabled him to illustrate his points most admirably. Tom Hopkinson, for instance, states that 'in discussion he [Collingwood] could explain a point by making a quick drawing, taking a musical instrument down and playing it, or with reference to the morning's newspapers'.[32]

Collingwood's attitude to teaching was ambivalent. He sometimes resented the fact that his heavy burden of teaching reduced the time he could use to write books. However, at the same time he believed that trying out his ideas on young lively minds helped him to further his own thinking on historical and philosophical problems.

There is no doubt that by today's standards Collingwood's teaching load as a tutor was very heavy. The system of individual tutoring placed a considerable weight upon the shoulders of young academics. In addition to his duties as a tutor and college librarian at Pembroke College, Collingwood taught philosophy to Lincoln College students between 1921 and 1928. When he was appointed university lecturer in philosophy and Roman history in 1927, his teaching commitments were slightly lightened. In his reports to the faculty of *Literae Humaniores,* for instance, he talks of the work he hoped to complete as a result of the new 'command of leisure' resulting from his new appointment.[33] However, even in 1930, after his burden was diminished, he still commented upon the encroachment of teaching upon his time to do other academic work. In a letter to E. B. Birley, for instance, Collingwood comments, with a hint of envy at the former's having secured a chair, 'When I think of myself teaching for 30–40 hours a week from the age of 23 to that of 40, barring the War, I rejoice to think how much you will be able to do that none of us could ever hope to do'.[34]

Collingwood could have freed himself from the predicament in which he found himself long before gaining his chair in 1935. As early as 1921 he was 'looking forward to the distant day' when he could leave Pembroke and do serious academic work, and in 1928, again, he maintained that 'unless I free myself of College teaching' work could not progress very far in 'formulating the problem of historical methodology'.[35] Yet despite many offers of professorships at universities in Britain and the United States, Collingwood refused to leave Oxford. This is quite difficult to understand, given Collingwood's own sense of intellectual isolation in Oxford, as expressed in *An Autobiography.* Indeed, he did not seek, nor, it appears, did he enjoy, the company of most of his philosophical colleagues at Oxford.[36] For many years during the 1920s he did not live in Oxford at all but travelled there on Mondays and returned home to North Moreton, near Didcot, on Friday evenings.

There is a combination of reasons why he continued to work in Oxford rather than move elsewhere. It can be inferred from *An Autobiography* that his principal reason for staying was that he felt an obligation, as Haverfield's sole remaining protégé teaching in Oxford, 'to keep alive the Oxford school of Romano-British studies . . ., and to make use of the specialist library he [Haverfield] had left to the University. It was this obligation that made me refuse all offers of professorships and other employments elsewhere which I received during the years that followed the War'.[37] However, even though he felt isolated as a philosopher in Oxford, he aspired to gain the recognition and respect of his colleagues. In 1924, for instance, Collingwood wrote to de Ruggiero, 'I think Oxford is the best centre for my present work, and I now find that *Speculum Mentis* is exciting a good deal of attention there and is regarded as possibly opening a new movement in English philosophy'.[38] This view proved, to Collingwood's chagrin, to be overly optimistic. A third reason why he stayed at Oxford was that although he often found the heavy teaching load onerous, he nevertheless derived a great deal of satisfaction from the response he got from students, and he also believed that the teaching helped to clarify his own philosophical ideas. He wrote to de Ruggiero, for example, 'This teaching does (I think) help a little towards getting one's mind clearer: at any rate I find myself beginning to make some sort of a mark. Not among my elders and contemporaries so far as I can see, but among the undergraduates . . . and my friends among them increase in numbers'.[39] In addition, he found the business of 'applying' and 'testing' his philosophical theories in his teaching of undergraduates much more congenial than expounding his views before his colleagues. Implied in his teaching were two principles: Determine the relevance of criticism before accepting its validity, and, before assuming that one has understood the argument of a philosopher, satisfy oneself that one has uncovered the question that the philosopher was trying to answer. In applying these principles in teaching, Collingwood found the tutorials 'no less salutory' than did his pupils.[40]

What, then, was the nature of Collingwood's perceived intellectual isolation, and with whom did he feel that he had philosophical affinities?

3. The place of Collingwood in contemporary thought

In the *Autobiography* Collingwood gives us an account of the intellectual environment in which he found himself. On the one hand there were the 'realists' like Carritt (his former tutor), Cook Wilson, and Pritchard, all of whom Collingwood associated with naturalism and a reverence for scientific explanation. The implication of 'realism' was that the knowing subject makes no difference to the object that is known. In respect of moral philosophy, this meant its relegation to the object of scientific study or its excision from philosophical enquiry altogether. On the other hand there was the new generation of idealists, following in the tradition of the school of Green, men such as J. A. Smith and H. H. Joachim, whom Collingwood criticizes for having nothing to say, and thus of having contributed to the demise of British idealism. Collingwood suggests that idealism never dominated philosophy and teaching at Oxford, and that its greatest impact was felt among those men who went out into the professions and put the creed into practice. He maintained that only the epigones of the movement of philosophers remained in Oxford. He was as concerned to disassociate himself from the remnants of the idealist school as he was to distinguish himself from the realists.[41] His reasons for doing so will be discussed in due course. What I want to argue at this point is that Collingwood's characterisation of British idealism and its contemporaneous disintegration is not altogether accurate. The roots of British idealism went far deeper into the philosophical culture than he wanted to allow, and its branches extended far wider during his lifetime than he was prepared to admit.

To be fair to Collingwood, he explicitly states in the *Autobiography* that his sketch of the idealist movement was not to be taken as a history. Although 'no one has yet written the history of this movement', he suggests, 'I do not propose to attempt it here'.[42] In fact, J. H. Muirhead had written a history of British idealism in 1931,[43] and it is difficult to imagine how this could have escaped Collingwood's attention – unless, of course, his comment is meant to be an oblique criticism of Muirhead or was simply the result of a lapse of memory. Whatever the case may be, Collingwood was well qualified to make a judgement upon any historical characterisation of the emergence of idealism in Britain because he had explored this area of research himself and intended to write a history of the thought of the Victorian period.[44]

When Collingwood became a fellow of Pembroke College in 1912, a number of leading idealists, such as T. H. Green (1836–1882), R. L. Nettleship (1846–1892), Edward Caird (1835–1908), D. G. Ritchie (1856–1903), and William Wallace (1843–1897), had died. However, during Collingwood's career many major and minor idealists lived on. For example, Bernard Bosanquet, erstwhile professor of moral philosophy at St. Andrews and leading light in the Charity Organization Society (1840–1923); F. H. Bradley, fellow of Merton College, Oxford (1846–1924); J. A. Smith and H. H. Joachim, friends and colleagues of Collingwood at Oxford, who were to die only a few years before him; G. R. G. Mure in Oxford, who lived many years after him; J. M. E. McTaggart in Cambridge, who did not die until 1925; and W. R. Sorley, the professor of moral philosophy in Cambridge, who held his position until 1933. M. J. Oakeshott, whose philosophy of history Collingwood regarded very highly, lectured on history in Cambridge during the 1930s. Sir Henry Jones was professor of moral philosophy in Glasgow University until his death in 1922. Others who were active during Collingwood's lifetime were J. H. Muirhead in Birmingham; J. S. Mackenzie in the University of South Wales and Monmouthshire, Cardiff; and H. J. W. Hetherington, who taught at Glasgow, Cardiff, and Exeter and who became vice-chancellor of the University of Liverpool and, in 1936, principal of the University of Glasgow; and, representing the younger generation, Malcolm Knox in St. Andrews and Michael Foster in Oxford, both of whom were 'disciples' of Collingwood. Indeed, although it may be said that idealism was certainly on the defensive by 1912, it still had enough troops to carry on the battle for some time yet, and those troops entrenched themselves in most of the leading chairs of philosophy in the country. Quinton suggests, for example, that 'until well into the 1920s idealists held nearly all the leading positions in the philosophy departments of British Universities and continued to be the largest group in the philosophical professoriate until 1945'.[45]

Collingwood's attitude towards the British idealists oscillates between admiration and rejection. His *Autobiography* shows that he had a great admiration for Green, Bosanquet, and Bradley. In *Speculum Mentis* Collingwood even described Sir Henry Jones as 'one of our most eminent philosophers'.[46] At the same time he was irritated by the encumbrances of carrying the label of idealism and was always at great pains to disavow the title of idealist, and thus to disassociate himself from its increasingly pejorative connotations. Why, then, did Collingwood want to part company with the British idealists? I have argued elsewhere that the British idealists brought about two fundamental changes in British philosophy. First, they maintained that there are no isolated individual facts. Each fact is implicated in a whole of interrelated facts, and it is this whole in which each fact has meaning and significance. Second, they argued that each philosophical problem could only be fully understood in terms of its genesis and the development of responses to it. These two aspects of British idealism, I suggested, implied a historical perspective. However, for the most part the implication did not manifest itself in practice.[47] This constitutes one of the main reasons why Collingwood found himself 'rather inclined to react against the British idealists'.[48] Throughout his life, Collingwood always emphasized the need for historical understanding of philosophical problems; indeed he regarded as his own subject 'the history of thought'.[49] In his mind the history of philosophy and the philosophy of history were always closely associated – even, at times, identical. Hegel, of course, had identified philosophy with its own history, but in doing so rendered both history and philosophy timeless.[50] Collingwood, however, wanted genuinely to establish history in its temporal concreteness. His very first publication was a translation of Croce's *Philosophy of Giambattista Vico.*[51] One of Vico's fundamental principles was that mind can know and understand what mind has made. The world of nations is eminently more knowable than the world of nature because the former is the product of human creativity, whose principles are to be found in the changing features of the human mind, while the latter is the creation of God and thus susceptible only to his understanding.[52] It was Vico, Collingwood used to say, who had influenced him the most.[53] Vico's emphasis upon the creativity and development of the human mind permeates the whole of Collingwood's work, and in Collingwood's writings we find presupposed at every point Dilthey's famous dictum that 'we are at home everywhere in this historical and understood world; we understand the sense and meaning of it all; we ourselves are woven into this common sphere.'[54]

Of more importance, perhaps, than the British idealists in disseminating and preparing the ground for the assimilation of the philosophy of history in Britain, and thus opening the way for Collingwood, was Robert Flint.[55] He did not himself make any original contribution to the philosophy of history, and it is for this reason that he is either forgotten or rebuked. He is mentioned now only because the new revival of interest in Vico credits Flint with the distinction of being the first writer in the English language to publish a monograph on Vico, although Vico was only Flint's third choice in Blackwood's series on philosophers.[56] What historians and philosophers seem not to recognise in respect of Flint is the distinction between the production of original thought and the dissemination of thought that is unfamiliar to the audience to which it is directed. It is in the latter category that Flint excels, and it is because the works of the more eminent writers he discussed are now more readily accessible that his contribution has been forgotten. Flint's books on the philosophy of history were all remarkably well received by readers in Britain and on the Continent,[57] and his monograph on Vico did much to strengthen his ties with Italian scholars; indeed, it was translated into Italian by Francesco Finocchietti and published in 1888.

In the same year as Bradley published his *Presuppositions of Critical History,* an essay which Collingwood described as constituting a Copernican revolution in the theory of historical knowledge,[58] Flint was arguing that the facts of history and their interpretation are not distinguishable entities: The facts *are* their interpretation.[59] Later he was to argue that thought must be shown to emanate from its context, because 'no life can be understood altogether apart from the environment in which it is developed', and no particular work can be seen in isolation from the whole of a person's life.[60] In large measure Flint was a professed follower of Vico and appropriated the latter's ideas in formulating his own conception of how history should be studied. For example, Flint tells us that the human mind and its history are eminently more knowable and more intelligible than any physical occurrence: 'Matter is the stage prepared for the drama of the spirit. There is, we may be sure, more significance in the drama than in the stage. . . . The truth is known by us only to the extent that we have made it'.[61] Although Flint was not himself an idealist philosopher, he did much to disseminate in Britain the ideas of idealist philosophers of history, but it was not until the second quarter of the twentieth century that British idealists, namely R. G. Collingwood and M. J. Oakeshott, made distinguished and sustained contributions to the critical study of history as a mode of enquiry and tried to establish its efficacy in relation to positivist claims to the autonomy, supremacy, and exclusiveness of scientific method.

In the first place, then, Collingwood reacted against British idealism because it was not fulfilling its potential of becoming a genuinely historical philosophy. In a letter to de Ruggiero dated 9 January 1931, Collingwood succinctly expresses his attitude and consequent sense of isolation:

Even the 19th Century idealists in England were not, in general, historically minded: there are traces of a historical point of view in Bradley and Green, and Caird – but they are not very strong, and in Bosanquet they vanish entirely, and the relics of that school in Oxford today are quite out of touch with history. Therefore a historically-minded philosopher here is a *vox clamantis in deserto.*[62]

Bosanquet, for example, was quite contemptuous, as Collingwood was well aware, of the historical mode of enquiry, describing it as 'the doubtful story of successive events'.[63] A number of the elder idealists were also quite intolerant of the new generation of historically minded philosophers on the Continent. Henry Jones, for instance, thought that 'the men some folk cackle about . . . Bergson and Croce etc.' were greatly overrated in comparison to Bradley and Bosanquet.[64] Bosanquet himself had a low opinion of Croce. In a reference to Croce and Jakob Böhme, Bosanquet says, 'Ask yourself if a reasonable man could sit down with either'.[65]

A second reason for Collingwood's rejection of the British idealists was that not only were they not historically minded enough; he also believed that they were much closer in thought to the British empiricist tradition than was commonly believed. Indeed, when he does enter into criticism of such people as Bradley and Bosanquet, Collingwood convicts them of lapsing from idealism into naturalism.

Let me illustrate this contention. Collingwood suggests that 'the break in English philosophy about 1870 is rather illusory' and convicts A. Seth Pringle-Pattison, Green, Bradley, Bosanquet, and MacTaggert of deserting 'Hegel for a more realistic view'.[66] In his specific criticisms of Bradley and Bosanquet this, again, is essentially the line he pursues. Bradley, for instance, implicitly denies Vico's idea that the historian, with great effort, can come to understand minds which are of a totally different character from his own;[67] instead the former suggests that evidence may come down to us which is totally incapable of being comprehended because it falls outside the present experience of the historian's world of ideas. In other words, historians have to verify their accounts by analogy with the present, and if their assumptions or presuppositions about the capabilities of people who lived then and of those who live now cannot be squared, the evidence, in effect, becomes unsusceptible to historical analysis. Bradley adds the proviso that 'the present experience which is open to our research, is so wide in its extent, is so infinitely rich in its manifold details, that to expect an event in the past to which nothing analogous now corresponds may fairly be considered a mere extravagance'.[68] Collingwood, although he considered Bradley to be the most systematic of British idealists, detected what was, for him, a serious flaw in Bradley's argument. In Bradley, Collingwood suggests, history is not in fact separated from the methods of the natural scientists but actually relies upon them for the general principles regarding what can and cannot have happened in the past. Collingwood believes that Mill's inductive logic permeates the whole of this aspect of Bradley's argument and that the logic itself embodies 'an inner inconsistency'.

On the one side, it claims that scientific thought reveals to us laws of nature to which there cannot be exceptions; on the other, it holds that this revelation is based on induction from experience, and therefore can never give us universal knowledge that is more than probable. Hence in the last resort the attempt to base history on science breaks down.[69]

In Italy, Croce, the doyen of Italian idealists, was leading the way, slightly later than the older British idealists had done, in attempting to devastate positivist logic. Croce, after extensive historical and literary studies, had arrived at a philosophical standpoint which he continued to develop. Two followers of Croce, Giovanni Gentile and Guido de Ruggiero, both of whom dissented in crucial respects from the views of their mentor, equally felt the necessity of having to immerse themselves in historical studies before, and while, developing their own idealist philosophies. While no one can deny Croce's historical-mindedness (indeed, he contended that 'philosophy and history are not two forms, they are one sole form: they are not mutually conditioned, but identical'[70]), this did not deter the younger Italians from convicting Croce of failing to emancipate idealism from naturalism, nor did it discourage Collingwood from systematically dismantling Croce's *Teoria e Storia della Storiografia*[71] and presenting its author as a bifurcated philosophical naturalist and historical idealist.[72] Croce himself noticed the similarity between the criticisms of

Collingwood and those of Gentile and de Ruggiero, suggesting that it was the latter of the two young Italians who had turned Collingwood against him,[73] at least the Collingwood up to and including *Speculum Mentis.*

I have suggested that Flint was responsible for introducing into Britain the philosophies of history of many continental thinkers, and in particular that of Vico. The ideas of Croce, the professed Vichian,[74] and those of Gentile were introduced into Oxford, and to a small extent to a wider audience, through the medium of published articles by J. A. Smith, who, while on a visit to Italy, fortuitously came upon the writings of Croce prominently displayed on many bookstands. It was Croce, Smith admits, who informed much of the inaugural lecture the latter gave in 1910,[75] and it was Gentile, H. S. Harris suggests, who influenced Smith's 1913 paper 'On Feeling'.[76] Smith later published an article on Gentile[77] and was an inspiration to H. Wildon Carr, who translated Gentile's *Theory of Mind as Pure Act.*[78] In addition, Smith lectured on Croce and Gentile at Oxford and gave a series of lectures, based on the ideas of the Italians, at Manchester College.[79]

Italian idealism was explicitly historical in character. John Passmore has summed this up well in arguing that 'Hegelianism in Italy was inter-preted concretely, as a philosophy of history rather than as a logic'.[80] Smith was immediately impressed by this aspect of Italian idealism and detected Vico's influence at work in its articulation. Smith emphasizes the stress of the Italians upon the influence of history in generating phi-losophy, and of setting philosophy the task 'of understanding History, and *imprimis* its own history'. Following from this, he suggests that for our-selves we might define 'the present-day problem of philosophy as the determination, organization, systematization of "the critical presupposi-tions of history" '.[81] It should come as no surprise, then, that Collingwood found the philosophical company of the Italians congenial, and in harmony with his own inclinations as a philosopher. If Collingwood's *Autobiog-raphy* can be relied upon, his acquaintance with Italian thinkers was in-dependently acquired during the time he was studying Greats at Oxford.[82] This would have been during the period when Smith was improving his Italian in order to familiarize himself more thoroughly, and more accu-rately, with the Italian thinkers.[83] It is reasonable to assume that Smith's enthusiasm for the 'New Idealism' would have, at least, acted as an in-spiration to Collingwood, and certainly E. F. Carritt, Collingwood's tutor in philosophy, whose aesthetic interests led him to examine and to sym-pathise (at least partially) with the aesthetics of Croce, would have dis-cussed such a topic of mutual interest with the young Collingwood.[84] Whatever the source of initial inspiration, Collingwood himself did much to give the Italian idealists a home in Britain, through translating and arranging translations of some of their works[85] and by incorporating some of their insights into his own arguments.

4. The Italian connexion

Much has been written upon the question of which Italian idealist influenced Collingwood the most. This issue is not relevant here. What is relevant is the extent to which the historical-mindedness of the Italians had a bearing upon Collingwood's conception and execution of his political philosophy.

The ideas of Gentile, especially the notion of the unity of the mind in the multiplicity of its manifestations, H. S. Harris contends, permeates the whole of Collingwood's philosophical endeavours.[86] In essence, Gentile had attempted to transcend the mind–object dichotomy by, first, reasserting, with the aid of Berkeley, the essentially subjective character of experience. Much more radically than, say, Bradley, who posited a level of sentient experience which exists prior to its mutilation by thought, and an absolute whose reality always remains just outside our grasp, Gentile wanted to move away completely from the question of the mind apprehending something external to itself. Vico had expressed an important principle in asserting the creative capacity of the mind in the genesis and modification of all things civil; he had, however, posited nature as a realm of experience beyond our understanding because it is not of our own making. Gentile eradicates the distinction and makes all experience self-, or mind-, created. He argues that 'there is no *theory,* no contemplation of reality, which is not at the same time action and therefore a creation of reality'.[87] Gentile disassociates himself from past thinkers by accusing them of separating truth and reality from the act of knowing.[88] All of reality, for Gentile, is immanent in the act of thinking. It is not the concepts produced by the act that call for our attention but the pure act itself, that is, the process of creation. In other words, for Gentile, nothing can be presupposed in experience; to presuppose is to set something outside the self-creating act of the mind. In philosophy, we presuppose nothing and take the act of pure thought as the foundation of the world of experience. The act of thinking, for Gentile, is the unity of the immanence of the pure act of thought with the transcendental process of thinking. Mind, or Spirit, is the infinite self-realization of itself in its own acts of pure thought: 'The transcendental point of view is that which we attain when in the reality of thinking we see our thought not as act done, but act in the doing', and we are able to do this because 'mind is not a being or a substance but a constructive process or development'.[89] Mind is what it is in the process of its own becoming, 'and becoming can have neither antecedent nor consequent without ceasing to become'.[90] This is Gentile's *actualism,* which identifies consciousness and creation: To be conscious of experience is to create it. For Gentile, the mind is unity and resolves into itself the seeming multiplicity of experience. Mind, in the process of self-realisation, asserts itself through art; this is its subjective moment. In its objective moment, mind asserts itself through religion. In knowledge – that is, the self-knowledge of the mind – the synthesis of subjective and objective is achieved. Knowledge itself is asserted in a triadic form; the subjective or questioning moment is the scientific activity of mind; the objective or answering moment is achieved in history.[91] Each mode of thought – art, religion, science, and history – is unsatisfactory in itself; each is one-sided and needs the insights of the others to complement its vision. Only in philosophy do we achieve an absolute synthesis. Philosophy interprets the unsatisfactory assertions of reality and assigns to them their places in the unity of the whole. Once history is conceived not as an object which stands outside the subject but as a unity created in the act of thinking, philosophy and the history of philosophy become one. For Gentile, then,

the identity of philosophy with its history is the typical form and culminating point of the resolution of temporal into eternal history, or indeed of the facts of mind into the concept or spiritual act. It is the culminating point, because philosophy is the highest and at the same time the concretest form of spiritual activity, the form which judges all the others and can itself be judged by none.[92]

In *Speculum Mentis* Collingwood conceives of philosophy as a philosophy without presuppositions, which examines the forms of experience that rest upon presuppositions, exposing their contradictions and resolving them into a linked hierarchy of forms of experience which culminates in philosophy. H. S. Harris has contended that this concept is in fact modelled on Gentile's five phases of experience. Indeed, Collingwood's five forms of experience – art, religion, science, history, and philosophy – are the same forms and occupy the same place in experience as a whole to which Gentile assigned them. Gentile, however, gives very little space to the analysis and structure of these forms in *The Theory of the Mind as Pure Act.* Also, following John Passmore, Harris suggests that implicit in the *Essay on Philosophical Method* is the same conception of philosophy, that is, the examination and interrogation of concepts with reference to their place on a scale of forms. Indeed, Harris further maintains that the remainder of Collingwood's books are a manifestation of the Gentilian method.[93]

There can be little doubt that the form in which *Speculum Mentis* unfolds owes much to Gentile, and indeed many reviewers saw it as an attempt to combine Hegelian, Crocean, and Gentilian insights. However, the conception of a philosophy without presuppositions was not a Gentilian invention. It was, in fact, quite common among the British idealists. For Bosanquet, for instance, philosophy is an activity 'without reservation or presupposition', and its aim is to pass from 'the contradictory and unstable in experience alike to the stable and satisfactory'.[94] The modes of experience 'have their attraction for the mind' and 'are linked together in a central enthusiasm when our attention is thoroughly focussed on thought as the determination of reality, and logic as the theory of thought'.[95]

I think that Harris, in his enthusiasm to demonstrate Gentile's significance, posits too strong a link between the Italian and Collingwood. In doing so Harris disregards one of Gentile's central points. In discussing philosophy and the history of philosophy, Gentile suggests that 'a choice of material is inevitable; and a choice requires a criterion. And the criterion in this case can only be a notion of the philosophy'.[96] Indeed, Collingwood's understanding of Gentile is not altogether that which others would see as immediately apparent, for the interpretation at which he arrives is coloured by his already thorough knowledge of the post-Kantian tradition in philosophy and by the problems that he sought to answer. When Collingwood attempts to summarise some of Gentile's arguments, the Englishman maintains that the positions stated are implied or assumed by the Italian rather than fully stated. And, as far as Collingwood is concerned, they constitute the common ground of idealism in general.

Collingwood emphasizes the historical character of Gentile's philosophy to a much greater extent than the latter emphasized it himself. For Gentile, Collingwood suggests, reality is history, and history is the knowing mind conscious of itself. It is only through self-consciousness of this history that mind has a history at all; 'Hence Gentile's philosophy is a "metaphysic of knowledge", that is to say, a philosophy which never loses sight of the question "how do we come to know what we know?" '[97] We will see that in *The New Leviathan* great emphasis is put upon the historical dimension of the European mind, and its character is discerned by means of the 'historical plain method'. 'Man as mind', we are told, *'is whatever he is conscious of being'*. In other words, Collingwood is, by implication, 'holding that mind is "pure act", so that the question *what mind is* resolves itself without residue into the question *what mind does'*.[98]

Second, Collingwood attributes to both de Ruggiero and Gentile the attempt to synthesize the transcendental and immanent moment in experience, a principle which de Ruggiero called *'absolute* immanence. . . . The absolute in this sense, is that which has reconciled its own opposite to itself, and therefore no longer stands in opposition to it'.[99] This, of course, is something that all idealists, in their different ways, attempt to achieve, and Collingwood, I will argue, is no exception. His 'law of primitive survivals', that is, the view that a residue of the lower forms of experience is always present in the higher, and his arrival at the notion of duty as the criterion of moral and political conduct, are, together, an exemplification of the principle of 'absolute immanence'.

Of greater importance and significance with respect to Collingwood's association with Italian idealism, in so far as it has a bearing on this study, is his understanding of de Ruggiero's notion of the development of liberalism. Collingwood himself gives us a summary of what he understands de Ruggiero to be doing in *The History of European Liberalism:*

Liberalism, as Professor de Ruggiero understands it, begins with the recognition that men, do what we will, are free; that a man's acts are his own, spring from his own personality, and cannot be coerced. But this freedom is not possessed at birth; it is acquired by degrees as a man enters into the self-conscious possession of his personality through a life of discipline and moral progress. The aim of Liberalism is to assist the individual to discipline himself and achieve his own moral progress; renouncing the two opposite errors of forcing upon him a development for which he is inwardly unprepared, and leaving him alone, depriving him of that aid to progress which a political system, wisely designed and wisely administered, can give.[100]

Indeed, the *New Leviathan* can be viewed as an attempt to formulate differently and more extensively the conception of liberalism that he outlines in the passage just quoted. There is some evidence to support the claim that Collingwood, after translating de Ruggiero's *History of European Liberalism,* incorporated some of the Italian's insights into his own work. In a letter to de Ruggiero dated 22 November 1928 Collingwood refers to an essay he was writing 'on the fundamental conceptions of political thought'. The writing of it, Collingwood claimed, brought him into constant contact 'with many ideas on that subject' which he had learned from de Ruggiero. The essay to which the letter refers could be 'Political Action', published in 1929, or it could be 'Stray Notes on Ethical Questions', written in 1928 but never published.[101] It is most probably the former, because Collingwood, in the same letter, expressed his intention to publish the manuscript.

It is well known that Collingwood greatly admired the work of Benedetto Croce, and in turn Croce thought Collingwood's work to be of great significance. Much has been written upon Croce's influence upon Collingwood, especially in the field of aesthetics. It suffices to say here that I will attempt to explore the relationship between the two thinkers from a different perspective. Croce's conception of liberalism is much narrower than that of de Ruggiero. The latter was, one might say, a 'New Liberal', who expressed admiration for L. T. Hobhouse and 'liberal socialism',[102] whereas the former views liberalism as a disposition of mind which opens itself up to alternative views and is therefore not a set of policies but is capable of adopting different policies compatible with individual freedom to suit the times.[103] Croce criticizes de Ruggiero for coming close to confusing the liberal ideal with empirical circumstances.[104] Despite Collingwood's close political affinities with de Ruggiero, however, he also sympathised with some of Croce's political views.

The aim of highlighting the affinities between Collingwood and other thinkers is not to detract from his originality but to demonstrate his sympathy for the ideas of the post-Kantian tradition. In rethinking the ideas of the past, making them his own, modifying them, and incorporating them into his own system, Collingwood was doing what all of the idealists had done before him. That Collingwood chose, in his *Autobiography*, not to express his debt to the Italians from whom he learned so much has been the occasion for some commentators to accuse him of deliberate concealment, or even duplicity, in order to exaggerate his own originality. H. S. Harris puts this criticism most forcefully. He says,

Gentile's name does not occur in any one of his books. . . . Worse still, Collingwood maintains absolute silence about Italian influences upon his thought in his *Autobiography,* and even represents his personal friend and immediate predecessor as Professor of Metaphysics, J. A. Smith, as an Idealist of the 'old school'. This fact seems to me to invalidate any hypothesis that would exonerate him from a charge of deliberate concealment.[105]

All these points, I think, lend themselves to a different interpretation which exonerates Collingwood from the charge of duplicity. Let me take them one by one, although some are obviously closely connected.

Although Gentile is not explicitly named in the *Autobiography*, Collingwood is alluding to him when he mentions 'a very able and distinguished philosopher who converted to Fascism. As a philosopher, that was the end of him'.[106] Given Collingwood's fervent hatred of fascism, he would hardly have been likely to admit, even to himself, that he had been influenced by Gentile to any great extent. Further, Collingwood had not in some of his earlier articles been reticent to express admiration for Gentile and de Ruggiero.[107] However, his hatred of fascism fails to explain why Collingwood does not express an intellectual debt in the *Autobiography* to Croce and de Ruggiero, although he does refer to the latter of the two as 'my friend Guido de Ruggiero'.[108]

Given Collingwood's expression of indebtedness in his correspondence with the Italians, J. H. Muirhead's opinion that Collingwood 'likely enough . . . developed his own ideas independently'[109] can be discounted. There are two much more plausible reasons why Collingwood does not express his debt to the Italians. First, the *Autobiography,* written after his first serious stroke, was primarily (with the exception of the archaeological material) concerned to outline conclusions that he intended to explicate further if his health permitted. Thus, he does not discuss his aesthetics, because he had already published his conclusions. He does, however, discuss in detail his views of history, metaphysics, and politics. The first of these found further expression in *The Principles of History* (1939), which he never completed; the second in *An Essay on Metaphysics*

(1940); and, the third in *The New Leviathan* (1942). Second, Collingwood might well have thought that his debt to the Italians was perfectly obvious. Reviewers of his books never tired of pointing out the similarities between Collingwood's and the Italians' theories. A few examples will serve to illustrate my point. Of *Speculum Mentis* it was said that 'the examples of Hegel and Bradley, Croce and Gentile have in a sense inspired and facilitated this latest adventure';[110] 'he is in substantial agreement with Hegel and Gentile';[111] 'his position ... is that of the Italian philosophers Croce and Gentile'.[112] Of *An Essay on Philosophical Method* it was said that 'it appears to owe a great deal to the Crocification of Hegel',[113] and of *The Principles of Art* it was written that 'this book, as I understand it, expounds without deviation Croce's theory that art is the expression of emotion';[114] and, 'This is substantially the view of Croce'.[115] It must be emphasized that in noticing the affinities between Collingwood and other idealists the reviewers all went on to praise Collingwood's original and important restatements of the theories. Collingwood was certainly aware that he was being compared to the Italians and made no secret in conversation, and in correspondence with his friends, of his admiration for Gentile, Croce, and de Ruggiero. In addition, Collingwood gave a series of lectures on de Ruggiero in the Michaelmas term of 1920, and Croce figured prominently in his lectures on aesthetics and the philosophy of history given in subsequent years. My point is this: Whatever reason, or reasons, Collingwood had for not mentioning his indebtedness to the Italians in his *Autobiography,* it is highly unlikely that he wanted or expected to dupe his readers on this matter.

Collingwood's view of the philosophical endeavour is not likely to have predisposed him to the expression of debts. Doctrines which appear in later philosophical writings, he argues, often to the retrospective eye look as if they had been contained in earlier philosophies.[116] Each philosophy, however, confronts situations and problems which are unique, and no philosophy can be accepted in its entirety by later thinkers: 'That each must reject the thought of others, regarded as self-contained philosophies, and at the same time reaffirm them as elements in his own philosophy, is due not to causes in taste and temperament but to the logical structure of philosophical thought'.[117] Similarly, in art each artist collaborates with his predecessors in that he grafts his own work onto the work of another.[118]

What I have argued so far, however, does not answer the charge that Collingwood deliberately misrepresented J. A. Smith as an idealist of the old school in order to conceal the former's indebtedness to the Italians. It is true that Collingwood does not mention Smith's interest in Italian philosophy, but this may be simply because he truly saw Smith as being more strongly related to the old school of British idealists. As I suggested earlier, the thought of the British idealists implied a historical dimension which was not, for the most part, evident in practice, and Collingwood was well aware of this. The same accusation could be made of Smith. He espoused the view that philosophy should be thoroughly imbued with, and grounded upon, history, but unlike the Italians he never went through the process, in the small number of articles he wrote, of demonstrating what his view of philosophy means when applied to particular problems. Gentile, de Ruggiero, and Croce had all published extensive historical surveys, and their philosophical conclusions are reached by grounding the problems addressed in the context of their genesis and development. In this respect, Collingwood, and certainly not Smith, was at one with the Italian idealists.

5. Contemporary reception of Collingwood's work

Collingwood's modest reputation during his own lifetime testifies to the perversity of the judgements often made by an author's contemporaries, compared with those judgements made after the passage of time has intervened to distance a text from its immediate context. In Collingwood's case the philosophical climate was not so much hostile as indifferent to the problems to which he addressed himself, and, if not to the problems, certainly to the answers he gave. Broadly speaking, the major philosophical journals, with the exception of *Mind,* took hardly any notice of Collingwood's books. However, his books were reviewed extensively in periodicals for the general reader, and in some specialist journals outside the academic confines of philosophy. In respect of his philosophical books, with the exception of *An Essay on Philosophical Method* (which was, incidentally, the only book which he considered to be completed and revised to his own satisfaction), Collingwood addressed them to the knowledgeable and intelligent sector of the general public. The issues with which he concerned himself, he believed, had a considerable bearing upon the problems of society as a whole and were not narrowly confined to the philosophical community. In so far as he addressed a broader audience, many of the publications in which his books were reviewed would have brought Collingwood's ideas to the attention of the very audience which he purportedly aimed to address. Nevertheless, it is evident that it was a great disappointment to him that the philosophical community never took up, in books and articles, nor took issue with, the arguments he propounded. Only Gilbert Ryle and L. S. Hearnshaw entered into dispute with him, and of general surveys of contemporary philosophy only de Ruggiero's *Filosofi de Novecento* discusses Collingwood's ideas.[119]

The reviews of his philosophical books, however, were, on balance, more favourable than unfavourable. While there certainly were critics who could not accept Collingwood's premises or conclusions, they always acknowledged his philosophical sophistication. A reviewer of Collingwood's first book illustrates this point of view admirably when he says that he 'finds himself at variance' with much of the argument but nevertheless concludes that the 'book is able and thoughtful, marked by great lucidity and precision of style as well as by considerable independence of mind'.[120] *Speculum Mentis,* for instance, also had its share of reviewers torn between admiration and rejection; it was not, however, nearly as badly received as Collingwood intimates in his *Autobiography.*[121] It is true that some reviewers, such as C. Delisle Burns and L. Susan Stebbing, thought *Speculum Mentis* suffered from the same deficiencies as the 'airy imaginings' of some of the Italian philosophers,[122] but the praise which the book elicited far outweighed these negative responses. For instance, F. S. Marvin asserted that 'it is one of the most profound and suggestive treatises of recent years'; C. E. M. Joad maintained that Collingwood had 'written an exceedingly brilliant book'; and, an anonymous reviewer pronounced that 'ce livre est d'un artiste autant que d'un philosophe. M. Collingwood, qui se défie du "jargon" scolastique et du verbalisme, a voulu écrire un livre attrayant; il y a réusse'.[123]

A similar story can be told about the remainder of philosophical books that Collingwood published in his lifetime, with the important qualification that the weight of praise, as opposed to criticism, became increasingly greater. In some quarters Collingwood's *Essay on Philosophical Method* was considered to be 'one of the best of recent philosophical books' and 'one of the finest restatements in contemporary British philosophy of a Platonic and Hegelian metaphysic viewed from a modern standpoint'.[124] For *The Principles of Art* Collingwood received very high praise indeed from some reviewers. The book was described as 'without doubt one of the most important contributions yet made by an English scholar to the study of aesthetics', and one reviewer went as far as to suggest that 'it is not often that one can pronounce a book great without reservation, but I do so here'.[125] The last three philosophical books that Collingwood published during his lifetime – the *Autobiography,* the *Essay on Metaphysics,* and *The New Leviathan* – all included, to a greater or lesser degree, overt political discussions. This is hardly surprising, given that in his later years he feared that irrationalism in the guise of nazism would destroy the values of European civilization. Of all his philosophical books published during his life, *The New Leviathan* received the most favourable reviews. Willoughby Dewar suggested that Collingwood 'is surely here in the right line of succession to the philosopher of Malmesbury', and Ivor Thomas maintained that the work as a whole is 'acute and profound, and deserves serious study'. John Laird was of the opinion that *The New*

Leviathan 'succeeds in its primary intention, that is to say, in restating and also to some extent in advancing the "classical politics".'[126] Many reviewers did, however, find the quality of the treatise variable. Collingwood anticipated this criticism in a letter that he wrote to the Clarendon Press on 6 August 1941, in which he suggested that 'if there are any signs of battiness in the whole work, they will occur in Part 4, which should for that reason be looked at with especial care; I find it very difficult to believe that, dictating to a typewriter, I can produce any thing but rubbish'.[127]

Collingwood, then, was certainly greatly admired, if little discussed, as a philosopher, among certain sections of the academic community. His books were extensively reviewed, and even those reviewers who could not accept the idealism of its latter-day exponent nevertheless expressed admiration for the intellectual manner, even if misguided, in which Collingwood pursued his conclusions. Having said this, it is fair to say that when he died Collingwood was better known and more highly respected, among the more general audience to which he addressed himself, for his archaeological achievements, which were reported occasionally in the *Times.*[128] It was the posthumous publication of *The Idea of History* that gradually attracted many philosophers to his ideas. In the last thirty years Collingwood's metaphysics, philosophy of mind, aesthetics, and philosophy of history have been extensively explored, yet the work that was most admired during his life, that is, his political philosophy, has been allowed to languish in obscurity. In this book I give something of the attention which Collingwood, having set aside the writing of the book that was to have been the culmination of a career steeped in the problems of the philosophy of history, thought that his deliberations on the fundamental principles of politics deserved.

6. Order of enquiry

This study of Collingwood's social and political thought is premissed on the view that the whole of his philosophy is interrelated, and that the whole illuminates and gives substance to the particular part which is the central focus of this study. Such a premiss entails selecting aspects from the whole and bringing them to bear upon the social and political arguments. The other aspects of his thought cannot be fully explored in their own right. Although I hope that the whole of Collingwood's philosophy has been brought to bear upon the part without distortion, my focus is necessarily upon the social and political thought.

In Chapter 2 I claim that *The New Leviathan* reflects certain of Collingwood's long- and short-term preoccupations. From early in his career Collingwood had been concerned to bring about rapprochements between philosophy and history, and between theory and practice. Furthermore, Collingwood's attempt to formulate a linked hierarchy of overlapping forms also constitutes a long-term preoccupation which is both implicit and explicit in his many works. All three concerns, I contend, are evident in *The New Leviathan*.

This is not to say that Collingwood's final work was the telos towards which his thought relentlessly progressed. Certain short-term considerations made it imperative that Collingwood should write *The New Leviathan* rather than complete his *Principles of History*. During the 1930s he became increasingly disillusioned with the response of 'liberal' governments to the rise of fascism in Europe. Fascism, he believed, was a form of irrationalism which threatened to engulf and destroy civilization. Civilization was under threat, not only from fascist irrationalism, which constituted a regression in mental development, but also from a fetish with utilitarian rationalism. Everything had to be justified in terms of its usefulness and its pleasure potential, at the expense of suppressing the emotional aspects of our characters. The outbreak of the Second World War impelled Collingwood to make a contribution to the war effort in the best way he knew. He hoped that *The New Leviathan* would clarify for people what was at stake in the war with Germany. In this Collingwood was caught up in the mood of the time. Philosophers in general were turning their attention to the issues which were integral to the serious predicament in which Britain found itself.

In Chapter 3 the focus turns towards the question of why Hobbes was chosen as the exemplar upon which to build a new theory of politics and society. In addition, the relationship between the two *Leviathan*s is explored, in terms of the triadic conception of the history of political thought. I argue that Collingwood formulated an entirely different criterion of conduct from that articulated by Hobbes. In relation to the levels of rational conduct, Collingwood is shown consciously to go beyond the transcendental intellectualism of Plato and the radical subjectivism of Hobbes in order to arrive at a concrete universal criterion of moral conduct in the form of immanent duty.

The idea of a hierarchical series of levels of rational conduct was, in his view, fundamental to, and a prerequisite of, civil association, or society and the body politic, but its character and significance cannot be fully appreciated without being aware of Collingwood's theory of how the mind develops towards the higher stages of consciousness at which social relations become possible. Chapter 4 is therefore devoted to Collingwood's theory of mind. In this respect special attention will be given to the role of language and emotion in the development of consciousness.

At the higher levels of consciousness the individual begins to free himself, or herself, from capriciousness. Freedom is equated with rational choice. In Chapter 5 Collingwood's view of classical politics is adumbrated. Hobbes, Locke, and Rousseau, Collingwood claimed, all theorized about the social community, but they failed to appreciate or incorporate in their philosophies a theory of the continuous and perpetual work of the body politic, that is, the conversion of the nonsocial into the social community. Classical politics failed to provide a theory of the nonsocial community and its relation to political life. Collingwood's aim in *The New Leviathan* was to rectify this deficiency by formulating a theory of the mixed community in which nonsocial and social elements coincide. Within the mixed community of the body politic three laws of politics govern the conversion process. Throughout Chapter 5 I argue that Collingwood's political views were thoroughly permeated with the ideas of European liberalism, in particular those of de Ruggiero and Croce.

For Collingwood, political activity is not monopolised by the state, nor are the functions of the state merely political. Indeed, the state often promotes economic and moral values in addition to attempting to secure the political value of order for the body politic. The state is not a synonym for the body politic: It is an empirical entity comprising a complex of political and other acts. Political activity occurs everywhere and anywhere in the body politic when rules are being formulated and obeyed. In Chapter 6 Collingwood's theory of mind and society is related to the role of the state in the body politic. In this respect, the principles of state intervention are identified and related to the role of punishment in preventing a regression from the social into a nonsocial condition. Furthermore, Collingwood's theory of international relations is introduced at this point. Aggressive war is, in the international sphere, equivalent to crime in the body politic. Just as punishment is necessary in the body politic to save society, war is necessary in the international sphere to save civilization.

Civilization, for Collingwood, is the principles of society and social behaviour universalised. Civilization is equivalent to socialization: Acting civilly is acting socially and freely. Acting civilly is manifest in three sets of relations: in those between members of a body politic; between members of a body politic and nature; and, between members of one body politic and another. It is shown that Collingwood's discussion is formulated in the vocabulary current during his lifetime. It was conventional to make a distinction between savagery, barbarism, and civilization. For Collingwood, savagery did not mean a total absence of civilization, nor civilization a total absence of aspects of savage life. To attain the level of free will is to have achieved the will to promote civilization. In every civilization elements of both barbarity and civility are present, because the conversion process is one that is perpetually in motion. There always remains a nonsocial element in the body politic, and therefore force, which characterises the relationship between the social and nonsocial elements, can never totally be eliminated. Force is anathema to the ideal of civility. Civilization contains within itself elements of the condition from whence it emerged, namely savagery. The difference between savagery and barbarism is that the former progresses towards civilization, whereas the latter actively attempts to retard or reverse the civilizing process. In this respect barbarism perverts rational consciousness by attempting to suppress the freedom of the will. Collingwood's views on savagery, barbarism, and civilization are taken up in Chapters 7 and 8.

One additional emphasis in this book remains to be mentioned. Collingwood's lifelong preoccupation with establishing the credentials of historical knowledge is manifest in his discussions of morality and civilization. His avowed aim was to articulate the principles of a historical morality and the conditions of a historical civilization. During the course of this book I hope to show what Collingwood means by these terms.

2

The New Leviathan in context

1. Introduction

This chapter is principally addressed to determining the place of *The New Leviathan* in Collingwood's long-term intellectual concerns. One such concern was the idea of a *scale of forms*. The theory of a scale of forms which is expressed in *An Essay on Philosophical Method* was formulated in *Speculum Mentis* and the moral philosophy lectures. The methodological considerations were excised from the lectures when the theory was published. The moral philosophy lectures form a large part of the subject matter of *The New Leviathan*. It is not surprising, then, that a version of the scale of forms, originally articulated in conjunction with the moral philosophy lectures, should emerge in *The New Leviathan*. Further, I argue that Collingwood's final work is in fact the culmination of his persistent endeavour to bring about rapprochements between philosophy and history, and between theory and practice. In this chapter the focus will be upon explaining what Collingwood understood the rapprochements between theory and practice, and history and philosophy, to entail. In this respect, it will be appropriate to give a brief indication of how these concerns become manifest in *The New Leviathan*. This is not to suggest a crude teleogical progression towards a culminating point. Indeed, the culminating point, for Collingwood, would have been *The Principles of History*. We therefore need to revert to various short-term considerations to explain why Collingwood produced *The New Leviathan* rather than the work on history which he had intended.

2. The long-term considerations

A complex congeries of reasons can be given for Collingwood's decision to write *The New Leviathan*. The reasons can fruitfully, although no-

27

tionally, be distinguished into his long-term and short-term, or immediate, concerns. The moral philosophy lectures that Collingwood revised copiously throughout his career formed the basis of what was to become *The New Leviathan*. The lectures included discussions of the method appropriate to philosophical enquiry, and the theory expounded provided the exemplification of the method. Having revised and expanded the methodological considerations for publication as *An Essay on Philosophical Method* in 1933, it is surprising that he took so long to publish its concrete exemplar. The relation between the two books, as theory and its application, has not gone unnoticed by commentators.[1] The unpublished manuscripts confirm that Collingwood himself was beginning to articulate the idea of a series of overlapping forms in the context of the moral philosophy lectures in the early 1920s. In this respect, *Speculum Mentis* and the *Outlines of a Philosophy of Art* are thoroughly imbued with the concept of philosophical method that was modified and published in 1933.

The scale of forms

The ostensible purpose of *An Essay on Philosophical Method* is to establish the peculiar character of the philosophical concept by comparing the method of philosophy with that of the sciences, both empirical and exact, or analytic. It is assumed, Collingwood suggests, that in the natural sciences the form of analysis is that of classifying instances into mutually exclusive species of a genus. The scientific concept has a variety of individual instances, all of which are differentiated into species of the genus by means of classification which unites groups of individual instances on the ground that they share a common characteristic. For example, each colour of each coloured thing is united in the concept 'colour': The form of unification which the concept achieves here is general. However, the concept also unifies specific instances of colour, such as green, yellow, and red, into species: This form of unification is generic. The exact sciences, such as mathematics, classify a priori, and are able to achieve distinct and exhaustive classes which constitute species of the genus, whereas the empirical sciences, such as natural history, encounter borderline cases which are difficult to place in any one species, but such exceptions are rare and can usually be accommodated within the classifications which comprise the concept without undermining its efficacy.[2]

Collingwood does not wish to enter into the question of how accurately the traditional theory of classification portrays the methods of the empirical and exact sciences: His point is that however true it may be of the sciences, such a theory of distinct, exclusive, and exhaustive species does not articulate the method of the philosophical explication of the concept. The species of a philosophical genus are characterised by a quite different logical relation. This is a point which Collingwood laboured quite frequently in both his published and unpublished writings. Simultaneously Collingwood was working out the character of a philosophical concept in his philosophies of spirit and of action. In 1923 he argued that within formal logic no one species of a genus includes within itself the universal to any greater degree than any other. Each species is an alternative, and complete, manifestation of the universal: Odd and even numbers are both equally good examples of the universal number. Collingwood objects to this view of the philosophical concept, arguing that if each specification of its species completely embodies the universal, then the distinctions between its forms are not explicable in terms of the universal itself. Such distinctions have to be explained by appealing to something extraneous to the universal concept. To explain why there are so many religions when each embodies the essence of religion perfectly is not possible without reference to reasons external to religion itself. We have to resort to a combination of religious factors, and other factors such as politics and economics, to explain the proliferation of species. The universal is now only one element in its instances, and religion is incapable of giving an account of religious facts: Each particular embodies religion and other diverse elements from outside itself.

This objection can only be met, Collingwood argues, by explaining the apparently extraneous elements not as alien but as in some sense derived from the universal. Such a view of the concept entails 'maintaining that the universal is not indifferently and completely present in all its specifications, but is realised in varying degrees and therefore in various forms'.[3] The coordinate and equal embodiments of the generic concept are now viewed as forms in a series, each of which embodies the generic essence more adequately than its predecessor, and less adequately than its successor. Aristotle was responsible for articulating this concept of a scale of forms, but his theory needs to be extended, or improved, by giving reasons why a specific form has to be succeeded by another. It is necessary to show, Collingwood argues, why no point on the scale should be regarded as its culmination. In each form there is a disjunction between what it is and what it tries to be, and in attempting to modify itself it becomes transformed into something else.[4]

This description of how best to explicate the universal concept of action is equally true of, and is exemplified by, Collingwood's philosophy of spirit. In *Speculum Mentis* he argues that he is concerned to dispel the theory that art, religion, science, history, and philosophy are all coordinate species of a genus, each autonomous and valid as a single part of the mind which is restricted to accounting for a limited part of reality.[5] These forms are not coordinate species of a genus, however, but experience as a whole, denying at the same time the validity of the other claims to absolute knowledge of the universe. Each form strives to be what it is not and in doing so transforms itself into a form of experience which stands above it in a linked series of overlapping forms. At the top of the series stands philosophy, which is experience as a whole, in that it makes explicit what was implicit in each of the forms and incorporates their positive aspects within itself. These forms are serially arranged in a logical order in which each is built upon its predecessors and is therefore not a completely new manifestation, or embodiment, of the universal, 'but is essentially a modification of the term before'.[6] None is autonomous, and each includes within itself the rest, but in denying this each presents a false view of itself. Basically, each of the forms is viewed as a philosophical error, overextending itself, and this is why each passes over into the next. In *Outlines of a Philosophy of Art* Collingwood sums up his view of the relation between the forms of the spirit:

The five phases of spiritual life which we have enumerated in this crude outline – and other phases which further analysis might distinguish – are not species of any common genus. They are activities each of which presupposes and includes within itself those that logically precede it; thus religion is inclusively art, science inclusively religion and therefore art, and so on. And on the other hand each is in a sense all that follows it; for instance, in possessing religion we already possess philosophy of a sort, but we possess it only in the form in which it is present in, and indeed constitutes, religion.[7]

The unity of the life of spirit, Collingwood goes on to argue, resembles that of an 'infinitely increasing spiral rather than the unity of a rotating circle. The energy which causes the spiral to expand is simply that pure activity which is the spirit'.[8]

Whenever Collingwood writes of the forms of practical reason (the useful, the right, and the dutiful); their associated forms of action (the economic or utilitarian, the political or regularian, and the moral or ethical); and their associated and integral forms of goodness (the economic good is that of individual utility, the political good is that of rightness or social orderliness in the body politic, and, the moral good is universal and good in itself);[9] and even when he writes of a serial form of goods which differ in matters of detail from those just mentioned, he always emphasizes that their relation is not that of species of a genus but that of overlapping series of forms in which the lower includes within itself the potential of the higher. The lower good denies that potential in asserting its own distinct principle, but in claiming to be practical reason, action or goodness in its universal aspect overextends itself and passes over into the next stage, which builds upon its predecessors and includes within itself the positive aspect of the lower, modifying it and denying its universal claim to validity, while accommodating its insights into a more adequate theory of the concept which sums up the position on the scale to that point: 'The higher thus negates the lower, and at the same time re-affirms it'.[10] None is exclusive, and none is autonomous: Each is an integral aspect of all the others. In an early attempt to delineate the forms of goodness, Collingwood recognises that the method necessary for such an exercise raises certain logical problems[11] if viewed as species of a genus, but when understood as a series of overlapping forms none is exclusive; thus utility is a characteristic of all actions,[12] and the same can be said of rightness and duty. In the 'Moral Philosophy Lectures' of about 1929 and after, which follow the serial form that anticipates the forms of practical reason discussed in *The New Leviathan,* Collingwood argues that 'the moral goodness of the good will contains in itself, as indispensable elements, the subordinate goods of utility and rightness. Without them it is a chimera, a false abstraction'.[13] They 'are not species of goodness but moments which imply each other in such a way that any rational act exhibits all three'.[14] In acting morally we do not ignore economic and political considerations; instead such considerations are conjoined with others more fundamental: We ask whether the end of economic action which determines the means is good, and whether the rule in political action is a good rule.[15] Essentially, then, duty 'sets right and expediency alike on a firmer basis than ever'.[16] Each action exhibits the characteristics of utility and right, but also exhibits those of duty. Collingwood maintains that

duty is thus the truth of action; it is what all action really is, it is so far as we act morally that we really act at all. Yet in acting morally we do not rid ourselves of such distinctions as that of means and end, law and the application of law, any more than we shake ourselves free of the physical world or leave our animal nature behind us. Moral action includes all these things within itself, makes of them the material out of which it builds its own world.[17]

This view of the relation between the forms of practical reason, rational action, or goodness also informs the 1933 and 1940 lectures on moral philosophy.[18] The idea of a linked series of overlapping forms of practical reason is pivotal and crucial to *The New Leviathan* in advancing his theory of society, politics, and civilization. It is therefore of some importance that we should acquaint ourselves with the theory of philosophical method which explains and justifies the manner in which the philosophical concept of action is articulated. This is not to say that *The New Leviathan* slavishly follows the theory as articulated in *An Essay on Philosophical Method,* but that the latter, in essentials, forms the basis of the method of the former.

Collingwood himself came to view *Speculum Mentis* as 'an introduction to a philosophy' which in *An Essay on Philosophical Method* was 'beginning to take shape'.[19] Mink has rightly pointed out that the latter is self-consciously an attempt to formulate the principles which informed the manner of philosophical thought employed in the former. Instead of pursuing the absolute philosophy which *Speculum Mentis* implied, in *An Essay on Philosophical Method* 'Collingwood moved from a dialectic of experience to a dialectic of concepts'.[20] In addition, as Donagan has contended, Collingwood changes his view of the relation of dogmatic, or false, philosophies to an overlapping scale of forms.[21] In *Speculum Mentis* Collingwood argues that each of the forms of experience, or spirit, is implicitly a philosophy without realising it. The explicitness of their philosophies is only realised when contemplation of their ostensible objects leads to the contemplation of what they take themselves to be, but because the view of their object is in error the subject is also deformed in the process of being contemplated.[22] These 'dogmatic' philosophies are 'dead by-products of the forms of consciousness': Each is a terminus from which there is no advance. In this respect, 'aesthetic philosophy is not the mother of religious philosophy but the corpse of art'.[23] In order to advance, one has to retreat and begin again in relation to another form of experience. In *An Essay on Philosophical Method* this view of inadequate or dead philosophies is repudiated, or at least radically modified. Collingwood argues that systematic philosophizing has as one of its tasks 'to show the truth of theories which, considered as self-contained and distinct philosophies would have to be condemned as errors'.[24] Ideally, even the crudest attempt at philosophy finds a place on a scale of overlapping forms.

What, then, is the character of this scale of forms which differentiates the philosophical concept from that found in other branches of knowledge? In essence, each of the species of a philosophical genus are related and overlap by 'combining differences of degree and kind, distinction and opposition'.[25]

In order to establish this, Collingwood argues that no philosophical method can be valid if it depends upon the notion of mutually exclusive species. Any attempt to treat the philosophical concept as exclusive species must result in committing certain fallacies. In the first place it asserts a disjunctive proposition which contends that any instance of a philosophical genus must belong to one of a number of specific classes. However, because instances overlap, they may fall into more than one class.[26] The disjunctive fallacy which divides a genus into exclusive species is a single principle which may be applied positively or negatively. When applied positively it results in the fallacy of 'precarious margins'. If, for example, we differentiate the generic concept of action into specific species, in the hope of being able to determine the characteristics exclusive to each, we would soon find that an overlap occurs in which certain

actions exhibit mixed motives, and which therefore defy exclusive classification. One way of attempting to get around such a problem is to
ignore the overlap by concentrating attention upon the margin where
the overlap between one form and another is not yet apparent. Enquiries
of this type assume that the overlap detected in a certain class can be
relied upon not to spread, and that beyond the affected area lies a region
in which the classification is pure and exclusive. This margin which exhibits the characteristics of the pure class is precarious, because to admit
of an overlap in the first place is to relinquish any grounds for assuming
it will not spread.[27]

If we apply the disjunctive fallacy negatively, in order to avoid the
fallacy of precarious margins, we fall victim to a different fallacy. To admit
that the overlap between classes is in principle limitless may lead us to
proceed as if the classes coincide in their entirety. Thus instead of distinguishing distinct species we conclude that they are identical. For example, the observation that the performance of one's duties often leads
to an increase in the general happiness provides the grounds for concluding that there is no distinction to be made 'between the concept of
duty and the concept of promoting happiness': This is the 'fallacy of identified coincidents'.[28]

Collingwood argues that even though the philosophical concept can
be divided into species of a genus, the species are not coordinate classes
embodying equally the essence of the genus. The instances exhibit differences in degree, that is, each may differ as subordinates and super-
ordinates in the extent to which it embodies the essence of the concept.
In other words, some are more adequate specifications of the concept
than others. The implication of this is that a species of a genus which
embodies a certain variable, or essence, will differ from the species in
kind to the extent that it 'embodies some variable attribute in a specific
degree'.[29] In so far as the species embodies the variable, it differs from
others in degree; in the way in which it specifies the generic essence, it
differs from the others in kind. If we apply this to *The New Leviathan*,
for example, utility, right, and duty are all forms of practical reason, each
embodying the generic essence of action whose variable goodness is embodied in different degrees; in so far as each asserts itself as goodness in
general, or as the universal essence of action, it differs from the others
in kind.

Differences in degree and kind, however, are not peculiar to philosophical method. A scale of forms can be constructed on the same principles in the sciences. Ice, water, and steam are different kinds of the
generic essence of water and thus constitute a scale of forms. They differ
in degree to the extent that they embody the common variable of heat.
The variable is extraneous to the generic essence of water, which is rep-

resented in its solid, liquid, and gaseous forms in the formula H_2O. Heat is extraneous to the formula, and whatever degree of heat water embodies, its generic essence remains the same. Even without the variable, at a temperature of absolute zero the generic essence would still remain H_2O.

The philosophical concept differs from the nonphilosophical concept in that 'the variable is identical with the generic essence itself'.[30] What this means is that a difference of degree cannot render the generic essence unaffected. For example, if goodness is identical with the generic essence of action, a variation in the degree of goodness entails a consequent variation in the degree to which the generic essence is embodied in the form. The lower on the scale an instance appears, the less adequate, satisfactory, or perfect its embodiment, or specification, of the essence of the genus. The generic essence, in a philosophical scale, is realised more adequately as the scale is ascended, and less adequately as it is descended.

Furthermore, Collingwood contends, differences in degree, with their consequent differences in kind, are not, on a philosophical scale of forms, quantifiable. In other words, the degree to which the form specifies the generic essence cannot be measured. We can measure degrees of heat, but not of goodness, pleasantness, beauty, or other philosophical concepts. The most that can be done is to estimate their degrees relative to each other and to the whole, but they resist measurement because there is never merely a difference of degree, but also and always fused with it a difference of kind: They are at once differences of degree and kind. Measurement can be applicable only to the quantification of differences of degree in a pure form. This, Collingwood argues, is the basis of the peculiarity of a philosophical scale of forms: Its forms are at once differences in degree and kind, whereas in a nonphilosophical scale 'there are differences of degree, and co-ordinated with them differences of kind'.[31]

The principle of overlapping classes serves to explain why differences of degree and kind are fused. Both are species of the genus 'difference' and consequently overlap, forming a difference which has the character of both.[32] To explain the fusion in these terms gives rise to a difficulty which remains unresolved in the *Essay on Philosophical Method*. In establishing the differentiae of philosophical method, Collingwood compares it with the method of the empirical and exact sciences. Both philosophical method and scientific method are species of the genus 'method' and, according to the principle of overlapping forms, should fuse to partake of the character of both. It looks suspiciously as though Collingwood himself has succumbed to the fallacy of precarious margins by identifying an area of philosophical method upon which the overlap of scientific method has not yet encroached, that is, a pure margin, on which to build his theory. This criticism aside, we must proceed with Collingwood's explication of a philosophical scale of forms.

So far we have seen that the philosophical concept has the character of an overlapping series of forms instead of that of coordinate species of a genus. It has this character because the variable in the philosophical concept is identical to the essence of the genus, and is therefore not extraneous to the philosophical specification. The embodiment of different degrees of the variable is responsible for a subordinate and superordinate relation between the species. Each level in the scale is a more adequate specification, or embodiment, of the generic essence than the one below it, and its specification, being more adequate, constitutes a difference in kind. The differences in degrees cannot be measured, because they are fused with differences of kind, this fusion itself being a result of the principle of overlapping classes where two species of a genus overlap to form a fusion which partakes of the character of both.

A further differentiation now needs to be added, that of the fusion of opposites and distincts. In nonphilosophical thought, opposition and distinction mutually exclude each other, but in the philosophical concept, because of the principle of the overlap of classes, they are fused into a single relation partaking of both. The implications that the fusion has for a scale of forms are as follows. If the variable in a philosophical scale of forms is identical to its essence, then there can be no point on the scale in which the variable is not present. The scale begins, then, not at zero, but at unity in which the generic essence is minimally embodied.[33] The scale therefore has no absolute opposite to the generic essence, but this does not imply that opposition is absent and only distinction present. The lowest form on the scale, in which the essence is minimally present, constitutes a distinct realisation which is the extreme, or limiting case, on the scale and which is 'opposite relatively to the rest of the scale'.[34] Collingwood illustrates this point by arguing that in the case of goodness, in its minimal manifestation, it is distinct in its relation to the other forms on the scale, but at the same time it stands in opposition to them as the negation, or privation, of goodness. The point is this: It is not adequate to call the act in which there is the minimal embodiment of goodness 'a very poor kind of good; we must go further and call it positively bad: the opposite of good'.[35]

Goodness and badness are not two distincts: The former is present to a low degree and considered bad, or opposed, in relation to those degrees above it. Considered in itself it has the character of good, but considered in relation to the higher embodiment it becomes thoroughly bad. At every point in the scale, opposition and distinction are fused. Each of two adjacent forms is distinct and considered good in itself, but in relation to the one above, it becomes bad and is hence opposed to it.

Further analysis of the fusion between opposites and distincts reveals more clearly the reason for the overlap in a philosophical scale of forms and more adequately reveals the specific character of that overlap. The lower of two forms on a scale not only embodies goodness in general, but also embodies it specifically, or in its own way. When compared to the higher of the two forms, the lower not only loses its general but also its specific goodness. The higher at once denies the specific goodness of the lower as opposed to the higher, but also affirms it by asserting the specific goodness in a modified and higher form. The reason why the lower gives way to the higher is because it is not able to deliver what it promises. The goodness the form purports to possess is only possessed inadequately and approximately: 'Just as it cannot wholly achieve goodness, so it cannot wholly achieve even that specific and admittedly imperfect form of it which is characteristically its own'.[36] It is the form above which achieves what the lower purported to possess, but the higher, when compared to the next specification above it, purports to be what that form is and fails, as its subordinate did, to possess genuinely what it claims to be. Each successive level is a more adequate embodiment of the generic essence, and is a distinct specification of it, while at the same time standing opposed to the lower as a higher and more adequate specification – that is, negating it as an inadequate embodiment of the generic essence, yet affirming it by including within itself the content of the form it denies. It does not, however, absorb into itself the negative aspect of the lower. Utilitarianism is right to affirm expediency in its description of action, but wrong to think that there is nothing else. A higher form denies this negative aspect of utilitarianism while reaffirming the positive.

This accounts for the overlap of the lower by the higher, but in what way does the lower itself overlap the higher? Collingwood argues that utilitarianism as a moral theory claims part of the content of the higher moral theories to be utilitarian doctrine itself, but rejects what it does not claim for itself as mistaken nonsense. Thus the overlap consists in the lower claiming for itself aspects of the higher, yet denying those aspects which it cannot accommodate. The relation which holds in the scale is not 'an overlap of extension between classes, but an overlap of intension between concepts, each in its degree a specification of their generic essence, but each embodying it more adequately than the one below'.[37]

What is asked of the higher of two forms is not that it agree with the lower, but that it should explain it. The lower constitutes the 'experience' given to the higher stage. This is the case at any point on the scale, and the task of each successive form is to construct a theory about that which precedes it. The content of the lower, by means of intense thought, is elevated to a higher level of rationality.[38] As we will see in the following chapter, each of the stages of practical reason – the useful, the right, and the dutiful – more adequately embody rationality by gradually eliminating caprice.

At each stage in the serially related sequence the whole of the scale is summed up to that point, and each form is its culmination, 'because the specific form at which we stand is the generic concept itself, so far as our thought yet conceives it'.[39] What we have at each stage, then, is a modification of that which precedes it: that is, experience raised to a more adequate and higher degree of rationality.

The principle which runs through Collingwood's whole account of a philosophical scale of forms is that philosophy is not a voyage of discovery in which things previously unknown become known. Instead, philosophy aims at understanding better something that is already understood.[40] In the 1929 moral philosophy lectures, for example, he argues that in enquiring into the character of action we have to assume that we already know what it is. Our knowledge of it, however, is confused and inadequate. We must begin a philosophical enquiry by making explicit those confused concepts, 'not to acquire brand new ideas that have never been in our minds before' but to 'go on to clear them up and improve them by degrees'.[41] The purpose of philosophy is to achieve, not new knowledge as such, but adequacy.[42] Each successive specification on a scale expresses more adequately the generic essence, where 'more adequately' means a more reasoned, or rational, form. This principle of coming to know better, or more adequately, something that is already known permeates *The New Leviathan*. In discussing the modern European mind, for example, Collingwood begins at the lowest stage of consciousness and ascends a serially related scale in which each form is a 'modification of the one before it' (*NL*, 9.36). The qualifications which *The New Leviathan* impose upon the theory of method in *An Essay on Philosophical Method* are more appropriately discussed in relation to the substantive issues which give rise to them. The point to be made here is simply this: The principles of method which inform *The New Leviathan* are in substance, with minor changes in detail, those exemplified in varying degrees in *Speculum Mentis, Outlines of a Philosophy of Art,* and later *The Principles of Art,* as well as in the lectures on moral philosophy, and articulated as a theory in *An Essay on Philosophical Method.*

Rapprochement between history and philosophy

Collingwood's attempt to bring about a rapprochement between philosophy and history has a considerable bearing on the form that his *New Leviathan* took, and, I want to suggest, constituted a reason for writing it.

It is by no means clear what Collingwood meant by the idea of a rapprochement between philosophy and history. A number of possibilities present themselves. First, it could mean nothing more innocuous than the belief that historians and philosophers should take more account of each other. Second, it could mean that philosophical issues have a historical dimension. The third, most controversial, and radical of the meanings could be that philosophy and history have the same order of enquiry: They are identified, if not identical. The first and second meanings have so little content that it is hard to imagine that Collingwood would have devoted his whole life to achieving such commonplace results. Only the third can match the grandiose conception that Collingwood had of his mission in life. Let us examine the evidence that this was his purpose, before proceeding further to investigate his views on the relation between philosophy and history.

It is my contention that *The New Leviathan* is, in fact, the concrete exemplar of the union of philosophy and history. There are good reasons for holding such a view. In a letter to Knox dated 11 September 1936, Collingwood makes it quite clear that for him the philosophy of mind, the subject matter of part I of *The New Leviathan*, is to be subsumed under the category of history: 'What I do wish to resolve without residue into history is the *Philosophy of Spirit*, or Theory of Mind, or Science of Human Nature'.[43] He goes on to argue that logic or pure metaphysics is prior to a philosophy of mind. It is clear that only some branches of philosophy should be resolved into history: Collingwood argues, 'It is only those philosophies which, despairing of a genuine metaphysics, resolve all philosophy into a philosophy of mind, which must fear "total dissolution into history if I had my way" '.[44] By 1939 Collingwood had even resolved logic into history. Logic, he claimed, was nothing more than the exposition of what principles give validity to thought during certain historical periods. For him, there was now no residue of philosophy which stood outside history: 'Philosophy as a separate discipline is liquidated by being converted into history'.[45] In this respect Collingwood was only doing something similar to that which his Italian sources of inspiration had done: Gentile had identified philosophy and history, and Croce had resolved the former into the latter.

It is important to bear in mind that *The Idea of History*, the structure of which is Knox's creation, does not constitute reliable evidence for the stage in the rapprochement which Collingwood had reached towards the end of his life. His unfinished book *The Principles of History* was to have given the theoretical exposition of the identity, and Collingwood himself had authorised the publication of that part which had been written. Knox, however, disregarded Collingwood's authorisation on the ground that the work was not of sufficiently high merit. Indeed, Margit Hurup Nielson claims that Knox told her in October 1975 that he went against Collingwood's wishes because it would have been 'disastrous' to have published the work.[46] Knox made no secret of the fact that he disapproved of Collingwood's later philosophical writings. He said that Collingwood's 'enthusiasm for history tended to make him "turn traitor" to his philosophical vocation'.[47] *The Principles of History,* then, written at a time when Collingwood had 'turned traitor' to the philosophical cause, was simply unacceptable to Knox, who thought that it did not represent the true Collingwood.

It is significant that Knox himself came to view *The New Leviathan* as the embodiment of Collingwood's resolution of philosophy into history. Initially Knox had viewed *The New Leviathan* as a diversion from, rather than as a continuation of, Collingwood's previous concerns. Knox belatedly intimated that a connection between the rapprochement of history and philosophy and its manifestation in *The New Leviathan* could be sustained. He argued that 'Collingwood regarded it as his life's work to bring about a *rapprochement* between philosophy and history. . . . The last of his works, The New Leviathan (1942), contains his only contribution to this result, but he had earlier made history the *Leitmotiv* of his work'.[48] Knox does not go on to show in what respects Collingwood's final work represents a contribution to the rapprochement between philosophy and history. What needs to be emphasized is that if *The New Leviathan* constitutes the embodiment of the rapprochement, then both history and philosophy are transformed into something beyond that which can be found in *The Idea of History.* On the principle of overlapping forms, one could argue, philosophy and history, two species of method, overlap and constitute a form of enquiry which partakes of both and in which differences of degree and kind, and opposites and distincts, are fused. Collingwood, throughout his life, attempted to define the relationship between history and philosophy, and he admired those writers, particularly the Italians Gentile, Croce, and de Ruggiero, who were attempting to liberate the historical mode of enquiry from its enslavement and subordination to the claims of natural science. Collingwood was clear in his mind that history constituted an entirely different form of knowledge from that achieved by invoking the procedures of natural-scientific enquiry,[49] but the question of the relation between philosophy and history was a problem which troubled him for over twenty years. It is not surprising that he did, from time to time, arrive at different conclusions. Collingwood was not one of those philosophers who was a slave to the principle of consistency. He did not mind reformulating his views, even if that meant abandoning a theoretical position he had previously held, in order to find a satisfactory solution to a problem. Indeed, he criticized Cook Wilson quite severely for refraining from publishing for fear of betraying a change of mind from one book to another, and he praised John Ruskin quite highly for repudiating the view that 'the wise man never contradicts himself'. Collingwood sees a certain merit in the view that 'truth is many-sided and that self-contradiction may easily be a mark not of weakness but of strength[,] not of confusion, but of a wide and comprehensive view which embraces much more truth than the one-sided consistency of the logicians'.[50]

In his first book, *Religion and Philosophy* (1916), we find Collingwood attempting to discern the relation between philosophy and history, and he concludes that they are identical activities. His argument in support of this conclusion is relatively unsophisticated in comparison to his later formulations of the problem. In this, his earliest book, Collingwood postulates the existence of a past, which he calls history, that exists independently of the knowing mind.[51] He appears to be subscribing implicitly to the realist concept of the correspondence theory of truth, which maintains that objects of knowledge exist independently of the mind that seeks to know them, and that the truth of our statements depends upon the extent to which the statements correspond to the objects described. History, for Collingwood, constitutes both the 'objective fact' and the mode of enquiry which determines it.[52] History, however, is not viewed as independent of philosophy; without the former, the latter is impossible. History designates what exists in experience; it is fact, and without it philosophy would have no object; indeed, 'no form of consciousness can exist without an object',[53] and therefore, by implication, no such form can exist without history. On the other hand, history cannot exist without philosophy: 'There is no such thing as an entirely non-philosophical history', because history makes complex philosophical assumptions. It needs to be emphasized that Collingwood is here transforming the notion of history as fact into history as the mode of enquiry that determines fact. It is history as a mode of enquiry that assumes philosophical presuppositions. History is concerned with evidence and has to weigh that evidence on the basis of epistemological assumptions about its value. Ethical thought determines the meaning of those actions that history attempts to describe. History also has to operate on the basis of metaphysical conclusions, in order to ascertain what events it believes could and could not happen.[54] History as a mode of enquiry, and philosophy, are the same thing. History as the object of historical research is the whole of existence, 'and this is also the object of philosophy'. History as subject, or mode of investigation, seeks to understand all that has occurred and all that is occurring, and this, too, is the concern of philosophy: 'History and philosophy are therefore the same thing'.[55]

In *Speculum Mentis* and 'The Nature and Aims of a Philosophy of History', Collingwood refines his arguments more rigorously, expunging any hint of the realist epistemology and of the correspondence theory of truth. Like Croce, Collingwood now argues that the various forms of experience do not stand outside of, and opposed to, their objects; they actually create them. Croce, for instance, had maintained in his *Logic* that the spirit has nothing external to itself, and that where we find concepts of something external, such as mechanisms and natural phenomena, we find that it is 'the spirit itself, which creates the so-called external, because it suits it to do so'.[56] Croce maintains that one cannot distinguish between a form of knowledge and its method. It is an abstraction to separate a method from the activity to which it belongs. It is the artificial distinction between form and method which leads to the interposition of the idea of an *object* of the form:

But since the method is the form itself, so form and method are the object itself. Certainly, all the forms of the spirit have a common object, which is Reality; but this is not because reality is separated from them, but because they are reality: they therefore *have* not, but *are* this object. Thus the forms of knowledge have not a theoretic object, but create it: they themselves are that object.[57]

In *Speculum Mentis,* Collingwood explicitly sets out to explore the various forms of knowledge, or *forms of experience,* as he prefers to call them. He blames the Renaissance for shattering the unity of the mind that had existed in the Middle Ages. Freedom, as it was conceived during the Renaissance, had the implication of severing the forms of experience from one another. Each resisted any interference from the others, and developed independently from the rest. Following from this, Collingwood suggests, 'Each tended to become a specialized activity pursued by specialists for the applause of specialists, useless to the rest of mankind and unsatisfactory even to the specialist when he turned upon himself and asked why he was pursuing it. This is the point to which we have come today'.[58]

Collingwood sets himself the task of restoring the unity that the Renaissance had shattered. It is the business of philosophy to examine the presuppositions and assumptions of each form of experience and to determine its place in experience as a whole. In 'The Nature and Aims of a Philosophy of History' (1924–1925), for instance, Collingwood maintains that philosophical reflection upon history must 'attempt to discover its place in human experience as a whole, its relation to other forms of experience, its origin, and its validity'.[59] In Collingwood, as we found with Croce, the forms of experience create their objects. The tests of the truth and error of the knowledge generated by the different forms of experience are the familiar idealist categories of coherence, or consistency, and contradiction, respectively; that which approximates consistency partakes of a greater degree of truth than that which is contradictory.[60] Collingwood follows both Hegel and Gentile in constructing a linked hierarchy of forms of experience which emerge in the course of a dialectical development. The actual specifications of the scale of forms were, as I suggested in Chapter 1, formulated by Gentile in a perfunctory and suggestive manner, but Collingwood takes the suggestions and transforms them into a comprehensive and rigorous exploration of the place of each form in relation to the others and in relation to the whole.

History, Collingwood believed, although more adequate than its rivals lower down on the linked hierarchy of forms of experience, is nevertheless, like them, a philosophical mistake; it cannot maintain what it asserts. W. J. van der Dussen cites a number of passages in *Speculum Mentis* which clearly support this claim.[61] Collingwood talks of history as asserting 'concrete facts', and as having as its criterion of truth 'nothing but historical fact itself'.[62] In other words, he is suggesting that the truth of a historical statement is determined by its correspondence to its object. He further asserts that 'the business of history is to state what happens and has happened, and that only'.[63] Van der Dussen acknowledges that Collingwood 'explicitly renounces realism; his discussion of historical philosophy makes this clear (SM[*Speculum Mentis*], 281–287). It is also clear, however, that at the same time his conception of history is a plainly realistic one'.[64] To put the matter this way is not inaccurate, but it is misleading, in that it assumes a contradiction which is, in fact, not there. To say that this is Collingwood's conception of history implies that the picture he gives is his own notion of what history is. However, it is clear throughout that Collingwood is giving history's *own* conception of itself.[65] It thinks itself to be determining concrete facts and recovering reality, and in so far as it thinks this it is deceiving itself. Let me emphasize, then, that Collingwood's philosophical method is idealist, and that he applies his philosophy to what he considers to be history's self-image, that is, its realist conception of itself. Indeed, he confirmed this in a letter to de Ruggiero in 1923 when he said 'Thus in each form there is a contradiction between its own view of itself and an outsider's, observer's, view of it (artist's theory of art and philosopher's theory of art, etc.) and this contradiction arises from self-ignorance'.[66] In the same letter he said that the argument of *Speculum Mentis* is 'all very commonplace and familiar; mostly stolen from Hegel, and other people'; in essence this confirms the sincerity of Collingwood's statement made three years earlier, in 1920, of his being 'quite ready to undertake the task . . ., of being the only English neo-Hegelian'.[67] Indeed, that Collingwood (pace his repudiation in *An Autobiography*) was quite happy to be associated with idealism at the time is evidenced by the excited tone in which he wrote to de Ruggiero, in the year of the publication of *Speculum Mentis,* that 'people, intending praise, say as T. H. Green was to Kant and Hegel, so is R. G. C. to Croce! and Gentile!'[68] This sentence appears to be an oblique reference to the debt that *Speculum Mentis* owes to the two Italians.

It is misleading, then, to suggest in the context of *Speculum Mentis,* as van der Dussen does, that Collingwood's conception of history at this time was realist in essence. It implies that Collingwood was himself a realist in this respect, rather than that he accepted history's view of itself and found that view to be a philosophical mistake. He found it to be deficient by applying idealist philosophical principles to it. Van der Dussen, in my view, is mistaken in his belief that Collingwood, at the time of writing *Speculum Mentis,* cannot be classified as belonging to 'any specific movement, either Idealism or Realism' on the grounds that elements of both are to be found in Collingwood's work.[69] Collingwood's principles of philosophical criticism throughout *Speculum Mentis* are thoroughly idealist, and he uses them consistently to expose the fallacies in the claims of realism. Thus, to say that Collingwood held a realist conception of history is to imply that it was at variance with the idealist aspects of the text. The whole enterprise is idealist – an attempt to reaffirm the unity of experience as a whole, and in so far as history claims to be knowledge of this whole, it has a false conception of itself and its object.

History breaks down, or reveals itself to be a philosophical mistake, because it purports to be knowledge of the entire world of facts, whereas this whole can never be known. The parts of history can only be known in relation to the context which gives structure to the whole, 'but since this context is always incomplete, we can never know a single part as it actually is'.[70] History conceives its object to be concrete fact, that is, 'fact to which its context is not irrelevant but essential';[71] and because the whole which it purports to know cannot be known, its parts are also rendered unknowable. History as a form of experience posits an object outside itself, the knowing of which makes no difference to it as object. However, Collingwood maintains, there is an object whose nature changes in the act of being known. An error reacts upon the mind itself and, in doing so, affects its behaviour: 'Mind is what it does'.[72] History, then, is wrong to conceive its object as something standing outside of mind, because the infinite whole of which there is possible knowledge is nothing other than *'the nature of the knowing mind as such'.*[73]

It is appropriate at this point, and a source of illumination, to compare Collingwood's enterprise with that of Gentile. Gentile conceives the business of philosophy, as does Collingwood, in so far as it is the ultimate form of concrete spiritual activity, as that 'which judges all others and can itself be judged by none. To judge philosophy, in fact, is to philosophize'.[74] In judging history, Gentile distinguishes between two modes of conceiving it. In the first place history is understood by some to deal with 'nothing but the historical fact in its multiplicity'.[75] This conception of history degrades mind from a spiritual entity to a natural entity. It posits mind as an object outside the activity of history, and it conceives act as fact: 'Nature *is,* mind *becomes'*.[76] It is this conception of history that Collingwood takes to be the historical form of experience and that he subjects to the dissolving attention of philosophical criticism. However,

Gentile's own conception of history, as opposed to the first he adumbrates, is one in which subject and object are united and where history and philosophy become identical. In this second conception of history, the actuality of the multiplicity of things is conceived as unity. Past and present are one in the process of the act of thinking. Empirically, history and philosophy are distinguished from one another, and this is because of the habitual mistake we make in viewing them abstractly, that is, as things 'external to the thinking in which alone their reality consists', rather than conceiving the two terms in 'the actuality of the thought which thinks them'.[77] For Gentile,

the facts of philosophy are in its past; you think them, and they can only be the act, the unique act of your philosophy, which is not in the past, nor in a present which will be past, since it is the life, the very reality of your thought, a centre from which all time irradiates, whether it be past or future. History, then, in the precise meaning in which it is in time, is only concrete in his act who thinks it as eternal.[78]

Collingwood makes it clear, in his 'Croce's Philosophy of History' (1921), that Gentile's view that history and philosophy cannot exist without the other and that every genuine act of thinking is at once both is preferable to Croce's theory that philosophy is a subordinate moment in history. Croce's view of the relation between philosophy and history, Collingwood suggests, conceives history as absolute thought which contains philosophy within itself. Philosophy is an inferior form requiring to be augmented by facts, or 'philology', in order to be 'converted into the perfect form of history'.[79] For Croce, Collingwood complains, philosophy becomes absorbed in history, whereas in Gentile 'the two are poised in equilibrium'.[80]

What, then, is the nature of the relation between history and philosophy in *Speculum Mentis*? Whereas history believes itself to be knowledge of the world of fact, that is, an object which stands outside of itself, in actuality the 'subject's consciousness of it makes a real difference to it as a whole and to all its parts'.[81] The subject is not separate from, but a constituent aspect of, the object. The transition from history to philosophy is affected by making explicit what is already implicit in history. Philosophy is self-consciousness, that is, mind is both the subject and object in the unity of thinking; philosophy, then, is the self-knowledge of the mind. The other forms of experience have an ostensible object outside the subject, but the real object is always mind in its unity. Thus the forms of experience are implicitly philosophy, but their true nature is 'concealed beneath an error in self-knowledge'; thus what they think they do and what they are actually doing betrays a marked inconsistency between theory and practice.[82] In essence, then, Collingwood is here agreeing with Gentile's view that immanent within them, all the forms of spiritual life have the substance of philosophy.[83] In other words, implicitly they are engaged in the achievement of self-knowledge of the mind, or self-consciousness. Both Collingwood and Gentile view philosophy as excluding nothing that is thinkable from its attention, but what is thinkable is a creation of mind. As Collingwood puts it, 'If the mind feels cold without an object other than itself, nothing is simpler for it than to create a palace of art, a world of mythology, a cosmos of abstract machinery, and so forth. In fact that is precisely what it does when it cannot achieve what it really wants – self-knowledge – without the help of these things'.[84] This, then, is an affirmation of both Gentile's and Croce's view that the forms of spiritual life do not have an object – they create it.[85] Similarly, like Gentile, Collingwood, but to a greater extent than the former, interrogates the forms of experience in order to overcome the abstractness of the multiplicity of things in the idea of the unity of the mind. Collingwood excludes from consideration the second conception of history to which Gentile adheres and interrogates only the first conception, which is found wanting, and out of which philosophy, which is implicit within it, makes itself explicit.

My purpose is not to trace in detail the changing fortunes of the relation between philosophy and history in the work of Collingwood. I have explored the relation between philosophy and history in *Speculum Mentis* in some detail here in order to specify terms of reference that will enable me to describe the subsequent changes in Collingwood's long-term preoccupation. At this stage, a clear distinction needs to be made. History conceives itself to be describing the objective world of fact in all its multiplicity; history is not concerned to ask whether the facts are right or wrong. Philosophy, as self-knowledge of the mind, asks explicitly the philosophical question whether what is asserted is true or false.

In *An Essay on Philosophical Method,* Collingwood still maintains a distinction between history and philosophy. It is no business of history, nor of the other forms of experience, for that matter, to reflect upon itself. If the historian reflects upon the historical form of experience, it is not in his capacity as historian, but as a philosopher. Philosophy is distinguished, however, in that self-reflection is part of itself.[86] Further, history is said to concern itself with the individual, whereas philosophy is more like science, in that it concerns itself with the universal.[87] Collingwood does not here suggest that it is the task of philosophy to interrogate the forms of experience and determine their place in the whole. Instead, as we saw, its task is to explicate the philosophical concept in terms of a scale of overlapping forms. Collingwood does not stress here, however, as he had in *Philosophy and Religion* and *Speculum Mentis,* that 'the mind *is* what it *does',*[88] nor does he talk of philosophy as the self-knowledge of the mind. This is probably explained by the fact that he is concerned more explicitly in the *Essay* with the method of philosophy and not with its object, mind. He also says very little about history, but this is not surprising, since he does not purport to be addressing the question of the relation between history and philosophy. However, implicit throughout the whole book is the notion that historical study of the philosophical tradition can inspire the philosopher to give new direction to the business of philosophizing.[89] Determining the truth and falsity of what is asserted is still specified as a fundamental preoccupation of philosophy.[90] Whether a philosophy is right or wrong is a distinctly philosophical question.

By 1936, when Collingwood wrote many of the lectures which now comprise much of *The Idea of History,* history had expanded its dominion. It is clear at this stage that Collingwood did not wish to resolve metaphysics into history. Metaphysics could not be studied, however, 'without *studying* the history of itself, to determine which of its problems mainly concern us here, and now, which have been tolerably well settled, and which are yet unripe for discussion'.[91] Nevertheless, what Collingwood had once regarded as the distinctly philosophical question of asking whether a philosophy is right or wrong now becomes part of the task of history.[92] Nevertheless, self-knowledge of the mind, hitherto the domain of philosophy, falls distinctly into the province of history. Collingwood contends, in the same letter, that 'the Theory of Mind' can, without residue, be resolved into history.[93] This is clearly expressed by Collingwood, in *The Idea of History,* when he suggests that history 'is the mind's knowledge of itself'; it is 'the self-knowledge of the living mind'; 'self-understanding of my mind is nothing else than historical knowledge'; and, 'the historical process which is the life of the mind is a self-knowing process'.[94] What, then, does this mean? Well, he is clearly not accepting history's self-description and self-conception of itself, as he had in *Speculum Mentis.* Indeed, there can be no doubt that *The Idea of History* is as avowedly against that realist self-description as *Speculum Mentis* was. The difference is that Collingwood now accepts what Gentile had accepted before him, that is, that history, because it has a false conception of itself, does not negate the possibility of achieving genuine historical knowledge. What Collingwood is doing in *The Idea of History* is specifying the conditions which make historical knowledge possible, and in doing so he overcomes the mind–object dichotomy which history's own self-conception postulates. He attempts to overcome this dichotomy by suggesting that

historical knowledge is the knowledge of what mind has done in the past, and at the same time is the redoing of this, the perpetuation of past acts in the present. Its object is therefore not a mere object, something outside the mind which knows it; it is an activity of thought, which can be known only in so far as the knowing mind re-enacts it and knows itself as so doing.[95]

In putting forward his own conception, rather than the self-conception of history, Collingwood is understanding differently something that is already understood. However, in so far as he does this he prepares the ground for converting history into what was hitherto conceived as philosophy. Thus, in the identification of philosophy and history Collingwood comes closer to the Italians – Gentile, Croce, and de Ruggiero – than he had previously been in *Speculum Mentis*. Instead of history being absorbed by philosophy after having become convicted of being a philosophical mistake, philosophy now stands poised to become absorbed by history. This facilitates Collingwood's claim in *An Autobiography* that there are no separate historical and philosophical questions. This claim is established by an argument, largely derived from Croce's *Logic,* which maintains that there are no permanent questions in philosophy.[96] What an author meant, and whether what the author asserted was true, become historical questions, in so far as the meaning and truth of what was said are correlative to the question-and-answer complex in the context of which the statement arose. Subsequently Collingwood develops this point further and considerably limits the application of the question of truth in metaphysics.

In his *Essay on Philosophical Method* the historical question of what is being asserted could be supplemented with the philosophical question of whether what is being asserted is true, because Collingwood then understood the various philosophical statements to be propositions which were capable of verification and falsification. In his *Essay On Metaphysics* the philosophical question is applicable only to propositions, or relative presuppositions, but not to absolute presuppositions. Metaphysics, understood by Collingwood to be a historical discipline, that is, concerned with self-knowledge and what mind has done in the past, can identify and reveal absolute presuppositions. For Collingwood, each question is itself an answer to a logically prior question, that is, it presupposes a question. Presuppositions are *relative* in so far as they are at once questions and answers depending upon the view, in terms of antecedents or subsequents, one takes of them. Questions, then, directly presuppose that which is logically prior to them, and if the presupposition is not made, the question simply cannot arise. A presupposition is relative in that it is both a question and an answer to a question – that is, relative to one question as its immediate answer, and relative to another as its immediate presupposition. We can, then, if we wish, trace back from each question the immediate presupposition that it entails and identify a logical series of questions and answers. However, there will come a point when we reach a question that presupposes nothing. This is an *absolute presupposition,* which is not itself an answer to a question. Absolute presuppositions are absolutely presupposed; they are not propositions, and therefore the question of whether they are true or false does not arise.

A complex of absolute presuppositions forms the foundation upon which all our intellectual activity, and indeed the very possibility of intellectual activity, rests.[97] These complexes of absolute presuppositions are perpetually subject to internal conflicts and strains, the intensity of which varies, but when the 'strains' become too great the structure collapses and is replaced by another. People are not ordinarily aware of their absolute presuppositions, and thus the changes occur through a process of 'unconscious thought', which in removing the destructive strains modifies the constellation.[98] The detection of absolute presuppositions and the changes that they undergo is, for Collingwood, a historical study, and since this is also the province of metaphysics, metaphysics is itself a historical science.

To sum up, in a metaphysical enquiry the appropriate question to ask is what absolute presuppositions were absolutely presupposed at a certain place and time. In this respect the concepts of truth and falsity pertain only to the metaphysician's statement that the absolute presuppositions were absolutely presupposed.[99] This does not preclude the metaphysician from asking whether the statements of other metaphysicians have been true or false. Metaphysics is critical in that it subjects claims about what absolute presuppositions were or were not being presupposed to the criteria of truth and falsity.

W. H. Walsh overemphasizes the extent to which Collingwood's theories in *An Autobiography* and *An Essay on Metaphysics* differ from the earlier theories. Walsh says, for example, that with the appearance of *An Essay on Metaphysics,* 'Collingwood took a step which marked a decisive break with his earlier thought. He now asserted, in effect, that philosophy cannot judge but only record'.[100] This is too literal a reading of Collingwood, difficult to sustain in the light of the fact that Collingwood himself engages in extensive criticism in *An Essay on Metaphysics*. Metaphysics, as a historical discipline, only records, because it deals with beliefs which are not propositions. Propositions themselves are susceptible to interrogation in terms of their truth or falsity, but this can only be determined in relation to the question-and-answer complex in which the proposition has arisen. Collingwood is in fact more explicit about the critical role of the metaphysician in a manuscript which he wrote shortly before *An Essay on Metaphysics*. The role of the metaphysician is historical and not critical, Collingwood argues, when the metaphysician detects and articulates the absolute presuppositions of his own community and those presupposed in others. Similarly, the work of comparison is historical and not critical:

But in his relation to other metaphysicians his function is critical. If for example the science of his own day really does presuppose the law of universal causation his business towards that presupposition is to detect it and state it. But if metaphysicians have got into the habit of thinking that this science presupposes the law of universal causation whereas really it does not, then his business is two fold: (a) to state the facts (b) to criticize the metaphysicians who have misrepresented them.[101]

There can be no doubt, then, that the function of the metaphysician is both historical and critical, but the criticism is reserved for propositions about whether absolute presuppositions are, or are not, being absolutely presupposed.

Collingwood's historicization of philosophy went beyond metaphysics. During the same voyage on which he wrote the *Essay on Metaphysics,* he also wrote 'Notes on HISTORIOGRAPHY', in which he argued that 'history is the only kind of knowledge'.[102] He maintains that all of the problems of metaphysics are historical problems, and, as I suggested earlier, he even attempts to demonstrate that the problems of logic are also historical. All that logicians do, Collingwood maintains, is to articulate the principles of valid thought acceptable in their own day. Similarly, all that ethical philosophers offer us is a vision of the ideal life towards which it is worth aiming. The people for which it is a worthy ideal are those contemporary with the composition of the theory.[103] It is in this context that Collingwood made his infamous statement about the liquidation of philosophy in its conversion into history.[104]

The question of the rapprochement between history and philosophy continued to preoccupy Collingwood even after he wrote *An Essay on Metaphysics.* In June 1937, prior to writing both *An Autobiography* and *An Essay on Metaphysics,* Collingwood was quite clear about his intention to 'give people a concrete methodology of present-day historiography, integrated in its own past, which will show them what the problems and methods of present-day historiography are'.[105] As late as 19 October 1939,[106] he remained true to this aim. On 9 February 1939 he had written a sketch of the contents for *The Principles of History.*[107] Between then and 21 February of the same year, Collingwood wrote about forty thousand words on the principles of history. He did not return to writing *The Principles of History* until 26 March. The following day he 'tried to begin chapter IV of *Principles of History* – stuff wouldn't flow'.[108] It seems that he never again made a sustained attempt to finish this work, even though on Easter Monday (April 1939) Collingwood wrote to F. G. Simpson saying that *The Principles of History* 'is the book which my whole life has been spent in preparing to write. If I can finish that, I shall have nothing to grumble at'.[109] He did not finish the book, and it seems that he could not, because he had reached a point in its writing, or theoretical articulation, beyond which he could not go. He could not find the words to express what he had to say. This would have been a very strong reason, then, for turning to something about which he did believe he had a great deal to say, namely 'the first principles of politics'.

Collingwood justifies his pursuit of this project by saying that in 'examining my own mind, I saw that I had plenty of ideas which it would be a public service to state'.[110] This does not mean, however, that he abandoned his attempt to bring about a rapprochement between philosophy and history. In a letter to E. R. Hughes, dated 8 December 1939, Collingwood said that he would continue to devote his life to 'the idea of a union of philosophy and history', an idea that 'could save Europe'.[111] It is a reasonable inference that Collingwood was here already thinking in terms of writing a political treatise that would constitute his contribution to the war effort. Indeed, there are many ways in which *The New Leviathan* can be viewed as the concrete exemplar of what he conceived the rapprochement to entail.

We saw earlier that Collingwood first accredited philosophy and then history with achieving self-knowledge of the mind. This entailed not looking at what mind is, but identifying what it does. Mind is nothing other than its acts. Throughout *The New Leviathan* explicit reference is made to mind as the fundamental subject matter of the book. The purpose of the book is to understand what civilization is, in order that the revolt against it can engender the appropriate response from the British. Such a purpose entails a voyage of exploration into the mind, 'for civilization is a thing of the mind. It follows that the "Man" into which we are inquiring in order to prepare for our account of civilization is a "Man" of the mind' (*NL*, 1.21). The enquiry is not concerned with what mind *is,* because mind is only what it does. Thus, in relation to exploring European civilization and the revolt against it, Collingwood is concerned only with what mind 'has done on certain definite occasions', and the occasions with which he is particularly concerned are those in the history of 'the modern European mind' (*NL*, 9.2–9.21). The development of this mind is 'not predictable' (*NL*, 9.43), and its study is 'entirely a matter of history' (*NL*, 9.23). However, the conception of history in *The New Leviathan* would not easily find a place in the more conventional genres of history books. He traces, for example, the development of mind through different levels of consciousness in which freedom becomes manifest in the capacity for, and the act of, uncoerced choice. It is this capacity for choice which enables individuals to confer authority and thus effect the process of conversion from a state of nature to a social community. Among the evidence that can be presented in support of such a view, Collingwood contends, is one's own mind. He suggests that everyone, in his capacity as mind, has the 'makings' of the answers to the questions to which *The New Leviathan* is addressed in his 'own consciousness. Reflect and you will find what it is. In the meantime', Collingwood says, 'I offer you the fruits of my own reflection' (*NL*, 1.87–1.88). His own mind is particularly appropriate because it is part of the 'modern European mind' and is 'peculiarly accessible' for answering certain questions. He even admits that much of what he has to say is conventionally not documented in history books, 'partly because "the history of what passes in a man's mind" (as Locke has it), though history, . . . is little noticed by their authors' (*NL,* 9.22).

In summary, then, what Collingwood means by history in *The New Leviathan* is self-knowledge of the mind, and knowledge of what mind has done in the past. In this respect, although the ostensible purpose of *The New Leviathan* is quite different, it can be viewed as the culmination and the embodiment of his lifelong preoccupation with effecting a rapprochement between history and philosophy. It must be emphasized, however, that the type of history offered bears little resemblance to what usually went under that title. It is, instead, the type of history which Collingwood had conceived as a result of his long and arduous task of bringing history and philosophy together.

Rapprochement between theory and practice

A third long-term problem to which Collingwood addressed himself was that of the relation between theory and practice. This is related to the first long-term preoccupation in so far as history and philosophy, whether conceived as separate or identical pursuits, are theoretical forms of enquiry, and the relationship between theory and practice often boils down to that between history, and/or philosophy, and practice, or the objects of the theoretical activity. Indeed, it is history which, for Collingwood, provides the key to overcoming the division between theory and practice.

Croce, for example, had always affirmed a strong connexion between theory and practice. He did not believe that people were either practical or theoretical; they were, for him, always both at once. The theoretical person acts, asserts his will, and lives like all other men. The practical person is also like the theoretical in that he has beliefs, engages in contemplation, reads, writes, and thinks, and also 'loves music and the other arts'.[112] For Croce, the theoretical and practical comprise 'a duality that is unity and a unity that is duality'.[113] In this duality and unity, theoretical activity is the presupposition of the practical. Practical judgement is nothing other than historical judgement, 'so that to judge practical acts and to give their history is really the same thing'.[114] It is this historical judgement, or knowledge, which forms the basis of all our future actions. Throughout Croce's work there is always a strong identification between the practical and contemporary concerns of the historian setting the problems and providing the inspiration for historical enquiry, the results of which provide the basis of future action. He says, in this respect, that 'a historical judgement is always the answer to a question which life sets us in order to generate further life. . . . Histories stimulated and guided by no practical problems would be at best virtuosities or fairy-tales, not serious history.'[115]

It is interesting that Croce himself saw one of the fundamental affinities between himself and Collingwood as being this emphasis upon the strongly practical dimension of historiography. Croce says, for instance, basing his view largely upon *An Autobiography* and *An Essay on Metaphysics*, that 'historiographic thought, for Collingwood and for me ... was based as far as we were both concerned, on contemporary politics to which it gave sharpness of concept, light of hope and firmness of decision.'[116] However, we should not assume that either Collingwood or Croce believed the relation between theory and practice to be causal or deterministic. Croce makes his own attitude quite clear when he says,

The relation between historiography and the practical activity, between history and action, establishes a link between the two, but not a causalistic or deterministic link. The antecedent to action is an act of knowledge, the solution of a particular theoretical difficulty, the drawing aside of a veil from the face of the real; but in so far as it is action it can only arise out of an original and personal inspiration of a purely practical sort, calling for practical gifts.[117]

In the writings of Collingwood the relation between theory and practice is always a close one. Often he was quite explicit about the practical intention he had in writing many of his books. They were addressed to a general, and not to a specialized, readership, and were meant to contribute something towards the understanding of the practical problems which loomed large upon the horizon of the civilization of his day and thus point the way to their resolution. Let me illustrate with a few examples. In *Speculum Mentis* Collingwood suggests that we have lost the capacity to be complete human beings. We all specialize in our own esoteric activities and as a consequence are 'wrecks and fragments of men', not knowing where to turn nor how to come to terms with life and achieve the happiness which we all so sadly lack. It is the detachment of the forms of experience from one another that has led to this sorry state of affairs. Collingwood's avowed aim is to give some indication of how we might escape from the crisis in which European civilization finds itself. The cure, as far as he is concerned, lies in the conception of a complete reunification of the fragmented forms of experience.[118] Even in his aesthetics, where one might expect Collingwood to renounce practical considerations, he affirms unequivocally that he is not concerned to present a merely theoretical treatise, of interest only to professional philosophers. Aesthetics he takes to be the attempt to arrive at solutions to problems that arise within the context within which artists themselves work. Thus *The Principles of Art* was 'written in the belief that it has a practical bearing, direct or indirect, upon the condition of art in England in 1937.'[119]

Indeed, Collingwood devotes the third part of this treatise to drawing out the practical consequences of his theory of art. In the context of a discussion of 'Aesthetic Theory and Artistic Practice', written in 1931, Collingwood raises the problem of the relation between philosophical sciences and the objects of their enquiries. In particular he is concerned to explore the impact of 'pure philosophy' upon aesthetics and, in turn, the impact of the latter upon artistic practice. He argues, for instance, that the revolt against naturalism and materialism in England and France, expressed in the philosophies of T. H. Green (1836–1882), Edward Caird (1935–1908), F. H. Bradley (1846–1924), and Bernard Bosanquet (1848–1923), on the one hand, and Jules Espirit Nicholas Lachelier (1832–1918), Charles Bernard (1815–1903), Emile Boutroux (1845–1921), Henri Poincaré (1852–1912), and Henri Louis Bergson (1859–1941), on the other, found expression in the art of the age. In Collingwood's view, history shows us that the ideas that find expression in the practice of art have filtered through to the artistic community through the medium of aesthetic theory. However, the ideas expressed in aesthetic theory first find expression in pure philosophy.[120] This is not to suggest that the artist merely follows rules laid down by the philosophers, but nor does the philosopher merely provide an ex post facto description of what artists do. Instead, there is a much more intimate relation between the theory and practice of art. Aesthetics is 'a statement of what art is, when it is really art; just as logic is a description not merely of how we actually think, but of how we think when we are really thinking. And this means that aesthetic tries to discover not merely what art is, but what art ought to be. This again is true of all philosophical sciences'.[121]

In relation to history, Collingwood was also attempting to bring about a rapprochement between theory and practice. He dismisses the view that theoretical enquiry can divorce itself from practical ends. Historians cannot be impartial in their enquiries. To write a history of poetry or of philosophy by necessity entails having strong views about what constitutes good poetry and good philosophy.[122] In a letter to Knox, Collingwood contends that he does not think it possible to treat thought and action as distincts; they are both one thing. He goes on to suggest that he 'would go a terrible long' way in repudiating the dualism between theory and practice.[123] It was Collingwood's intention that *The Principles of History* would overcome the division between theory and practice. This traditional distinction would be negated by history itself in that the object of history is enacted and is thus no object at all. In this respect Collingwood is similar to Gentile: Both overcome the distinction between theory and practice by eradicating the idea of objects external to the mind. In *Speculum Mentis* it was philosophy which unified the mind and its object, but later, for Collingwood, this unification takes place in history. In his

54   The social and political thought of R.G. Collingwood

proposed book on the principles of history Collingwood intended to provide 'a characterization of an historical morality and an historical civilization, contrasting with our "scientific" one'.[124] That *The Principles of
History* was abandoned does not mean that he gave up the attempt to
reconcile theory and practice nor the characterisation of a historical civilization and morality. Indeed, in *The New Leviathan* Collingwood (as
we will see in Chapters 3, 6, and 7) actually provides us with the characterisations of historical morality and historical civilization that he had
intended to articulate in *The Principles of History.*

  The New Leviathan itself is the paramount manifestation of Collingwood's commitment to the close relation between theory and practice.
In the preface Collingwood, by implication, envisaged his book as an
attempt to articulate the principles for which the Second World War was
being fought. The occasion for writing such a book, he said, was the fact
that people were ignorant of what they were defending in the war and
that the contemporary leaders in society were either not able, or perhaps
not willing, to tell them (*NL*, p. vi). Collingwood described the purpose
of his enterprise as being 'purely practical' in that he was attempting to
discern what could be done in the face of 'the present attack on civilization' (*NL*, 9.2).

  However, to know that Collingwood's writings were informed with a
practical intention does not tell us what he thought was the nature of
the relation between theory and practice, and it is to this that I now wish
to turn. In the first sentence of the prologue to *Speculum Mentis* Collingwood declares that

all thought exists for the sake of action. We try to understand ourselves and our
world only in order that we may learn how to live. The end of our self-knowledge
is not the contemplation by enlightened intellects of their own mysterious nature,
but the freer and more effectual self-revelation of that nature in a vigorous practical
life.[125]

The role of the philosopher, or historian, in informing the conduct of
practical life is not, however, to supply principles of conduct to guide
action, nor to tell others (at least not directly) what they ought to do.
The relation between theory and practice is far more subtle than this.
Philosophy, in its capacity as theoretical understanding, is neither un-
interested in nor noncontributory to the subject matter upon which it
reflects. On the other hand, this form of theoretical understanding does
not intrude excessively upon, nor attempt to direct, the activities about
which it theorizes.[126] Theory should not address itself to the solution of
practical problems, but to clearing up 'misunderstandings which make
their solution impossible.'[127] It is for theory to open the way to the solution
of practical problems by demonstrating that they are, in principle, sol-

uble,[128] that is, theory should generate a faith in the possibility of the problems being solved.

In *An Autobiography* Collingwood castigates the realist philosophers for teaching that philosophy makes no difference to what is known. He suggests that from the time of Socrates moral philosophy 'had been regarded as an attempt to think out more clearly the issues involved in conduct, for the sake of acting better.' Up until the latter part of the nineteenth century the school of Green taught young people 'that by thinking about what they are doing, or were about to do, they would become likely on the whole to do it better.'[129] This, in fact, is what Collingwood himself said to students in his lectures on moral philosophy. The lectures of 1933, for instance, end with a section advising students of the value of moral philosophy for their future conduct. However, he offers no injunctions to act in any particular way, nor does he favour any course of action. He offers, in essence, a cautionary note to the effect that one should think clearly before one acts, for the more clearly one thinks, the greater the possibility of acting wisely.[130]

If we look once again at *Speculum Mentis,* the efficacy that such advice would have had, at least in Collingwood's mind, becomes clear. The self does not stand opposed to its objects: The self and its world are correlative; each is what it is because of the other. The world I know is the world as my mind knows it. If we are in error about the theory of what it is we do, then the world in which we do it, for us, is a reflection of that error: 'The mind, having formed a false conception of itself, tries to live up to that conception.'[131] This is also applicable to our conceptions of our own actions: To misinterpret them is to make them different from what they would have been. Collingwood argues that the 'action itself, not merely our conception of it, becomes confused, and this confusion is evil. Thus absolute action, or action which truly understands its own nature, is good action, and good action alone is truly intelligent'.[132] The point implied in all this is that we are thinking beings whose thought makes a difference to the world in which we act. Changes in our theories of economics, politics, and morals, for example, entail changes in the fabric of our society. Similarly, one's own theories of life and morality affect the way in which one not only perceives one's relation to society but the way in which one actually is related to society.[133]

By the mid-1930s Collingwood believed that the only way of overcoming errors in self-knowledge was by means of historical understanding. Such knowledge enables the person to discern the various threads in the past which have a bearing upon a present situation, and enables the same person to pronounce other aspects of history as invalid for the situation. In doing so, self-knowledge is enhanced and self-criticism facilitated, thus enabling mind to raise itself to a higher power of rationality or mindhood by becoming self-conscious, and thus possessing in a new manner the self of which previously it was unaware. The self-awareness of mind, which is history, is at the same time the self-enlargement of mind by developing in itself this new power.[134]

In *An Autobiography* Collingwood argues that he gradually came to realise that the relation between theory and practice is that of mutual dependence. Thought depends upon that which we have learned from our experience of acting, and action depends upon how we see ourselves and the world in which we live. Further, the ostensibly theoretical activities of scientific, historical, and philosophical thought rely on our moral integrity just as much as upon intellectual qualities, and moral problems depend for their resolution just as much upon clear thought as moral force.[135]

It is the practical problems and predicaments in which we find ourselves, Collingwood suggests, in agreement with Croce, that set the historical problems we choose to pursue. The study of history enables us to clarify the situations in which we are constantly having to decide how to act: 'Hence the plane on which ultimately, all problems arise is the plane of "real" life: that to which they are referred for their solution is history.'[136] What Collingwood means by this is best clarified in the context of *The New Leviathan.*

Historical problems arise out of the practical problems encountered on 'the plane of "real" life', and the practical problem in which Europe found itself was that of preserving civilization in the face of the onslaught upon it by the rising tide of barbarism, manifest in the late 1930s and early 1940s in the various fascist movements in continental Europe. The response to this crisis of civilization was not immediately apparent to a people uncertain of the reasons for which it was fighting and starved of a clarification of the issues by leaders who were either unable, or unwilling, to tell them. Thus Collingwood was faced with an eminently practical problem, and given that he thought contributions to the solutions of such problems can only be found in history, it is not surprising that throughout *The New Leviathan* he describes his mode of enquiry as being historical in character. In anticipation of the discussion to follow in the next chapter, it suffices to say here that Collingwood viewed acting through a sense of duty as the highest form of practical reason, and therefore as the counterpart of the highest form of theoretical reason, namely history, from which caprice is almost entirely eliminated. To know what one's duty is in relation to any particular situation, one must turn to history for the answer. In *The New Leviathan,* too, as we will see in due course, Collingwood gives a detailed analysis of the relation between practical and theoretical reason, arguing that the former always has priority over the latter.

To sum up the relation between theory and practice: Both Collingwood and Croce postulate a similar order of procedure. Life – that is, the contemporary issues and problems which resonate in one's soul – sets the issues towards which history attempts to point the way to a solution. History is not in this respect didactic; it is not, as Machiavelli believed, a storehouse of examples from which we can choose the most appropriate to follow as a response to a particular situation. The role of history, for Collingwood and Croce, is much more complex than this. It facilitates self-knowledge, and in doing so it enhances our ability to understand the present in the light of what came before it. History opens up for us the potential inherent in human nature, thus contributing towards our formulation and enactment of an appropriate response to the practical and immediate problems which face us.

Three fundamental preoccupations, we have seen, provided the long-term foci of Collingwood's interests and formed part of his motivation for writing *The New Leviathan.* First, the preoccupation with articulating the theory of a scale of overlapping forms is manifest in *The New Leviathan.* Second, the rapprochement between history and philosophy finds its concrete exemplification in Collingwood's final work. Third, the rapprochement between theory and practice, the latter of which provides the problems to which the former addresses itself, also finds its concrete exemplification in *The New Leviathan.* The crisis of civilization could provide no more complex a practical problem towards which Collingwood, through historical enquiry, might offer some theoretical clarification in order to facilitate a solution.

I do not want to suggest that I have exhausted the exploration of a scale of forms analysis, the relations between history and philosophy, and between theory and practice, but I have said as much as is necessary to show the place of *The New Leviathan* in the context of Collingwood's self-professed fundamental long-term concerns.[137] Other long-term concerns also formed part of the motivation for writing this political treatise and received their mature formulation there, but discussion of the preliminary arguments for these theories is best reserved for later discussion. It suffices to say that Collingwood had thought a great deal on the questions of language, morality, politics, and civilization which appear in *The New Leviathan* and had written down his deliberations in the form of lectures and in published and unpublished papers. Many of the arguments found in these sources appear in revised form in Collingwood's last work.

3. The short-term considerations

What were the short-term, or immediate pressing reasons, for the composition of *The New Leviathan?* The answers given in this chapter are necessarily brief, because more detailed analysis of Collingwood's hopes and fears is more appropriately introduced in later chapters. In this chapter the scene is set for these later discussions.

It is always difficult to distinguish clearly between long- and short-term considerations, and the distinction, although useful, is always to a certain extent arbitrary. For example, Collingwood's concern with practical political problems became highly accentuated by the mid-1930s. Occasioned primarily by the rise of fascism in Europe and his increasing conviction that the British government lacked the ability or the will to respond positively and honestly to the challenge, his harsh criticisms of the policies of the British leaders and his claims that they were undermining the values of liberalism in British society[138] led many of his acquaintances to believe that his politics had turned sharply to the Left; a number of reviewers commented that he appeared to be well on the road to Moscow.[139] Professor Joseph Needham, for example, in a letter to the *New Statesman,* was deceived by Collingwood's praise of Marx. Collingwood had expressed admiration for Marx by describing him as a gloves-off philosopher whose philosophy was eminently practical in intent. Needham interpreted this as an endorsement of historical materialism.[140] Nothing could be further from the truth. As we will see in Chapter 5, Collingwood's admiration for Marx was strictly limited and severely qualified. However, Collingwood's concern with practical politics, as he tells us himself,[141] had begun a long time before the rise of fascism in Europe.

It is true that during and after the First World War Collingwood wrote much with a general practical import, including *Speculum Mentis.* However, by the 1930s more immediate and pressing concerns than Collingwood had had in 1919 inspired the highly political tones of parts of *An Autobiography* and *An Essay on Metaphysics,* and culminated in *The New Leviathan.* The rise of fascism as a caricature of the worst features of socialism posed a threat to the liberal-democratic tradition in Europe. Even though he said that he preferred socialism to fascism, because the former purportedly desired the social and economic welfare of the whole of a nation while the latter disguised its desire to promote the interests of capitalists by asserting the claims of the nation in the international context, Collingwood ultimately rejected socialism, because he believed that the parliamentary system of government could avert the outbreak of class war.[142] By the mid-1930s a whole series of social, cultural, and political trends, some of long duration, appear to have awakened Collingwood's crusading instinct against what he perceived to be their cumulative threat to civilization. The threat now became much more tangible than the breakup of the unity of the life of mind and the consequent retreat into the different forms of experience. He became concerned about the reproduction of art by mechanical means and the failure to educate the public in the appreciation of original art.[143] In a paper written after that in which he expressed his concern about the debasement of art, it becomes clear that Collingwood perceived other, more sinister, threats to civilization, which to some extent echo the argument of his address to the Belgian students of 1919,[144] but the paper betrays a far more pessimistic tone than had hitherto been discernible in any of his work. Writing shortly after the Spanish civil war had begun (an event which, due to lack of support for the Spanish government by the British government, made Collingwood extremely disillusioned with liberalism),[145] he suggested that civilization was dying and that little could be done to save it. The symptoms of the disease that had beset civilization were, for Collingwood, quite clear. First, nations found themselves in the paradoxical position of spending ever-increasing amounts of money on arms in order to maintain peace. They were driven to this because it had become the test of nationhood that the nation had the ability to wage war. 'War', Collingwood maintained, 'is the ultimate end of the modern state. All forces that go to make up the modern state combine to drive its activity in the direction of warfare.'[146] In Collingwood's view, the new militarism of modern states projected an individualist concept of sovereignty in which the absolute and unlimited state stood opposed to all others.

A second reason for the impending death of civilization was the collapse of liberalism. By the term *liberalism* Collingwood understood essentially what de Ruggiero saw as its character, that is, a political doctrine that had as its goal the creation of a society in which free expression is fostered and political opinions freely articulated. Liberalism sought a unity in the multiplicity of views, by means of a dialectical method in which opposing views were freely discussed until their exponents began to uncover beneath the opposition some underlying common ground which would help them move forward.[147] A third reason given for the sorry condition of civilization was the severing of our emotional life from the traditional ways of society. The civilization of Europe had been fundamentally an agricultural one, but the destruction of the countryside by advances in modern technology had led to a perversion of our emotions, especially towards the land. That the people of the countryside could not resist the encroachment of the town and its values upon themselves was a sign that the vitality of the countryside had already been sapped of its energy.[148]

Some of the themes discussed in 'Art and the Machine' and 'Man Goes Mad' are taken up in both *An Autobiography* and 'Fascism and Nazism'. They are evidence of the extent to which Collingwood was consciously applying his views on the rapprochements between philosophy and history, and theory and practice. Immediate practical problems provide the subject matter about which to theorize, and the mode of theorizing is essentially historical with a practical intent. Collingwood unequivocally states that there is no greater practical problem 'at the present time than Fascism and Nazism.'[149] These two tendencies were conducting a successful attack on civilization because they were 'specialists in arousing the emotions'.[150] In *An Autobiography* Collingwood goes as far as to suggest that the Chamberlain government was undermining democracy, deceiving the electorate and itself, and promoting fascism, by its betrayal of Czechoslovakia, Abyssinia, and Spain. The tactics of the government, that is, the manipulation of emotions, he suggests, were akin to the methods of the fascists, but whereas the latter appealed to the allure of national glory, the British prime minister defused opposition to appeasement by terrifying the masses with the threat of war.[151] In two letters to Knox, Collingwood makes it clear that what he fears is not military defeat but the total abandonment of democratic ideals in the face of the novelty and the emotionalism of fascism.[152] To become Nazi in order to defeat nazism would be a fate worse than military defeat. It is interesting to note here that Collingwood was so passionately opposed to the policy of appeasement that it provided the occasion for him to become actively engaged in practical politics. He lobbied the Labour party headquarters in an effort to persuade the party to adopt an anti-appeasement policy.[153] Collingwood also supported the candidature of A. D. Lindsay in the 1938 Oxford by-election. Lindsay stood as an Independent Progressive (the Liberal and Labour candidates having stood down in support of him) against the Conservative candidate, Quentin Hogg. Lindsay's platform was vehemently anti-appeasement and pro-rearmament. The day before Collingwood left for the East Indies to attempt to regain his health he wrote to Lindsay, saying,

I am appalled by the apathy with which our situation is regarded by a great many of us, and by the success which the Government has had in keeping the country as a whole from knowing the truth. Your candidature shows that the spirit of English democracy is not extinct. I hope that it still survives among those who have to vote next week.[154]

In addition, in response to a letter from E. R. Hughes, Collingwood became involved in the Standing Committee for Intellectual Cooperation with China.[155] In a letter to Hughes, Collingwood testified to his belief in the power of thought to bring about changes in action. The union between philosophy and history, Collingwood suggested, was a Chinese idea which could have practical consequences in saving Europe. He goes as far as to say that 'nothing else can'.[156]

What is suggested is this: The accentuation of Collingwood's fears for the future of civilization, precipitated by events in Europe after the mid-1930s (especially the Second World War), led him to bring together his many and varied thoughts on aspects of morals and politics, mind and language, and civilization and barbarism, to compose a comprehensive study of the fundamental presuppositions of European civilization, in order to educate the masses in the principles for which (and against which) they were fighting. The clarification of these principles was Collingwood's contribution to the war effort. In making what contribution he could to raise the morale of those fighting against the new barbarism, Collingwood was reflecting a widespread desire among philosophers of the time to address themselves to issues which had a bearing upon contemporary events. Collingwood's desire to respond to the circumstances was enhanced by his determination to bring about a rapprochement between theory and practice. Collingwood suggests, for instance, that his article 'Fascism and Nazism' was inspired by C. E. M. Joad's 'Appeal to Philosophers'. Joad argued for a truce to be called between philosophers, and a return made to the classical tradition in which the great philosophers addressed themselves to the practical problems of conduct. It has become incumbent upon the modern philosopher, even if he, or she, has nothing very original to contribute, to make the wisdom of the ancients 'available for the comfort and guidance of our distracted times.'[157] It is the duty of the philosopher, he suggests, echoing Collingwood's *Autobiography,* to guide the present generation towards principles and ideals by which it can live – a task which has become even more pertinent 'when traditional ideals have been repudiated and traditional principles abandoned. It is partly because of this repudiation and this abandonment that our civilization has reached its present *impasse*'.[158]

Collingwood's *New Leviathan* does return to the classical tradition in philosophy and attempts to update the wisdom he finds in it to suit the differing circumstances of the twentieth century. In the same volume of *Philosophy* in which Joad's and Collingwood's articles appeared, H. D. Lewis published a two-part paper concerned with the question 'Is There a Social Contract?' Lewis, in agreement with W. J. Gough, says that it would be a very strange thing if the idea of a social contract, having been invoked by many philosophers over the centuries, turned out to be totally erroneous. Indeed, such important thinkers as Hobbes, Locke, and Rousseau, although differing in other fundamental respects, all rely upon social-contract theory in their political philosophies.[159] The author discusses the theories of each of these thinkers, pronouncing something of value in each. However, he regrets the tendency in Green and Ritchie to regard the 'demands of the State as ultimate and morally infallible',[160] and he alludes to Hobbes in suggesting that because of the tendency to reify the state in times when faith and a respect for philosophical truth are discarded values, it is a salutary consideration to 'emphasize the ultimate artificiality of the State.'[161] Lewis further suggests that he could not envisage a time when a thorough understanding of the social contract would

be of more value than in the time in which he wrote. Collingwood, as
we will see, in returning to the classical tradition, stresses the value of
the social contract in Hobbes, Locke, and Rousseau; its value, for Collingwood, is that it emphasizes that stage in human development when
the rational consciousness has attained the level of freedom of choice,
thus enabling individuals to confer authority upon those who rule over
them. The theory of the social contract is found wanting because it does
not provide a consideration of how those having attained the level of
freedom of choice can facilitate the conversion to civility of those who
are still in a state of nature. Collingwood, in providing this missing element,
attempts to make the social-contract theory, and by implication the classical tradition, relevant to his times.

Finally, with regard to the short-term reasons for writing *The New Leviathan,* philosophers and the educated public were asking the question
'With whom are we at war?' J. H. Muirhead, taking his lead from 'a lively
discussion going on in *The Times',*[162] takes up the question in that same
issue of *Philosophy.* The point of contention is essentially this: To what
extent is it the German government that constitutes the enemy, and to
what extent are the German people also implicated in the actions of their
government? On the one hand, some say that one cannot indict a whole
nation, and that we must find a way to appeal to the greater part of the
German nation to reject the enemy within, that is, its own government.
On the other hand there are those who suggest that every people gets
the government it deserves.[163] Collingwood, in *The New Leviathan,* allies
himself with those who are of the latter opinion. Herd worship, Collingwood suggests, is 'an immemorial condition of the German people'; they
possess 'insufficient civilization' (*NL,* 45.88), and therefore, by implication,
have leaders that reflect the lack of civility in their society.

In summary, then, we may venture to say that *The New Leviathan* was
occasioned by the times in which it was composed but is also thoroughly
integrated into the philosophical and historical concerns of Collingwood's
whole intellectual and practical life.

3

The two *Leviathan*s and the
criteria of rational action

1. Introduction

The last chapter showed how the long-term and short-term problems
with which Collingwood concerned himself coalesced to inspire him to
write *The New Leviathan.* * In this chapter I will be principally concerned
with two related questions. First, why did Collingwood take Hobbes as
his exemplar? This question is not as naive as it may first appear. Indeed,
there is no immediately apparent reason why Collingwood, given his affinities with the idealist tradition in philosophy, should have chosen
Hobbes as the beneficiary of his lavish praise, and as the touchstone for
his own ideas. The second of the questions, and by far the more important
of the two, is this: What is the philosophical relation between the two
*Leviathan*s? In this respect, an arbitrary and capricious selection of issues
for comparison simply will not do. Comparison has to be systematic, and
what is compared has to be compatible and appropriate. For this reason,
I invoke a triadic conception of the history of political thought, in order
to place Hobbes and Collingwood in perspective. There are three aspects
to a text which can bear fruitful comparison. In the first place we have
the questions to which the philosopher addresses himself or herself. Second, there are the answers given, or conclusions reached. Third, and
most important, are the reasons given for those conclusions. Similarities
can always be found between the thought of one thinker and another in
terms of the first and second aspects of a text, but no genuine similarity
exists, that is, no fundamental philosophical compatibility can be determined, unless the reasons they give for their conclusions are in harmony
with one another.

In attempting to unravel the relationship between the two *Leviathan*s,
it will become apparent that one of the main purposes of the exercise

* This chapter is a greatly revised and expanded version of sections 1–3 of my article 'The
Two *Leviathan*s: R. G. Collingwood and Thomas Hobbes', *Political Studies,* 35 (1987).

is to provide an overview of Collingwood's general aims and method, in order to prepare the reader for the descent into the detailed arguments of *The New Leviathan* and their precursors in his earlier writings which follows this chapter.

2. Why Hobbes?

Before proceeding with a comparison of the two *Leviathan*s we must try to determine why Collingwood chose Hobbes as his exemplar in writing a political treatise. It is incontrovertible that towards the end of his life Collingwood expressed great admiration for the Sage of Malmesbury. In the preface to *The New Leviathan* Collingwood refers to Hobbes's *Leviathan* as 'the world's greatest store of political wisdom' and 'the greatest work of political science the world had ever seen' (*NL*, p. iv). In the preliminary draft of the preface, which was altered considerably for publication, Collingwood's book is dedicated 'To the Memory of Thomas Hobbes of Malmesbury', and Collingwood generously suggests that many of the things said in *The New Leviathan* 'have already been said by Thomas Hobbes in his Leviathan: so many that the present writer has stolen Hobbes's title and dedicated his book to Hobbes's memory'.[1] Both the dedication and expression of indebtedness are absent from the published work.

Collingwood mentions Hobbes from time to time in both his published and his unpublished works. In *Speculum Mentis* Hobbes is cited once and alluded to on one occasion; in 'Economics as a Philosophical Science' he is mentioned briefly; in *The Principles of Art* he appears four times; and in 'The Limits of Historical Knowledge' and 'Fascism and Nazism' his name is invoked once in each article.[2] Collingwood uses Hobbes in *An Autobiography* to substantiate his argument that there are no perennial problems in the history of philosophy.[3] In *The Idea of History,* published posthumously but written before *The New Leviathan,* there are three brief mentions of Hobbes.[4] The unpublished manuscripts contain a number of references to Hobbes, principally in those lectures which contain Collingwood's early thoughts on the issues and problems that were to preoccupy him in *The New Leviathan.* In the 1921 and 1923 lectures on moral philosophy Hobbes is associated with the 'hedonist or sensationalist view of action'.[5] In the subsequent revisions of 1929, 1932, 1933, and 1939–1940, the emphasis upon discussing particular thinkers goes, and along with it Hobbes almost completely disappears. That Hobbes is not the subject of discussion at all in the 1939–1940 lectures (he is merely listed, along with a number of other thinkers, in relation to the doctrine that it is human beings who make and break laws) is quite surprising in view of the fact that these lectures were the basis for parts of

The New Leviathan and that very shortly after these lectures were written Collingwood was praising Hobbes in the most glowing terms. Nor does Hobbes appear as a worthy subject for discussion, although he is mentioned, in the many other unpublished writings on politics and ethics.[6] Nowhere in the published and unpublished works do we find such enthusiastic praise of Hobbes as that in the preliminary draft of the preface for *The New Leviathan* itself.

Given that Collingwood, following common practice among the idealists, thought that it was unnecessary, for the most part, to acknowledge one's sources of inspiration, it is quite possible that Hobbes's influence might be strongly implicit in the work that Collingwood did prior to the composition of *The New Leviathan.* However, when one looks for affinities between Collingwood's books and the arguments of Hobbes, there is no great evidence that Collingwood found anything of profound value in him. This is not particularly surprising, because idealist philosophers had long discounted and rejected the one-sided hedonism of Hobbes. Indeed, it was only during the 1930s that a significant revival of interest in Hobbes occurred – significant enough, that is, to inspire a fellow idealist, Michael Oakeshott, to review the literature.[7]

It is clear from the available evidence that Collingwood's admiration for Hobbes never extended beyond part I of the *Leviathan.* Of Hobbes's three hundred ninety-six pages (in the original pagination of the *Leviathan*), Collingwood, out of twenty-two or so citations in *The New Leviathan,* quotes only the first sixty-three pages, with one exception, namely page 386, which he cites in order to substantiate a historical point. All but one of the citations from Hobbes are taken from part I of the *Leviathan,* the part which, in fact, is implicitly invoked and criticized in the 1921 and 1923 lectures on moral philosophy. In other words, Collingwood's admiration for Hobbes was largely restricted to what Hobbes had to say 'of Man'. Collingwood had always thought this aspect of Hobbes's work an important contribution to the history of political thought; it was only towards the end of his life, however, that Collingwood came to regard it as 'the world's greatest store of political wisdom'. What interested Collingwood in Hobbes always appears to have been the same; however, Collingwood's evaluation of it changed. This remarkable continuity of interest in only part I of the *Leviathan* needs some demonstration.

In *The New Leviathan* Collingwood quoted from the Clarendon edition of the *Leviathan,* using the original pagination parenthetically inserted in that edition for the purposes of referencing. However, Collingwood's early working copy of the *Leviathan* was his personal copy of the Routledge edition. We have in that annotated copy a clear record of the aspects of Hobbes's *Leviathan* which Collingwood thought significant in his early career, substantiated by his discussions of Hobbes in the early lectures on moral philosophy, and we also have testimony, in the form of *The New Leviathan,* to what he considered significant in the *Leviathan* at the end of his career. All the marginal references and marked passages in the Routledge edition, with the exception of one occur in the pages preceding page 94 (page 72 in the original pagination). The one exception is a marked passage on page 121 (page 94 in the original edition) which reminded Collingwood of one of his favourite fairy tales.[8]

In the early lectures on moral philosophy we also find that what most attracts Collingwood's attention is Hobbes's analysis of the springs of action. This analysis occurs in part I of the *Leviathan,* and, in particular, in the chapter on the passions (chapter 6). The equation of good with desire, and evil with aversion, forms the basis of Hobbes's ethical system. Placing expediency and morality upon a radically subjectivist foundation enabled Hobbes to bridge the dichotomy between the expedient and the ethical. Collingwood believed that Hobbes, by equating morality with the 'springs of human nature', was providing a powerful alternative to the excessive intellectualism of Plato.[9] We will see in due course why Collingwood found Hobbes's subjectivism to be deficient. All that needs to be emphasized at this point is that the evidence strongly suggests that Collingwood's interest in the *Leviathan* was always confined to part I, even though he described the whole book as the world's greatest store of political wisdom. We are still left, then, without an answer to the question of why Hobbes became the exemplar for Collingwood's political treatise.

Collingwood's own explanation of his sudden enthusiasm for Hobbes, stated in *The New Leviathan,* is not entirely convincing. Collingwood argued that it was only recently, 'towards the middle of the twentieth century', that people had begun to appreciate the true worth of the *Leviathan.* Hitherto this appreciation had been clouded by the 'rising tide of ethical and political sentimentalism'. The wars of the twentieth century, Collingwood suggested, had enabled men such as himself 'to blow away the mists of sentimentalism' (*NL,* p. iv). However, Collingwood himself had criticized the sentimentalist reaction to Hobbes a long time before the Second World War began. The sentimentalists, Collingwood had argued in 1921, had admitted that "subjective" feeling acts as the criterion of activity, but they appended to Hobbes's subjectivism the 'existence of altruistic feeling'. This, for Collingwood, constituted a contradiction in terms: 'If it is *feeling* then it is a wholly immediate source of action: if it is really *altruistic* it is no longer immediate but contains something beyond mere feeling'.[10] The clouds of sentimentalism, then, had long been dispelled in Collingwood's mind before he came to regard 'Hobbes's *Le-*

viathan as a work of gigantic stature, incredibly overtopping all its successors in political theory from that day to this' (*NL*, p. iv).

We get nearer to an explanation when we bear three factors in mind. Collingwood's aim in moral philosophy had always been to overcome the one-sidedness of intellectualism and the one-sidedness of subjectivism. Plato was the most sophisticated of the theorists associated with the former, and Hobbes provided the most systematic and eloquent statement of the latter point of view. Collingwood had very early in his career recognised the direction that modern ethics had to take: 'The task is to think on from Plato to Hobbes and then from Hobbes to something new which shall overcome the defects in Hobbes'.[11] It is not surprising, then, that Collingwood called his book *The New Leviathan,* for he believed that the next step in ethics was to move on from the moral theory of Hobbes.

A second reason why Collingwood chose Hobbes as his exemplar is that the former, like his distinguished predecessor, endeavoured to ground his theories of ethics and politics in a philosophy of human nature, or philosophy of mind. Both authors felt compelled to begin from first principles. For Collingwood, European civilization is a thing of the mind, and an understanding of the former cannot possibly be attained without an enquiry into that which created it. Similarly, for Hobbes, to compose a society in which human beings can best associate with one another necessitates the knowledge of the prime movers of action. Despite the differences of their accounts of human nature, or mind, the main connection between Collingwood and Hobbes is the primary place which the theory of mind occupies in their respective political philosophies.

The third factor to bear in mind is that Collingwood obviously perceived certain similarities between the 'revolt against' civilization which was occurring in his own day and the 'miseries, and horrible calamities, that accompany a Civill Warre', that is, the events of Hobbes's own day.[12] Both situations constituted, for Collingwood, retrograde steps in the progress of civilization, and a consequent advance in the forces of barbarism. Hobbes's response was to return to first principles, in order to point the way out of the predicament which faced his countrymen. Collingwood, in the light of the predicament that faced modern European civilization, appears to have come around to the view that Hobbes's realism had been an appropriate response to the seventeenth-century calamities, and that something of this same realism might be appropriate to the crisis of the twentieth century. Indeed, in a letter to H. T. Hopkinson, Collingwood suggests that 'by recovering the hard boiled Hobbesian attitude to politics one can make sense even of the politics that is going about in the world now'.[13] Collingwood had long recognised the significance of Hobbes's hardheaded subjectivism as a corrective to in-

tellectualism in the history of political thought. It was only with the advent
of the Second World War, however, that Collingwood realised its appro-
priateness in discussing contemporary practical political problems. This
is not to suggest that Collingwood abandoned his view that there are no
perennial problems in philosophy. He did not believe that Hobbes could
supply us with answers to twentieth-century problems. This is why it
was necessary 'to bring the Leviathan up to date, in the light of the advances made since it was written, in history, psychology, and anthropology' (*NL,* p. iv). Hobbes had to be adapted to meet the demands of
the new circumstances.

3. The apparent relation

Before proceeding to look at the general philosophical relation between
the two *Leviathan*s, it is necessary to dispel two common partial mis-
conceptions about the apparent relation. Many reviewers of *The New
Leviathan* detected immediately a very obvious resemblance between
the two *Leviathan*s,[14] a point of comparison which Collingwood himself
encouraged in the preface to his political treatise.[15] Louis Mink echoes
the many reviewers when he suggests that

> when Collingwood wrote *The New Leviathan* he consciously modelled the or-
> ganization of the book on the predecessor whose title he adopted. It has four
> main parts, 'Man', 'Society', Civilization' and 'Barbarism', corresponding to Hobbes's
> sections 'Of Man', 'Of Commonwealth', 'Of a Christian Common-wealth' and 'Of
> the kingdome of Darknesse'.[16]

Collingwood did not, however, initially intend consciously to model his
Leviathan upon that of Hobbes. It is to some extent fortuitous that both
the *Leviathan*s have four parts. In fact, Collingwood's treatise was to
have a fifth part. It was to be the culminating part, to which the four
prior to it were merely preliminary. The fifth part was to be addressed
to the question of 'how a society which considers itself civilized should
behave in the face of' the threat to civilization posed by the new barbarism.
Indeed, in a statement which devalues somewhat the 'preliminary' four
parts of *The New Leviathan,* Collingwood suggests that the fifth part was
to be the 'real subject of the book'. He even went as far as to say that
the question to which part V would be addressed constituted the real
purpose for writing *The New Leviathan.* In Collingwood's view it was
imperative that the question be answered 'pretty soon', or there would
be no civilized societies in a position to 'react to the revolt against civilization'.[17] It is regrettable that this was the very question which his
chronic ill health prevented him from addressing directly in the proposed
fifth, concluding part. It was only with tremendous resolve, during periods

of intermittent lucidity, managing sometimes only one or two sentences a day, that he completed what now stands as the final part of *The New Leviathan.* When the author explains in the published preface that what he offers 'to the reader is not what [he] should call a finished work',[18] he is alluding to much more than the fact that the published work is not as well revised as he would have liked it to have been; the work was actually unfinished, because it did not contain what he considered to be the most important part.

The most obvious difference between the two *Leviathans* was, like their most obvious similarity, immediately noted by reviewers. Most of the reviewers who commented upon the difference expressed their disappointment that Collingwood, in contrast to his exemplar, had chosen to present his arguments in short aphoristic paragraphs. Here are some representative comments upon the manner of presentation adopted in *The New Leviathan:* 'The logical demonstration of his conclusions is reminiscent of Spinoza. . . . It is unfortunate that he has numbered every short paragraph on a kind of pseudo-decimal system';[19] 'One of Dr. Collingwood's innovations is to write his entire book in numbered sections *à la* Wittgenstein';[20] 'Why has Dr. Collingwood, a writer of limpid English prose, chosen to imitate Spinoza rather than Hobbes in the matter of presentation?';[21] and, finally, 'He borrows from modern logic the device of designating the main topics in his argument by using whole numbers and of indicating the development of the argument and subordinate topics by using decimals. This device makes for ease of reference, but the logical progress and dependence it purports to indicate is not, in fact, achieved'.[22]

These observations on Collingwood's method of analysis raise two related problems. First, why did Collingwood adopt this uncharacteristic mode of presentation? Second, what inspired him to adopt such a method? I will attempt to answer the latter question first. On the basis of mere resemblance it has been suggested, as the quotations just given indicate, that Collingwood was following modern logic, Spinoza, or perhaps even Wittgenstein. It is assumed that Collingwood was employing a logical deductive system, and that this is why he numbered each paragraph. However, a more plausible explanation can be given of Collingwood's source of inspiration, one which relates *The New Leviathan* more closely to Hobbes.

Collingwood's interest in the philosophy of religion and his thorough knowledge of the Bible[23] give us a clue. It seems to me that it may have been the King James authorised version of the Bible that provided Collingwood with a useful exemplar. There are a number of arguments to support this suggestion. The King James Bible, although presented in short numbered paragraphs, does not purport to employ the deductive method. *The New Leviathan* itself does not proceed by means of deductive argument. Collingwood is quite clear that his own method is historical. By this he means the asking of relevant questions, and the gathering of information and data to answer them. Those reviewers who attribute to Collingwood the use of a deductive model are soon forced to conclude that he failed to make a very satisfactory job of it. It does not occur to them to question their own assumption about whether or not Collingwood actually was employing such a model.[24] Indeed, Collingwood had argued strongly elsewhere against the attempt to apply deductive methods to a philosophical enquiry. He praises Kant, for instance, for distinguishing clearly between mathematical and philosophical thinking. Kant, in making such a distinction, has the 'touch ... of a master'.[25] Collingwood agrees with Kant in believing that

philosophy knows no demonstrations: its proofs are not demonstrative but acroamatic; in other words, the difference between mathematical proof and philosophical is that in the former you proceed from point to point in a chain of grounds and consequents, in the latter you must always be ready to go back and revise your premises when errors, undetected in them, reveal themselves in the conclusions.[26]

In addition, Collingwood gives us good reason, in the form of a direct criticism, for discounting the view that Spinoza was the source of his method and system of numbering:

It follows that the literary form of a treatise in which a metaphysician sets out to enumerate and discuss the absolute presuppositions of thought in his own time cannot be the form of a continuous argument, leading from point to point by way of quasi-mathematical demonstration, as in the *Ethics* of Spinoza. It must be the form of a *catalogue raisonné*, as in the fourth book of Aristotle's *Metaphysics* or in the *Quaestiones* of a medieval metaphysician.[27]

These suggestions about Collingwood's method do not, of course, point us directly towards the King James Bible; we are in need of more evidence.

Everyone familiar with the Bible will know how remarkably easy it is to be extremely precise in referencing Bible verses. For example, 1 Cor. 14.10 points us, without ambiguity, to the following sentence: 'There are, it may be, so many kinds of voices in the world, and none of them are without signification'. Hobbes, of course, used this system of referencing extensively, throughout the *Leviathan*, in order to invoke the specific sections in the Bible which supported his claims. Thus, when Hobbes cites the Book of Judges to suggest that at times the term 'the *Spirit* of God' denotes 'an extraordinary Zeal' he is able to list the following numbered references: 'Judg. 3.10. 6.34. 11.29. 13.25. 14.6. 19.'[28] This is not conclusive proof, but it does seem reasonable to infer that Collingwood's newfound enthusiasm for the *Leviathan* extended to borrowing, and slightly modifying, the system of referencing he found there. There may, of course, be more than one source that served as Collingwood's exemplar. It could be suggested that Hobbes's *Elements of Law* offers itself as a worthy candidate in this respect. However, the system of numbering in the *Elements of Law,* and in the works of Grotius and Pufendorf, for that matter, differs considerably from the system employed in *The New Leviathan.*

The question of why Collingwood departed from his usual style of presentation – that is, lucid, clear, and flowing prose – has not been answered. I have argued that his reason for adopting the new style was not that he wanted to employ the deductive method of logical inference. Given that Collingwood's treatise purported to take as its starting point many of the problems and ideas articulated in the seventeenth century, he may have wanted to emphasize this link by using a method of presentation common during that century. However, in the light of the information we have concerning how ill Collingwood was while he was writing *The New Leviathan,* a more pressing reason can be inferred. In order to cover the ground that he had hoped (and we must remember that he fell short of completing his initial plan), he probably viewed aphoristic paragraphs as the best way of maintaining continuity in his arguments and of presenting only so much as he needed in order to advance his views further. The system of numbering would have had the added attraction that it could facilitate internal cross-referencing with extreme precision and thus aid his own thought processes at a time when his powers of concentration were failing him.

4. The philosophical relation

The aim of this section is not to detect resemblances and differences in the details of the two *Leviathans.* Such comparison would not adequately reveal the true relation between these books. In order to come to a more satisfactory understanding of Collingwood and Hobbes, it is necessary to invoke an appropriate framework to use in comparing them. What is, then, the appropriate framework to adopt?

Given that Collingwood's avowed purpose in writing *The New Leviathan* was to bring the *Leviathan* up to date, our starting point should be Collingwood's own perception of the manner in which he thought he was updating Hobbes. Without a familiarity with Collingwood's own understanding of the history of philosophical thought, the fundamental difference between the two *Leviathans* may not be apparent, nor will their significance or place in the history of philosophy be immediately intelligible. Invoking Collingwood's conception of the history of philosophy enables us to pinpoint exactly what he thought his relation was to Hobbes. The recovery of his conception of the history of philosophy is of immense value in our task of comparison, because it is not a mere chronology; it is a triadic understanding of political and ethical thought, in terms of which every thinker, including Hobbes, could be appraised.

Hegel, in his *History of Philosophy,* did much to formulate the perspective that Collingwood was later to adopt. It was Hegel's view that before coming to understand any of the details of the history of philosophy there is an imperative need to formulate a conception of the whole: 'Just as we first desire to obtain a general idea of a country, which we should no longer see in going into detail, so we desire to see the relation which single philosophies bear to the whole; For in reality, the high value of the detail lies in its relation to the whole'.[29] For Hegel, philosophy is a developing system, and the development occurs dialectically, exhibiting in its motion an inherent rationality. Each philosophy has value; none is without worth in this history. Each, however, is limited and partial in that it is a reflection of the level that consciousness has attained in the rational development of philosophy up to its own time. In formulating the category of the subjective, Hegel argued that the view of experience it generates is deficient, because of its excessive concern with finite matter. Instead of revealing to us the content of philosophy, we are offered only its 'formal and subjective moment'.[30] Under the category of the 'objective' we are offered a view of experience which is deficient because it ignores the subjective moment and has in common with philosophy only its 'objective moment'.[31] In Hegel's view, 'philosophy demands the unity and intermingling of these two points of view'.[32] The unity is to be found in the synthesis of these antithetical moments, that is, in what is immanent in the history of philosophy itself. Philosophy, as the thought which is universal, incorporating both the subjective and objective moments, has its content revealed little by little in the history of philosophy. Philosophy and its history are one and inseparable.

The British idealists, in agreement with Hegel, viewed the history of philosophy as a dialectical system in development. In the realm of ethical and political philosophy, they postulated that each thinker was concerned to formulate a criterion, or standard, of conduct. The criteria, they suggested, can be grouped into three categories, which are related to each other dialectically. They maintained that an anthropocentric, or subjective, criterion was nascent in the non-Platonic element in Greek political thought and that it became gradually more explicit and refined throughout the centuries. The antithesis of this subjective criterion was the transcendental, theocentric, or objective standard of moral conduct formulated by Plato and his successors. These antithetical traditions of the subjective and objective criteria of conduct coexisted until the eighteenth century, when Rousseau explicitly attempted to formulate a new criterion of political and moral conduct to overcome the deficiencies of the two antithetical criteria. Hegel, acknowledging Rousseau's lead, took on the task of synthesis and formulated a criterion of moral conduct that was immanent in the historical development of each society. The British idealists (and Collingwood is no exception) implicitly, and often explicitly, assumed this triadic conception in their historical and philosophical enquiries.[33] This contention needs to be illustrated.

F. H. Bradley, for example, the most systematic and sophisticated of the British idealists, sets out in his *Ethical Studies* to formulate a criterion of moral conduct. He proceeds by means of dismissing the subjective and objective alternatives. First, the subjective criterion posits that morality is a means to pleasure, but this, for Bradley, can be 'no standard for morality', because on this idea 'fixing the relation of means to end must always be a matter of opinion' and 'the rules are not laws; I can please myself about them; and a standard which is no standard, a law which is no law, but which I may break or keep, which is at the mercy of changing judgment and fleeting opinion is no practical basis for me to regulate my life by'.[34] Second, Bradley is equally dismissive of the 'universal laws' of the abstract criterion, because there are no universal laws that 'can never be overruled'. Within this idea of an objective, transcendental, and eternal criterion is entailed the notion that we act 'for the sake of a good will to realize oneself by realizing the will which is above us and higher than ours; and the assurance that this, and not the self to be pleased, is the end for which we have to live. But as to that which the good will is, it tells us nothing, and leaves us with an idle abstraction'.[35] Third, the synthesis of the two one-sided, abstract, and partial criteria becomes manifest in the idea of 'my station and its duties'. The criterion of conduct is immanent in the social situations to which individuals as social beings are inescapably related. The 'individual apart from the community is an abstraction'; thus, 'to know what a man is (as we have seen) you must not take him in isolation. He is one of a people, he was born in a family, he lives in a certain society, in a certain state. What he has to be depends on what his place is, what his function is, and that all comes from his station in the organism'.[36]

Having established that the triadic conception of the history of moral and political thought is one to which the idealists subscribe, it remains to ask where Hobbes fits into the triad. In order to answer this question it is necessary to look at some idealists who discussed Hobbes's arguments. Bernard Bosanquet, in a very succinct and lucid manner, characterises the whole essence of the idealist view of past thought when he compares Hobbes, Locke, and Rousseau, each of whom is archetypical of the subjective, objective, and immanent criteria, respectively. Bosanquet maintains, 'For Hobbes, then, we might venture to say, political unity lies in a will which is actual, but not general; while for Locke it lies in a will which is general, but not actual', and 'if it were possible to inspire a logic as coherent as that of Hobbes, with a political content as large as that which animates Locke, a new ground would be won. And this is what Rousseau has attempted in his conception of a will at once actual and general'.[37] Bosanquet concurs with T. H. Green in placing Hobbes in the company of those who tried to formulate a subjective criterion of moral conduct. Green interprets Hobbes as having built morality upon base animal appetite. The sense of desire for something is accompanied by the impulse to appropriate that which we desire: 'Appetite, transformed (it is not explained how) into deliberate self-interest, is thus the source at once of the idea of duty, and of the "moral sentiments", or the affections which dispose us to realise the idea'.[38] Green goes on to suggest that such superficial analyses of 'composite feeling' were obviously satisfying to the taste of the age, 'seeking deliverance from the idea of an absolute divine law'. In terms of analyses of the grounds of morality such as that offered by Hobbes, 'men would not only please themselves (as they had always done), but take credit and account to themselves for their pleasure'.[39] Green is, then, clearly placing Hobbes in opposition to the objective criterion of conduct. In the *Lectures on the Principles of Political Obligation* Green concludes that Hobbes's subjectivism leads to a radical individualism which inhibits and frustrates the formation of a concept of the common good. Hobbes is convicted, in this respect, of being one-sided and abstract.[40]

A common appraisal and criticism of the subjective criterion was that, on the positive side, it stressed the importance of the interests and desires of individuals in guiding their conduct. On the negative side, such a criterion was deemed to legitimate almost any expedient course of action and could not, therefore, act as a genuine moral criterion of conduct. This is exactly the line of appraisal which Collingwood takes against Hobbes in the early lectures on moral philosophy and, to a large extent, in *The New Leviathan*. In the lectures of 1921 and 1923, Collingwood is explicitly trying to formulate a criterion of ethical conduct which 'concretizes' the subjective and objective criteria.[41]

Collingwood argues that it was Plato who formulated the first complete ethical theory. Plato is identified as the foremost exponent of 'Realism or Objectivism in Ethics'.[42] The criterion of moral conduct formulated by Plato stands entirely outside of the people who have to act in accordance with it.[43] It is 'a law given to the mind but not by the mind'.[44] What is right and wrong is 'a matter of objective fact'.[45] Those things which it is right to do depend for their rightness not upon being done, or being thought about and imagined, but upon the external and objective standard of the good. The transcendental laws of morality are 'an absolute standard by reference to which the intellect can and indeed must set itself up as a judge of the will'.[46] Intellect is fundamental to human action, and the will is its mere subservient derivative. The will has to be brought into alignment with an intellectually apprehended form to which it contributed nothing in the making. All action is dependent upon thought; the former presupposes the latter, but the same is not true in reverse.

Objectivist ethics shares with commonsense realism the supposition that there is an objective reality which has 'an existence and character of its own independently of any perceptive activity on the part of a knowing mind'.[47] The objectivist view of ethical activity is, for Collingwood, unsatisfactory in that it requires us to apprehend the form of the good by the exercise of pure reason or intellect, unassisted by the will, which is subservient to intellect and not in a position to give it assistance. If we fail to grasp the laws correctly, our actions are vitiated from the outset. Metaphysics, then, forms the basis of morality, and only the philosopher capable of determining the moral law, through the exercise of intellect, qualifies to be a statesman. This is not to say that the objectivist, or intellectualist, theory of moral action has nothing of value to offer. Indeed, Collingwood states quite emphatically that the 'intellectualism of Plato is not by any means all error. The impossibility of acting without thinking and of acting well without thinking well, has never been more forcibly stated, and it remains a permanent truth'.[48]

Aristotle, according to Collingwood, is also an intellectualist, 'that is to say one who denies the special character of activity and transfers the centre of his theory to the intellect regarded as a faculty of passive contemplation'.[49] For Aristotle the good, or the end of action, is right action in accordance with rule. We apprehend right rule by means of an act of the intellect. The apprehension of the right rule is a presupposition of right action.[50] Aristotle is, for Collingwood, intellectualist through and through, and the former's concept of God as the unmoved mover in the universe, towards which we direct our action and which we contemplate as an object of love, is testimony to the dualism that is characteristic of Greek intellectualism. This dualism is evident in Plato's doctrine of the transcendent forms, and in Aristotle's distinction between God and the world. The good, for Aristotle, Collingwood argues, is placed outside of human existence: It can be contemplated but never attained, and must therefore continue to be 'an object of the purely theoretical intellect.'[51]

Christianity initially rejected this intellectualism of the Greeks by emphasizing human activity. Activity was viewed as being at the basis of thought. Wisdom, conceived as intellectual contemplation, was replaced by the idea of the creative and passionate energy of love. God is not the object of this love 'but a life incarnate in man himself: the Aristotelian static self contemplation of God becomes the atonement in which God's spirit wins back his children to unity with himself, a dynamic or creative self-knowledge'.[52]

Christian philosophy was only at first able to articulate its corrective to the intellectualism of the Greeks in the symbolism of its creeds and theologies. The fall of the Roman Empire stimulated philosophical thought, but the medieval mind, in reviving the philosophical heritage, returned to the Greeks to find its bearings. The result was a Christianity imbued with Hellenism. The Gospels became permeated with the intellectualism which they had originally opposed. When the new revolt against intellectualism occurred during the Renaissance, Christianity itself was on the opposite side, 'and the new anti-intellectualism was ostensibly anti-christian as well.'[53]

The moral theory which the Renaissance produced, and which was the antithesis of objectivism, or intellectualism, was hedonism. There had always been opponents of intellectualism, existing side by side with their antagonists.[54] However, the former had been distinctly in the shadow of the latter until Machiavelli capitalised upon the disarray in which Christian intellectualism emerged from the Middle Ages. The intellectualism of medieval Christianity had resulted in a rigid concept of law in accordance with which society should be governed. This, of course, was anticipated in the intellectualism of the Greeks. The implication was that human nature was excluded from politics, and human life or the well-being of society was to be regulated by rigid and unalterable precepts. It was during the Renaissance that hedonism, although always evident, became dominant and intellectualism was forced onto the defensive.

Machiavelli's prince, while recognizing the common morality founded upon abstract principles, denies its claim upon the affairs of statecraft. The prince has to be perceptive and astute, capable of responding, without constraints, to the varied and many potentially dangerous situations which confront him. The prince, then, is not looking upwards to the heavens for guidance in action, but down to the immediate practical predicaments that face him. This 'concrete historical imagination of the prince' enables him to understand and come to terms with 'the movement of the actual world of men'.[55] In a very Crocean interpretation of Machiavelli, Collingwood maintains that

Machiavelli never denied that the prince ought to be loyal and merciful so far as he can, and that when he cannot he is really breaking a moral law, however unavoidably. Hence Machiavelli's work is permeated by a sense of tragedy, the claims of morality and expediency stand over against one another in unreconciled antagonism, and if morality must yield to expediency, it is only because of the world's incorrigible wickedness.[56]

Collingwood views Hobbes's *Leviathan* as a sequel to Machiavelli's *Prince*. Hobbes succeeded in resolving the dualism in Machiavelli between morality and expediency. He did this 'by making morality itself an outgrowth of expediency'.[57] Whereas Machiavelli rests content with providing no answer to the question of why the people should allow the prince to rule, Hobbes provides an explicitly hedonist answer. In the chapter in the *Leviathan* on the passions, Hobbes makes human appetite and desire the criteria of what is good; evil, in contrast, is that to which human beings are averse. Morality, then, becomes correlative with expediency. Because what is good is ascertained by subjective feelings, and individuals come into conflict in the pursuit of their desires, it is deemed expedient to invest in an authority the powers that can alleviate the conflict, and above all minimise the threat which everyone fears more than anything else, that is, sudden and violent death.[58]

Hobbes's hedonism was a considerable advance on the ethics of the Greeks, because, unlike the latter, it emphasized the self-assertiveness of every action. Action is self-willed, creative, and spontaneous, and not something imposed upon the individual from outside the self.[59] Hobbes and Descartes did great services to the theories of ethics and epistemology, respectively, in that the former emphasized the radical subjectivism of action and the latter made the same point in respect of thought.[60] Both, however, failed to move beyond the one-sidedness of subjectivism.

For Collingwood, all forms of subjectivism, including hedonism, rest on the mistake of combining a true insistence on the subjectivity of action with a misconceived distinction between subject and object. The subjectivist separates the world into two parts: Everything which falls outside of its own understanding of the world is rejected as irrelevant. The subjectivist distinguishes those things which belong to the self and those things which are alien to it. Those which belong to the self and constitute its personality are the only things which have a claim upon it.

The implication in Hobbes is that our motive for action lies within our immediate consciousness, but this further implies the independence of each moment of consciousness. Present feelings are severed from those of the past. In Collingwood's view, feeling constitutes the only spring of action for Hobbes; feeling determines conduct. Collingwood argues that this view of action is mistaken. Present feelings are undoubtedly affected by one's past feelings and by one's anticipation of future feelings. We are not, then, dealing with pure feeling at all, but with the capacity to remember and imagine feelings which are not being immediately enjoyed. This reflective power gives us the capacity to transcend immediate feeling and constitutes an aspect of 'our nature wholly distinct from feeling itself'.[61] The strength of Hobbes is his radical subjectivity, but this starting point is undermined by his separation of the subjective from the objective;

the self is conceived as something fixed and complete, standing in opposition to a world which is hostile. In Collingwood's view, the self is
not like this at all: 'The self is really in constant flux, a process of creating
itself and its world'.[62]

The mind is something which the hedonist takes to be ready-made. A
moralist, for example, is deemed to have the tastes and inclinations of a
moralist, and to find pleasure in things appropriate to moral activity. This,
however, does not explain how a person with these characteristics came
to possess them. To prefer one activity, or to have one taste, in preference
to another presupposes reflective thought, and it is only this which 'can
bring into existence the types of character which the Hedonist is content
to observe ready made'.[63] Character is constantly in the process of being
formed, and as we reach the higher and more rational levels of action in
which the human being is fully developed and civilized, to view character
as static is an implausible fiction.

In Collingwood's view, 'Hobbes's moral theory may be defined as a
pure hedonistic subjectivism, precisely antagonistic to the pure intellec-
tualistic objectivism of the Greeks.'[64] Utilitarianism constitutes a modification of hedonism in that it attempts to unify the multiplicity of divergent feelings by reducing them to a central principle. This principle,
or standard, of what feelings ought to be still rests upon the principle of
feeling itself. Instead of a pure subjectivism, a privileged consciousness
is postulated whose feelings are set up as the standard. The theological
utilitarianism of the eighteenth century postulated God as the privileged
consciousness, and the political utilitarianism of the nineteenth century
postulated society.[65] Rewards and punishments bring the feelings of the
individual in line with the standard. The sanctions are formulated and
enforced by the standard consciousness itself, that is, in the form of legislation, whether it be divine or political.

Hedonism had the merit of emphasizing the radical subjectivism of
action, but it did so (and this is its downfall) by asserting the ultimacy
of feeling as the criterion. Utilitarianism preserves the latter while rejecting
the former. It uses as its criterion the feeling of society as the measure
of the greatest happiness of the greatest number. The system of rewards
and punishments ensures that individual actions conform to such a criterion, which values the presence of pleasure and the absence of pain.
However, the radical subjectivism and autonomy of the will, the strong
points of hedonism, are sacrificed by subjecting the individual to an external authority which is beyond question.

This is, in fact, a form of intellectualism in which the greatest happiness
is not a feeling at all, but an object which stands outside the individual,
inviting contemplation. The difference between this form of intellectualism and that of Plato is that utilitarianism tries to philosophize about
irrational feelings: 'Thus we have lost all the spontaneity of hedonism

and revert to an authoritarianism which only differs from that of the Greeks in that authority is rested no longer in reason but in the caprice of a capriciously chosen master'.[66] Utilitarianism is the 'degradation of hedonism'[67] in that it preserves the errors and denies the truths of that out of which it grew. It does have genuine philosophical value, although one-sided, in that it demonstrates that utility 'is one of the permanent and necessary categories of ethical thought'.[68]

Each of the criteria sets up a dualism which it fails to overcome, and in asserting its positive principles denies what is also essential. The objectivist, or intellectualist, tends to ignore or suppress the subjective element of action, which is desire, and tries to explain the impetus of action solely in terms of the exercise of reason. The intellectualist fails to recognise that reason is 'the regulative unity of consciousness', which must have 'a consciousness to unify.'[69] In suppressing desire the intellectualist has rejected the content which reason unifies and thus is left in the position of having to convert reason into a constitutive, rather than a regulative, principle, which, in Collingwood's opinion, 'debases it into a special kind of desire.'[70]

On the other hand the subjectivist suppresses reason and tries to explain action in terms of the sole operation of desire. He destroys the unity of consciousness and is left with a multiplicity of desire which cannot issue in action. The subjectivist is forced to reintroduce a unity by postulating degrees of desire, which enables him to explain action as that which issues from the strongest. The attainment of such a unity 'is exactly the kind of thing which his principles forbid.'[71] What is needed, then, is a theory which unifies objectivism and subjectivism, desire and will, in order to overcome the one-sidedness of each of the deficient and antithetical theories.

Rousseau's significance in the history of ethical thought is that he gave direction to future attempts at overcoming the deficiencies in the subjectivist and objectivist traditions. Hobbes, Collingwood suggests, had given a mythological account of 'the process by which the manifold of desire is unified into action', and it is Rousseau who is given the honour of 'bringing the myth into closer union with the thing signified'.[72] Rousseau realised that the unity of consciousness in a body politic cannot be symbolised by a single person, because that would be to introduce a single desire in place of the multiplicity of desires. The unity of consciousness has to be found in the relation which pertains between the individuals who comprise the commonwealth. Rousseau tried to formulate such a unity in the idea of the General Will. Kant's ethical theory is, similarly, an attempt to overcome the dualism of reason and desire. For Kant, 'desire is constitutive and reason regulative, so that each apart from the other is an unreal fiction.'[73]

It is incontrovertible, then, that Collingwood used the triadic conception of the history of political and ethical thought as a reference point in appraising the arguments of past philosophers. Although the discussions of specific thinkers disappeared from the revisions of the lectures on moral philosophy after 1923,[74] the idea of the three criteria of rational conduct still remained.[75]

In relation to the general philosophical aims of the two *Leviathans*, Collingwood was attempting to formulate a different criterion of conduct from that of Hobbes, one which he hoped would overcome the deficiencies of the subjectivist and objectivist traditions. We can, then, take the title of *The New Leviathan* to mean *new* in the sense that it would attempt to establish the criterion of moral conduct upon a different foundation; namely, upon the idea of duty rather than upon the principle of utility. Collingwood felt able to call his book *The New Leviathan* because he did not think that his project entailed refuting what Hobbes had argued. Collingwood, in fact, had never wished to refute Hobbes. In the early lectures he states quite explicitly that 'nobody wants to refute Hobbes except people who want to go back to the middle ages and re-establish a neo-Hellenic objectivism. . . . One does not refute philosophies, one continues them'.[76]

Collingwood did not believe that Rousseau, Hegel, Bradley, or Bosanquet[77] had succeeded in going beyond Hobbes in formulating a satisfactory account of ethical conduct; therefore it must have seemed quite appropriate to Collingwood to call his book *The New Leviathan* rather than the *New Social Contract, New Philosophy of Right, New Ethical Studies,* or *New Philosophical Theory of the State.* Collingwood's view, expressed in the early lectures, that we do not refute, but rather continue, past philosophies is quite in keeping with the view he held in *The New Leviathan.* In the latter work, echoing the *Essay on Philosophical Method,* he subscribes to the Platonic distinction between *eristical* and *dialectical* discussion. Eristical discussion is confrontational and adversarial in character. It is the activity of trying to prove that one's own arguments are right and that those of others are wrong. In contrast, 'the essence of dialectical discussion is to discuss in the hope of finding that both parties to the discussion are right'.[78] Collingwood's method in *The New Leviathan* is to advance his argument, not by refutation but by discussion, and by incorporating other views into a more adequate understanding of the European mind and its manifestations.

5. Collingwood's synthesis: constrained by convention

I have argued that Collingwood consciously attempted to formulate a criterion of moral conduct different from that of Hobbes. Let me now substantiate this claim more fully with reference to the theories that Collingwood developed gradually over the years and that culminated in the argument of *The New Leviathan*.

In *An Autobiography* Collingwood says that shortly after World War I he began to reconsider all the familiar problems of ethics associated with economics, politics, and morals in terms of the principles which were informing his work, namely, the rapprochements between history and philosophy, and between theory and practice. (One may also add that these problems were addressed in the context of developing a scale of overlapping forms.) He says that he first subjected the problems to a historical treatment, in order to demonstrate that each had a history and was not intelligible without an understanding of that history.[79] This, as we have seen, he conveyed in his lectures on moral philosophy up to and including 1923 (which also include revisions probably made during the period up to 1927). Second, Collingwood claims that he subjected the problems to an 'analytic' treatment. He explains, 'My notion was that one and the same action, which as action pure and simple was "moral" action, was also a "political" action as action relative to a rule, and at the same time an "economic" action as means to an end.'[80] Although this view of action was not published in a fully articulated form until *The New Leviathan,* it appears to have been taking shape about 1920, but he declared himself at that time to be dissatisfied with the attempt he had made to distinguish right from duty. He said of his account of duty, 'This of course is weak: a positive account of duty must be given.'[81] From 1921 to 1927 Collingwood reverted to identifying rightness and duty and associated both with law-governed activity, or regularian action. In *Speculum Mentis* and the moral philosophy lectures of 1923, as well as in the revisions made prior to 1927, he envisaged a stage beyond duty, that of absolute ethics, or absolute action. The 1927 revisions, and 'Economics as a Philosophical Science', including the earlier drafts, nevertheless still identified right and duty. In his article 'Political Action', Collingwood reverted back to distinguishing between right and duty, but he concentrated his efforts on specifying the character of politics, which he associated with right, and thus avoided giving a positive and distinguishing account of duty. He employed a similar tactic in an essay read to the Exeter College Dialectical Society on 3 March 1930. After talking of utility and rightness as two forms of goodness, Collingwood said, 'Concerning duty, which I take to be a third form of goodness, I prefer to say nothing here, because I have already trespassed long enough on your patience.'[82] He was less reticent about expounding upon the distinction in his moral philosophy lectures of 1929, 1932, 1933, and 1940. After the publication of W. David Ross's *The Right and the Good* in 1930, Collingwood was able to invoke him as an ally, albeit only partially, for having distinguished some forms of duty from rightness.[83] Nevertheless, Collingwood did not feel confident enough to distinguish clearly between right and duty in

An Essay on Philosophical Method, the main points of which accompanied his moral philosophy lectures up until 1933, nor in *The First Mate's Log,* published in 1940.[84]

For our purposes Collingwood's attempts to specify the character of action can be distinguished into two categories. First, there are those accounts of action which wholly, or substantially, conform to the sequence, at the level of rational will, of utility, duty, and absolute ethics. Utility is abstract ethics; duty is concrete ethics; and absolute ethics is the concrete universal concept of action, that is, action which has overcome the abstractness of utility and the mere concreteness of duty. In this sequence of the forms, or concept, or action, duty and political activity are correlative. The second sequence with which Collingwood characterises the concept of action is that of utility, or the useful, which is associated with economic action; right, or regularian action, which is associated with politics; and duty, or ethical action, which is action in its totality, or the concrete universal concept of action, which is associated with morality proper.

Both sequences are concerned to demonstrate how at each successive level capriciousness is gradually eliminated. Capricious choice is what Collingwood calls a 'mere decision, uncomplicated by any reason why it should be made in this way and not that: in fact, *caprice'* (*NL*, 13.12). Both sequences conform to the analysis which is exhibited in the triadic conception of the history of political and ethical thought, that is, the specification of an abstract and a concrete concept of the criterion of action, followed by its synthesis in a concrete universal. In both sequences the concept of action is expounded in terms of a scale of overlapping forms. This means, of course, that the Hegelian dialectic becomes modified into the dialectic of a scale of forms analysis. The difference is clearly expressed by Croce.

Croce argues that Hegel's important contribution to philosophy was his handling of the idea of opposites. The philosophical concept, Croce suggests, is not defined in terms of a genus and its species. The philosophical concept includes within itself distinct forms which are united with the others and with the whole.[85]

A unity is inconceivable without distinction: What is there to unify if there are no distincts? The distinctions of the concept do not stand outside it, nor do they negate it: They are the concept itself.[86] For example, the *'spirit',* for Croce, is a philosophical concept which is subdivided into the theoretical and the practical. The former is further distinguished into intuition and thought; the latter is differentiated into utilitarian will and ethical will. These four activities of the spirit are found in the doctrines of aesthetics, logic, economics, and ethics.[87]

These four forms are, in relation to the spirit, philosophical concepts:

They are not beneath spirit, nor outside it, but the particular forms of spirit itself. They are distinct, but not separate; the one implies the other.[88] None, however, is arbitrary, and each has its place and function in a succeeding order of degrees of the concept. That which precedes provides the material for that which succeeds, and that which succeeds includes within itself that which preceded it. The series of implications is not arbitrary, but necessary:

The four moments imply one another regressively by their concreteness. The concept cannot exist without expression, the useful without both and morality without the three preceding degrees. If the aesthetic fact is in a certain sense alone independent while the others are more or less dependent, then the logical is the least dependent and the moral will the most.[89]

Classification is, then, rejected, and the scheme of degrees of the spirit, or of reality, put in its place. The scheme is one in which unity and distinction are correlative.

Distinct concepts render possible the unity of the philosophical concept, but the same does not appear to be the case with opposed concepts. Opposite or contrary concepts cannot be reduced to distincts. Rather than imply each other, they deny each other; rather than compose a unity, they seem to demand and compel diversity. A series of distinct concepts such as beauty, truth, the useful, and the moral cannot have added to them or inserted among them the ugly, false, useless, and evil.[90] Hegel's great discovery, according to Croce, was that opposites are not an illusion, nor is unity illusory. Opposites stand in opposition to one another, but they do not stand in opposition to unity.[91] This is because two abstract opposites negate each other but are preserved in the synthesis which overcomes their abstractness. Thus being and nothingness are opposites whose synthesis – becoming – overcomes their abstractness.

Hegel's failure was to conceive the theory of opposites and the theory of distincts as the same thing, and thus he formulated the connection between degrees of reality as a dialectic of opposites, instead of a series of implicated distincts. For Hegel the beautiful and the ugly were two opposed concepts, which would find their synthesis in a third concept. This, for Croce, was a mistaken view of the relation between a concept and its contrary. The concept includes as part of itself, and not something outside of itself, its opposite. Beauty is what it is because of its denial of the ugly, and good is such because it denies evil. The positive and negative are inherent in the same concept.[92] For example, evil is not a concept which stands outside of, and negates, goodness: It resides within the concept as a degree of goodness, although its privation.[93] Collingwood makes a similar point when he argues that within a scale of forms, goodness and badness are exhibited in varying degrees according to the place on the scale from which the generic essence is viewed. The lower of two levels in the scale loses its intrinsic goodness and takes on the character of badness in comparison to the one above: 'In it [the lower level] the abstract idea of evil finds a concrete embodiment, and at this point in the scale the achievement of goodness simply means the negation of this one thing'.[94]

Both Croce and Collingwood contend that philosophical thought includes within itself the affirmative and the negative. To affirm something is at the same time to deny something else, and to deny something is at once also to affirm something. Croce, for example, argues that thought is '*affirmation* and *negation;* it does not affirm save by denying, and does not deny save by affirming.'[95] This is what Collingwood refers to as 'concrete affirmation' and 'concrete negation'.[96] As we saw in the preceding chapter, each point on a scale of forms summarises the whole scale to that point. What this means is that the truth of the proximate form, and of the other levels below it, are preserved in the highest form. On the other hand, when affirming the highest form, the proximate is the embodiment of the errors we wish to deny.[97]

In summary, for Croce, Hegel's important contribution to philosophy was the formation of the concept as a concrete universal; the development of the doctrine of degrees of reality as opposed to coordinate species of a genus; and the recognition that opposites are not opposed to unity. Hegel's error lay in conflating the ideas of distincts and opposites, which led him to misconceive the relation between a concept and its contrary as the dialectic of opposite concepts, whereas, Croce argues, the distinct concept has within itself its own opposite. Therefore the relation between concepts is not that of contradiction, but of implication.

Collingwood's idea of the concept as a fusion of differences in kind with differences in degree, and a fusion of opposites and distincts, owes more to Croce, it seems, than it does to Hegel. Collingwood denied the dialectic of opposites and conceived the philosophical concept as a series of distinct degrees, each of which implicates the others and includes its opposite within itself. Collingwood does not, however, follow Croce's division of the spirit into the two theoretical and two practical forms. As we saw earlier, the sequence and order of the forms of experience in *Speculum Mentis* constituted a development of Gentile's ideas. Nevertheless, Collingwood's understanding of the concept of action, especially in its economic form, owes a good deal to Croce.

In the first sequence of theories of action which Collingwood formulated, the forms of action are related to the forms of the spirit. In both *Speculum Mentis* and the 1923 lectures on moral philosophy, Collingwood precedes his discussion of the three higher forms with discussions of play and convention, the former being related to art, and the latter to religion.[98] It is in the life of reason, having left mechanical, reflexive, and instinctive action behind, that we meet with choice, the very lifeblood of the mind. The life of conscious choice, or reason, is one characterised by temptation and struggle, in which we are faced with the predicament and burden of choosing between good and evil, often without knowing which is which, and often wishing that we could return to the life of instinct, in which we are able to do anything which comes to mind without the question of right and wrong ever entering into the activity. The wish, however, is forlorn, because to wish for a different state of affairs is itself to negate instinct:

Our very revolt against the law of reason is inspired by the principles of reason, and we can only recover the life of instinct not by anything so rational as to revolt, but only by sinking down into a dull animality in which choice itself becomes a lost art and our mind shrinks into the narrow confines of unconscious habit.[99]

The consciousness of choice – that is, when we do one act in the knowledge that an alternative was open to us – is to exercise our will. In its elementary form, will is caprice, and 'we decide simply for the sake of deciding; our newly found power of volition runs riot in mere self assertion whose only aim is to be self action. Caprice is will for will's sake.'[100] In the choice, we choose ends which are good, and this consciousness of choice brings about the distinction between good and evil. It is possible to choose, however, Collingwood argues, without realising that one is choosing a good, and one is thus oblivious to the fact that the choice is shot with moral issues.[101] Choice of this kind is play.

In *Speculum Mentis* Collingwood argues that play is action in its most rudimentary form and that play corresponds to art, which is thought in its rudimentary stage. In the 1923 lectures on moral philosophy, play is not the most rudimentary form of action; it is the most rudimentary form of rational action.[102] In play our choice is explicitly rational, and it is as a consequence free, but only to a small degree, because we do not know why we make the choice.[103] The end we choose in play is not chosen because we think it right, useful, conventional, or customary: 'It is simply chosen'.[104] Whatever motive there is in play is only implicit, and the actor is unaware of it: Such motives are made explicit only at higher levels of consciousness.

Play is the activity natural to children, but it is also the proper form of relaxation for adults. Play, although distinct, is not separate from the higher forms of activity. Play implicates the higher levels of action in that it is in them that it finds its own explanation and justification. In itself play exhibits a self-contradiction, in that it makes believe that the ends chosen are the result of pure caprice, untainted by considerations of usefulness or morality, but this is self-deception. The discovery that life cannot be guided by our own subjective caprices is the lesson which passes us beyond the activity of play.[105] The reasons we have for acting are not really absent; they are concealed. In asking oneself why one chose the ends one did, an attempt is made to convert the implicit into the explicit. The simplest answer to the question is that I chose this action because other people chose it, and here we have entered the world of convention.

When an individual decides to eat dinner wearing a clown's nose and a red curly wig, he or she is engaging in play, but when a society decides to dine in formal dress, it is convention, and this is corporate play. To the extent that play is often corporate, in the form of joint activities or team games, it contains an element of convention. In play, however, the conventional element is implicit. We play a game of rugby because we want to, not because others want to, but implicitly we only want to play because we have seen others play and it looks as if it could be enjoyable. The conventional element is there, but only implicitly. The matter is different when we dress formally for dinner. Our reason is not merely that we want to, but that it is the done thing, it is customary and conventional, that is, it is what is expected of us on certain occasions.[106]

In *Speculum Mentis* the morality of religion is associated with convention. In play one has a subjective radical individualism; that is, the I asserting itself as will. At the same time there is a rejection and denial of any constraint which emanates from outside one's will. Play is, then, abstractly concrete, which means that it is one-sided and incomplete. Religious morality is a conventional morality in which action is guided by commandments which emanate from a source outside the individual. 'This', Collingwood argues, 'is the type of action in which the agent does a given thing not because he chooses it, but because his society chooses it'.[107] If the agent begins to reflect on the act and thinks that he, or she, must do it because society would disapprove of one who broke the convention, then the act becomes one of utility, because it is no longer done because others do it but because to do it is advantageous in so far as it avoids harm. If the agent reflects further and comes to believe that the society of which he, or she, is part has a moral claim which obliges the act to be performed by its members, then the act becomes one of duty. Thus at every stage the act is performed, and becomes a different act, because thought thinks it so.

Convention, nevertheless, is just as necessary as play to the development of the moral consciousness: The value of having everything arranged is a source of satisfaction and a relief from pure caprice. The attachment to a common purpose is a higher form of rationality than play, but it is still a rationality of a very low level. In answer to the question 'Why do I do this?', I reply, 'Because others do it', but others do it because other people do it, and therefore we all do it for no other reason than collective caprice.[108] The continuation and perpetuation of conventional action is a clear sign that recognition of the power to initiate is not yet explicit to the mind. The fact that other people do something is no reason why I should do it. To discover this is to be an inhabitant of a higher level of consciousness in which life is no longer completely guided by convention. In this higher level 'convention still has its place as a subordinate principle, regulating matters which we regard as unimportant'.[109]

It is consciousness of the consequences which lurk behind the non-performance of conventional activities, that is, the threat of punishment – of, for example, being ostracized by society for deviating from the customary thing to do – which elevates us to the level of utility, in which choice is no longer immediate but mediate – that is, we choose a thing not for itself, but in order to arrive at a certain consequence or to achieve a certain end.[110] The utilitarian aspect is always implicit in convention, just as convention is implicit in play. It could be said of every conventional act that we perform it because society rewards us for doing it and punishes us for failing to do it, but the act remains conventional only if these aspects are implicit. It need not be laboured that here we see Collingwood's form of philosophical analysis being applied to the substantive problems of articulating the concept of action. Each action is distinct but not separate, in that the lower has implicit in itself the higher, and the higher, while denying the lower, absorbs what it supersedes. Each is a different kind of action, yet embodying the generic essence in different degrees: None is a coordinate species of a genus; all are implied in an overlapping scale of forms; and, each sums up the whole of the scale to the level which the form has reached. In other words, the analysis is one in which there is a fusion of differences in degree with differences in kind, and a fusion of distincts and opposites.

It is at the level of utility and beyond that we begin to see more clearly the connection between Collingwood's historical treatment of the problems of ethics, that is, in the form of a triadic conception of the history of political thought, and the higher levels of action in an overlapping scale of forms. This is because we now enter the realm of ethical theories. In science, the third form of experience, or spirit, we find distinctions which are evident in 'an indivisible reality',[111] such as thought and action, intellect and will, and the universal and the particular, that is, scientific abstractions. Scientific abstractions separate knowledge from conduct and give rise to the utilitarian doctrine of the will. Science asks itself, 'What common characteristic is shared and invariable in a multiplicity of instances?' When applied to action, the answer which it comes up with is that action is purposive and is thus directed towards an end: 'Hence to be means to an end is the invariable characteristic of all action'.[112] From concrete actions utilitarianism abstracts only their purposiveness and identifies it as utility. The science of utility is economics.[113] Economics is an empirical science if it 'conceives its object as substance or thing', whose aim is to study wealth scientifically. Economics is a philosophical science when it conceives its object as 'the study of economic action'.[114] Croce had made this distinction quite forcefully by arguing that the economic, or useful, must not be conceived empirically but philosophically, as a fundamental and necessary category, or concept, of the spirit.[115] Collingwood acknowledges Croce's importance in this respect when he argues that Croce 'insists upon the philosophical validity of the concept of "economicity" and regards the useful as a fundamental philosophical notion on a level with the beautiful, the true and the good'.[116] Collingwood's inclusion of economics in the category of philosophical science is more clearly asserted in an early manuscript when he says that utility, or the economic good, is an ethical category which is a priori, and which therefore 'is a branch of philosophical ethics, i.e. an integral part of the spirit.'[117]

In economic action, two elements are evident: an immediate act and a mediate act, where the former is done in order to bring about the other.[118] In other words, we do something that we do not want to do, in order to do what we do want.[119] Here the particular act is never isolated, but always thought of as having an end beyond itself.[120] The act does not have a goodness as such; it is useful in relation to its end. In accordance with his theory of overlapping forms, Collingwood argues that

all action is useful: that is to say, the infra-utilitarian types of action when more clearly understood reveal a utilitarian quality or pass over by their own dialectic into utility, and the supra-utilitarian types imply utility as a transcended or negated moment within themselves.[121]

In recognising this we do not obviate the need for making the distinctions characteristic of the forms of action.

Action, under the category of economics, is regarded as a means to something that is not the action. Thus something not emanating from the actor and presented to consciousness by an external world possesses the good to which the action itself is directed. Utility is more free and rational than play or convention because the individual becomes conscious of his, or her, strength to initiate action and take a stand against convention. The action fails to be wholly rational, however, because it is deficient. We know why we choose to act, that is, because the action is useful in procuring a good which stands outside the act. It cannot give an answer, however, to the question of why the end is sought. Such an answer can only be achieved at a higher level of consciousness.[122]

Utilitarianism, Collingwood argues, in its attempt to be a calculus of conduct, 'is the most abstract and dialectically primitive of all the possible kinds of ethical theory.'[123] Utility, raised to an organized and logical level and presented as a guide to conduct, is found in the life of business, industry, and commerce. It is a life of abstract individualism in which conflicts of interest, whether they are at the individual, group, class, national, or racial level, are endemic. A second area of conflict is apparent as a consequence of the abstract separation of the will from the intellect. The businessman, as man of action, stands in opposition to the man of science, the former exhibiting a practical ideal and the latter a speculative ideal, yet they are mutually dependent. Industry and commerce depend on the discoveries of science, and scientists benefit from the profits of industry and commerce, but their 'ideals are in permanent conflict'.[124] A third area of conflict is evident between business and the state. Business, Collingwood claims, is essentially individualistic and rests upon the principle of laissez-faire. Regulation by the state is alien to its principles. Nevertheless, businessmen must cooperate and cannot perpetually be in conflict, and thus their way of life already implies the existence of law and order. The theory of the 'social contract' emerges when what is implicit in the business world, namely cooperation, is explicit. The world of business, which is contractual in character, is recognised to be based upon a fundamental contract, that is, the compact which obliges us to observe contracts. Business, Collingwood claims, 'rests upon the concrete truth of duty or law'.[125] This takes precedence over expediency and leads to the renunciation of profits, profits which on economic grounds would be sound and legitimate. If this claim is acknowledged, the economic viewpoint is transcended, and we enter the political or historical view.

The question which utility fails to answer, that is, why we choose the ends we pursue, is given its answer when we can say simply that we choose them because they are good. To pursue the good as good is an act of duty,[126] and an 'act is an act of duty, and its goodness is rightness, when it is the act of consciously determining one's whole life – acting under the consciousness that one's acts have infinite consequences, and accepting the responsibility for these consequences'.[127] Every act is charged with the potential of infinite consequences, and the lightness of heart or capriciousness with which each is chosen only betrays our ignorance of the fact. All actions can be viewed as moral from the point of view of a person reflecting upon them. It is from the point of view of the agent that they lack a moral dimension.[128] Croce put this point well when he argued that 'morality has complete empire over life, and there is not an act of life, be it small as you will, that morality does not or ought not to regulate'.[129] He goes on to add that morality, however, does not have absolute sway over the categories of the spirit and cannot destroy or modify them.

In *Speculum Mentis* Collingwood argues that historical thinking is the world of fact and that in it the universal and the particular are partially unified. The means and end of utility coincide: 'The means becomes an end in itself and the end becomes the means to itself'.[130] Action is now not a means to an end but an end in itself and done for its own sake. Historical ethics, however, cannot tell us clearly what duty is, and this is because it embodies a contradiction which must be overcome in a concrete, universal concept of action. On the one hand historical ethics presents a subjective answer to the question 'What is duty?' by asserting that the will is its own guide to conduct and that there is nothing outside it to determine it.[131] This is what Collingwood calls conscience. It is the sense of responsibility that we feel intuitively – a burden which bears heavily upon us and upon others in the situations we face daily.[132] Conscience is an intuitive sense of what our duty is: It is a moral sense unable to give an explanation of itself. Each of us might intuitively have different judgements about what it is right to do, but if it is to be more than caprice the end must be obligatory, not merely for myself but for everyone. Such a paradox cannot be transcended by conscience itself and leaves the problem of how to reconcile conflicting consciences unresolved. For Collingwood, 'The "coherent and solid life of duty" can never be realised by an intuitive conscience taking every case on its merits: but only by a will which wills, not the bare particular, but the universal'.[133]

The historical world of concrete fact also puts forward an objective answer to the question 'What is duty' which conflicts with its first answer and stands in unreconciled opposition to it. This answer puts forward an objective moral order manifest in law and directed towards determining the conduct of the subjective will.[134] Law is, for Collingwood, the moral judgement, or the collective conscience, of the whole community.[135] Conscience is moral choice in its immediacy, that is, as judged on each individual occasion, whereas 'law is moral choice in its ideality': In law, morality is 'abstracted from the actual in order to assert the ideal'.[136] Nevertheless, law is something external to the agent, something which imposes itself and serves to limit his, or her, freedom.[137] Thus conscience has its opposite in authority. Command and obedience in the political world have their logical parallels in the economic distinction of means and end. Collingwood goes on to suggest that 'authority has within the sphere of duty the same function which utility has within the sphere of rational choice as a whole'. Because of this logical parallel, economics and politics are often viewed as being integrally related.[138] Here Collingwood is alluding to Croce's identification of law and economics.

For Croce, laws are the springs of classes of practical acts. In other words, laws are volitional,[139] or, because they are abstract and have to be applied to single acts, they are, strictly speaking, aids to 'real volition'.[140]

Legislative activity, that is, the 'will that wills classes of acts', can be either moral, which includes within itself the economic, or merely economic. Laws, although abstract in classifying certain actions, will be conceived with a view to good or bad ends, for reasons of utility, or out of strong moral convictions. Law is for Croce '*generically practical,* or taken in itself, *merely economic*'.[141] The act of executing the laws, the juridical act, is also generically practical. Unlike law, however, juridical activity is identical with economic activity. Legislative activity enters the economic, but is distinguished from it in that it is abstract or indeterminate volition, that is, willing classes of action rather than willing concrete action. Juridical activity, the execution and application of the laws, is 'concrete and determined' and cannot be distinguished from economic activity,[142] that is, activity under the category of the useful. In *Politics and Morals* Croce argues that the state 'is nothing but a series of useful actions performed by a group of persons or by individual members within a group'.[143]

Collingwood's identification of law and morals, or politics and morals, follows Kant and Hegel rather than Croce. Collingwood argues that obedience to law is misconceived when it is viewed as action motivated by self-interest or punishment. Legislation is not the promotion of the interests of a particular class, and government is not an economic function.[144] Obedience to the law rests on duty, not utility. Politics, for Collingwood, is a branch of ethics, not of economics. Duty is integral to the idea of rule. The ruler rules in order to promote the good, and 'it is impossible for anyone actually to rule without feeling absolutely convinced that rule is a duty'.[145]

Collingwood argues that the legal mind is not that of the scientist but of the historian, whose knowledge is immersed in concrete facts. Law is an organic unity of statute and case law. The generality of law is directed to a concrete end, that is, law is used in the determination of specific cases. Both law and history include within themselves abstract generalisations which are subsidiary to their character as determinants of concrete fact, and therefore only part of their substance. Nevertheless, the fact that law is external, standing in relation to the agent as something other than himself, or herself, makes it abstract and still bound to scientific thought.[146]

In historical ethics, or duty, the law claims to embody right, yet the individual conscience may stand against it in the name of right. The two aspects of duty, individual conscience and external authority, can be reconciled only at a higher level when the ruled and the ruler become one and the same person, and when the ordering of other people to do what is right becomes unnecessary because everyone can be relied upon to do it without command. This, for Collingwood, is the perfectly free society in which each person is both subject and citizen. It is, then, a Kantian kingdom of ends.[147] We have not reverted to the anarchy of conscience, because we obey both ourselves and others. Such obedience is forthcoming because we think both our own commands and those of others to be responsible: We appreciate that the rationality we deem ourselves to possess is also present in others.[148] We have now entered the realm of *absolute ethics, absolute will,* or *absolute action,* and in relation to the forms of experience adumbrated in *Speculum Mentis* we have passed over into the realm of philosophy, in which all remnants of abstraction have disappeared. The agent is prepared for action in unique circumstances by identifying himself, or herself, with the world of fact in its entirety. The act is not one of duty, because there is no sense of an objective law, whether it resides in conscience or in the political sovereign. The agent embodies and is identified with absolute mind, and the act is a 'pure act of self-creation'. The act and self-knowledge are identical, 'and thus the abstract distinction of the will and the intellect is transcended'.[149]

This is no mere ideal; it is one whose character we glimpse here and there in our own society. It is an immanent ideal, slowly being realised.[150] The realisation of the ideal does not mean the absence of a legal system as a guide and constraint. The legal system of a society has been developed to ensure an ordered and civilized life in which citizens can devote themselves to pursuing their own highest ends. In so far as we wish to live an ordered and civilized life, we view the legal structure as necessary to this aim. Law is not to us an external force compelling us to obey; it becomes the expression of our own free will.[151]

All action is absolute action, when understood correctly. Absolute action is the consummation of all action, including within itself all the levels which have been transcended: 'It is not opposed to desire, for it *is* desire, desire fulfilled and consummated; nor to mechanism or instinct or play or convention or utility or duty; for all these are all included in it together with their own opposites'.[152] Collingwood goes on to suggest that we must go to religion for descriptions and images of this absolute freedom – for example, the image of God creating the world. But this is no mere illusory image or abstract ideal: It is in fact experience itself, and we are all God, creating the world in our actions.

Here, then, we have the first of the two general categories of attempts made by Collingwood to solve the problems of ethics in articulating a concrete universal concept of action. It conforms with a scale of overlapping forms analysis, and the latter part, that is, the level at which theories of ethics appear, has its parallel in his conception of the problems of ethics in their historical dimensions. Utilitarian, or economic action, could not resolve the false opposition of means and end, and this is the category under which Collingwood placed Hobbes's ethical theory. Such an opposition could be transcended only at the next stage of ethical action.

Duty, however, posited a false opposition between conscience and authority which could only become resolved in the sphere of absolute action, in which the legal system does not stand opposed to me but is conceived as the product of my own will. Here again we see Collingwood's endeavour going considerably beyond that of Hobbes. On this characterisation of the concept of action, Hobbes would be viewed as an exponent of a variety of *abstract ethics,* that is, abstracting from concrete actions only that aspect which is purposive. Collingwood himself, as we saw, attempted to go beyond both abstract and concrete ethics in his concrete universal concept of action as absolute ethics.

6. Collingwood's synthesis: utility, right, and duty

In the preceding section it was suggested that at the level of rational choice, that is, the level of consciousness at which we ask ourselves why we do certain acts, the answers associated with utility, duty, and absolute ethics were analogous to the history of philosophy as the idealists in general, and as Collingwood himself, had depicted it. The second category of answers which Collingwood gave to the problems of moral philosophy are similarly analogous to the idealist conception of the history of philosophy. It has already been suggested that in the first sequence right and duty were conflated: Duty was itself a form of regularian action. In the second sequence right and duty are distinguished. This, however, is not the full extent of the differences between the two categories of answers. Duty is not merely separated from right, and absolute ethics jettisoned from the scheme. Duty and absolute ethics become the third form of practical reason in a scale which includes utility and rightness prior to it in a sequential and overlapping relation. Duty, then, now includes within itself the sphere of absolute ethics. There are further differences which serve to add weight to my contention that *The New Leviathan* is a concrete exemplar of the rapprochement between philosophy and history.

In *The New Leviathan* Collingwood differentiates reason into practical and theoretical forms. Rational thinking entails making a distinction between the self and the not-self, and such thinking is primarily practical in that its function is to ask and answer questions about why we choose to do particular acts (*NL,* 18.1). People need to reassure themselves about the choices they make, and about the knowledge they possess, by asking the question 'Why?' Having formed an intention to do 'something', we may hesitate and ask why we wish to do it. In other words, we look for a ground of which the 'something' is a consequent (*NL,* 14.32). We may satisfy ourselves that we wish to do a certain action by saying that it is

94   The social and political thought of R.G. Collingwood

useful as a means to an end, or because it conforms to a rule, or because it is our duty to do it. All real thinking, Collingwood claims, begins with 'practice and returns to practice; for it is based on "interest" in the thing thought about; that is, on a practical concern with it' (*NL*, 18.13). Theoretical reason arises when we have satisfied ourselves why we wish to do something, or why we make a certain choice, and then go on to ask why we should think the ground and consequent are so (*NL*, 14.35). The practical problems of relating the self to the not-self are addressed by theoretical reason; therefore the latter form of reason is never pure, and always includes within itself an element of practical reason. Collingwood argues that the theoretical forms of thought are more completely dependent upon the practical than are the practical upon the theoretical (*NL*, 1.67). This is, in fact, the relation which Croce believes pertains between the practical and theoretical forms of spirit.

Collingwood goes further and suggests that our practical attitude towards something has a strong bearing upon our theoretical attitude towards it (*NL*, 18.2). We saw, in relation to the first sequence of answers which Collingwood gave to the problems of ethics (to use the idiom of *The New Leviathan*), that in the practical form of reason utility had its theoretical counterpart in science; duty had its in history; and absolute ethics had its in philosophy. The second category of answers postulates an entirely different set of relations. Utility – that is, action conceived as means and end – gave rise to a view of the not-self as teleological. That Greek view of action led to nature being viewed as having ends and as devising means to those ends (*NL*, 18.31). The medieval view of right as obedience to law gave rise to the theoretical view of nature in terms of laws and conformity to law (*NL*, 18.44). Duty, conceived as a unique individual doing a unique act in a unique situation, and doing that act because it was the only one which as a unique agent the person could do, gave rise to history as the theoretical counterpart of duty.

The culmination of theoretical reason in history in *The New Leviathan* suggests to me that the rapprochement between philosophy and history is complete, with philosophy having been liquidated, or absorbed, by history, which is the theoretical counterpart of duty, the highest form of practical reason. In other words, duty and its theoretical counterpart history absorb absolute ethics and its theoretical counterpart philosophy, and thus become the culmination of the series.

This contention would be severely weakened if it could be shown that Collingwood envisaged a stage of practical and theoretical reason beyond that of duty and history but did not enter into a discussion of it because he was concerned only to address himself to the level which the European mind had reached up to his own day. Lionel Rubinoff has argued that 'in the same way as philosophy supersedes history so will the ethic of duty

be superseded by a philosophical ethic'.[153] Rubinoff is deceived by the
fact that duty, in both *Speculum Mentis* and *The New Leviathan,* is associated with history, and he cites the transcendence of history in the
former as evidence that a similar transcendence is implied in the latter.[154]
Rubinoff's view completely ignores the fact that duty in *Speculum Mentis*
is not equivalent to duty in *The New Leviathan.* Indeed, duty, in the latter
work, transcends the inadequacies of duty in *Speculum Mentis,* which
were a consequence of the identification of duty with regularian action.
My point is this: *The New Leviathan* does not imply a further development
of mind towards absolute ethics, because duty is already absolute ethics.
This can quite easily be substantiated by referring to the 1929 lectures
on moral philosophy, in which Collingwood puts forward the second
category of answers to the problems of ethics. There are, he suggests,
only three reasons for acting: the useful, the right, and the dutiful; 'No
fourth answer is possible'.[155] More significantly, when Collingwood discusses duty he does so under the sub-heading 'Duty, or Absolute Ethics'.[156]
Duty is 'as rational as activity can be'[157] and 'triumphs over every form
of its own opposite passivity, and therefore becomes for the first time
absolutely free and absolutely responsible for itself.'[158] Duty, Collingwood
suggests, 'is best defined as absolute action.'[159] It is difficult to envisage
how there could be a form of action beyond the absolute. This is not to
say that Collingwood foreclosed any further development of the European
mind. He did not speculate upon it because he believed that the mind's
future development is not predictable (*NL,* 9.43).

Collingwood's second category of answers to the problems of ethics,
like the first, complies with a scale of forms analysis. He says, for example,
that the 'three forms of goodness – utility, rightness, duty – are not species
of goodness but moments which imply each other in such a way that
any rational act exhibits all three'.[160] In *The New Leviathan,* however,
he introduces a principle which modifies the argument of *An Essay on
Philosophical Method.* It appears that his anthropological studies led him
to conclude that within modern society throwbacks of former ages still
continue to exist unmodified. Edward Tylor had argued that in comparing
civilized peoples with 'barbarous hordes' it is surprising how often one
finds elements of the lower culture existing scarcely modified, or not
modified at all, in the higher.[161] Although Collingwood is extremely critical
of Tylor's functionalist approach to anthropology,[162] he does nevertheless
adopt Tylor's idea of primitive 'survivals' for his own work. We will see
in Chapter 7 that this idea is important for his understanding of civilization.
At this stage we can be content with familiarizing ourselves with the
principle as it is formulated in *The New Leviathan.*

Collingwood calls this principle the 'law of primitive survivals' (*NL,*
9.5), and he defines it as follows: *'When A is modified into B there survives*

*in any example of B, side by side with the function B which is the
modified form of A, an element of A in its primitive or unmodified
state' (NL, 9.51).* Thus, for example, in a series which contains appetite,
passion, and desire, each successive stage modifies that which precedes
it, but the modification includes an element 'pure and simple' of the unmodified forms it has superseded (*NL,* 9.55). The principles, or laws,
serve to explain 'why theoretical reason always contains a primitive survival of practical reason' (*NL,* 14.38).

The law of primitive survivals entails two clear qualifications to the
doctrine of *An Essay on Philosophical Method.* First, Collingwood is no
longer arguing that there is a complete overlap of forms on the scale:
We find now that something of the lower form remains 'pure' in the
higher form – that is, modification is only partial and never complete.
Second, following from this, the law of primitive survivals is at variance
with his principle of the 'fallacy of precarious margins', which 'consists
in assuming that the overlap which has already affected a certain area of
the class in question can be trusted not to spread, and that beyond its
limits there lies a marginal region in which the instances exhibit only
one of the specific forms, uncontaminated by the presence of the other'.[163]
In so far as *The New Leviathan* exhibits a scale of forms analysis, one
must acknowledge that Collingwood's conception of it has become altered
in these crucial respects.

It is now appropriate to turn to Collingwood's criticisms of utility and
right, in order to see how he thought their deficiencies were transcended
in the idea of duty.

A person is free, Collingwood argues, when he is able to exercise his
will freely. On the positive side this means that he makes choices freely,
and on the negative side it means that he is free from desire, that is, he
is not at the mercy of his desires (*NL,* 13.2–13.27). Everything, Collingwood contends, is good, but only to a degree. To call something bad, or
lacking in goodness, simply means that its share, or degree, of goodness
is so small that it falls below the standard which we are applying.[164] A
thing is good by the fact that it is chosen.[165] Consciousness of choosing
something belongs to one of two kinds of choice. In the first kind of
choice the agent is conscious of choosing, but not of the reason for making
the choice. This means that there is consciousness of possible alternative
actions, and of choosing one of them and rejecting the other (or others),
but there is no consciousness of the reason why the choice is made.[166]
The choice, Collingwood argues, is 'capricious' (*NL,* 13.12).

The second kind of choice is that in which the person who chooses
is conscious of having reasons why this, rather than that, was chosen.
This is called 'rational choice'.[167] In rational choice there is consciousness
of alternatives and of choosing one and rejecting the other (or others),

but in addition we ask why we choose this and not that; why we consider this alternative good, and better than that. In other words, practical reason raises the question 'Why do I choose this?'[168] There are three answers to this question, which, in the 1929 lectures on moral philosophy, Collingwood calls the 'three kinds of reason for acting'.[169]

Collingwood does not attempt to explain why there are only three reasons. He contends that an examination of European history reveals only three, and he confesses that he neither knows, nor asks, why this should be so. Pace Plato, Collingwood looks to the individual in order to reveal the nature and content of each of the reasons before venturing to define their place in the society in general. In the context of European history, Collingwood maintains that he can discern three different answers to the question 'Why did you do that?' (*NL*, 14.65). The answers to the question are, first, because it was useful; second, because it was right; and third, because it was my duty. Each answer is the manifestation, on an ascending scale, of a different level of practical reason, each, as I have suggested, having a theoretical counterpart in which there is a primitive survival of the practical.

The first of the reasons, or criteria, for acting is the utilitarian. 'All good acts', Collingwood argues, 'are useful, and their utility is the way in which – or one of the ways in which – they are good'.[170] The merit of utilitarianism as a philosophy is that it recognises the permanent and necessary character of utility as a form of goodness.[171] This form of practical reason posits a means–end relation. The means–end relation can be divided into its positive and negative parts. The relation is positive because it is a rational relation and does serve partially to explain why I choose something as a means to an end (*NL*, 15.22). The means-plan and the end-plan are logically interrelated and are appraised and modified in relation to each other. The relation between the two is that of logical priority, that is, of ground to consequent. In planning the end, the means is implied: that is, the end is the ground, and the means is the consequent. In execution, as opposed to willing, the means imply the end. In other words, the ground–consequent relation is reversed when we pass from the will to the deed. When we plan an action, the means is chosen because of the end which is chosen. It makes no difference to the utilitarian relation whether the end is a capricious choice or the result of good reasons. All that is required is that the end is chosen and that the choice should 'logically necessitate' the choice of the means (*NL*, 15.42). In the execution, or deed, the necessity flows in the opposite direction. It is the means which necessitates the end. Collingwood sums up his argument by saying that the positive aspect of utility entails a relation between two second-order choices: (1) the choice of a means, and (2) the choice of an end, in which the choice of the end logically constrains the person

to do the act constituting the means as well. In addition, to carry out
the decision to enact the means also logically constrains the person to
bring about the end.[172] The means is said to be useful, then, because it
is an element in this complex situation (*NL,* 15.5). This positive aspect
of the utilitarian means–end relation is a universal characteristic of all
forms of practical reason, and in this respect 'utility is identical with
rightness and duty' (*NL,* 15.51).[173]

It is the negative aspect of utility which distinguishes it from rightness
and duty. This is because utility falls short of a fully rational explanation:
Utility explains, at least partially, why the means is chosen, but it cannot
give reasons for the choice of the end. To say that the end is chosen
because it is useful would be to convert it into a means to something
else,[174] and eventually an end must be reached which is not good for
something, but good in itself, and therefore it would no longer be useful.

In order to illustrate the limited rationality of utilitarian explanations
of action, Collingwood asks us to imagine his going into a tobacconist's
shop in order to purchase a pound of tobacco. The fact that he receives
a pound of tobacco explains why he pays the tobacconist a certain sum
of money. However, in his pocket he had a variety of coins and notes,
and was also able to charge purchases. The choice of what combination
of coins, notes, and credit to exchange for the tobacco is left entirely
open. Nevertheless, the choice has to be made before the transaction is
completed, but the choice cannot be made with reference to the end:
'It can', Collingwood suggests, 'only be made by what from a utilitarian
point of view, is caprice; in other words, something that a utilitarian point
of view leaves unexplained' (*NL,* 15.63). Similarly, the utilitarian is unable
to explain, or make determinate, the end. The plan to purchase a pound
of tobacco cannot tell me which of the many different brands to buy. In
Collingwood's view, utilitarian thinking leads to an 'indefinite individual'.
Utilitarian action is individual but abstract, in that each act is said to
conform to certain specifications but is variable in other respects, as long
as it complies with the specifications (*NL,* 15.72).

In the 1929, 1932, and 1933 lectures on moral philosophy the discussion of utility is followed by an analysis of economics as the science
of utility. In its empirical form, economics is said to restrict itself to a
limited field of action. It does not study actions in general, but only those
which exhibit 'the characteristic features of exchange'.[175] Empirical economics is therefore concerned mainly with commerce, manufacture, finance, and other business-related activities. Such an investigation unearths
a number of 'fundamental concepts', such as exchange and 'production,
wealth, capital, labour, money'. Some of these concepts are applicable
beyond the field of economic facts, and 'thus the subject-matter of economics tends to widen until it becomes co-extensive with rational action

in general'. This is when economics becomes the province of philosophy, that is, the study of 'one of the necessary and universal forms of value'.[176]

In *The New Leviathan,* the nature of the enquiry results in a much greater emphasis upon politics. Given that all action is useful, right, and dutiful, Collingwood sees politics as capable of exhibiting all of these goods, or values. In what way, then, does the utilitarian principle manifest itself in political action — that is, in the joint will of society exercised by the rulers of the body politic?

Utilitarian political action entails making a distinction between means and ends. The utilitarian form of political action is *policy.* The end and the means to achieve it are determined by the ruling class and imposed upon the class which it rules. Because the end and the means stand in a logical relation — that is, the achievement of the means entails the achievement of the end — only the means need be explained to the ruled. The end can be hidden. In consequence, the utilitarian form of political action 'facilitates the concealment of a ruler's purposes from the ruled' (*NL,* 28.52). During the Renaissance, Collingwood maintains, the moral authority of the Church was in disarray. Lip service had to be paid to it in theory, while in practice it was ignored. Machiavelli believed that the Church had authority in morals but that political questions were essentially utilitarian and fell outside its domain. This division gave the state control over all of the substantive acts of men and left the Church with little but a shadow with which to play. The association of politics with utilitarian action expelled morality from the political sphere. Policy guided by the utilitarian principle is capricious, because it does not clearly show the ruler which end the body politic should aspire to attain. The ruler is left free to choose on capricious grounds towards which of a number of different ends to steer society. In relation to the external policy of a state, the principle of utility leads rulers to think of quarrels between states in terms of a conflict of interests (*NL,* 29.58).

Collingwood does not, at this point in his argument, associate Hobbes with Machiavelli, nor with utilitarian politics. This may be because he did not want to undervalue Hobbes's philosophy, which he had called (referring specifically to the *Leviathan*) 'the world's greatest store of political wisdom'. However, as I demonstrated earlier, Collingwood did associate Hobbes with Machiavelli, and also with this one-sided point of view, attributing to Hobbes the faults Collingwood ascribed to the political tendency in general, while at the same time acknowledging that Hobbes was an especially valuable and sophisticated exponent of the doctrine. In *The New Leviathan* itself, Collingwood, in discussing the attempts of classical political theorists to explain why civil society replaces a state of nature, makes a comment which expresses again Collingwood's whole criticism of utilitarianism and also implies an indirect criticism of Hobbes.

The classical political theorists, Collingwood says, have given us an account of the transition to civil society 'in the exaggeratedly utilitarian style of the age' (*NL*, 32.62). It follows that Collingwood's criticism of utilitarian political action in *The New Leviathan,* although taking Machiavelli as its focus, is also probably an oblique criticism of Hobbes.

The answer given at the practical level of reason to the question 'Why did you do that?' has implications for how one explains the world at the level of theoretical reason. For someone who has not gone beyond the level of utility in his, or her, personal conduct, rationality and utility are regarded as equivalents: 'To understand a thing is to think of it in terms of ends and means. In the question: "Why does this thing do what we find it doing?" The word "Why?" always means "to what end?" ' (*NL*, 18.3). As we saw, this practical attitude was further projected upon nature and, in the sphere of theoretical reason, gave rise to the Greek teleological science in which nature was deemed to have ends and was portrayed as devising means to those ends.

Utilitarian action, then, in which the whole is divisible into a means part and an end part, is a perfectly legitimate explanation of a universal characteristic of action, but it nevertheless falls short of a complete explanation. Utilitarian explanation, however, fails to recognise its limitations and takes its partial explanatory power to be the complete and only characterisation of action. The second, and antithetical form of, or reason for, action, namely *right,* utilitarians claim not to be opposed to utility at all. Right and utility, they suggest, are different names for the same thing. This view, Collingwood argues, is mistaken. Bradley is invoked both in the moral philosophy lectures and in *The New Leviathan* to define the meaning of right; for Bradley, right is always a rule and conformity to that rule. A *right action,* then, is that which conforms to a rule.[177] Etymologically, Collingwood insists, *right* does not mean 'useful'. A right key for a lock, for example, is any one among a number of right keys which conforms to the rules governing the mechanics of the lock: 'A thing is useful, or the opposite, in relation to the end it achieves; it is right, or the opposite, in relation to the rule it obeys' (*NL*, 16.23). A bent hairpin and a key designed to open a different lock may both open the lock one wishes to open, and if they do they will be useful, but not right. Conformity to a rule is the form of goodness which a right act exhibits, and an act which conforms to a rule 'implies that it falls in with a plan of action'.[178]

A rule is a generalised purpose 'to do things of a certain kind on all occasions of a certain kind' (*NL*, 16.31). This is what Collingwood calls a *regularian principle,* which entails defining a specified act to be performed when all occasions of a specific kind arise. In the 1940 lectures on moral philosophy, Collingwood calls a rule a 'practical universal',[179] and he argues that it is the consciousness of understanding action as conforming to the practical universal, of which it is an instance, which makes people aware of a goodness that is not utility but rightness.[180] Like a utilitarian action, however, rightness involves bifurcating the action, not into means and end, but into a universal and an instance of that universal. The universal has to be chosen, and also the individual instance of that universal is subject to choice. To put it simply: We choose the rule and choose whether or not to obey it. Such an act is both practical and intellectual: practical because it is an act of the will, and intellectual because obeying the rule entails being conscious of obedience to it.

A rule is a generalised intention to do an act of a certain kind on occasions of a certain kind. The difficulty is that many different acts may conform to the general specifications of the rule. There may be a few or many acts which satisfy the specifications, but this is not dependent upon the rule but upon the circumstances to which the rule is acknowledged to be applicable. I have to choose between the alternatives, and the rule cannot do this for me. The regularian view of action fails to explain the reason for the choice of the particular instance. It can explain why an act of a certain kind was performed, that is, why an act conforming to the rule was performed – namely, because it was right – but not why, out of the alternatives, this particular instance was chosen in conformity with the rule's specifications (*NL*, 16.63).[181]

Further, a right act which conforms to one rule may be wrong in relation to another (*NL*, 16.64). Both rules, however, may be applied to the situation, and their applicability depends not so much upon the rule as upon the sort of person one is and the sort of life one wishes to live. We do not all live by the same rules: Different rules define different ways of living. The person has to choose, from among the many different rules that appear to be applicable, which one to follow in the unique circumstances of this particular case and which accords with the sort of person he, or she, wants to be. The rules cannot help one to make, nor to explain, the choice. There are, for example, many different rules which concern the telling of the truth. If one is the sort of person who believes in telling the truth at all costs, then, when someone planning a murder asks the whereabouts of a prospective victim, one will convey the information one has. Collingwood sums up the position thus: 'Even the best-thought-out rules leave much to caprice and accident. . . . For any man who tries to live rationally there are always conflicts between one way of life and another' (*NL*, 16.77).

Collingwood associates regularian action with politics. Empirical theories of politics essentially focus upon the state and its functions, but regularian action is not exhausted by the state.[182] Like utility (or economic action), right (or political action) is a universal aspect of action in general. The state is an empirical fact which concerns itself with much besides political activity, such as economic planning, scientific research, and promotion of the arts. Political, or regularian, action, in so far as it is characteristic of action in general, 'is bound to overflow the limits of the state and to appear whenever there is action of any kind'.[183]

Regularian action entails two decisions: first, to do things of a certain kind when occasions of a certain kind arise. This is the making of a rule. Second, there is the individual, as opposed to the general, decision to act in a specific way because a certain specific occasion has arisen. This is the act of obeying a rule. When translated into the political form of right action, the rule becomes a law, and the act of formulating the law is legislation. The capricious element in law appears in the fact that one law defines one sort of life for a body politic and another law directs us to another way of life. The body politic is capable of conforming to either way of life. The ruler, or ruling class, in choosing to enact one law and reject the other, makes a capricious choice. In relation to external policy, differences of opinion between states, conceived in terms of right, or international law, are viewed as a conflict of rights (*NL*, 29.58).

Regularian practical reason gave rise to its counterpart in theoretical reason. Consciousness of law and obedience to law, Collingwood says, had long been a feature of early civilizations. The Roman law and the religion of the Jews ensured that the regularian tradition survived in European society. To the European of the Middle Ages, familiar with Christian principles, 'right took precedence of utility; the business of man was not to achieve ends but to obey laws' (*NL*, 18.42). By the law of primitive survivals, however, an element of utility had survived in this regularian tradition. An act principally recommended on the basis of regularian criteria was also recommended on utilitarian grounds. The rewards and punishments of heaven and earth were often invoked to impel action, but these impellents were subordinate to the regularian motive for action, namely, respect for the law.

Just as people became accustomed to thinking about themselves in terms of laws and conformity with law, Collingwood states, so they came to view the world in the same terms. The idea of a 'Law of Nature', Collingwood contends, is crucial to the structure of modern science (*NL*, 18.44). Its defects as an explanation of nature are those of the form of practical reason, from which regularian science derives. It is not wholly rational and leaves much to caprice in its explanatory laws and instances of the universal. Its rationality consists in the fact 'that it is logically derived from a regularian or legalistic view of human life' (*NL*, 18.45).

The third level of practical reason arises when one responds to the question 'Why did you do that?' with the answer, 'Because it was my duty'. The first and second levels of practical reason each has a distinct form of goodness, but the goodness consists in relation to something else. Utilitarian action is useful, or good, because it relates to an end. Regularian, or right, action is good because of its relation to the rule of which it is an instance. Dutiful, or moral action, or simply the 'good will', 'is good in itself and apart from any relations whatever'.[184] It is distinct, but not separate, from the other two forms of good, containing within itself 'the subordinate goods of utility and rightness'.[185]

Etymologically, Collingwood tells us, what it is my duty to do and what I ought to do mean the same thing. In order that some act may become someone's duty, two conditions have to be met. The act must be determinate, and it must also be possible. Duty does not allow of any alternatives. As a free agent I am called upon to do *this* act, not an act of a particular kind, nor one of a number of alternatives: Only *this* act will do, and it is *my* duty and no one else's (*NL*, 17.5–17.53). Unlike utility and right, then, the idea of duty is without caprice. It relates so tightly to the consequent that no alternatives are possible. Collingwood sums up his view when he says, 'Dutiful action, among these three kinds of rational action, is the only one that is completely rational in principle; the only one whose explanations really explain' (*NL*, 17.55). This is because duty overcomes the abstractness of utility and rightness. Utility is abstract because any one of a number of acts is useful if it leads to the end. The act is required merely to fulfil that condition, and any other features which it may exhibit are 'irrelevant to its utility'.[186] Similarly an act is right in that it conforms to a rule, and any other characteristic it may have is irrelevant to its rightness. An act is right in that it is 'an act of this kind, not by being this act'.[187] Duty, however, is concrete and not abstract: It is an individual act to be performed by a specific person on a specific occasion. Whereas a right act is right no matter who performs it, 'a duty is always someone's duty, and presents a claim which no other agent can discharge'.[188] No other agent can perform my duty, because it is *my* duty, and therefore as a concrete action 'it involves the whole of my character, circumstances and history, which no one else can entirely share'.[189] I am, then, conscious of my unique situation, not a situation of a certain type, and conscious of what it is my duty to do on that occasion.

To perform one's duty, Collingwood argues, is to be responsible for one's own actions. By implication, dutiful action refuses to accept unquestioningly that the ends of other people are necessarily those to which one can subscribe, or that the rules of others are those by which one wishes to guide one's own conduct. The responsibility entailed in duty means making up one's own mind and being accountable to oneself for one's own acts.[190] This, in turn, requires an acknowledgement of a similar capacity possessed by other individuals. We have a duty to cultivate in ourselves the moral will capable of action of a concrete character. To determine myself as will and to be conscious of duty is, for Collingwood, the same thing. Thus, duty is 'to act in such a way that in acting I take the entire responsibility not only for acting thus and not otherwise, but for acting at all. Here every trace of passivity has disappeared; action has become absolute, and absolutely free.'[191]

As a concrete action, then, duty is in *principle* completely rational, because it has eliminated caprice from rational choice. Duty is only in principle completely free, because in reality duty is an abstraction and not a first-order object of consciousness. However, duty is an immediate form of consciousness in relation to its first-order object and is therefore as nearly infallible as it is humanly possible to be. Its infallibility consists in making me aware that I am under an obligation, not in specifying the nature of the obligation. Such a specification entails a logical thinking process beyond the intuitive awareness that I am under an obligation. In other words, after having ascertained that I am obligated, I have to ask myself what the obligation is by asking, ' "Is it this?" "Is it this?" "Is it this?" ' (*NL*, 17.59). The obvious objection to this view is that if duty is abstract and partially indeterminate, is it not like utility and right, that is, allowing realisation in different ways and thus guilty of mere specification? Collingwood answers this objection thus:

Duty in general is such a specification. But my present duty is not. 'My present duty', like 'the present king of England', is a phrase which at any given time applies to only one thing or person, although many different persons have been kings of England at different times, and many different acts have been at different times my present duty (*NL*, 17.83).

If freedom, for Collingwood, is equivalent to the freedom of rational choice, it would appear from his characterisation of duty that the element of choice is absent. If duty allows of no alternatives, in what sense are we exercising freedom of choice? This is an apparent difficulty which Collingwood chooses not to address in any detail in *The New Leviathan*, but he does give it a good deal of thought in the moral philosophy lectures. We are fully free, Collingwood argues, only when we act morally.[192] It is not a matter of choice, as such, between alternatives, because 'consciousness of alternatives disappears'.[193] Alternatives appear before the mind not as possible acts, but as acts which are rejected as out of the question. They appear not as alternatives, but as temptations which are conceived and abjured. There is a sense of urgency to do what I have to do, and nothing else. In a sense, then, the choice is already made, and we express this kind of action which one does out of duty by saying that given the kind of person I am, there was nothing else I could do.[194]

Although choice is not consciously present, the consciousness of freedom is intense. The freedom is one not of doing what we want to do, but what we must, as a moral will, do on this occasion. It is a self-creating moral will, which is at once free and bound by necessity.[195]

Duty entails a special and unique obligation which precludes the type of freedom associated with capricious action. A person who performs his, or her, duty has no options; every aspect of the action is covered by one's consciousness of the obligation. This may seem to imply that freedom is completely negated. However, this implication arises only if one falsely identifies freedom with caprice. Someone who is aware of what he, or she, has to do, with no alternative left open, is completely obliged only in so far as the person is consciously resolved to do his, or her, duty. The resolution is an act of free will, 'and hence the apparent absence of freedom is not a genuine absence of freedom'.[196] Action which is capricious is irrational, and duty, which excludes caprice, is perfectly rational action.[197]

Collingwood's account of duty in *The New Leviathan* gives the barest essentials in order to distinguish duty, right, and utility. A. J. M. Milne has complained that Collingwood's account of duty is unsatisfactory. On reflection, Milne argues, duty, as Collingwood discusses it, turns out only to be a special case of right. Milne argues that 'a duty is a certain kind of right act: namely an act of the kind which meets the requirements of the moral rule that people should always do what they have freely undertaken to do'.[198] This, perhaps, would be a valid criticism if Collingwood was purporting to classify the genus 'goodness' into distinct and separate species. Duty does not exclude regularian action; the latter is the material upon which duty builds. The moral will 'seeks to express itself in an action displaying not one form of goodness but all the forms together'.[199] The moral consciousness, however, necessarily overrides rules, not this or that rule in particular, but the general spirit of obedience to rule. The moral consciousness is the ultimate court in which one decides that an act is appropriate and accepts it as one's duty, that is, as the only act possible for one to do, being the person one is, in this particular case. In doing one's duty one does not affirm a particular good, but good as a whole. Such a spirit 'creates a new law out of the ashes of the old, affirms new ends more desirable than those it renounces, and so sets right and expediency alike on a firmer basis than ever'.[200] In the 1929 lectures on moral philosophy Collingwood argues that duty includes within itself its own criterion of action. We cannot look to something outside it as a justification of doing one's duty: Duty does not need the certainty which an external criterion can provide, because it already possesses certainty in itself. Thus, in judging whether an end, or rule, is one which obliges me to act, duty 'is its own criterion'.[201]

In 1930 the provost of Oriel College, W. D. Ross, published *The Right and the Good,* in which he suggested that what is right and what is my duty are not synonymous. There can be a number of acts which it would be right to do in certain circumstances, but only one which I ought to do. Similarly, it may be right to bring about a number of states of affairs, without it being my duty to bring about any one in particular. However, while acknowledging that right has a wider application than what ought to be done, Ross blurs the distinction, for convenience, by suggesting that the word *right,* for his purposes, means 'morally obligatory'.[202] Thus duty and right are equated, but acknowledged not to be synonymous. What Ross is really concerned to show is that the 'morally obligatory' act is different from the morally good act. If I borrow a book and promise to return it, I am morally obliged to return it. The act of returning it is not right because it is conducive to a certain end – that is, the goodness of the act does not consist in a result which is different from itself. Ross suggests that the act 'is right because it is itself the production of a certain state of affairs',[203] namely, ensuring that the book is returned safely. A person is morally good in possessing a certain kind of character, and actions or feelings are morally good because they emanate from such a character. In summary: 'Moral goodness is quite distinct from and independent of rightness, which ... belongs to acts *not* in virtue of the motives they proceed from, but in virtue of the nature of what is done.'[204]

Collingwood mentions Ross in *An Essay on Philosophical Method* and *The New Leviathan.* In the former Ross is invoked as illustrative of a scale of forms analysis,[205] and in the latter he is associated with Kant and Bradley for, 'in spite of misgiving' (*NL,* 17.72), identifying right and duty. In the lectures on moral philosophy for 1932, 1933, and 1940, Collingwood gives a good deal of attention to Ross, identifying their points of agreement and disagreement. Collingwood was already distinguishing between right and duty prior to the publication of Ross's *The Right and the Good,* but subsequently Collingwood invoked the authority of the provost to support the contention that right and duty are not synonymous.[206] He made it clear, however, that he could not follow Ross in qualifying the distinction and identifying the two.[207] Given that duty is determinate, that is, only one act can be *my* duty, it follows for both Collingwood and Ross that there cannot be a conflict of duties for the individual, whereas there can be a conflict of rules, or right actions, which apply to a particular situation. Collingwood also agreed with the provost in believing that morally good action emanates from a virtuous character,[208] but could not accept that virtue is a condition, or state, of the will. The provost, Collingwood claimed, does not tell us how we become of virtuous character, but it is clear that Ross did not think that it is by means of an act of will. Collingwood thought this mistaken, because 'nothing can be finally good which includes in itself an element of passivity'.[209]

To return once again to politics: When it is conceived as duty, the elements of caprice associated with utility and right disappear. The policy which the ruling class formulates will be the only policy that it regards as open to it. This is because the traditions inherent in a body politic will reduce the options for the type of life it prescribes to only one. Concrete thinking of the act as individual is a prerequisite of political action conceived in terms of duty. The duty of the ruling class will be revealed to it through its practical consciousness of the concrete facts of its traditional inheritance. The rational will of the body politic becomes explicit in the process of this concrete understanding. The many alternatives that are open to utilitarian political action are reduced to one when political action is conceived as duty. This is because 'the body politic[,] having the traditions it has, . . . would repudiate all but one' (*NL*, 28.89). Differences in external politics, conceived in terms of duty, are viewed as a conflict of duties (*NL*, 29.58).

The practical reason of duty in which each act is individual, and in which one conceives oneself as a unique agent acting in unique circumstances, performing the actions which one does because one can do no other, has implications for one's view of the world of things other than oneself. Historical thinking is the consciousness that the world consists of agents other than oneself, all of whom are unique, related to unique situations, and performing duties uniquely appropriate to the circumstances (*NL*, 18.52). In Chapter 2 we saw how Collingwood, in suggesting that we can overcome the distinction between theory and practice by means of historical thinking, foreshadowed the formulation and articulation of a historical morality. In the 1940 lectures on moral philosophy, Collingwood argues that 'the idea of history is the idea of action as individual'.[210] It is an idea which has emerged gradually since the eighteenth century, but which has not yet reached full maturity. On this view, duty itself, being so closely allied with the historical consciousness, is still in the process of developing and has not yet attained the degree of maturity potential within it. In the past there has been an idea of history based on utilitarianism, viewing events in terms of means and ends. Similarly, there has been an idea of history based on the regularian principle, in which actions are viewed in terms of rules and obedience to these rules. The modern idea of history seeks to emancipate itself from the utilitarian and regularian ideas of action in providing individual reconstructions of unique actions and events in the past. Such an emancipation, however, has only been partial, and the utilitarian and regularian principles are still influential in the historical consciousness. It is Collingwood's view that 'until these obsolete tendencies in historical thinking have become wholly obsolete, we shall not have a fully-developed consciousness of duty'.[211]

To be conscious of action as individual does not deny it the possibility of explanation in terms of the utilitarian and regularian principles. By being conscious of the individuality of the action, utilitarian and regularian methods of analysis become divested of the residue of irrationality they retain. Taken by themselves, neither the utilitarian nor the regularian methods are capable of overcoming caprice. Utilitarian action is capricious both in terms of the choice of ends and in the choice of means to realise those ends. By means of historical understanding we can come to know why a certain person chose a certain end, and why that person chose a particular means to pursue it. Each choice is no longer viewed as being capriciously made, but instead 'is regarded as the end which one chooses because one has got to choose it', and 'the means by which one realizes it is no longer regarded as one possible means capriciously chosen from many various possible means; it is regarded as the means which one chooses because one has got to choose it'.[212] Similarly, regularian action is capricious both in the recognition of an appropriate rule and in choosing one from among a number of possible ways of obeying it. The historian would hope to show that the choice of the rule, and the choice of the manner in which it was obeyed, were both the only choices the individual could have made on that occasion.

On what criterion does the historian make such judgements? We saw how duty, or the moral will, required no criterion outside itself in judging the moral character of ends and rules. What is fully rational includes within itself its own criterion. History, as the highest form of theoretical reason, is fully concrete, and it too is the criterion of its own judgements. The historian does not accept the sources uncritically; he uses his own a priori imagination to interpolate between the sources an imaginary construction which provides, or constitutes, his picture of the past.[213] The criterion of the validity of this picture is not the sources, but the historian's a priori imagination itself. It is the historian's picture which justifies the sources, not the sources which justify the picture.[214] It is the coherence of the construction which acts as the criterion of its truth.[215] In other words, everything is accounted for; there are no capricious elements left unexplained. Just as the completely free moral agent does not accept another person's ends as his own, nor another's rules which bind him unquestioningly to obedience, the historian does not accept the facts as given. Just as the completely moral will is activity, an achievement of self-creation which excludes all passivity, the historian does not passively accept the facts as given: The facts are an achievement of the historian's activity.[216]

Collingwood is not concerned merely with the individuation of action, but also with the forms of explanation which are apposite to it. More will be said of this in the next chapter. I want to emphasize here that Collingwood was convinced that the problems of the modern world were not those posed by nature, as interesting as these might be, but those posed by history. And it was to history that Collingwood turned to understand the character of the predicament of war-torn Europe, its civilization, and the threat to its traditional values.

I have demonstrated earlier that in both the historical and the more 'analytic' treatments of the problems of moral philosophy Collingwood, like other idealist thinkers, held a triadic conception of the history of moral and political thought when he approached Hobbes. The triad was not a dialectic of opposites in the Hegelian sense, but a scale of overlapping forms of rational action in which opposites and distincts are fused. In this respect it is a Crocean, rather than a Hegelian, characterisation of the concept. Further, it is clear from what has been said that Collingwood never intended to 'update' the theory of Hobbes in a piecemeal and arbitrary fashion. Collingwood wanted to replace the very foundation of Hobbes's philosophy with the idea of duty as the criterion of conduct. The idea of duty is in fact the fulfilment of Collingwood's promise to replace the excessively scientific or utilitarian morality of the day with a historical morality. In wanting to go beyond Hobbes, Collingwood was always consistent. In the 1921 lectures on moral philosophy in which he discusses the arguments of particular thinkers, he maintains that 'by throwing itself wholeheartedly into the new subjectivism thought can progress through it and so recover in good time, the half-truths of the old objectivism'.[217] On the general philosophical level, then, Hobbes and Collingwood represent different traditions in ethical thought. Hobbes's *Leviathan* falls firmly into what Collingwood called the subjectivist, or utilitarian, tradition, while Collingwood's *Leviathan* is representative of the immanent, or rational will, tradition.

4

The development of the European mind

1. Introduction

In the preceding chapter it was argued that at the level of rational action Collingwood attempted to articulate a criterion of conduct which would eliminate the capricious aspects of the criterion offered by Hobbes. Collingwood gave two different series of 'analytic' answers to the problems of ethics. Both series, it was suggested, are analogous to his 'historical' treatment of the problems found in the 1921 and 1923 lectures on moral philosophy. In all three treatments, Hobbes is representative of a tradition quite different from that to which Collingwood belongs. We saw how the stages of practical and theoretical reason constitute the higher levels of consciousness: that is, the striving of the will towards fully rational action, and the intellect towards fully rational thought, the latter being a modification, and containing within itself primitive survivals, of the former. It is now appropriate to examine how consciousness develops to the level of rational will, that is, how consciousness attains the freedom necessary to the achievement of a fully rational life. In other words, in order to understand fully the good will, we must understand how consciousness develops to the level of will.[1]

In this chapter, following from the individuation of action in Chapter 3, I begin by discussing the explanatory model which Collingwood used for the study of mind and its activities. It will be seen that the subject matter of history is conceived differently in *The Idea of History* and in *The New Leviathan*. This is because in the former Collingwood wishes to emphasize that thought and feeling are distinct and, for the purposes of historical enquiry, quite separate, whereas in the latter he emphasizes at every stage the overlapping character of thought and feeling. I next present an uncomplicated account of the levels of consciousness, in order to demonstrate the overlap of feeling and thought in a modified scale of

110

forms analysis. I supplement the theory by demonstrating the importance of emotion, imagination, and language in Collingwood's theory of mind. Emotion, Collingwood stresses, is closely associated with imagination and language. In *The Principles of Art* Collingwood argued that language comes into existence with the emergence of imagination. It is consciousness which converts sensa and their emotional charges into imagination, and the function of language at the level of consciousness, or imagination, is to express emotion. We become conscious of an emotion only by expressing it, and expressing it is an acknowledgement of the emotion. In attending to sensa selectively we distinguish between emotional experiences that we wish to acknowledge and those that we do not. Failure to express an emotion amounts to disowning, or repressing, it. If this occurs, intellect finds itself in receipt of distorted or false emotional expressions upon which to construct its thought.

2. Mind and history

In *The Idea of History* Collingwood argues that knowledge of the mind is historical knowledge,[2] and that this historical knowledge entails the study of mind's activities.[3] History has only recently emerged as an autonomous form of thought. Its potential in the modern world has yet to be fully explored.[4] In this respect Collingwood's new form of history might be viewed as the exploration and articulation of a mode of understanding that he saw as being potential in history. In both *The New Leviathan* and *The Idea of History* Collingwood professes himself to be a follower of Locke's 'historical plain method'.[5] The study of mind must be conducted in accordance with such a method. In *The New Leviathan* Collingwood does not attempt to elaborate upon what he takes Locke's 'historical plain method' to be. However, in *The Idea of History* it is evident that Collingwood's understanding of what Locke meant is different from what Locke understood himself to be doing. Collingwood sees Locke as being of importance in the history of philosophy because the latter formulated anti-Cartesian principles which implied a reorientation of philosophy towards history. Locke's understanding of the 'historical plain method' was that it is the procedure of accounting for 'the ways whereby our understandings come to attain those notions of things we have'.[6] Locke's aim was to achieve knowledge of the human mind by means of methods analogous to those used in the natural sciences; that is, the observation and collection of facts which could then be arranged into classificatory schemes. In Collingwood's view, Locke was ambiguous in describing the historical plain method and displayed little understanding of its significance and implications.[7] Fortuitously, Locke was right in believing that the study of the human mind required the use of a historical plain method, but he was mistaken in believing that the conclusions of such an enquiry would result in knowledge of a universal human nature. Additionally, Collingwood believed that Locke contributed little to the problem of unravelling what human understanding is. For Collingwood, then, Locke points the way forward for achieving an understanding of the human mind, but falls short of providing a method by means of which to attain such knowledge.

For Collingwood, the essence of the method adopted in *The New Leviathan* is a concentration upon *facts,* by which he means deeds, or things done and things that are made. A thing made is the result of a deed, and it is the business of the historical method to concern itself with both the deeds and their results. This entails asking what mind has done on specific occasions. Modern European civilization, the phenomenon that Collingwood seeks to understand, is the result of the deeds of mind. In order to know the civilization, we must know the minds whose deeds have produced it. The idea of mind as substance is rejected; mind is what it is wholly on account of what it does. The mind is activity (*NL,* 9.1–9.3), and as such is creative of itself and its environment.

In rejecting the idea of mind as substance, Collingwood declares himself in agreement with Locke. However, and more interestingly, he is also echoing Gentile. For Gentile, mind 'is act or process not substance'.[8] As I suggested in Chapter 1, Gentile, in viewing mind as pure act, had reached a philosophical position which de Ruggiero termed 'absolute immanence'. Collingwood viewed absolute immanence as 'the philosophy whose primary principle, that of immanence, has overcome its own abstractness by including in itself its own opposite, namely, the principle of transcendence'.[9] Both philosophy and history are *actual* in the mind that thinks them; they exist only in the process of thinking. It is only when we conceive them as external to thinking, that is, as the objects of mind, that history and philosophy are viewed as different from, and external to, each other.[10] In Gentile's view, the mind attains self-consciousness by bringing about a unity in historical reality. This unity consists in knowledge of what mind does and of its manifestations. The past is continually recreated in the present of our own minds. Philosophy is itself self-consciousness of the mind, and in so far as it is, it can only be so by also being history.[11] De Ruggiero sums up Gentile's doctrine when he says, 'Philosophy, in creating its own history, creates itself. Hence an absolute immanence of philosophical truth in the historical process, which is at the same time the phenomenological process of the spirit'.[12]

Gentile's distinction between *act* and *fact* is closely connected to his doctrine of the identity of history and philosophy. Facts are what the mind has created. Facts have a temporal existence and are posited in time. The mind as act is *causa sui,* the cause of itself. It initiates change without being subject to change, but at the same time it exhibits change. The act as *causa sui* creates time and in this respect stands outside it. However, acts and facts are not separate and divided entities; they are a unity. The act realises itself in the fact. The mind as act has life only in the facts which are of its own making. If there were no identity between the act and fact, each of mind's creations would be a sterile, impermanent, isolated object in a mere multiplicity of facts – a mere object, or substance, posited as external to the mind. Gentile's argument for the unity of act and fact echoes the quite common idealist doctrine of unity in diversity, or identity in difference.[13] Gentile's view is that there must be a permanent identity for change to be possible. This permanent identity, or transcendental reality, is immanent in the process itself. The permanent without change, and change without permanence, are illusory fictions. That which changes must sustain a permanent identity throughout change; otherwise there would be nothing but a series of discrete, disconnected facts, severed from the act of their creation. The doctrine of fact and act, viewed in terms of the identity between philosophy and history, has the following implications:

The facts of philosophy are in the past; you think them, and they can only be the act, the unique act of your philosophy, which is not in the past, nor in the present which will be past, since it is the life, the very reality of your thought, a centre from which all time irradiates, whether it be past or future. History then, in the precise meaning in which it is in time, is only concrete in his act who thinks it as eternal.[14]

This, then, is the foundation upon which the idea of absolute immanence is built, that is, the unity between immanence and transcendence.[15] This is not to say that Collingwood followed Gentile's views without modification. My point is that Gentile's views help us to understand those of Collingwood.

It is now possible to understand more fully what Collingwood means by the 'historical plain method'. When he tells us that it involves the 'concentration upon *facts*', he does not mean 'facts' in abstraction from the acts that create them. Collingwood suggests that we may call something a fact when it is abstracted from the act of its creation. However, history is about facts – that is, facts and the deeds of which they are the result. The word *fact*, then, is Collingwood's term for that which is the unity of the immanent and transcendent aspects of experience. A fact is Collingwood's idea of absolute immanence; it is 'both mental activities and their results' (*NL*, 9.15). Immanent in the facts is the transcendental and eternal activity of the mind. This does not mean, however, that the activity of mind is the same everywhere and anywhere. Human nature is historically determinate, in that people think and act differently in different situations. Where the historical context remains the same, it may be possible to make generalisations about the activity of mind under such circumstances, but the generalisations are historically limited to situations of that kind, and not applicable to the activity of mind in general. It is not possible at the level of thought to make generalisations about the 'mind of man as it always has been and always will be'. Philosophers, or historians (in Collingwood's special sense of the latter word), can do no more than expound 'the position reached by the human mind in its historical development down to their own time'.[16] Because Collingwood makes a distinction between 'historical and non-historical human actions',[17] the former being applicable to rational activity and the latter to feelings, or the psyche, it was possible for him to subscribe to the view that whereas human nature at the level of thought has a historical determination and is susceptible only to limited historical generalisations, human nature at the level of feelings, or the psyche, is universal and unchanging, that is, explicable in terms of universal laws.[18]

Although Collingwood does not attempt to offer a defence of the view that 'what mind has done on a certain definite occasion is typical of what it always and everywhere does' (*NL*, 9.19), it is clear that he holds this to be the case with reference to the European mind. By looking at what minds do on certain occasions, it becomes apparent that immanent within the deeds is the transcendental activity of the modern European mind. In other words, we have a unity in diversity, a continuous identity amid the flux and change. In understanding the mind as pure act, Collingwood is subscribing to the doctrine of absolute immanence. Thus Collingwood is using the term *history* in a very special sense, that is, one which is inspired by Gentile, and this is why *The New Leviathan* is unlike other histories with which we may be familiar.

In Gentile's view, as I have already suggested, the activity of thinking is *causa sui,* the cause of itself. This, for Gentile, is what constitutes its freedom.[19] Freedom, for Collingwood, at its highest level, as we saw in the preceding chapter, is activity divested of all elements of caprice. It is activity independent of 'information or persuasion from anyone', in which the 'intentions or purposes are similarly independent'.[20] This type of activity, Collingwood suggests in *An Essay on Metaphysics,* 'could be called self-causing (*causa sui*); an expression which refers to absence of persuasion or inducement on the part of another'.[21] Gentile believed that the activity of thinking, and thus acting (for all thinking is action), is *causa sui,* while for Collingwood this is the case only at the higher levels of rational activity. In other words, caprice mitigates the self-causing activity of thinking.

The language of causation is not alien to the historical explanation of human action, nor is it appropriated from the practical and theoretical

natural sciences. Collingwood actually reverses the conventionally accepted relation between history and the natural sciences by claiming that
all cosmological theories are inspired by analogies. Modern cosmology,
Collingwood claims, is founded upon an analogy with human history.
The ideas of process, change, and development were embraced by modern
cosmologists and applied to the characterisation of nature. The analogy
first found systematic expression in Bergson's radical evolutionism.[22]
Collingwood goes on to make the contentious claims that natural science
is dependent upon history, 'and that no one can answer the question
what nature is unless he knows what history is'.[23] A second way in which
Collingwood subordinates the natural sciences to history is by arguing
that history possesses the primary sense of causation, of which the senses
of causation found in the practical and theoretical natural sciences are
modifications.[24]

Collingwood argues that free, conscious, and deliberate acts are those
which can be said to be 'caused', in the historical sense of the word. Such
words as *urge, compel,* or *persuade* may be substituted for the word
cause in this sense. The historical sense of the word *cause* is comprised
of two elements: the efficient cause (*causa quod*) and the final cause
(*causa ut*). The former is that which exists, or that with which the agent
is confronted – but not merely this, because the agent has to be aware
of the situation and believe such a state of affairs to exist. The latter,
namely, the final cause, does not refer to mere wishful thinking. The final
cause is an intention which demonstrates that the agent really meant to
act in the way he did.[25]

A historical causal explanation of human action can be legitimately
given where a first consciousness acts upon a second by informing or
persuading the latter that he is in a certain situation and where the latter
believes, or is convinced, that he is in that situation. Alternatively, where
two consciousnesses are concerned, the first may cause the second to
act by persuading that person to formulate an intention. The act performed
is still an act of free will, but the person said to cause it may be said to
share in the responsibility. The language of historical causation is still
applicable, however, to those circumstances in which the agent may be
said to be solely responsible for the act performed. Even in these circumstances there is both an efficient cause and a final cause, because
the agent 'has done for himself, unaided, the double work of envisaging
the situation and forming the intention'.[26] In other words, the agent conceives a situation and believes himself to be in it, and on the basis of this
he forms an intention to act. If an agent constantly acts in this way, the
complex of his actions could be described as self-causing.

W. J. van der Dussen has criticized Collingwood's concept of historical
causation on the grounds that it does not admit of natural events being

the causes of human actions. Collingwood, van der Dussen suggests, is inconsistent in his views, because he uses the following illustration for the historical sense of the word *cause:* 'Bad weather causes [a man] to return from an expedition'.[27] This apparent inconsistency should have alerted van der Dussen to the fact that he may have misunderstood Collingwood. There is nothing in Collingwood's idea of historical causation which would exclude natural occurrences from the situation (or efficient cause) in which the agent believes himself to be placed. Take, for example, a person driving a car. All of a sudden smoke begins to billow from under the bonnet. The situation is conceived by the person as potentially dangerous, that is, his conception of the situation is the efficient cause of his intention to stop the car and run for cover. In this example we have both an efficient and a final cause, which constitute a case of historical causation. The natural occurrence is an aspect of the situation believed by the agent, rightly or wrongly, to constitute the predicament in which he finds himself, and this belief comprises the efficient cause of the intention, or final cause. The cause of the action is, strictly speaking, human activity – that is, the conception of the situation – whereas that which is conceived is a natural occurrence. Thus in a historical explanation of human action, natural phenomena are not excluded. The natural phenomena alone cannot be the cause, because an efficient cause is both the situation, or occurrence, and our awareness of it.

The example I have given relates to a person acting 'on his own responsibility', where his belief about the situation is free of information received from, or of persuasion by, another person. Similarly, the intention is independent of an external consciousness acting upon it. But can natural phenomena enter into causal explanations where one consciousness acts upon another? The answer is yes. When Collingwood says that all 'history is the history of thought',[28] he means that human action is explicable in terms of the conception the agent has of a situation. The situation may be a mountain range which stands as an obstacle between places A and B. The agent's conception of the situation may be one which he believes because another person has convinced, or persuaded, him that that is the situation in which the agent must act. In other words, the physical obstacle may be insurmountable for the agent, not because he has conceived its insurmountability free of persuasion from another consciousness, but because another consciousness has taught him to believe that the mountains are inhabited by devils. This efficient cause leads him to form a final cause, or intention, not to cross the mountains.[29] In summary, then, there is no reason to believe that natural events are excluded by Collingwood as causal historical explanations.

One of the purposes of *The New Leviathan* is to explore the European mind, but so far we have looked only at its highest levels of development.

History is self-knowledge of the mind, the activity formerly ascribed by Collingwood to philosophy. It is therefore necessary, in order to understand mind fully, to trace its development up to the stage where rational consciousness becomes possible. What is to be excluded, and what is to be included, in a study of the development of the mind? In 'Human Nature and Human History', written in 1936, Collingwood gave an unequivocal answer. History, as self-knowledge of the mind, has no business with anatomy and physiology, nor with mind in general in so far as it includes feeling, sensation, and emotion.[30] These aspects of mind are the psyche or soul, and not spirit. Spirit is the rational mind of thought. The irrational elements in the psyche are the subject matter of psychology. Sensations, feelings, and appetites 'form the proximate environment in which our reason lives, as our physiological organism is the proximate environment in which they live'.[31]

Under the heading 'The Subject-Matter of History', in *The Idea of History,* Collingwood explicitly addressed himself to the question 'Of what can there be historical knowledge?' His answer was 'Of that which can be re-enacted in the historian's mind'.[32] That which can be reenacted is the activity of thinking – not merely thought, but 'reflective thought'. It is thought that is not mere consciousness, but self-consciousness, which involves having a conception of what it is we want to do as well as an awareness of the fact that we have done it when we have done it; further, knowing that we have done it is determined with reference to the criterion of our original conception of it.[33] Thus, the historian can have no historical knowledge of 'immediate experience, a mere flow of consciousness consisting of sensations, feelings, and the like'[34] though they are 'the activity of a mind', they are 'not the activity of thinking'.[35] If we relate this to Collingwood's concept of action, we arrive at the following conclusion. The subject matter of history is comprised of those acts which can 'be roughly described' as acts done on purpose. Collingwood himself identifies economic, political, and ethical actions as human activities of this kind and therefore appropriate as the subject matter of history. Their purposive character is not something incidental to them, because they could not be what they are unless they were purposive.[36] So far as the subject matter of history is concerned, then, Collingwood, in *The Idea of History,* wishes to maintain a rigid distinction between rational thought and feelings.

In both *The Principles of Art* and *An Essay on Metaphysics,* Collingwood still maintains the distinction between the psyche and the spirit and continues to designate the psyche as the proper subject matter of psychology.[37] Psychology, being a noncriteriological science, that is, having no concern for the self-critical aspects of thought, can appropriately have anything valid to say only about feelings and emotions which occur at the psychical level of experience. As soon as it permits itself to offer conclusions about thought, in the absence of acknowledging the criteriological character of thought, it becomes a dangerous pseudoscience.[38] However, the scope of the historical plain method, or science of mind, in *The New Leviathan* is expanded to include the psychical level of experience in its investigations. What is Collingwood's reason for making such a change? The answer is intimated, I think, in *The Idea of History* and becomes explicit in *The New Leviathan*.

In *The Idea of History* it is maintained throughout that all understanding is contextual. Nothing can be understood in isolation. As we saw, Collingwood allows the fact that sensations, feelings, and appetites constitute the proximate environment in which reason resides. Reason, he suggests, can discover and study these psychical phenomena, but in doing so it is not studying itself: 'By learning to know them, it finds out how it can help them to live in health, so that they can feed and support it while it pursues its own proper task, the self-conscious creation of its own historical life'.[39] By the time Collingwood wrote *An Essay on Metaphysics* and *The New Leviathan*, he perceived the condition of civilization, the various manifestations of which he had often warned about before, to be at crisis point. He may therefore have come to think that the psychical house needed to be put in order, since it was the foundation of thought and of the rational life, before he could offer any worthwhile conclusions about the workings of mind in general. If the psychical level of the mind was malfunctioning, that is, passing on misleading data to the higher levels of consciousness, then consciousness was bound to become corrupt. More than this, however, he had come to view a single act as comprising a number of types of activity: 'For example the individual act which I call "seeing my inkpot ten seconds ago" includes a function or group of functions belonging to sensation, and also a function or group of functions belonging to thought' (*NL*, 9.31), both of which appear to be integral to the understanding of mind. In *The New Leviathan* Collingwood is concerned to show that thought and feeling overlap and that both are the appropriate subject matter of the historical plain method.

Collingwood still makes a distinction between the psyche and the soul, but prefers to express it in different terms. He makes a clear division between body and mind. Body, the subject matter which physicists, chemists, and physiologists study, is explicable only in terms of natural science, and is on that account excluded from the ambit of the historical plain method. They are logically distinct orders of enquiry creative of their own objects of study. It is a fallacy to think that we can proceed so far with one, and then swop horses to continue the enquiry with another. Each is a legitimate form of enquiry, but each can proceed only in accordance with its own methods. Each recognises and identifies separate problems, and each can solve only those problems which it acknowledges as problems within its own terms of reference (*NL*, 3.1., and 2.6–2.74).

Body and mind are not two different aspects of man; each is the whole of man as understood from the perspective of different orders of enquiry. However, there is another sense in which the term *body* is used which allies it with the mind. This Collingwood calls the *'psychological sense of the word body'* (*NL*, 3.54). By this he means *'bodily appetite', 'bodily pleasure',* and *'bodily exertion'* (*NL*, 3.2). Thoughts belong to the various levels of consciousness, and consciousness is a constituent of mind. Feelings, on the other hand, are not thoughts. Feeling is an appanage of mind, that is, it is a prerequisite of simple consciousness, the object of which we become conscious. Thus feelings and thoughts stand in different relations to mind. As in *The Idea of History,* feelings are the context in which thoughts occur, but unlike the view propounded there, feelings, as appanages of mind, are the subject matter of the historical plain method. In order for this to be the case, one of the fundamental conditions of historical understanding outlined in *The Idea of History* has to be modified, namely the principle that historical knowledge consists solely in the reenactment of past purposive thought. Collingwood is quite explicit in *The Idea of History* about the fact that feelings cannot be reenacted[40] and that they are the proper domain of psychology. There seems to be no alternative but to conclude that psychology, like metaphysics, logic, and ethics, in the later writings of Collingwood becomes converted into history.[41] Consequently, however, the subject matter of history becomes something different from what it was understood to be in *The Idea of History.* History remains self-knowledge of the mind, in his subsequent work, but what he understands to be the subject matter of history is broadened to include what he had termed the psyche. In this respect history can no longer concern itself only with past purposive thought and its reenactment. It must also concern itself with thought at all the preceding levels of consciousness, and thought in *The New Leviathan* begins at the level of simple consciousness, that is, at the level he had previously termed the psyche.

3. The levels of consciousness

In *An Essay on Philosophical Method,* as we saw in Chapter 2, Collingwood stresses a principle which he feels is particularly important in articulating a theory about the method of philosophy. A philosophical enquiry is not directed at discovering things of which we are totally ignorant. Its principle is to come to understand better something that we already know, and our object is 'not to know it better in the sense of coming to know more about it, but to know it better in the sense of coming to know it in a different and better way – actually instead of potentially, or explicitly instead of implicitly'.[42] This is the principle that informs the 'sciences of mind' whose procedure of enquiry is the historical plain method. A natural scientist may reasonably expect, in the course of his enquiries, to gain knowledge of things of which he was previously ignorant; 'the sciences of mind', however, teach the inquirer 'only *things of which he was already conscious*' (*NL*, 1.71). Each person has it within himself, or herself, to reflect upon the levels of consciousness. Any of the forms of consciousness in the mind are capable of becoming the object of reflection for another form. To be conscious of something, and to be conscious that we are conscious of that something, involves two levels of consciousness; consciousness of the first entails calling into being a second level at which reflection upon the first takes place.

The levels of consciousness, Collingwood argues, form an integrated hierarchy in which each level is serially related to the next. The levels of consciousness form an irregular series. We are not in a position to be able to predict the development of mind. There is nothing in any of the levels of consciousness to necessitate that which comes after them (*NL*, 9.43). Collingwood had made this quite clear in *The Idea of History* when he suggested that 'the historical study of mind ... can neither foretell the future developments of human thought nor legislate for them'.[43] Collingwood refers to the indeterminacy of future developments in the mind as the 'law of contingency' (*NL*, 9.48). The intellectual foundations for this view are to be found in Hegel's writings. Hegel had maintained that in the sphere of nature there is constant repetition. Causes and effects stand outside each other and are externally related. Nature is a perpetual cyclical process in which occurrences are precipitated by external necessity.[44] In the realm of spirit, or mind, there is an internal relation, distinct from external necessity, with the propensity for creating and developing novel ideas and things. The mind is not mere repetition; it is capable of producing genuine novelty, and this is because we have an overwhelming desire to achieve perfection.[45] In nature, because of continuous repetition, events are predictable. In the realm of spirit, the logic of the past does not enable us to foretell the future.

A second principle which Collingwood views as integral to the study of mind is that of the 'law of primitive survivals' (*NL*, 9.5). This law, as we have seen, is a modification of the principle, articulated in *An Essay on Philosophical Method,* that each specification of a concept is related to other specifications in a linked hierarchy of forms, where the essence of what went before survives as a modification in what comes after.[46] Collingwood argues that without the operation of the law of primitive survivals there could be no development in the mind. If, for example, we take consciousness, and second-order consciousness, which reflects on the first, such reflection would not be possible unless something of mere consciousness survives to be reflected upon. In his 'Notes towards a Metaphysic' Collingwood explicitly relates the study of mind to *An Essay on Philosophical Method.* Collingwood says,

In the *Essay on Philosophical Method* it has been argued that a philosophical concept is differentiated into specific forms arranged on a scale; at the bottom of the scale comes the most rudimentary or primitive, which hardly exhibits the generic essence of the concept at all; the higher forms exhibit it more and more completely and at the same time in a more and more developed and elaborated way: the essence acquiring new increments as it realises itself more fully.

On this principle, the first thing to ask about consciousness is not whether it is essential to mind, but whether it constitutes the minimum essence of mind: the last determination left when mind is stripped of all its attributes, before it vanishes altogether. Now, the answer to this question is simple. Pure sentience is not the same as consciousness, and seems to be something yet more primitive. In framing a philosophical theory of mind, therefore, we must treat sentience and consciousness separately; and thus find the minimum essence (or pure being) of mind in sentience, with consciousness as a further increment.[47]

In formulating his theory of mind in *The New Leviathan,* Collingwood makes a distinction between feeling and consciousness. The human mind, in his view, is thought, both theoretical and practical. Thought is consciousness; thus mind *is* consciousness (*NL,* 1.61–1.63, and 4.2). Consciousness is not passive; it is an activity which is a constituent of the mind. In contrast, feeling is not something which mind *is;* it is something that mind *has.* By this Collingwood means that feeling, as an appanage of mind, is not a state of consciousness but its object: It is what we have consciousness of. This object of which we have consciousness consists of two closely related elements. In the first place we have 'a *sensuous* element such as a colour seen, a sound heard, an odour smelt' (*NL,* 4.1). Closely associated with this we have an *emotional charge* upon the sensation. One may, for instance, see the colour cheerfully; be afraid when one hears the noise; and be disgusted by the smell. In *The New Leviathan* Collingwood argues that to experience feelings is an act of simple, or first-order consciousness, the object of which is simple feelings. First-order consciousness is equivalent to what Collingwood had called, in *The Principles of Art,* psychical experience, but not in every respect. In *The Principles of Art* Collingwood reserved the term *feeling* for experiences which occur at the psychical level. Within this category he included sensa and their emotional charges. He was not denying, however, that thought at its various levels of consciousness brings into being new and more sophisticated emotions appropriate to itself.[48] To avoid possible confusion, he declined to call these emotions, which take place at the level of thought and above, feelings. In *The New Leviathan* Collingwood refers to feelings that are experienced at the first level of consciousness as 'simple feelings'. 'Simple consciousness' is consciousness of simple feelings; there is nothing else of which it can become conscious. Feeling at the level of first-order consciousness is sensuous-emotional, but is also capable of taking more 'specialized forms'. A person *has* feelings both of the simple and specialized kinds (*NL,* 4.2). The specialized forms come into being by means of the work of practical consciousness, and practical consciousness, taking stock of, or reflecting on, what it has created, makes the feeling an object of theoretical consciousness. Feeling, in all its forms, at whatever level of consciousness, is given, or immediate.

Simple, or first-order, consciousness is not in itself knowledge. We do not attain knowledge until we bring into play more sophisticated and specialized forms of consciousness. Simple consciousness must be reflected upon before knowledge is achieved. It is by an act of selective attention that we bring our diffused feelings and our diffused consciousness of them into focus (*NL,* 4.5). This Collingwood calls second-order consciousness. It involves three notionally distinct procedures. First we make suppositions about the object, that is, the first-order object, or feeling, present in simple consciousness. This involves attending to it and making suppositions about its origin. In the case of a noise, for instance, I have to make a supposition about whether it originates inside my head or from a source outside me. Second, I subject it to questioning; I ask what could have made it. Third, I attempt to answer the question by comparing the noise with other noises I imagine, or recollect, that I have heard (*NL,* 4.3–4.37). Second-order consciousness is the level at which conceptual thinking takes place.

In *The New Leviathan* it is argued, on methodological grounds, that feelings have no objects. The doctrine that he wishes to undermine, and the one to which he appears earlier to have subscribed himself, is that '*seeing* is an activity which has a proper object, namely *colours. Hearing* has a proper object, namely *sounds*' (*NL,* 5.23). Sounds, for example, on this view would be first-order objects to sensation, and second-order objects to simple consciousness, the first-order object of which is sensation itself. This is a scholastic doctrine that Locke reaffirmed. Descartes denied that feelings have objects, on the ground that a colour is not the 'object of a transitive verb *to see,* as a dog may be the object of a transitive verb to kick' (*NL,* 5.34). A colour is a mode of action, an experience, not an object; it has 'an *adverbial* function in the sentences in which it occurs' (*NL,* 5.35). To feel a colour, say blue, means that I am conscious of it. It does not mean that that colour is the object of feeling; the colour is the mode of feeling of which I am conscious. The theories of both Locke and Descartes are consistent with the facts. Neither theory is nonsensical. Working on the principle of Occam's Razor, Collingwood asks 'whether a theory of feeling needs objects as well as modes. The Lockian theory does; the Cartesian does not. By Occam's Razor the Cartesian theory is preferable' (*NL*, 5.39).[49] Thus, on methodological rather than positive grounds, Collingwood denies the existence of objects of feeling.

In *The New Leviathan,* Collingwood reaffirms the view he held in *The Principles of Art,* that feelings are transitory. They are fleeting sensations that begin to fade as soon as they are experienced (*NL*, 5.5). It was this point of view which informed Collingwood's criticism of Hobbes in the early lectures on moral philosophy. Feeling could not be the basis of ethical activity, simply because feelings are immediate, here and now, unaffected by feelings we have had in the past or feelings we may have in the future. The fact that feelings are coloured by comparison with past and anticipated feelings means that something in addition to feeling is at work in forming the grounds of our actions. It is the power of imagining feelings that we are not at present experiencing that enables us to rise above the flux of transitory feeling. It is this principle of imagination that distinguishes feeling itself from recalling or anticipating feelings. In the early lectures Hobbes's theory is pronounced inadequate because he fails to detect that two different levels of experience are in operation in the awareness of feelings: 'Now for Hobbes feeling is the only source of action: that is what is meant by hedonism. Whatever feeling we actually have determines according to him our conduct: and there is no fraction of conduct which is not so determined'.[50]

At this stage Collingwood does not venture to explain why Hobbes failed to understand the relation between what Collingwood called, in *The Principles of Art,* psychical experience and consciousness, or what he called, in *The New Leviathan,* first-order and second-order consciousness. In both books Collingwood does indicate an answer. In *The Principles of Art* Collingwood attributes to Hobbes the view that it is impossible to distinguish between real and imaginary sensations by means of direct inspection, and that is the only means by which such knowledge could be acquired. The immediacy of our sensual experience and the impossibility of distinguishing the real from the imaginary led Hobbes to deny the distinction and employ the two terms synonymously.[51] Even though, in *The New Leviathan,* Collingwood only alludes to this criticism, it is clear that he still stood by it. He argues that a person who participated in the colour-vision experiments conducted by J. S. Haldane might well have concluded that real feelings do not exist. We experience 'only ghosts of non-existent feelings'. Such a person, Collingwood suggests, 'would at any rate have Hobbes on his side, who wrote that "sense in all cases, is nothing else but original Fancy" ' (*NL*, 4.48).[52] Hobbes, then, had made the mistake of confusing sensation and imagination, or first- and second-order consciousness.

At the second level of consciousness we see clearly how feeling and thought overlap. At the first level we have simple feeling, or feeling proper, which mind *has* as an appanage to what it *is,* namely, consciousness. At the second level we have appetite, but this is also the stage at which conceptual thought arises. In second-level consciousness the activity of attending to, or selecting, feelings takes place within a framework of evocative thinking. To evoke feelings, other than those to which one is attending, is to arouse in oneself, by means of thought, feelings that are not immediately given. The evocations form a context inseparable from the activity of selecting. The evocation provides contrasts to the feelings attended to and facilitates the identification of those feelings. At this level of consciousness such selective attention in the context of evocations is the process by which we encounter appetite in the forms of hunger and love, and it is at this level that we become conscious of passion in the forms of fear and anger.

Appetite is the first-order object of the second level of consciousness. By means of thought, appetite is identified. The evocation of a context enables mind to contrast the feeling with a state in which that feeling is absent, that is, a condition of pleasure potential in which the appetite is satisfied. The practical move towards attaining this condition is impelled by the concept of pleasure potential. Thought, then, converts simple feeling into appetite; it makes partially determinate what was completely indeterminate. Because it is an abstraction, appetite is made determinate in limited ways. The object of appetite, that which will bring about satisfaction, is conceived only as the thing that will satisfy. Apart from this, everything else is indeterminate. Mind is inherently restless, and appetite is the name which designates this restlessness. It is appetite which constantly drives us from the "what is" to the "what ought to be": 'a quest due to no choice, guided by no reason, directed on no goal. Choice and reason and goal are not among the sources or conditions of appetite, they are among its products' (*NL,* 7.69).

Appetite is the unsatisfactory feeling-state that Collingwood calls the *actual self.* The satisfactory feeling-state he calls the *ideal self.* Hunger, one of the two forms which appetite takes, is a dissatisfaction with oneself. It is a dissatisfaction with the actual self for being weak, and a corresponding, or concomitant, wanting to be strong, that is, wanting to be the ideal self. Appetite specifies no limit to the strength to be achieved in the ideal self. It is a blind impulse towards an indeterminate, ideal feeling-state. God is the ideal self towards which the appetite of a hungry man strives. God is the ultimately strengthened ideal self, 'the infinite satisfaction of man's hunger: man himself become omnipotent' (*NL,* 8.29). It is, then, an idiomorphic god, the ideal self of the hungry man.

Love, as the second form of appetite, is a modification of hunger. It is only through love that we come to differentiate between the self and not-self. We are not conscious of this distinction until we reflect upon it 'as something ready-made' (*NL*, 8.18). To love something is to think of it as other than oneself, but in addition to this, it is to think that the loneliness which is the source of one's present dissatisfaction will be satisfied by coming into contact with that which is other than oneself. What is other than the person who loves is his second self: 'The idea of a second self is the abstract idea of anything, no matter what, to which his practical relation is that he looks to it to cure his loneliness; he wants a satisfaction, no matter what, which he expects it to supply' (*NL*, 8.32).

The lover rejects the idea of an idiomorphic god and seeks instead a heteromorphic god who is the object of his love. The lover loves a heteromorphic god, that is, whoever is the object of love. Lovers worship each other, and each is the other's heteromorphic god. Love is satisfied, or at least holds out the hope of satisfaction, in this religion of earthly love. The religion of unsatisfied love wants a not-self unaccessible in our world, that is, a god who is transcendent and to whom the lover calls but gets no answer, 'because there is nothing there' (*NL*, 8.38).

In love we create the object of our satisfaction; we establish a relation between ourself and an other self. In establishing such a relation lies the origin of both the self and the not-self. The act of creating a not-self, or an other self, highlights a centre of activity, that is, the creative centre, which, in the act of creation, circumscribes a unique self differentiated from all that is not self. The self and not-self are abstractions from the act of reflecting on love, but why does love emerge at all? It arises because of the impossibility of the hungry man achieving omnipotence. He is not able to recognise or acknowledge the impossibility of his quest until he has reached a level of mental development far beyond that of second-level consciousness. It is the repeated frustration of his quest to be omnipotent that turns blind appetite towards another course of satisfaction. Having failed to satisfy the self by attaining the ideal omnipotent self, satisfaction is sought in something that is not self. Of what does this not-self consist? In Collingwood's view, 'No answer is possible, for the not-self is an abstraction, determinate only in being other than the self; in all else indeterminate, as (for that matter) the self is' (*NL*, 8.56). Love comes into existence when the quest for omnipotence, or the absolute satisfaction of wants, becomes modified into a limited range of demands.

The not-self, in frustrating the satisfaction of even the limited range of demands, has the power to throw one into a passion. In reflecting upon this, all a person can ascertain is that a not-self of indeterminate character has in some way acted upon one and in doing so provoked a reaction. This, then, is passion, and it appears in the forms of fear and anger. Collingwood is critical of both Hobbes's and Spinoza's understanding of fear, because they attribute rationality to something that is simply not rational. In Hobbes's view, to experience fear is to have an aversion to something on the ground that the object may cause me harm.[53] Thus, fear of a bull would entail identifying the animal as a bull; recalling that bulls are dangerous to men; and, to complete the syllogism, concluding that this particular bull can do harm to me. Contrary to this view, Collingwood argues that someone overcome by fear is in no position to rationalize his situation. A regress may occur in the mind if the rational higher functions are displaced by fear. This is possible, because, due to the law of primitive survivals, fear is never totally extinguished at the higher levels of consciousness and can take charge when a person becomes really frightened. Fear contains an element of conceptual thinking, that is, the act of abstracting the self and the not-self, and then contrasting the two. Fear does not, however, pace Hobbes, contain an element of propositional thinking. Fear is the practical reaction to the contrast, but not to every contrast – only those which become accentuated in the act of attention. Love is converted into fear when the not-self is seen as independent, existing in its own right, and not merely for the benefit of satisfying one's own appetites. Fear contains within itself an element of the love out of which it developed. Fear creates its own object; it is one's thinking an object to be alive, having an independent existence, whether it is the case or not, that makes a person frightened (*NL*, 10.26–10.33).

Anger is the second of the two forms of passion, and once again both Hobbes and Spinoza are criticized for attributing rationality to something that lacks it (*NL*, 10.4–10.42).[54] We become conscious of anger, Collingwood maintains, only when we reflect upon it. In anger one is only aware that there is something which contrasts with one, something which contradicts and threatens one. This is the intellectual element present in anger, which corresponds to 'the intellectual element in fear' (*NL*, 10.43). To succumb to the threat of the not-self is fear, and to rebel against it is anger. We do not choose which course of action to take. Choice is a rational activity developed at a higher level of consciousness. Anger develops out of fear because the inclination towards complete submission to that which one fears is an impellent, at the same time, towards the annihilation of the self. It is shame that converts fear into anger:

10.5. Shame, which is the critical point in the process converting fear into anger, is in a larger sense a critical point in the whole development of mind: for unlike a man in a condition of appetite a man in a condition of shame knows what he wants: he wants to be *brave*; not devoid of fear, but triumphant over fear.

It is anger which forms a bridge from the lower levels of consciousness, where thought is capable of receiving what is given and of conceptualizing abstractions from it, to the higher forms in which propositional thinking develops, followed by rational consciousness, or will. Anger, Collingwood appears to be saying, is the intermediate stage between conceptual and propositional thinking. The second level, as we saw, is the home of conceptual thinking. Conceptual thinking has 'an intellectual element'. This intellectual element consists of the development of the distinction between the self and the not-self. Fear and anger are the practical responses to the contrast which intellect makes (*NL*, 10.26–10.27 and 10.43–10.44).

At the third level of consciousness we encounter desire and happiness, both of which are feelings, and it is at this stage that propositional thinking arises. Desire is the activity of wishing for something, and is distinguished from appetite in that the latter is the mere wanting of one knows not what. Wishing for something entails knowing what it is that one desires. To desire something implies that one may not desire, or may have an aversion to, something else. In desire one is faced with alternatives and has to ask oneself, 'Which do I want?' This is propositional thinking, in which the acceptance of one alternative involves the rejection of the other. Truth and error are the corollaries of desire. It is possible to have both true and false desires. In answering the question 'Which of these alternatives do I want?', the answer given is a proposition which is either true or false. The very first step in 'knowing yourself is knowing what you want' (*NL*, 11.39). We can know nothing else before we know what we desire.

Collingwood agrees with both Hobbes and Spinoza in thinking that what is desired is good, and that that to which we have an aversion is bad. Collingwood believes, however, that their formulations of the theory are hopelessly confused. Hobbes fails to distinguish between appetite and desire, and Spinoza identifies good with 'four very different things: conation, volition, appetite, and desire' (*NL*, 11.4–11.42).[55] In other words, Collingwood is suggesting that Hobbes and Spinoza failed to understand that appetite and desire are the products of two different levels of consciousness. It is desire, the product of the third level of consciousness, which makes things good, or worthy to be desired. Desire bestows goodness upon the thing it desires, and it may be wrong in doing so only in so far as it is mistaken about the fact that the object is really desired. In desiring something, the mind 'for the first time assumes the form of knowledge. . . . and good is the first thing we come to know' (*NL*, 11.68–11.69). We do not desire things because they are good; their goodness consists in being desired. It must be emphasized here that at every stage the law of primitive survivals is operating. Each stage is a modification of what went before, but also contains an element of that prior stage in an unmodified form. Collingwood makes this point quite clearly when he says,

9.55 If appetite, passion, and desire form a series, each is a modification of the one before; but any individual example of passion contains, over and above the appetite which has been modified into passion an element of appetite pure and simple: any example of desire contains a primitive survival of passion and also one of appetite: and so, as the series goes on, the structure of the functions grows more complex.

In general terms, what human beings desire is happiness – happiness, that is, in Aristotle's sense of the term. To achieve happiness is to dominate circumstances, and to be unhappy is to be dominated by them. In relation to the self, happiness is goodness, and in relation to the not-self it is 'the power to prevent the not self from doing to him anything at all' (*NL*, 12.55). In relation to the self, unhappiness is being at the mercy of one's passions, and in relation to the not-self it is to be weak, not being able to do anything and having everything done to one. Its twentieth-century manifestation is the powerlessness with which we face the overwhelming might of economic, social, and political forces. In Collingwood's view, Hobbes and others made it abundantly clear that it is we who created these creatures; they are the work of artifice intended for our own protection and defence. This optimistic hope has turned to despair as we are confronted with the realisation that it is those very agents whose protection we expected to enjoy that are now the perpetrators of the evils they were meant to end. Collingwood's *New Leviathan* is explicitly meant to help restore our hope that we can overcome the evils that have befallen humanity. In this respect he offers 'a science of politics appropriate for the modern world' (*NL*, 12.96).

In the first, second, and third levels of consciousness, action is at no time informed by reason. At the first stage, as we saw, action is what Collingwood had previously termed *mechanical*. The agent acts in a world from which he is unable to differentiate himself. His acts are impelled by blind will, in which everything is a blooming, buzzing confusion. This is action at its most primitive, in which no element of cognition is present. It is wholly irrational action, that of an agent producing changes in the world, unaware of himself doing so and unaware of the world in which it is done. The agent experiences a mass of diverse and conflicting sensations in which the world and himself are an undifferentiated whole. There is no awareness of consciousness and no thought, just sensations and their emotional charges blindly impelling fortuitous, gratuitous, and irrational acts of 'blind will'.[56] The second level of consciousness exhibits a form of action which resembles that which Collingwood had identified as *instinct* in the 1927 conclusion to the 1923 lectures on action. In instinctive action the agent is unaware of any purpose in his acts. As instinctive agents our freedom consists of delighting in the satisfaction of our appetites. We are free to indulge our appetites, in so far as our indulgences are not frustrated, but at the same time we are slaves to our appetites.[57] The third level of consciousness seems to have appropriate to it a form of action which Collingwood had described, in his 'Economics as a Philosophical Science', as *impulsive*. When we act from impulse we do what we want to do. Our desires act as the springs of our actions.[58] Desires, however, are not choices. We do not choose what we desire: 'A man who "prefers" *a* to *b* does not choose at all; he suffers desire for *a* and aversion towards *b*, and goes where desire leads him' (*NL*, 13.14). Although he had an apparent alternative, the alternative is closed because desire directs him towards one and away from the other.

When the alternatives are open, we are able to make a choice. We do not become free by making a choice; choice presupposes freedom. The way to attain this freedom is through self-liberation – to break free from desire and make decisions. In its positive sense this means that we are free to exercise our wills; in its negative sense it is freedom from the domination of desires. To liberate ourselves is not something we choose to do; we are capable of choice only after liberation. Further, it is not something that anyone else can do for us. How, then, do we become liberated? This process can occur only when we refuse to let desire dictate to us. Such acts of denial provide the only means to achieve consciousness of freedom, and that means the attainment of self-respect. We do not indulge in acts of denial in order to achieve self-respect; that is a utilitarian act in which one thing is exchanged for something better. Self-respect is not something we could value above what our desires direct us to pursue, namely happiness. Why human beings liberate themselves is a mystery, for they can have no conception of the rewards that are to be gained. How they liberate themselves, however, is explicable. They do so by naming the desire. Having done so once, men and women can do so over and over again. Once again language is imperative in the development of the mind. The linguistic act liberates us from the third level of consciousness and precipitates the transition to the fourth level, in which we encounter the life of reason. It is the business of both government and education, Collingwood suggests, to ensure that those who have attained the level of freedom – that is, those who have become capable of free choice – become conscious of having done so. Thus persons who are only preconsciously free, that is, who have not become aware that they possess freedom, must have their self-respect aroused. Conversely, if one wishes to deprive a person of the capacity to make choices, then one should undermine his, or her, self-respect.

At this fourth level of consciousness a distinction is made between the will and the deed. The will is the decision between alternatives, and the deed is putting that decision into effect. To be conscious of making a decision makes that decision a first-order object of consciousness; 'what I decide to do is a second-order object, an abstraction from that' (*NL*,

13.72). No abstraction is ever completely determinate. This explains why even at the level of duty there is a minute trace of caprice. A decision always leaves open a certain degree of flexibility for the enactment of the deed. Even the best-laid plans can never be complete down to the fine detail. The flexibility for extemporization is a necessary feature of carrying out a deed: 'an over-detailed plan is an impediment to its own execution' (*NL*, 13.75). The thought is the practical act of will in which an intention is formulated. This intention is progressively converted into performance, but not always in its entirety, because intentions are often frustrated.

Mind has now reached the level of reason, that is, the point at which capricious choice and the criteria of rational action come into play. The process by which mind gradually eliminates caprice while passing through the stages of utilitarian, regularian, and dutiful action was demonstrated in the preceding chapter. Hobbes had not, it was suggested, gone beyond the analysis of utilitarian action. In this chapter further differences between Hobbes and Collingwood have emerged. First, Collingwood believed that Hobbes had confused sensation and imagination. Second, he thought that Hobbes had wrongly attributed rationality to fear. Third, he criticized Hobbes for failing to distinguish between appetite and desire. Similar criticisms, Collingwood believed, were also applicable to Spinoza. In essence, then, Collingwood had a very different conception of the nature and content of mind from that of Hobbes or Spinoza.

On the positive side of the relation between Hobbes and Collingwood, the latter acknowledged that Hobbes, among others, had once and for all emphasized that the social, economic, and political powers which overawe us are creatures of our own artifice. Hobbes also held out the hope of liberation. However, the liberators have become the main perpetrators of the very things against which we empowered them to protect us. Furthermore, as we will see in the next section, Collingwood developed a great admiration for Hobbes's theory of language.

4. Emotion, imagination, and language

The exposition of the levels of consciousness now needs to be supplemented with a discussion of the importance of emotion, imagination, and language in Collingwood's theory of mind. Such a discussion is not a digression, for, as we will see in subsequent chapters, Collingwood draws upon his theories of emotion, imagination, and language in expounding his views on society, civilization, and the threat to civilization. Emotion, imagination, and language are integrally related. Sensa and their emotional charges are converted into imagination by consciousness, and it is at the level of imagination that emotion is expressed in language. This is the theory which Collingwood explicated in *The Principles of Art* and modified in *The New Leviathan*.

We must turn to *The Principles of Art* for a better understanding of the distinction between sensation and emotion. The relation between sensation and emotion is more intimate than that between two species of a genus. The sensation and its emotional charge are not two separate experiences; they are one experience. A child who is terrified by seeing a red window curtain blazing in the sunlight is not experiencing a sensation of red and an emotion of fear: 'There is only one experience, a terrifying red'.[59] The experience combines the sensual and emotional elements in accordance with a structural pattern in which the sensation has precedence over the emotion. This does not mean that the sensation precedes the emotion in a time sequence. If it did, there would be two experiences.

At the psychical level of feeling, or first-order consciousness, as he was later to call it, Collingwood argues that there is a mode of expression wholly independent and distinct from consciousness. This is what Collingwood terms 'psychical expression', which is unrelated to linguistic expression, the latter being inextricably associated with consciousness. Each emotion that occurs at the purely psychical level is accompanied by physiological changes which express it. Dilated pupils, for instance, may express fear, while facial distortion may express pain. To observe and interpret these psychical expressions is the work of intellect. However, the expression of emotions may affect us without our being aware, or conscious, of what is happening. A terrified person, for example, may precipitate panic in a crowd. Each person becomes terrified without reflecting on the feeling, but because the fear is contagious it presents itself in each person as a complex pattern of sensa emotionally charged with terror.[60]

In order to bridge the gap between feeling and intellect, that is, in order to provide a mediating category, Collingwood formulated a theory of imagination. The problem which Collingwood is trying to answer in bridging the gap between feeling and intellect is that of providing an adequate account of how we come to make connections between the various sensa. Sensation is immediate and discrete; sensations are not retained in the act of sensing. In order that comparisons and connections can be made between the discrete sensations, there must be another form of experience, closely related to feeling, in which sensations are retained and recalled but cease to be sensed. This form of experience is imagination. Before comparisons can be made between sensa, sensa must be distinguished, or attended to. This means that we must become conscious, or become aware, of what it is we are sensing. In Collingwood's view consciousness converts sensa into imagination. *Consciousness* and *imagination* are synonymous terms for the same level of experience. Within this level of experience, however, a distinction has to be made between that which effects the conversion and that which has undergone the process of conversion. Consciousness converts sensa, and imagination is what sensa become after being converted. It is intellect that establishes the relations and makes the inferences. Imagination, then, is 'the point at which the life of thought makes contact with the life of purely psychical experience. . . . It is not sensa as such that provide the data for intellect, it is sensa transformed into ideas of imagination by the work of consciousness'.[61]

We have to expand further upon the place of imagination in the life of the mind, because, as we will see, its proper cultivation is of considerable importance for personal development and for the survival of civilization. In *Speculum Mentis* Collingwood argues that art is 'purely imagination'.[62] In this 'world of imaginations', propositions, assertions, or 'facts' about reality are absent.[63] Children and savages, Collingwood suggests, are natural artists whose imaginations are unconstrained. This artistic experience can only be achieved by civilized adult human beings by shutting out the objects which they are accustomed to seeing historically or scientifically, in order to be able to apprehend them aesthetically.[64] The mind is not a machine which manufactures artistic objects; instead the mind 'creates itself, as the activity of imagination by creating these works of art which are its imaginary objects'.[65]

In relation to the forms of experience, the most rudimentary form of thought is art. Play is the counterpart of art in that it is the form which the most rudimentary form of action takes. Aesthetic consciousness has a theoretical side, which is art, and a practical side, which is play. The importance of the aesthetic consciousness is that its innocence affords us a foretaste of the condition of mind after it has faced its problems and overcome them. Art enables the mind to reach out into the unknown, whereas play treats the world as a place in which adventures can be perpetually enacted. Collingwood contends emphatically that 'the spirit of play, the spirit of eternal youth is the foundation and beginning of all real life'.[66] Art, which is imagination, is the foundation upon which all other forms of experience are built,[67] and imagination is 'the first step in the growth of knowledge'.[68]

In *The Principles of Art* Collingwood moves away from the idea that art is pure imagination and argues that art is the expression of emotion at the level of consciousness which he calls imagination. The ability to express one's emotions is particularly important in the development of consciousness. As we saw in Chapter 2, we become conscious of experiencing an emotion only by expressing it. When we are conscious of the emotion, we are acknowledging what we feel. By means of selectively attending to sensa, we distinguish our emotional experiences into those we wish to acknowledge and those we do not. By failing to express an emotion, we fail to acknowledge it and, therefore, effectively disown it. In this respect consciousness fails to convert psychical emotions into imaginative expression. In this 'corruption of consciousness', intellect receives a series of false emotional expressions upon which to build its thought.[69]

Magic and various other folk practices are also necessary vehicles of emotional expression and emotional arousal. We look with disdain upon the magical ceremonies of savages, and the rituals and customs of agricultural people, or even upon those of the uneducated classes. We view such practices as the irrational and senseless acts of ignorant people. But to view such practices in these terms is a misconception: 'for magic, which sums up all that we dislike in savage life, is beginning to reveal itself as the systematic and organized expression of emotion'.[70] Activities such as dancing, singing songs, drawing, and modelling are artistic elements in magical rituals. Magic differs from art in that it is directed towards preconceived ends, which allies it more closely with craft.[71] The purpose of magic is the arousal of emotions which are channelled into the performance of our practical and necessary activities. The survival of any society depends upon the vital emotional energy generated by magic.[72] We tend to think that we have passed the stage of mental development in which magic has a place, but we are only deluding ourselves. Numerous magical practices survive in the customs of modern society,[73] and in the absence of these magical practices emotional expression is artificially suppressed. A healthy society needs magical practices to channel its emotions into positive enterprises. Dance, for example, is a magical practice, and in its modern forms it is, for the most part, a ritual associated with courtship. The emotion aroused and expressed is not fully expended in the dance but is intended to bear fruit in the creation of a future partnership.[74]

Towards the end of the 1933 lectures on moral philosophy, Collingwood includes a discussion of rational emotion. Each of the three levels of practical reason has a corresponding emotional colouring, or emotional charge. These emotions are appropriate to rational beings in that they are emotions of a special kind. In this respect the distinction between utility and right is a reiteration, at a higher level, of the distinction between hunger and love. We have an emotional attitude towards utility, that is, the value of an act conceived as means to end, which is a rational form of hunger. It is 'rational or intelligent hunger, an appetite qualified by rational understanding of what it is that we want'.[75] We also have an emotional attitude towards rules which we acknowledge and obey. This is commonly called respect or reverence for the law, and it is a form of rational love. As universals, laws are appropriate objects of love, and in so far as they are apprehended by intellect the love we feel for them is intellectual. Just as appetite has a place in rational consciousness, so does passion. We have 'a rational fear' of being frustrated in pursuing our ends, and 'a rational anger' when acknowledged rules are breached.[76]

Although hunger is the emotional attitude we have towards utility, or the useful, an element of love is also present, but it is self-love, devoted to attaining our own interests, not blindly and irrationally, but in a way which we think will be advantageous. Whereas rational self-love is characteristic of economic life, love of others characterises our respect for law, or regularian activity. It is the desire to have everyone, without discrimination, equal before the law. It is a rational desire to create a harmonious order in the life of human activity. Collingwood claims that the rational love of our neighbour is the emotional spring of the expression of political activity. There is also a rational form of love which corresponds to duty, and this is the love of God. Collingwood argues that when we do our duty we are trying to realise in ourselves 'an absolutely good will' which is 'the will of God', and to devote ourselves to this ideal is to love God.[77] The rational emotion of love of God, which is an intelligent love, excludes passion from the sphere of duty, because here our will is wholly active and has no place for fear or anger. Only in so far as our will is impeded by its own inadequacies and intellectual shortcomings do we live in fear of God, and because we do not understand him we are angry at those who deviate from his will. In this respect our love of God is not complete. Collingwood sums up his discussion of rational emotion by arguing that

the love of God is the sea into which all our passions and appetites flow. At first we think that we have two appetites, hunger and love; but hunger, when we understand it, turns into self-love. We think that we love ourselves and our neighbours, but when we come to know our own minds better we recognize that in these various loves we have from the first been loving God, from whom all love comes and to whom it all returns.[78]

The importance of language in Collingwood's philosophy of mind cannot be overestimated. Language is absolutely crucial to the development of mind. Each conversion from one level of consciousness to another is brought about by a linguistic act. Given the importance Collingwood attributes to language when discussing the levels of consciousness in *The New Leviathan*, one would expect a similar emphasis to be found in the series of lectures upon which part I of the book is based. This, however, is not the case. In none of the series of lectures on moral philosophy does he devote a separate section to language. He tends, rather, to assume, or presuppose, the role of language in the development of mind. There is no question, however, of the chapter on language in *The*

New Leviathan being a belated afterthought to the theory of mind. He had on many prior occasions addressed himself to the question of the nature and character of language. Indeed, a theory of language is crucial to Collingwood's concept of art, a subject to which he returned again and again throughout his career.[79] In fact, the theory of language articulated in *The New Leviathan* is a development and modification of that in *The Principles of Art.*

As we saw earlier in this chapter, Collingwood, in *The Principles of Art,* made a distinction between psychical expression and linguistic expression. Language, to continue his argument further, comes into existence at the conscious level of experience. Imagination, that which feeling becomes when transformed by consciousness, is inextricably related to language. Language, in its original form, is both imaginative and expressive. Language 'is an imaginative activity whose function is to express emotion'.[80] There are emotions which arise only at the level of consciousness, for example, 'hatred, love, anger and shame'.[81] They all presuppose a self-awareness and cannot, therefore, arise at the level of psychical experience. They can, however, be psychically expressed. If we take shame as an instance, we see that it is the awareness of how weak or ineffective we are. Such emotions of consciousness are able to be expressed by language. They also find expression at the psychical level. Shame may be expressed involuntarily in a blush, but shame is not an emotional charge upon a sensum. There is no corresponding sensation, because shame is an emotional charge upon a level of consciousness. Why, then, is it susceptible to being expressed at the psychical and conscious levels of experience? The answer to this, Collingwood suggests, is that each different level does not supersede its predecessor; instead, it is superimposed upon it. They differ from each other in that they have different principles of organization, but in the higher type the lower continues to be perpetuated.

In order to undergo the transition from one level to the next, the lower stage must be consolidated by organizing the principles upon which it is built. Shame, in this respect, although capable of psychical expression, must be expressed linguistically in order to become consolidated at the level of consciousness. No transition from consciousness to the next level of experience, that is intellect, can occur until expression at the conscious level has taken place.

Collingwood takes language, at the conscious or imaginative level, to be any form of controlled expression, as long as we conceive the expressions and are aware that we are controlling them. Thus, bodily gestures as well as the use of the vocal organs are encompassed by imaginative and expressive language. In fact, the use of speech is a refinement and specialization of one aspect of the ' "original" language of total bodily gestures'.[82] Language, at the level of consciousness, or imagination, must undergo certain modifications before it can serve the purpose of intellect. Intellect divides, determines, and establishes relations between experiences in converting imagination to the higher level. At the level of consciousness, 'imagination presents to itself an object which it experiences as one and indivisible'.[83] Alan Donagan articulates Collingwood's distinction well by suggesting that 'unlike imagining, thinking is essentially analytic and abstract'.[84] In order to accomplish analytic and abstract thinking, language itself must become the object of the intellect. Grammarians analyse and adapt language in order to facilitate the expression of thought. The grammarian fulfils this function only in a limited and partial way: Language always retains elements of the vitality it displays at the conscious, or imaginative, level of experience. Similarly, the logician tries to convert language into the perfect vehicle of thought, but fails to do so because language resists complete intellectualization. Language at the level of intellect is never devoid of emotional expressiveness. Emotional charges accompany every activity:

> The emotional charges upon thought experiences are expressed by the controlled activity of language. Taking next the distinction within thought of consciousness and intellect, the emotions of consciousness are expressed by language in its primitive and original form; but intellect has its emotions too, and these must have an appropriate expression, which must be language in its intellectualized form.[85]

The example which Collingwood gives to illustrate this is that of Archimedes on discovering specific gravity. The cry of 'Eureka' expressed the complex emotional charge on the level of intellect. In the merely written form we would not be able to distinguish between the levels at which such a term is used to express an emotion. Understanding such an expression of emotion is contextual and depends upon the audience having reached a similar level of intellect to oneself. The contextual nature of understanding had been strongly emphasized by Vico, Dilthey,[86] and Croce, three philosophers whom Collingwood greatly admired. Croce, for instance, argued in his *Logic* that 'a word no longer has meaning ... when it is abstracted from the circumstances, the implications, the emphasis, and gesture with which it has been thought, animated and pronounced'.[87] Collingwood, however, went much further in that he formulated a theory of meaning similar to that which we commonly attribute to Wittgenstein. Wittgenstein, in his famous formulation of a definition of meaning, says, 'The meaning of a word is its use in the language'.[88] Collingwood, independently of Wittgenstein, intimated such a doctrine in *The Principles of Art* when he said, 'One does not first acquire a language and then use it. To possess it and to use it are the same. We only come to possess it by repeatedly and progressively attempting to use it'.[89] In an undated, unpublished manuscript, 'Observations on Language', which appears to have been a preliminary study of language for *The New Leviathan* that was not used,[90] Collingwood makes an unequivocal statement linking the meaning of language with its use. Because the manuscript is available for consultation only in the Bodleian, it is worth quoting at length, or at least to the length permitted by the literary executor. Collingwood's argument is as follows:

1.   Language is not a tool or instrument which we use in order by its use to do things which we would not do without it. It is a mode of conduct, an activity.

1.1   It is therefore a mistake to think of language as an 'invention' or the like, comparing it with fire or other instruments invented at a certain time (or at various times) by men.

1.2   It is a mistake to think of it as having certain properties or powers in itself and apart from the 'using' of it: for since it is an activity, not an instrument, it does not exist save in being 'used'.

2.   Significance or meaningfulness, the attribute which is essential to language, is therefore an attribute not of an instrument (as sharpness or heaviness is of a chisel or hammer) but of the linguistic activity, or rather the agent engaged in that activity.

2.1   . . . .

2.2   When language considered in itself is divided for the convenience of grammarians into separate words, and the question is then raised, what does this or that separate word mean? there is properly speaking no answer; for (a) since words are never used except in a context, and have no meaning except as used, they have no meaning except in a context; (b) since it is the speaker not the word, that means, the nearest we can get to an answer is 'it means whatever people mean when they use it'.[91]

These observations are confirmed in the scattered statements on language in the 1940 lectures on moral philosophy. There Collingwood argues that 'the correct usage of words is determined only by usage itself'. In this respect, 'a word is a social custom: and to define a word is to describe the type or types of occasion on which that social custom comes into play'.[92] It is clear, then, that Collingwood held both that the meaning of language is in its use, and that all understanding is contextual.

In *The Principles of Art*, Collingwood makes a distinction between symbolism, which is intellectualized language, and language proper, which expresses emotions. Language, he suggests, in its imaginative form has expressiveness but no meaning. Intellectualized language, however, is both expressive and has meaning: 'As language, it expresses a certain emotion. As symbolism, it refers beyond that emotion to the thought whose emotional charge it is. This is the familiar distinction between 'what we say' and 'what we mean'.[93] The purpose of his analysis of language, in *The Principles of Art,* was to arrive at a theory of art. Art, he concluded, is both expressive and imaginative, and therefore it must be language. Artistic experience is generated at the level of consciousness, or imagination.[94] Collingwood therefore denies all theories that place the origin of art in the psychical and intellectual levels of consciousness.

Collingwood's theory of language in *The New Leviathan* is a modification of that propounded in *The Principles of Art.* The modifications are quite significant and are designed to bring his theory of language into line with the changes he formulated in his theory of mind. Simple consciousness, or first-level consciousness, replaced his earlier notion of psychical experience. Similarly, psychical expression had to be jettisoned in order to accommodate this change. Language, which had appeared only at the second level of experience, namely consciousness or imagination, now emerged at the level of simple consciousness: 'Language in its simplest form is the language of consciousness in its simplest form; the mere "register" of feelings' (*NL,* 6.58). Collingwood takes language to be any form of bodily movement, including the production of sounds, the use of which is designed to mean or signify something. This entails the abandonment of the distinction he had made earlier between language, which is expressive, and intellectualized language, which has meaning. All language now has meaning, because language makes its appearance in the act of naming things. Feelings are immediately present to consciousness, and we become conscious of them by means of language. To feel something entails naming that feeling, whether it be by means of speech or by the use of a gesture which is the equivalent of the name articulated in speech. Naming the feeling awakens consciousness of it. The feeling does not come first and the name following after: 'Until you name it, feeling is preconscious. When you name it, it becomes conscious' (*NL,* 6.28). The act of naming our feelings occurs at the level of simple consciousness. To become aware that we have named a particular feeling, or selectively to attend to the act of naming it – that is, to be conscious that we are conscious of a particular feeling – is an act of second-level consciousness.

There is no point in asking why human beings bring about various changes in the mind which initiate development. The process is not intentional, because intentions do not feature in consciousness until the fourth level has been achieved. Nor are any of the steps ever necessary. No law governs the development of the human mind. Language, however, is crucial in this development because each transition from one stage to another is brought about by a linguistic act (*NL,* 7.25–7.29). The linguistic act which initiates the transition from the first to the second level of consciousness is conceptual thinking:

Concepts or abstractions are not things lying about in the world, ready-made, like blackberries, for the sedulous *micher* to find; they are things that man makes (and perhaps not man alone, but man alone is what we are studying) by an act of practical thinking; and if he then finds them ready-made it is because that act has made them (*NL*, 7.22).

Language and consciousness develop in unison. The transition from the second to the third level of consciousness is brought about by language developing indicative sentences in terms of which propositions can be stated. The step from the third level to the fourth level of consciousness, that is, the stage at which consciousness becomes reason, is accomplished when 'language becomes demonstrative discourse wherein sentences are so linked together as to state verbally "the Consequences of one Affirmation to another" ' (*NL*, 6.59).

In *The Principles of Art* Collingwood believed that he had detected an error in Hobbes's theory of language. Hobbes, in suggesting that 'the primary use of speech is for "acquisition of science", for which purpose "the right definition of names" is the first requisite',[95] committed the error of associating language in general with language in its intellectualized form. This criticism, however, is no longer pertinent in *The New Leviathan,* and Collingwood gives due credit to Hobbes for having made an invaluable contribution to the theory of language. This contribution has been noticed by R. M. Martin and, more recently, by Terence Ball. Martin, for instance, argues that Hobbes's theory of language is in many ways the forerunner of modern semantics. Truth, for Hobbes, is an attribute, not of objects or things, but of speech, in particular of affirmations and sentences.[96] Ball goes even farther and credits Hobbes with ideas that we now associate with Wittgenstein and J. L. Austin. Hobbes, Ball contends, understood speech 'as the medium through which we *do* things with words' and, 'to borrow a distinction from Saussure, we might say that Hobbes became progressively less interested in *language* and more in *parole,* or language-in-use'.[97]

Neither Martin nor Ball appears to have been aware that Collingwood had, long before them, credited Hobbes with having held views which foreshadowed modern linguistic theories. Collingwood argues that it was one of Hobbes's greatest achievements to discover that language is a prerequisite of knowledge. Without language there can be no knowledge, communication, nor society. In arriving at this conclusion Collingwood places considerable emphasis upon Hobbes's comments on numbering. In Hobbes's view, some forms of mental activity cannot even begin without the use of language: 'Without words, there is no possibility of reckoning of Numbers; much less of Magnitudes, of Swiftness, of Force, and other things'.[98] In order to make this applicable to knowledge more generally conceived, Collingwood suggests that Hobbes believed that science, with mathematics at its foundation, was knowledge of anything, with the exception of isolated facts, which related 'the Consequence of one Affirmation to another'. On the basis of this very broad understanding of scientific thought, Collingwood concludes that, for Hobbes, 'from being an indispensable means to the diffusion of knowledge, language has become the precondition and foundation of knowledge, so far as knowledge is scientific' (*NL*, 6.47.).[99]

In summary, then, Collingwood argues that language is a prerequisite of knowledge. Without language there could be no mental development. Even at the highest level of consciousness it is language that begets reason, and not reason that begets language. Furthermore, without language there can be no society.

5

Collingwood's liberal politics

1. Introduction

In the preceding chapter we saw that Collingwood's theory of rational action, discussed in Chapter 3, is the culminating phase of his comprehensive philosophy of mind. At the level of first-order consciousness, feelings and their emotional charges, which are the appanages of mind, are merely registered, without discrimination or differentiation. Feelings are something which the mind has; consciousness is what mind is. By selectively attending to feelings, we enter the second level of consciousness, in which conceptual thought and appetite overlap. At the third level, mind is capable of propositional thinking, which overlaps with desire. At the fourth level, the mind is will, capable at first of making capricious choices and distinguishing between good and evil. The gradual elimination of caprice takes place when mind develops through the three stages of practical and theoretical reason. Each of the levels of practical reason has its concomitant theoretical counterpart: Utility contributes to a view of the world which is teleological; right has its counterpart in modern scientific explanation in terms of the laws of nature and conformity to these laws; and duty, as a form of practical reason, has its theoretical expression in historical explanation.

In this chapter we will begin by examining Collingwood's dissatisfaction with classical political theories and will then go on to explore his theory of society, which he believed supplied the element missing in the classical theories. Classical theorists such as Hobbes, Locke, and Rousseau had much to say about the social community but, Collingwood thought, failed to discuss adequately the nonsocial community out of which the social is continually replenished, if society's lasting existence is to be ensured. Collingwood saw the body politic as a mixed community, comprising nonsocial and social elements, the primary function of the latter being

141

to promote and encourage the former to complete the process of transition from the nonsocial to the social spheres.

During the course of this chapter Collingwood's affinities with liberalism will become more and more evident. Even though he owed a good deal to the actual idealism of Gentile, Collingwood could not accept nor condone the fascist conclusions which Gentile drew out of his philosophical theory of the will. Instead, Collingwood saw freedom of the will, not in conflict with other free wills and therefore compelled to dominate them, but instead as necessarily implying the acknowledgement of and respect for the freedom of other wills, without which there could be no society and no civilization. In this respect Collingwood was in sympathy with de Ruggiero's social liberalism and, to a certain extent, with Croce's more restricted conception of liberalism.

2. Classical politics and the problem it fails to solve

In Chapter 2 of this book, in discussing the reasons why Collingwood wrote *The New Leviathan,* I suggested that C. E. M. Joad's exhortation to philosophers to return to the classical tradition, and H. D. Lewis's suggestion that the idea of the social contract had much to offer political philosophy, formed a context within which Collingwood's own thoughts were developing. Let us now see how Collingwood took up these suggestions and used them in formulating the problems that he hoped that *The New Leviathan* would solve.

Joad was of the view that Plato and Aristotle, in particular, exemplified the classical tradition, and that it was to them that we should turn for inspiration in the troubled times of twentieth-century Europe.[1] Lewis, on the other hand, believing that the idea of a social contract had much to offer modern philosophy, turned to Hobbes, Locke, and Rousseau for inspiration. It is clear from Lewis's argument that he believes that of the three contract theorists Hobbes had by far the most significant things to say. Lewis's high opinion of Hobbes is illustrated, for example, in the following assessment: 'As regards the account of the essential nature of the State itself, it would be hard to improve upon the *Leviathan*'.[2]

Collingwood, by implication, disagrees with Joad's evaluation of the importance of Plato and Aristotle as sources of theoretical insights into the political condition, but is in implicit agreement over the question of the need to return to the classical tradition. What Collingwood means by *classical* is different from the meaning which Joad employs. For Collingwood, the *classical politics* refers to the attempt to formulate a science of political life; the initiator of this effort was Thomas Hobbes. In Collingwood's view, Locke and Rousseau restated the theory in ways which are only marginally different from that of the founder. The return to the classical theorists is important, not because they made the definitive and final statements on the topic of political society, but because they point the way towards a better, or more adequate, understanding of political life. The theory towards which these three theorists contributed is 'classical in the sense that every beginner in the subject, on pain of going ill-grounded, must start with it' (*NL,* 31.23).[3] What makes the three classical theorists particularly well suited to the formulation of such a theory was the fact that they were not professors, but men whose interests in politics were formed by participation, and by conversations with those whose lives revolved around political activity.[4] The audience to which they addressed themselves was deemed to possess certain qualities: namely, enough experience of political life and social relationships to enable its members to know intimately the kinds of problems that the political theorists were tackling. Such experiences, Collingwood suggests, were 'general throughout the civilized world' (*NL,* 32.82) – so general, in fact, that the *Leviathan* 'could be understood without a commentary not only by another Englishman like John Locke but by a Portuguese Jew living in Holland' (*NL,* 32.9).

An admirable feature of the work of the theorists of the classical politics is that they all set limited objectives. They did not attempt to explain everything about political life – only that which they believed to be apposite to the circumstances about which they theorized. Their objective was to explain a certain class of political facts in relation to the notion of *society.*[5] They took their lead from the Roman idea of *societas,* and explained the partnership as one which had its origins in a *social contract.* It is that contract which gave rise to the obligations indicative of social relations. The partnerships which informed their deliberations were not those of the Roman citizen, but those partnerships which arose in medieval and modern Europe, imbued with the tradition of Roman law. The aim of the theorists of classical politics was to limit themselves '*to study the social elements in political life'* (*NL,* 32.16). They were aware that political life combined both social and nonsocial elements, and they referred to the latter as *nature,* or the state of nature, out of which mentally mature human beings emerged into society by entering into a social contract. Political life, to these theorists, Collingwood tells us, was a dialectic between the polarized opposites of *society* and *nature,* the former of which referred to that element comprised of mentally mature persons entering into agreements with a view to collective action, and the latter of which referred to everything else that was not to be found in political life. In Collingwood's view,

32.3.   The great merit of the classical politics is that it knows political life to be dynamic or dialectical. It teaches that, of the two ends between which political life is polarized, one is positive and the other negative. It teaches that the positive end is social in character: that is, consists of relations between human beings established by their free adoption of a joint purpose.[6]

This entails the view that people in the state of nature must be educated to a level at which they attain the capacity to exercise free will, and hence become converted from the nonsocial into the social condition. The responsibility for facilitating such a process falls squarely upon the shoulders of those who already constitute a society. Rousseau, Collingwood maintains, saw more clearly than either Hobbes or Locke (although such a view is implied in both) that 'the life of politics is the life of political education' (*NL*, 32.34). The fact that political life is dynamic, that is, involves the conversion of individuals from one condition to another, entails a heightened understanding of the end towards which this process is directed. Such knowledge is imperative in the conduct of political life: imperative, that is, to the rulers, or ruling class in the body politic, who are charged with the duty of providing the means by which the conversion process can occur.

Rousseau was confused, however, in believing that man is born free and everywhere found in chains. To possess freedom entails having a will which is not constrained by forces outside the self. To be chained implies that the will is hindered from finding expression in action. In Collingwood's view, a baby simply has no will, that is, has not reached the level of consciousness appropriate to will, nor can it do so without the conditions conducive to such an end. People are born without a will and are thus rendered totally at the mercy of their parents, and 'that is what no science of human community, social or nonsocial, must ever forget' (*NL*, 23.97).

Collingwood admitted, as we saw, that the political arguments expressed in de Ruggiero's *History of European Liberalism* were everywhere Collingwood's own. This emphasis upon freedom being an achievement and not an innate attribute of human life is a view firmly espoused by de Ruggiero, who was in turn, as Collingwood himself recognised, echoing some of the ideas of Green, but in a far more organized and complete manner.[7] In de Ruggiero's view, 'Men are not born free, they become free by means of society and the State. . . . This is the great distinction between the liberal conceptions of the eighteenth and nineteenth centuries. The one places liberty at the beginning, the other at the end, of the historical process'.[8]

If it were the case that the nonsocial is eliminated in the process of conversion into the social, then, Collingwood believes, the theorists of classical politics would have been justified in not having provided, or in not wanting to provide, a theory of the nonsocial element in political life. These theorists were not, however, optimistic about the possibility of the social condition wholly superseding the state of nature. Hobbes, for instance, thought that in certain respects individuals remain in the state of nature even after having entered civil society. Furthermore, Hobbes believed that some people never emerge from the state of nature at all. What is more disturbing, however, Collingwood states, is the fact that progress is not inevitable. Hobbes was in no doubt that the process of conversion was reversible; the social element in the community could revert back to the nonsocial (*NL,* 32.42–32.6).[9]

The theorists of the classical politics, in acknowledging the perpetual danger of regression, merely postponed rather than eliminated the necessity for a theory of the nonsocial community. This, for Collingwood, is the failure of the whole classical politics, that is, the inability of the theorists 'to attach any positive meaning to the phrase "state of nature", . . . into which babies are born and hence not born free' (*NL,* 33.18). One of the purposes of Collingwood's enterprise was to make good this failure of the classical politics and formulate a science of politics in which the nonsocial and social elements in political life are adequately accounted for.

3. Collingwood's solution to the problem of classical politics

Collingwood maintains a clear distinction between a *society* and a *community.* Every society is a community, but not every community is a society.[10] The 'true and proper sense' (*NL,* 19.11) of the word *society* Collingwood takes to signify a whole which is composed of parts. It is a kind of whole, or form of group cohesion, unlike a *class.* A class is a whole whose parts are related to each other by having a particular *kind* and *degree* of resemblance. Determining what the kind and degree are is a classificatory act which has to be performed by some specific person. This is a practical distinction, circumscribing one class of facts from another. A society, however, is a relationship of a different kind. In modern Europe, deriving its source from Roman law, a society, or *societas,* is a relation between persons who are capable of suing and of being sued, that is, individuals who possess the capacity of free will and who are capable of joining together to take joint action. The relationship is established by means of a consensual contract. Under Roman law such contracts must satisfy three criteria. First, the agreement must be reciprocal. Second, there must be a common interest whereby the parties derive benefits from the partnership. Third, there must be a genuine intention on the part of those who invoke the relationship to form a partnership.

Variations of the term *society* that disregard the idea of free will are dismissed as being perversions of its true meaning. There can be no society among people or objects that have not attained the level of rational consciousness. A society has 'a *suum cuique*, that is, a one–one relation between sharers or participants and shares', (*NL*, 19.11), and 'the establishment and maintenance of the *suum cuique* is effected by their joint activity as free agents' (*NL*, 19.8).

A community also has a *suum cuique*. It makes no difference to its being a community what that *suum cuique* is, but it does make a difference to what type of a community it is. A community can, for instance, consist of a group of children who constitute a community of apple sharers and whose communal habits have developed in the course of their practical activities. A community is a community because it shares something. In this respect a society is a kind of community in that its members share a *social consciousness*, or possess a will. To be socially conscious is to be conscious of freedom. It is to be conscious of oneself as free, and it is the acknowledgement of others as the possessors of freedom. In other words, a social consciousness requires those who are conscious of their freedom to have reached the level of rational consciousness in the development of the mind. Without such an attainment, consciousness of freedom, and hence social consciousness, are impossibilities.[11] A society, then, can consist only of mentally adult persons, each one of whom

is bound to recognize in others the same kind of freedom which he claims for himself; and therefore each must recognize the will of these others as a source of rules binding on himself. And this is not a mutual slavery, because the joint enterprises out of which these rules grow are pursued by each party of his own free will.[12]

Given Collingwood's emphasis upon the inextricable relation between freedom and society, it is now clear why he felt the need to plot the stages through which the mind must develop in order to achieve such a prized possession. Freedom, that is rational consciousness, is something to be valued above all else, and it is something without which no society can exist.

Gentile's doctrine of the mind as pure act places the knowing mind in the centre of creating that which it knows. Thought as pure act is the foundation upon which the world of experience rests. Thought is its own criterion of truth: The world is made in the act of knowing it. Thought and will, or theory and practice, are unified in the self's creation of reality. This radical autonomy of the will, as Richard Bellamy has pointed out, gives us all 'equally valid grounds for regarding our own will as an autonomous spiritual creation, and those opposed to it as objects to be absorbed and organised within it'.[13] The conflict between these competing

autonomous wills is overcome by the domination of all wills by one will.
This is the idea from which Gentile's fascism stems. The state is such a
will, which has emerged to impose its will and absorb that of others
within itself. The will of the individual and the will of the state are identified. The universal will is that will which possesses the force to make
itself so. Law and force are therefore correlatives. In being forced to recognise the compulsion of the will which imposes this law, we are, according to Gentile, free and united with the universal will.

For Collingwood, however, the autonomy of the free will cannot be
undermined in this way without ceasing to be autonomous and free. Consciousness of freedom implied for Gentile the imposition of one's free
will upon others, whereas for Collingwood consciousness of freedom
necessarily entails consciousness of the same capacity for acting in others.
This is the sole basis of a social community, which is a collection of
individuals capable of free choice, having chosen to pursue a joint purpose
with others whom they deem equally as free and rational. Without such
consciousness there can be no society, only a nonsocial community in
which mentally immature people without the capacity of freedom of
choice are ruled over by force, and in which those who rule pervert or
suppress the development of consciousness and thus inhibit, or even destroy, the process of conversion from the nonsocial to the social.

In prizing so highly freedom and its development Collingwood was
echoing the sentiments of many British and Italian idealists. Kant, of
course, was a major source of inspiration, but Kant could give an account
of freedom only as it had developed up to his own day. For most of the
British and Italian idealists, the development of freedom was correlative
with the development of liberalism in Europe, that is, it made its greatest
strides in the latter half of the nineteenth century and in the early part
of the twentieth. In Italy, both de Ruggiero and Croce were the champions
of liberalism and freedom. Croce explicitly equated 'philosophical idealism
... with the liberal concept of life'.[14] The liberal concept of life, for Croce,
was not merely that of free enterprise; to elevate the economic to the
status of ethics is to posit a hedonistic or utilitarian morality. Liberty, or
freedom, for the liberal, does not 'accept as prized possessions only those
which satisfy the pleasure of the individual'. For Croce, 'the "Liberty" of
which liberalism means to speak is intended to promote spiritual life in
its entirety and, consequently, only in so far as it is moral life'.[15]

Liberalism, the love of liberty, is an eminently practical doctrine which
should oppose economic measures only on the ground that they impede
'moral development and progress'. Ethical liberalism is compatible with
many measures that abstract theorists may classify as socialist. Indeed,
Croce suggests that it is 'even possible to speak of a "liberal socialism",
as I remember is done in a beautiful English eulogy and apology for lib-

eralism by L. T. Hobhouse'.[16] The liberal concept of freedom is opposed
only to authoritarian socialism, that is, only to that element which impedes
the development of the freedom of the will. It is compatible with that
type of socialism which shares liberal principles, and which can therefore
easily be absorbed into, or accommodated by, the latter. Liberalism is
able to learn from socialism, and did indeed benefit from the inadvertent
impetus that the latter gave to breaking the too close association, almost
to the point of identity, 'between liberalism and economic freedom, morals
and economy, ethical institutions and economic institutions',[17] because
liberalism for Croce was not so much a definite list of political practices
as a disposition of the mind towards openness in assessing different view-
points. Such openness allowed liberalism to respond to different conditions in a variety of ways, even to the extent of absorbing some aspects
of socialism which did not impair liberalism's disposition towards openness. In terms of ideals, then, there could be no compromise between
socialism and liberalism, but in terms of political practice the one could
contribute something to the other. Similarly, de Ruggiero maintains that
liberalism and freedom have developed correlatively. In the eighteenth
century, he suggests, a negative freedom developed. The emphasis was
upon doing what one liked, on the assumption that individuals possessed
rights which should not be hindered. Out of this concept grew the positive, constructive notion of freedom: 'According to this, freedom is not
indeterminate caprice, but man's ability to determine himself, and thus
by the spontaneous act of his own consciousness to rise above the ne-
cessities and the bonds in which practical life imprisons him'.[18] To permit
capricious freedom, de Ruggiero maintains, is to sow the seeds of destruction for civil life. The liberal concept of freedom guarantees that
different free wills are able to coexist in the same society. Freedom can
develop only within society, and society cannot flourish without freedom.
Freedom is an achievement, not a benefit conferred.[19] For de Ruggiero
the fundamental principle of liberalism is its assumption that human beings
have a spiritual freedom which is not explicable in terms of reductionist
interpretations. Liberalism 'posits a free individual conscious of his capacity for unfettered development and self-expression'[20] and capable of
creating the institutions within which this spiritual development can take
place. The individualism of classical liberalism had, in de Ruggiero's view,
given way to a more organic conception of society in which the antinomy
of individualism and authority is resolved. In the theoretical and ideo-
logical realm, T. H. Green and L. T. Hobhouse had contributed greatly
to the articulation of this form of liberalism. Green, de Ruggiero argues,
recognised quite clearly that freedom is not enhanced by a mere lack of
restrictions, nor can it be enjoyed at the expense of others. Freedom is
a capacity, or power, which enables us to do or enjoy, in common with

other members of society, those things that are worth doing and enjoying. It follows for Green, and for de Ruggiero, that contracts which demean or effectively enslave an individual are void. Society is therefore justified in restricting freedoms which are detrimental to, or are at the expense of, the freedom of others.[21] Liberalism's hostility to the state, de Ruggiero contends, has diminished because of liberalism's involvement in government and administration and also, partially, because the state has become more capable of synthetically expressing the varied interests in society. In addition, changes in social life have generated problems so complex that individuals left to their own devices could not be expected to solve them. Individuals create for themselves the state under whose auspices they develop their characters, and the state 'has become conscious of its duty to contribute positively to the individual's education, and to broaden and strengthen the energies of individuals and of their free and voluntary associations'.[22] In summary, then, liberalism's transformation from a predominantly libertarian conception of society to a more collectivist view had, as far as de Ruggiero was concerned, been a change for the better. Collingwood's own account of the development of the freedom of the will and its gradual elimination of capriciousness is a theoretical and extended articulation of de Ruggiero's point that freedom is an achievement rather than an endowment.

The British idealists were no less vociferous in their support of liberalism[23] and in equating it, not with mere laissez-faire doctrines, but with a positive concept of freedom. The role of government within society was, in their view, to promote freedom. Green, for instance, espoused a similar view to that of Collingwood in suggesting that it is 'only so far as a certain freedom of action and acquisition is secured to a body of men through their recognition of the exercise of that freedom by each other as being for the common good, is there an actualisation of the individual's consciousness of having life and ends of his own'.[24] Henry Jones, to give another instance, argued fervently against the negative concept of freedom. An isolated will opposed to the state and society is no will. This excessive individualism is nihilism.[25] Freedom and society are truly compatible; neither is possible without the other. Freedom is something that we have to attain: What we constantly overlook is the fact 'that man is not born free. He is born capable of becoming more and more free by his intercourse with his fellows and his experience of the world'.[26] Jones was opposed to 'some forms of modern Socialism' because they had not taken to heart the fact that no legislation can be good which weakens individuality or restricts the enterprise of the people.[27] Generally speaking, British idealists denied that liberty is doing what one desires; instead, liberty can only be promoted in relation to obedience to the laws. Self-realisation is possible only in a social context.

L. T. Hobhouse also must be mentioned in this context, because his social liberalism was admired by de Ruggiero and complimented by Croce. Hobhouse was hostile to some aspects of idealism, especially the authoritarian implications he detected in Hegel's and Bosanquet's theories of the state.[28] Hobhouse, nevertheless, admired Green and was sympathetic to his organic view of society, in which each individual was conceived as an element in an interdependent whole. Thus, suffering and degradation could not be isolated and allowed to go unchecked, because of their implications for the moral and spiritual life of the organism in general. The state, in Hobhouse's view, was one 'among many forms of human association' which had a responsibility 'for the maintenance and improvement of life'.[29] Human freedom, Hobhouse suggests, is exhibited in our ability to determine the social institutions and practices in which our ends are formulated and pursued. Freedom, he claims, depends upon the use of compulsion which is both limited and defined. If compulsion prevents others from frustrating my enjoyment of a common liberty, then it augments my freedom, but it is a fallacy to suggest that freedom is augmented by laws which prohibit me from drinking or compel me to serve in the army. Restrictions of the latter kind may be justified if other freedoms are enhanced, but they do not make a difference to the fact that restrictions have been placed upon freedoms, even if others are secured at the expense of those restrictions. Political freedom, Hobhouse claims, exists when differences are tolerated and when they are valued as contributions to a life which is richer and more varied. Freedom is something which members of a community share, and that which frustrates such sharing can justifiably be restrained. A society is free when its laws ensure that the potential for the development of the person and for free association are unhindered. A society, then, is free only 'where all minds have that fullness of scope which can be obtained if certain fundamental conditions of their mutual intercourse are maintained by organized effort'.[30] In addition, political freedom is correlative with citizens actively participating in the decision-making process. The freedom of citizenship consists, not in the fact that common decisions coincide with my own, but in the fact that I enjoy the same scope for expressing my views 'as anyone can have if all are to have it and yet live and act together'.[31]

New Liberals, in general, saw themselves as moving away from the negative concept of liberty which emphasized the importance of the lack of constraints upon, or government interference in, spontaneous and free human development. Instead, they embraced a positive concept of liberty, which emphasized equality of opportunity and the duty of society to make it possible for those who were less fortunate to have ample opportunity to develop fully their potential. Ramsey Muir was representative of this new tendency in liberalism when he argued that 'liberty is not merely a negative thing, mere absence of restraints; it is a positive thing. No man is really free until he possesses, in sufficient degree the material basis of liberty'.[32] Andrew Vincent and Raymond Plant go as far as to suggest that the idealists, practically committed to liberalism, were the only ones in late nineteenth- and early twentieth-century Britain who had a coherent theory of positive liberty.[33] This theory denied that liberty entailed doing what one desires; instead liberty could only be promoted in relation to obedience to the laws. Self-realisation is possible only in a social context.

This distinction between negative and positive liberty, which was commonly made by liberals whose sympathies lay with intervention, may in retrospect appear facile in the light of more recent philosophical discussions of the concept of freedom. Gerald C. MacCallum, Jr., has argued that the distinction made between positive and negative freedom has served to confuse our understanding of the concept. Such a bifurcated view of liberty has resulted, he suggests, from a lack of clarity in identifying the nature of the disputes between those who wish to determine the specifications of the concept. MacCallum claims that negative and positive freedom are not two separate and distinct types of freedom. On the contrary, freedom is one concept, or model, comprising a relation among three variables. Every statement about freedom, even if only implicitly, has three distinguishable referents: It is a statement (first) about an agent who (second) is constrained or unconstrained to (third) do a particular act or be a particular something.[34] Freedom is never either/or, negative and positive, but always both at the same time. For example, freedom *from* hunger entails being free *from* certain barriers, such as agricultural, social, economic, and political obstacles, which renders me free *to* acquire sufficient food to stave off hunger. Disputes about freedom are not about what freedom *is,* but about the ranges of the variables, 'for example about what persons are, and about what can count as an obstacle to or interference with the freedom of persons so conceived'.[35]

Collingwood's concept of freedom escapes MacCallum's criticism. There are different kinds of freedom, Collingwood argues, but of course they are not separate species of a genus. Freedom is a philosophical concept which includes within itself a unity of differences in kind with differences of degree, and a fusion of opposites and distincts. Each kind of freedom is both negative and positive. In its positive aspect, it is freedom to do certain things; in its negative aspect, it is freedom from certain compulsions. In Collingwood's view, 'Freedom of the will is, positively, *freedom to choose;* freedom to exercise a will; and, negatively, freedom *from desire;* not the condition of having no desires, but the condition of not being at their mercy' (*NL,* 13.25). MacCallum has argued that much of the confusion about the idea of freedom has emanated from the 'tacit presumption that persons can be free or not free *simpliciter*.'[36] This again is a criticism which cannot be applied to Collingwood. In his view, freedom of choice is not a matter of absolutes, but of degrees. Capricious choice is free choice, but it embodies the generic essence in a low degree. Compared to the stage above it, in which freedom finds expression in utilitarian choice, it is relatively crude, irrational, and unsophisticated, because freedom in the higher stage is more fully developed and less subject to caprice. The same relation pertains between each form and that which supersedes it.

Collingwood was thoroughly familiar with the practical and theoretical concerns of both the Italian and British idealists. Like these theorists, he was in full sympathy with the European liberal tradition and the gains it had made in the realm of personal freedom. In his *Autobiography* Collingwood readily confesses that his political inclinations had always been 'democratic' or 'liberal'.[37] His praise of Marx in the same book, although qualified, is compatible with the view that the modern generation of liberals took towards socialism. De Ruggiero, for example, praised socialism very highly indeed for its compassion towards the poor. He saw socialism as having played a positive role in forcing liberalism away from laissez-faire economics and towards a more humane concept of society. 'Socialism has been of great value to Liberalism' in that the former taught the latter that abstract formulations and declarations of individual rights and duties were often a vindication of the power of the strong over the weak. Such declarations must be accompanied by positive sanctions, in order to assure these rights for everyone. De Ruggiero went on to suggest that 'by following the action of Socialism for the improvement of wages and the general condition of the working classes, Liberalism has had occasion to see how groundless were the arguments by which employers justified their stubborn resistance'.[38]

It is not this liberal socialism, but mechanical socialism, that liberalism rejected. Mechanical socialism equates social life with economic forces which themselves give rise to class warfare. Such rigid distinctions among the interests of the classes are, in de Ruggiero's view, nonexistent',[39] because in modern society there is an increasingly complex system of interactions among class interests which defy simplification. Property, for instance, cannot be attacked in the name of labour without at the same time encroaching upon the interest that labour has, indirectly or directly, in the maintenance of property. The work of Henry Jones is again illustrative of the compatibility of liberalism and socialism. Ramsey MacDonald, for instance, responding to Jones's attack on the class appeal of the Labour party and its potential for promoting divisiveness, claimed that Jones's accusations were unfair and that the ethical grounds upon which they were based were at every point those of the Labour party.[40]

It is clear from Collingwood's published and unpublished works that his attitude towards Marx, communism, and socialism was similar to that of other idealist liberal philosophers. There were, he believed, many positive aspects to the doctrines associated with the Left, but they always presented only half truths, whereas fascism and nazism perpetrated downright lies. Collingwood argues, for instance, that the 'Marxian interpretation of history was legitimate and in its day valuable' in emphasizing the need to study economic history, but in so far as it claimed that economic facts are the only facts that are important 'and form the *real* skeleton of history, it is simply a philosophical blunder'.[41] In his *Autobiography,* Collingwood states quite clearly that he had never been convinced by Marx's economics nor his metaphysics; what he admired was Marx's fighting spirit, that is, his courage to stand up and announce his intention to change the world.[42]

Collingwood, like other liberal idealists, associated communism and some forms of socialism with class war. If class war were ever to win out in Europe, it would mean the destruction of all that we hold dear.[43] Government by class is not wrong because it promotes a particular interest; it is wrong because it 'governs with a partial conception of the interest of the whole'.[44] This was also true, nevertheless, of unrestrained capitalism: 'The dictatorship of the capitalist will destroy things no less precious'.[45] This does not mean that Collingwood wanted to see the demise of either socialism or capitalism. Instead he saw them as 'co-existent tendencies in the economic organisation of one single age'.[46]

The suggestion that Collingwood moved radically to the Left[47] in his *Autobiography* is largely illusory. Collingwood did not abandon the principles of liberalism; he believed that everyone else had. In 1936 he was suggesting that people were abandoning all attempts to live by liberal principles. There was much too strong an emphasis upon distinguishing between private interests and public interests, with too little concern for the common good.[48] The *Autobiography* itself castigated the politicians and the popular press for having attacked liberal principles.[49] Similarly, Collingwood continued to bemoan the subversion of liberal principles in his article 'Nazism and Fascism'. In this article he held up for adulation the fundamental beliefs in freedom of thought, freedom of enquiry, and freedom of political persuasion. Such freedoms are derived from Christianity: 'The real ground for the "liberal" or "democratic" devotion to freedom was religious love of a God who set an absolute value on every individual human being'.[50] Collingwood was convinced of the wisdom of liberal and democratic thought but pessimistic about the passion with which people treasured it.[51] In a later essay Collingwood maintained that part of the very idea of a body politic connoted the notion of freedom. The problem with the liberal political doctrine was that in stressing the positive concept of liberty it ignored the fact that 'there is always in any body politic a ruled element whose function in the body is to accept the initiative of an element stronger and more active than itself'.[52]

It turns out, then, that not only is the lack of a theory of the nonsocial community, that is, the nonsocial element which is converted into the social, a defect of the classical politics; it is also a defect of liberalism. *The New Leviathan,* in making good this defect, is at once furthering classical politics and reaffirming the principles of liberalism by placing them on a firmer foundation.

A society, in Collingwood's view, entails consciousness of freedom, but a community does not. A community is logically, but not necessarily temporally, prior to a society, and is, in its presocietal state, a nonsocial community. A community maintains its cohesion because its members share in something they think desirable, in whatever proportion the shares are allocated; those members remain faithful as long as they agree with the allotment. Maintaining the *suum cuique* is 'the essence of its communal character' (*NL,* 20.34). Ruling is the business of establishing and maintaining the *suum cuique.* In this respect, Collingwood makes an important distinction. By implication, from what has previously been said, those who lack the capacity of free will lack the capacity to rule, because ruling requires the faculty of freedom of choice. A nonsocial community, then, is incapable of ruling itself and is incapable of existing without being ruled. A society, on the other hand, is self-ruling. Its members, who are mentally mature, have the power of self-determination. This Collingwood calls *immanent* rule; a condition in which the ruled and the rulers are the same people. Rule is *transeunt* when the rulers rule over something other than themselves. A nonsocial community, if it is to exist at all, must be subject to transeunt rule, whereas a society, or social community, is self-determining in that it exercises a joint will. Such a community originates and maintains itself. Its genesis is the result of an act on the part of the joint will. This same joint will is capable of bringing into existence a nonsocial community over which it exercises transeunt rule. Between the two communities the relation is that of dependency by the nonsocial upon the social. Such a relation is not one of the latter having authority over the former, because those who comprise the nonsocial community are not in a position to confer authority. Authority, then, is a relation which pertains to the social community, or society, which entails a person who has authority and another person (or persons) who authorises (or authorise) the authority. In the case of the relation between the social and nonsocial communities, authority may be conferred by one person upon another in society. That person would then be authorised to perform certain functions in relation to the nonsocial community. The exercise of such functions may require the use of force. What force means in this context is one person's mental superiority over another (*NL,* 20.1–20.6).

A society, then, is comprised of agents who possess and exercise free will. Free will is, nevertheless, subject to gradation. The strength of will a society possesses must be equal to, or greater than, that needed to execute the joint enterprise upon which it has embarked. Without the strength of will, such enterprises may fail. Such societal enterprises must be freely entered into by means of any form of expression recognisable to the other members. In addition, by what Collingwood calls 'the *Principle of Limited Liability'* (*NL,* 20.65), the obligation of the person to the society is limited to that which the chosen enterprise implies. The society of marriage, for instance, entails obligations implied by, and appropriate to, the enterprise embarked upon. Where one partner is unable to discharge such obligations, perhaps because he, or she, lacks the strength of will to do so, then that person ceases to be a partner in the society, and, because in this case only two partners comprise the society, the partnership ceases to exist.

We see again that Collingwood's theory of mind is the foundation upon which his theory of society is built, because this theory explains how people become capable of possessing a social consciousness. A person whose mind has developed far enough to be able to think 'I will' has, in the process of doing so, become accustomed to distinguish the self from the not-self. To distinguish oneself as a self of a certain kind entails the idea of something other than oneself of the same kind. Similarly, 'the idea of oneself as having a will is correlative . . . to the idea of someone other than oneself as having a will' (*NL,* 21.14). To think of oneself as a free agent is inseparable from thinking of others as free agents. The idea of free agency is correlative with the idea of free agents other than oneself and among whom social relations exist. Consciousness of oneself as free entails association with others who are free, and this association can become manifest only in the form of social relations. Rational consciousness and social consciousness are two sides of the same coin: 'No man can think himself free except as integrated in a context of other free men constituting with himself a society' (*NL,* 21.76). De Ruggiero says something similar in maintaining that it is only the fact that we have attained freedom which enables us to recognise it in others. Only in asserting oneself as a person, an autonomous free will, does one recognise the right of others to assert themselves as persons: 'This understanding or recognition does not imply a merely theoretical observation; it also signifies a respect for that which it observes, a personal moral adhesion'.[53]

Naturally there are points of similarity between Collingwood and de

Ruggiero, since they are both, in their different ways, dealing with the same subject matter. The principles of liberalism with which de Ruggiero is concerned, namely the establishment, maintenance, and guarantee of positive liberties for every adult human being, are the same principles with which Collingwood is concerned in relation to the development of the European mind and the social and political institutions to which it gave rise. Collingwood and de Ruggiero were both sympathetic to liberal values, so it is not at all surprising that they should come to similar conclusions as to their place in European history.

In Collingwood's view, 'Most communities, if not all, are mixed communities' (*NL*, 22.11). The nonsocial community is comprised of those persons who have not yet attained rational consciousness, and the social community is comprised of those who have. Even if the whole of the nonsocial element becomes converted into the social, there always remains an element of the former out of which the latter develops (*NL*, 21.44). It appears, then, that the law of primitive survivals which operates in relation to the development of the mind also pertains to the development of societies. This view is confirmed by the position that Collingwood advances in a manuscript on fairy tales. He argues that the emotional life of the savage found expression in the various rituals and magical practices of primitive cultures. Modern societies still retain distinct traces of the primitive cultures out of which they grew. In order to understand our own culture, we must understand the cultures of primitive peoples. We can do this only by learning to 'face the savage within us'.[54] Following the same line of thought, it is necessary to understand the nonsocial community in order to understand the social community.

A family constitutes an example of what Collingwood means by a *mixed community*. A family is comprised of a social element instituted by the free will of mentally mature persons, and a nonsocial element which is the nursery, or the children, who did not choose to be part of such a community because they simply lacked the free will to do so. Similarly, the same deficiency makes them ill equipped to run the nursery themselves. In such a mixed community there are parents who replenish the nursery and nurses who run it. In most instances parents discharge both functions. The nursery is not self-filling, but it is self-emptying, because, with few exceptions, the children attain the level of mental maturity required to enter a society. In savage cultures puberty indicates the emergence from childhood and heralds entry into the adult membership of the tribe. In European life, however, the complexities that surround our cultural practices require a longer 'educational preparation' (*NL*, 22.32) before one is initiated into the society, or social element, of the family.

The society which is the nucleus of the family is what Collingwood calls a *temporary society*, that is, one which is instituted with the intention of it coming to an end within a certain period of time. In the case of the society set up by the marriage act, it is 'for "so long as ye both shall live" ' (*NL*, 21.93). Not every culture has deemed its women capable of entering into the marriage contract. In some cultures women were not believed to possess the requisite degree of free will required to make such a decision. In Collingwood's view, there need be no contradiction between modern beliefs about the capacities of women and those different beliefs held in the past. Such differences in belief can probably be accounted for by differences in the education of women (*NL*, 23.38). Even in the modern marriage practices of Europeans, traces of past rituals survive. It is still customary, Collingwood suggests, for the bride to be given away by the father, or someone representing him, as if the bride were incapable of entering into a contract. The survival is not a mere anachronism, but the expression in ritual of a repressed belief, held correlatively with the belief that women are capable of entering into contracts:

23.4.   Modern Europeans, with the top of their minds, conceive a marriage as a contract between a man and a woman; but at the bottom of their minds they are not so sure; they are haunted by the idea which in their saner moments they know to be savage, the idea that it is the transference of a chattel from one owner to another.

In marriage, then, there is a sense in which individuals act freely in instigating the society, and a sense in which such freedom is constrained by the parents and relatives. Freedom comes to us in degrees, and what begins with a small degree may develop and grow as each of the partners matures and faces the responsibilities and obligations associated with the society they have initiated.

The enterprise for which the society of marriage was primarily initiated in the past was sexual gratification, with children being a consequence of this enterprise. With the advent of contraception the society of marriage is increasingly becoming understood, not as a partnership for sexual gratification, but as a partnership primarily intended for the procreation of children. It is children, for the most part, who comprise the nonsocial family community and over whom parents exercise transeunt rule. The parents exercise this rule with a view to bringing the children to a state of intellectual and physical maturity. Such maturation entails a process of education, conducted by others and by the self. The educative process must always hold out the promise of future incorporation into the society. In the family the parents have to make it clear to the child from an early age that he, or she, will be welcomed as an equal as the signs of mental maturity become manifest. This is an aspect of the child's education that parents cannot delegate. There are, of course, many things that may work to frustrate this process. Parents may try to prolong unduly the process of maturation because they enjoy being depended upon. Some parents even enlarge the nonsocial family community by incorporating nonhuman pets, whom they can rely upon always to be dependent and never to reach the level of free will.

The kind of community to which political theorists direct their attention is the body politic. For the Greeks it was a society of citizens who ruled themselves corporately. To the thinkers of the Middle Ages the body politic was a nonsocial community: 'a human herd which strong men rule and good men would wish to rule well' (*NL,* 24.5). One of Hobbes's great discoveries, according to Collingwood, was that the sovereign or the state does not rule by force, but by authority. The body politic is neither social nor nonsocial; it is a mixed community, some of the inhabitants of which, having crossed the line between the nonsocial and the social, are capable of conferring authority. The life of the body politic is that of the continuous process of conversion from the nonsocial to the social, that is, the dialectical process of growing up in a body politic to share the business of rule. A body politic, in this simple formulation, differs from a family in that the social element in the former constitutes a permanent society in which no termination date is implied (*NL,* 21.92 and 25.22). 'The council or "state" or "sovereign" [that is the social element in the mixed community of the body politic] is a permanent society because its work is never done' (*NL,* 25.23). The council, or social community, is charged with the pursuit of dealing with three broad problems. First, to determine an appropriate way of life for the sovereign or council. Second, to determine a way of life for the nonsocial, or nursery, element in the body politic. The third problem is to determine the relation between the two. These three tasks of the council are, for Collingwood, part of the constitutional problem of the body politic.

A further constitutional problem relates to the subdivision of the nonsocial, or ruled, and the social, or ruling, elements in the body politic. The minimal prerequisite for eligibility of membership in the ruling class is very low:

25.44.   People having that qualification and no more are capable of free action only when the problem to be solved is the easiest possible kind of problem and the circumstances in which they have to solve it are the easiest possible kind of circumstances.

Because different people are capable of attaining differing strengths of will, where the problems of the body politic are complex and the strains of solving them greater, it is those with stronger wills, capable of resisting the strains and able to exercise freedom of will, who must be vested with the responsibility. On these grounds, Collingwood maintains, the class of rulers must be subdivided into a multiplicity of grades, membership of each one being determined by the differing strengths of will apposite to each grade.

The ruled class itself also becomes subdivided. This subdivision is based on the principle of induction. A person who is unable to exercise free will, or only able to exercise it in a very low degree, may come to behave as if he, or she, possesses such attributes on account of his, or her, proximity to those who do. A person who does not have the capacity to choose freely, or cannot because the circumstances prevent it – for example, the emotional charge of fear having deprived the person of his, or her, rational capacities – may nevertheless on the outside perform actions which appear to exhibit free will, even though the actions have been induced by force. A soldier may appear to face the enemy bravely, because he is forced into battle by an officer's gun. There is a third possibility in addition to those of the person who is incapable of, or unable to, exercise free will, and one who only appears to do so because he, or she, is forced: This is the case of a servile agent who is weak in will and only capable of responding to example – in other words, the person who is capable of being led, 'but incapable of standing alone' (*NL*, 25.55). This is what Collingwood means by 'induction' – the inspirational effect that someone of stronger will has on the person of weaker will. This inductive process can also occur in instances where a person is not quite able to exercise free will but is in contact with one who is. The inductive process therefore enables people who are not quite qualified to enter the ruling class to do so on account of the quality of leadership they have received. The higher the quality of the ruled class, the greater the propensity of their example to 'elevate sections of the ruled to temporary and induced membership of the rulers' (*NL*, 25.58). Collingwood likens this process of induction to the business of education. It is, in fact, an important aspect of education. The qualities of good leadership are developed in responding to leadership, and conversely a good leader is always concerned to teach his, or her, followers to be good leaders.

The inductive function of the rulers is explained by Collingwood more clearly and forcefully elsewhere. He maintains that such a function is implied in the Greek word ἀρχή, which is usually translated 'rule'. This concept, for the Greeks, referred to the opening of new paths that introduced new horizons to which other men could aspire. Rulers, in performing public activities, had to set high standards which acted as exemplars for future rulers or followers to imitate: 'The ruler as path-finder is the ruler as setter of examples'.[55] The concept of rule is relative to the ruled. It is nothing in itself, except something, whatever that something might be, which the ruler possesses, and is acknowledged to possess, in a greater degree than those over whom he rules.

Collingwood attempts to summarise his theory of the body politic in what he calls the three 'laws' of politics. First, 'that *a body politic is divided into a ruling class and a ruled class*' (*NL*, 25.7); that is, 'the class which decides how to deal with a political problem, and the class which, with regard to a political problem now being dealt with, does what the first class tells it'.[56] The distinction, essentially, is between the part that has the initiative and the part that does not.[57] The second of the laws of politics refers to the fact that the division between the rulers and the ruled must be permeable. The ruling class must make provisions for its own perpetuation. The provisions that it makes to bring about such a result are not self-fulfilling. They have to be promoted, and the rulers have to be active in ensuring that the process of conversion is effective.[58] The third law of politics postulates that there is 'a correspondence between the ruler and ruled' (*NL*, 25.9). By this Collingwood means that there is a tendency in any body politic for the ruled, whether consciously or not, to imitate the rulers.

This law is explained in more detail in 'The Three Laws of Politics'. We have inherited from the Greeks, Collingwood suggests, the idea that intelligence confers upon men the power to rule over others. A group of men possessing such intelligence build up a scale of values pertinent to their own community. The values imputed to intelligence and rationality, however, can be subverted in any particular body politic.[59] In other words, the third law may operate *inversely* (*NL*, 25.92). The ruled may not allow itself to be ruled over by any rulers who are out of tune with its demands. This Collingwood calls the 'reversed action of the Third Law of Politics'.[60] The third law does not work automatically, and unless the rulers work hard to promote it the community is left devoid of good exemplars to follow. The second stage of this reversal is that the resulting 'democracy' which occurs throws up leaders from its own ranks who are 'so much jetsam, floating on the surface of the waves' they pretend to control.[61] In Collingwood's view, the mob 'elevates to a position of supremacy over itself whatever is most devoid of free will, whatever can be entirely trusted to do what is dictated by the desires which the mob feels' (*NL*, 25.98). In circumstances such as these, the mixed community of the body politic reverts back to a nonsocial community, yet still retains the function of rule, devoid, however, of free will, or is reduced at least to a condition of being capable only of capricious will. What Collingwood is implying in his third law of politics is that although the ruling class rules over the ruled class by means of force, the relationship between them cannot merely be based on force. The third law of politics postulates a certain reciprocity. It behooves the rulers to prepare the ruled for rule by providing exemplars that the ruled will be inspired to follow. Such inspiration will affect only those who have almost reached the level of free will. This requires cooperation rather than confrontation, a dialectical rather than an eristical (that is, adversarial) relationship.

Force and deceit are necessary to the business of ruling, especially in dealing with those who are the most backward in the ruled class, that is, those who are possessed of very little political education. For those who are less backward, force and fraud 'are differentially replaced by "induction" (25.5) and other forms of partial and progressive sharing in the liberty of the ruler' (*NL*, 27.38). The rulers must never forget, then, that the members of the ruled class are the potential recruits to the ruling class, and that they must be treated as sharing, to a degree, the freedom of will 'which in an eminent degree is peculiar, by the First Law of Politics, to the rulers' (*NL*, 27.34).

In summary, the body politic is a mixed community. It is comprised of a nonsocial and a social element. Each element is subdivided: in the nonsocial according to the level of consciousness attained, and in the social according to the degree of strength of will attained. The more complex the problems of rule, the greater the degree of strength of will required to deal with them. The social element, or ruling class, exercises immanent rule over itself, and transeunt rule over the ruled class.

There is a certain amount of ambiguity in Collingwood's account of the body politic. For example, is the transition from the ruled to the ruling class automatic once a person has reached mental maturity, that is, once a person has gained the capacity persistently to exercise free will? Apparently not, because the transition involves the passing of a judgement by the rulers upon the members of the ruled class as to their suitability for ruling. That is what Collingwood calls the quality of *rule-worthiness*, which is not a fixed quality and actually changes according to the characteristics of those who exercise rule.[62] What are the implications of this? First, it appears that the ruling class, that is, the permanent society in the mixed community, determines the composition of the nonsocial element as well as the composition of itself. In other words, it is not the capacity of free will which qualifies a person for entry into the ruling class but the judgement of rule-worthiness being conferred upon the person by the ruling class. If such a judgement is conferred upon all those adults (with a few exceptions, such as mentally retarded people) who have reached a certain age and are able to cast a vote in elections and thus confer authority, then few problems are envisaged. However, if the qualifications become more rigorous, such as the passing of literacy, numeracy, and initiative tests, or even heredity tests, then the nonsocial, or ruled, element in the mixed community will quite likely include a number of people who have reached the level of rational will, but who are formally denied this recognition.

Collingwood does, as we saw, allow for the possibility of the induction of those who are not quite capable of the exercise of rational will into the society of rulers. What this means is that the nonsocial community is not necessarily comprised of people who lack the capacity to exercise free will, and the social community is not necessarily comprised of those who do (*NL*, 26.25–26.27). It is therefore not so much the possession of a certain quality as its recognition that qualifies a person to enter the ruling class – or is it? What is the ruling class? A class, according to Collingwood, is not a society. A class is 'a collection of many things into one, in virtue of their resemblance' (*NL*, 19.37). Does this mean, then, that having certain attributes makes one a member of a class, whereas their recognition qualifies one for membership of the society of rulers? Is it the members of the society, after all, who have to confer the title of rule-worthiness upon a person? If this is the case, the ideal character of the body politic, that is, where the nonsocial and social correspond to the nonrational and rational, or the ruled and the rulers, would seem to be radically out of step with the empirical character of the body politic.

Second, to avoid further confusion, we need to distinguish more clearly than Collingwood does between those who comprise the society of rulers and those who actually rule. As we saw, Collingwood suggests that sometimes we encounter cases where something capable of ruling itself appears to submit to the rule of something else. The illusion of such a relationship pertaining is created by the conferment of authority on the latter by the former. In the case of the society of rulers, sub-divided as it is into a hierarchical series of degrees of strength of will, it would appear that some are more qualified than others to be vested with authority. Among this society of rulers, some have only the minimal qualifications which would suit them only for dealing with the least complex problems. Those members of the ruled class, who are not rulers in the sense of taking the initiative, and who confer authority upon others to make decisions in their names, can still be said to rule themselves, presumably, because they have conferred authority freely. In this respect, although they are not rulers themselves, but are members of the ruling society, they can still be said to exercise transeunt rule. Furthermore, these people who have conferred authority and who are members of the ruling society, are, like the members of the nonsocial community, the subjects of the rulers, that is, those upon whom authority is conferred. As subjects, those who have conferred authority appear to be entitled to a greater amount of respect in the business of ruling than those who are not capable of making such conferments. Such an interpretation is consistent with the remarks which Collingwood makes about the use of fraud and force in politics. He suggests that the subjects of the ruler 'include people of all kinds from the intelligent to the foolish, from those who almost call out to be bullied to those who rebel at the slightest suggestion of force' (*NL,* 27.42).[63] Those who rule, then, rule over both the intelligent and un-intelligent, or the social and nonsocial elements of the body politic; the intelligent, because they confer authority, can be said to share in this rule, or to exercise immanent rule over themselves.

Croce, in his *Philosophy of the Practical,* argued that contrary to pop-ular opinion, aristocracy is not incompatible with democracy. The true aristocrat, Croce maintains, has promoted democracy in being the bearer of the universal values of liberty and freedom; 'hence the more we are aristocratic the more we are democratic, and inversely'.[64] In a later essay, Croce put forward the view that liberalism denies equality, and that the advancement of liberty is not correlative with democracy, but in fact promotes aristocracy. In what appears to be a partial endorsement of what Collingwood later formulated as the second law of politics, Croce, purporting to be following Gladstone, asserts that 'aristocracy is truly vigorous and serious when it is not a closed but an open aristocracy, firm in rejecting the crowd, but always ready to welcome those who have raised themselves to its level'.[65] The whole emphasis of British idealist liberalism was aristocratic in character. Its purpose was not to admit the 'denizen of the London yard' (Green) to the society of rulers, but to remove those obstacles, or hinder those hindrances, which hampered self-enhancement and self-development. The aim was to promote the de-velopment of the self towards the attainment of freedom of the will.[66] In ceasing to be a slave to one's passions the individual moves closer to satisfying the qualifications for citizenship. To possess citizenship is to possess the morally autonomous will, that is, to be subject to self-rule.

Collingwood shares with many liberals the view that democracy and aristocracy are compatible and complementary. In answer to the question concerning how the ruling class can be strengthened to its optimum, the democrats and aristocrats offer partial answers. For the democrat such an optimum will be achieved by enlarging the ruling class as far as possible. For the aristocrat the desired effect will be achieved by restricting it as far as need dictates. It is Collingwood's contention that

26.16   There is no quarrel between these answers. The inevitable recruitment of a ruling class from its correlative ruled class is a dialectical process, part of the process which is the life of the body politic. Democracy and aristocracy are *positive and negative elements in that process.*

The principles of aristocracy and democracy provide, then, correlative rules for facilitating the process of conversion in a body politic. There is no such thing as a pure democracy, nor a pure aristocracy; each includes elements of the other.[67] There are two parts to every body politic, the ruled and the rulers. Inclusion in the second, if the body politic is to function well, should be determined solely on the ground that the aspirant has the required ability to do the work. In other words, the qualifications for entry fluctuate in accordance with the degree of difficulty of the tasks that face the rulers. What this implies is that one's capacity for exercising freedom of choice, or being mentally mature, is relative to the complexity of the demands placed upon the ruling element in a body politic. It seems then that under certain circumstances, where the demands of ruling are light, persons may be in a position to exercise their will freely. If circumstances change and the demands of rule become heavy, those very same people may lose their capacity of free will, thus altering the balance between the social and nonsocial elements in the body politic. The principle of aristocracy is equated with force: The stronger rule over those who are less strong. The principle of democracy is that of self-rule, that is, the society exercises self-rule (*NL*, 27.47).

The relation between the principles of democracy and aristocracy is dialectical rather than eristical, but in practice the relation is often mistaken. In such cases false victories are claimed where the proponents of one principle claim to have vanquished those of the other. To adopt this eristical, or adversarial, style of politics is a denial of liberal principles, one of which is the recognition of the necessity of the coexistence of democracy and aristocracy in the body politic. In Collingwood's view, 'The one essential of liberalism is the dialectical solution of all political problems'. It is liberalism, rather than socialism, 'that has proved the true heir of the dialectical method'.[68] The regulation of the conversion process from the condition of the nonsocial community to the social is a dialectical process between those who would hasten the conversion and those who would retard it.

In nineteenth-century England, Collingwood suggests, the dialectical method in politics was understood very well. The Conservative party represented the negative, or retarding element, in the conversion process, and the Liberal party represented the positive element. Both parties knew that the relation between them was dialectical. They were in fundamental agreement on many assumptions regarding the body politic. The percolation of freedom throughout the community must be facilitated. Circumstances may require a variation in the rate, but there is an optimum which, through trial and error, may be more or less discoverable. The Conservative party consciously acted as a brake upon the more impetuous Liberal party. Although the relation was dialectical, it seems that consciousness of this fact in both parties was not equally evident. A dialectical system of politics depends upon the recognition, by those who hold one point of view, that the other must be represented. The failure by one party to acknowledge such a necessity leads to adversarial, or eristical, politics, in which the party becomes a faction. The reason for the demise of the Liberal party in Britain was the failure of that party to recognise the necessity of conservatism and thus set itself in an eristical rather than a dialectical relation with it. Liberals considered Conservatives to be part of the dead weight that was holding back human progress. In other words, England had a Liberal party that did not understand the fundamental principle of liberalism, namely, the belief in the dialectical solution to all political problems.

Collingwood's view of the dialectical relation between Liberal and Conservative parties differs in certain respects from that of de Ruggiero. For de Ruggiero the dialectical relation is unconscious, and indeed it must be unconscious if liberal principles, which are not restricted to Liberal parties, are to triumph. It is a presupposition of Liberal parties that people develop through competition, and that in doing so they overcome the constraints of habit, tradition, and unquestioning obedience which are assumed to be hostile to progress. These negative forces are nevertheless necessary, but a Liberal party which is partial and partisan cannot incorporate within itself the principles of its opponent: 'If it recognized the necessity of the thing against which it was fighting, this recognition would end by paralysing its activity'.[69] This partiality of Liberal parties is both a weakness and a strength. If they were to be more comprehensive, they would recognise 'the dialectical ground of the antithesis and would see resistance and movement, conservation and progress, justified and validated in a higher synthesis which is political life in its concreteness'.[70] Thus the alternation between Conservative and Liberal parties in government does not represent an alternation between darkness, or unfreedom, and light, or freedom, but a necessary rhythm in the progress of liberty. No Liberal party, however, is likely to regard its defeat as a victory for liberalism. The liberal state, or government, is not the province of one party: It is the synthesis of the opposing tendencies. Croce, de Ruggiero, and Collingwood agree that current trends in criticism and the growing intolerance of parliaments, on the grounds that they are mere talking shops, are ill conceived and show an ignorance of, and a hostility to, the essentially dialectical character of politics.[71]

This section has described the affinities between the principles that Collingwood advances and those of avowed liberals. At every point his principles accord with his own understanding of liberalism. In attempting to encapsulate de Ruggiero's understanding of the development of liberalism, Collingwood is also summarising his own position. Liberalism, he says, is the recognition that men and women are free. The freedom is not a gift, but a capacity which is achieved by degrees, as people gradually become conscious of their personality 'through a life of discipline and moral progress'. Liberalism attempts to facilitate this progress without forcing it upon those who are unprepared, and at the same time renounces the idea of leaving people to their own devices, choosing instead, not to deprive them of the aid to progress but to aid that progress in whatever way possible.

These principles lead in practice to a policy that may be called, in the sense above defined, Liberal; a policy which regards the state, not as the vehicle of a superhuman wisdom or a superhuman power, but as the organ by which a people expresses whatever of political ability it can find and breed and train within itself. This is not democracy, or the rule of the mere majority; nor is it authoritarianism, or the irresponsible rule of those who, for whatever reason, hold power at a given moment. It is something between the two. Democratic in its respect for human liberty, it is authoritarian in the importance it attaches to the necessity for skilful and practised government.[72]

We must at all times make a clear distinction between liberal principles and liberal parties and governments, he asserts. While the parties and governments may fail to realise, or may even compromise, liberal principles, in Collingwood's view the principles themselves are beyond reproach.

This chapter has presented Collingwood's views on the failure of classical politics and has outlined his theory of the body politic and its close connexions with British and Italian liberalism. In part his theory makes good the deficiency that he detected in classical politics, in so far as it attempts to locate the state of nature, or the nonsocial aspects of life, within the framework of the body politic itself. It remains to identify the role of the state in the body politic and relate the forms of political action, which were discussed in Chapter 3, to the activity of the state.

6

The state and the body politic

1. Introduction

In the preceding chapter we saw that Collingwood identified a defect in
the classical politics of Hobbes, Locke, and Rousseau. They failed to provide a theory of the nonsocial community and thus ignored the important
question of how a society can continually recruit new members for itself
who are mentally mature and responsible, and who can exercise their
free will in the joint enterprise of ruling. Collingwood's solution to the
problem that the classical theorists failed to address was thoroughly imbued with the liberal principles of the idealists, from whom he derived
philosophical as well as political inspiration. This chapter looks at how
Collingwood's theories of mind and society have a direct bearing upon
the role of the state in the body politic; the place of punishment in preventing a reversion to the nonsocial community; and the relations between
bodies politic.

2. The state as activity

In Collingwood's view, the state, understood as substance – that is, as an
entity having certain functions, characteristics, and attributes – provides
the focus for the empirical study of politics.[1] Croce, in believing that the
sphere of 'political action is co-existensive with that of useful action',
denies that the state as a focus of attention can adequately demarcate
the political from the nonpolitical in human life. He says, for example,
that 'there exists . . . not the State, but political actions'.[2] Collingwood,
while disagreeing with Croce's identification of the political and the useful,
nevertheless agrees with him in viewing the philosophical understanding
of politics not as a theory of the state but as a theory of political activity.
The state, for Collingwood, 'is not a substance but an activity',[3] and in

167

this respect the state neither exhausts the sphere of political activity, nor are all its actions political. Political activity, as we saw, is coextensive with obeying and making rules. Political action and regularian action are equivalents. The state is not merely concerned with the 'making and carrying out of rules';[4] it concerns itself with much more besides which is not (strictly speaking) political, because 'as a concrete historical institution ... it must to some extent interest itself in economic and moral questions'.[5] Similarly, there is no institution nor individual that is not concerned, to some extent, with making, implementing, and following rules. Political action is transcendental in that it is identical with action in general and is therefore bound to overflow the mere empirical limits of the state.[6] Political activity, then, 'is coextensive with human life',[7] and from an understanding of regularian activity we are not able to deduce the functions of the state, which have developed in relation to empirical circumstances. This does not mean that a theory of the state is redundant in understanding politics: On the contrary, empirical and a priori theories of the state 'are indispensable to any political theory'.[8] Politics is rightly associated in a special way with the state in that it exists to perform political works — not all that there are to perform, but those deemed necessary to the maintenance of a body politic, and any work additional to the political which the state undertakes to do is an outgrowth of its primary task.[9]

What is the state, and what is its relation to the body politic? It is a mistake, Collingwood argues, to use the term *state* as a synonym for the body politic. The concept of the state designates not the body politic, but the ruling class within it. Philosophically we should 'think of the state not as a thing but as the collective name for a certain complex of political acts'.[10] What this means is that the state is mind, because 'any organized system of acts is itself an act, and ... therefore any loyal member of a community wills the whole organization of that community.... The mind of the state is the mind of any member of the state, so far as he genuinely shares in its life'.[11]

As we saw in Chapter 3, political action is the penultimate level of practical reason in Collingwood's philosophy of mind. Political action is regularian, or action according to rule. It is the making and obeying of laws. The individual, for example, is a source of laws, and, in so far as the laws are made and obeyed, is engaged in political conduct. In this respect, as a member of the ruling society, he is 'bound to recognize in others the same kind of freedom which he claims for himself; and therefore each must recognize the will of these others as a source of rules binding on himself'.[12] The purpose of political action is to create order, or orderly existence, through the establishment and maintenance of, and obedience to, rules. Thinking out a scheme to regulate or organize action is the essence of politics, and there is no substantive difference between devising a plan to guide my own actions or those of other people. Political activity is self-government, in the sense that a person who devises a scheme for a society or community is part of that community for which it is devised. On the other hand, those who are members of the body politic and whose actions are to be organized by the scheme cannot be compelled to acquiesce, but obey 'of their own free will'.[13]

The forms of action, or levels of rational consciousness – that is, the utilitarian, regularian, and dutiful – all have political manifestations. Political action is, as I suggested, regularian, but the reasons for which rules are made and enforced differ. For instance, where one has will pure and simple – that is, a capricious will – political activity or political rule is by *decree*. A decree is an executive act imposed upon the ruled by the rulers: It is 'the simplest form of political action because it represents the simplest form of will, namely caprice transposed into the key of politics' (*NL*, 28.3). When we reach the stage of rational will, we find that political *utility* is that form of political action which distinguishes between means and ends in the making and obeying of rules. Its political manifestation is *policy,* and, as we saw, the choice of both means and ends is relatively capricious. The second form of rational action finds its political expression in *law*: 'Law is the political form of right; *it is regularian action in its political form'* (*NL*, 28.6). A law must satisfy three criteria. First, it must emanate from the rulers as an act of will. Second, the rulers themselves should obey it, and third, the members of the non-social community should obey it, as they are forced to do by the rulers. The making of such law still retains an element of caprice in that the type of society, or type of life, that the laws direct us towards is a matter of capricious choice on the part of the rulers. Finally, political duty is the free choice of the only course of action available to a body politic. The accentuated historical awareness of what it behooves the rulers to choose, being the only option open to them, eliminates the element of caprice found in policy and law. Collingwood's enterprise is in many respects similar to that of Plato. The elements in the mind or pysche correspond to those in the body politic. Order and harmony prevail in the body politic when the highest level of rational consciousness, exhibited in its corresponding rational action, prevails over and dominates the subordinate levels.

The good that political activity seeks to promote is that of a society, or community, 'whose members live together under good laws well administered and loyally obeyed'.[14] The state, philosophically conceived, is that collection of activities conducive to such a good. Its function is the maintenance of order in the community. This is not a moral good, but a political good. This needs further explication, because the character of its goodness is not self-evident. A political value is one that applies to all people equally and is inseparable from obedience to rule, orderliness, and regularity. Keeping a promise, for instance, is a political good: 'Its goodness is the goodness of orderly conduct, observance of rule: for a promise has something of the nature of a self-imposed law'.[15] Rightness, or the political good, is equivalent to 'law and order, civil peace, and the various other phrases which the political consciousness has used as names for its own proper end'.[16]

Politics and morality are distinct, but not opposed to each other. If something is politically good, that does not mean that it is morally bad. It is the moral duty of the politician, for instance, to enact good laws. It is the moral duty of the magistrate to enforce them. Obedience is demanded as the moral duty of the subject.[17] The relation of the state to duty, or morality, is that its activities respect freedom of conscience and ensure that the laws do not undermine this liberty. The orderliness which the state creates is the foundation upon which the life of morality can flourish. What the state is primarily concerned with, however, is that the laws are obeyed. It is a matter of indifference to the state for what motive they are obeyed. It is no business of politics to promote morality. The political good is different from the moral good. Paying one's taxes is a political good irrespective of whether one does so for morally good reasons. The political and the moral are connected, however, in that one may discharge one's political obligations from a sense of duty. The state may command me to provide for my children, and the reason for which I obey such a law is of no consequence to it because I am in my action promoting the political good. The state 'leaves me perfectly free' to maintain my children from 'a sense of duty'.[18] What Collingwood is suggesting is this: If a person has responsibility in respect of the work of the state (and that means almost every adult in communities where there is universal suffrage based upon certain age and mental qualifications), then that person has a duty to facilitate the work of the state. The subject who is part of the political community, and whose function it is, in terms of the political good, to obey the rulers, is also the bearer of a duty to fulfil his obligations in the 'common political task'. A ruler who rules badly and a subject who refuses to obey the law are at once politically and morally bad.[19] However, what concerns the state is that the actions are politically bad and must be condemned for being so.

The state, or the social element in the body politic, is also distinguishable, as a body of actions, from economic life, or the utilitarian mode of action. The relation of the state to utility is that the state provides the framework of 'law and order', and 'civil peace', which allows individuals to pursue their own 'interests or utilities'.[20] The laws that the state enacts are not designed to bring about an economic good: 'A society makes a law not because it will thereby become more wealthy, but because it will thereby achieve a good of another kind – a political kind'.[21] Like many of the New Liberals in Britain, Collingwood fully acknowledged that economic principles have an important place in the community: 'Conflict of interest, competition, the will to drive a hard bargain, is the essence of economic action, and a society in which economic action has no place is certainly a utopia'.[22] Economic principles, however, are not the only ones, and this is something of which we should never lose sight, nor should we ever underestimate the human need and desire to satisfy personal interests. This, of course, is an allusion to the importance of the subjectivist tradition in the history of political thought.

There are not, as such, separate classes of economic and political facts, because each action can be viewed from the economic or political perspective. Every act can be viewed as a means to an end, and in this respect the person enacting it really makes it a means to an end. Every act can also be viewed as the exemplification of a rule, and when it is thought to be so by the person performing the action, 'he does it in such a way that it really is an example of a rule, and possesses genuine rightness'.[23] Every act can, similarly, be viewed as a dutiful action, and if the person enacting it thinks that it was the only course of action that was possible and morally defensible to do on that occasion, then that person really makes that action one of duty.[24] The very same act, or what appears to be the same act, can at once be utilitarian and economic, regularian and political, dutiful and moral, depending upon the view one takes of it. Each act, however, has a distinguishable good, which it as an activity alone promotes: Economic action is an individual good; political action aims at the good of the community, or body politic; and, moral action is directed towards the universal good.[25]

Given that Collingwood philosophically distinguishes these three spheres of action, can it ever be legitimate for the state to enter the spheres of the economic and moral and attempt to regulate their activities? If one looks at the state empirically, 'as a concrete historical institution', it is clear, as far as Collingwood is concerned, that it 'cannot confine itself to the making and administering of rules or laws, it must to some extent interest itself in economic and moral questions as well'.[26] When we understand the state philosophically, rather than as substance, Collingwood still believes, however, that the state should concern itself with the economic and moral modes of activity. What is of crucial importance is that the state does not intervene in the economic and moral spheres for economic and moral reasons. Political intervention should be for political reasons, designed to achieve a political good.

What, then, are the principles upon which the state should intervene? The state should interfere in matters that are likely to precipitate disorder.

The promotion, maintenance, and protection of the political good of orderliness is the justification for political, or state, intervention. Some examples of particular cases in which state intervention becomes desirable will serve to illustrate the extent to which Collingwood would endorse state action in the economic and moral spheres.

The housing conditions of the poor, for instance, should be improved. Slums are a social evil indicative of disorder and 'corporate slatternliness in the body politic'. As for other evils in addition to these that may arise from poor housing conditions, 'a well-ordered state would not tolerate them, not because they are a danger to happiness or health or morals, if indeed they are, but because they are an offence against order'.[27] A person who is forced to work for a low wage because his poverty leaves him no other option is in a position which is not reproachable on economic grounds, because the labourer is willing to enter into such an arrangement, but it may be asked whether such arrangements ought, on moral grounds, to be allowed. The person should perhaps, instead, receive maintenance rather than be allowed to become a victim of sweated labour. The demand for legislation to establish a just wage is rational, in Collingwood's view, if it rests upon the claim that certain special circumstances induce workers to accept a lower wage than they would if the adverse circumstances were removed. It is a reasonable demand, in that it asks for legislation to amend 'the condition of society' in order to ensure fair bargaining.[28] In an economic relation between the rich and the poor, the former are in a position to use force upon the latter, and even though Collingwood thinks that the demand to amend the conditions of society is a fair one, he is pessimistic about the effectiveness of such legislation. Once a contrast between rich and poor has been condoned in the community, it sets up a force 'which henceforth it is idle to resist' (NL, 38.7). Collingwood seems to be suggesting that a certain structural power operates to establish a relation of dominance and dependence: 'However men work to minimize that result, there will always be one law for the rich and another for the poor; for that is what being rich and being poor are' (NL, 38.71).

From the turn of the century in Britain, a growing number of liberals had come to view poverty as a social affront which was inimical to the civil condition. C. F. G. Masterman, for example, a most vociferous critic of the social squalor in England, argued that the survival of civilization 'is incompatible with the continuance of poverty'.[29] Collingwood, too, took the view that the social disharmony that a marked difference between the rich and poor displays within a community is out of keeping with the ideal of civilization.[30] Some disparity, he thought, may be necessary in order to stimulate the communal wealth of the whole. The contrast, however, has to be justifiable on the grounds that it is necessary in order to preserve what the community has come to regard as a tolerable living standard. If adjustments can be made, they should be made, 'for the *raison d'etre* not only of bodies politic but of every community is that men should live, as Aristotle says, a good life' (*NL,* 38.81). The accumulation of wealth is only justifiable if it is used to pursue civilization. The accumulation of wealth by those who seek to create a greater contrast between rich and poor leads to a perversion of the ideals of civilization, that is, those positive freedoms and the social relationships which they entail and to which we have become accustomed (*NL,* 38.81–38.83).[31]

In the realm of morality, Collingwood argues, 'the state must have the power of suppressing seditious or obscene publications'.[32] Protests by artists who assure us that the works subject to censure have artistic merit should not sway the state to surrender this function. The state intervenes to suppress, not literature as such, but particular works of literature which violate 'the order which it has to maintain in society'.[33] The rules which we frame and obey in this respect 'do not bring our lives into harmony with the idea of duty but with the idea of orderliness, which is the governing conception of political action'.[34] If the justification for such state intervention is that a certain work of literature is not conducive to order, and the plea of artistic merit does not exempt a work from being suppressed, upon what grounds can one object? Collingwood replies, 'The only valid objection to such interference by the state with literature would be that it is not necessary for the maintenance of this order, and that is a political question, not a literary one'.[35] The relation between orderliness and obscenity is not further explored by Collingwood in this context, but it can be inferred from what he says elsewhere. Pornography is a form of amusement designed to stimulate the easiest of emotions to play upon, namely, sexual desire. Every emotion has two phases: 'charge or excitation, and discharge'. To prevent the emotional discharge from affecting practical life, artificial or make-believe situations are created in order to 'earth' the emotions. The prevalence of sexual fantasy betrays a degeneracy in modern Europeans, who substitute titillation for action and who have devalued sexual passion to the level of mere amusement. The obsession with pornography is testimony to 'a society where the instinctive desire to propagate has been weakened by a sense that life, as we have made it, is not worth living, and where our deepest wish is to have no posterity'.[36] It appears, then, that the threat which obscene literature presents to orderliness is to direct the individual's emotions into a form of antisocial escapism inimical to the positive and practical values upon which a flourishing community can thrive.

The point which Collingwood wants to make is that the question of state interference is not one of politics intruding into institutions and areas of life which are nonpolitical. Political action is universal and therefore not the preserve of the state. The question really boils down to which political actions are best dealt with and regulated by particular associations such as the family or a factory, and which are more appropriately dealt with by the state. Collingwood illustrates this point with reference to the work of a laboratory.

For the state to interfere with the laboratory organisation would be wrong (if it *was* wrong) not because the state is politics and the laboratory science, but because the state's political problems are not those of the laboratory, and it had better leave the laboratory to solve its own political problems. The case of the Factory Acts shows that state interference with a laboratory need not be wrong. The laboratory may prove unable to solve its own political problems and the state may be compelled to take charge of them.[37]

In summary, then, political intervention can be justified only on political grounds, and the principle employed should always be that of intervention for the maintenance of order, orderliness being the ultimate political good.

3. The state and punishment

H. L. A. Hart has argued that it is a mistake to believe that an acceptable account of punishment has to rest upon one supreme value, whether that value is retribution, deterrence, or reform. Instead, we have to be aware that different principles may be appropriate at different stages in giving a morally acceptable, or justifiable, account of punishment.[38] Although the British idealists (for example, Green, Bradley, and Bosanquet) did not make the various stages explicit nor discuss the problems in the same way as Hart, they nevertheless had implicitly grasped the necessity of discussing the different aspects of punishment in terms of different principles, and thereby acknowledged that each one may be appropriate at a certain stage and inappropriate at another.[39] Collingwood is also of the view that retribution, deterrence, and reform must all be accounted for in a justifiable theory of punishment. Each can be viewed as a rival account of punishment, or all can be understood as coexisting elements of punishment in general. Collingwood contends that only one of the principles constitutes the 'essence', while the others are the 'properties' of punishment. It is unlikely that any system of punishment could be just if it did not in some way improve the criminal and raise the level of obedience to the law in general, but neither of these effects is morally defensible unless the punishment which brings them about is deserved. Retribution, he claims, is the essence of punishment, but 'it seems likely ... that the deterrent and reformatory characters of punishment, though they are certainly not its essence, may be properties in the logical sense of the term, that is attributes following necessarily from the essence'.[40] The value of Hart's account is not so much his assertion that all three principles must be accommodated in a theory of punishment as the framework in terms of which he demonstrates it. The different principles may be given in answer to different questions concerning definition, the general justifying aim, and the distribution. The question of distribution refers both to who qualifies for punishment and how much is to be administered.[41] Hart's differentiation of these question categories can be usefully invoked to elucidate Collingwood's thoughts on the nature and aims of punishment.

Before the question of justification of punishment can arise, one must establish what exactly one wishes to justify. The question of what punishment is must therefore precede its justification. For Collingwood, punishment belongs to the sphere of action in general and is therefore not limited to a state-instituted judicial process or designated apparatus. Punishment, because it belongs to action as such, is any penalty administered for breaking a rule, and if the breach does not incur a penalty in the courts of the land, that may be because it is punishable outside the judicial system.[42] Punishment is simply the penalty inflicted for breaking a law. The idea of a society entails the choice of a common good in which its members share, and the conscious construction of a system of laws which protect and promote the common life they have chosen.[43] Any violation of this order subverts the aim of promoting the common good of the community. Punishment is the condemnation of the criminal by the community whose order he has violated, 'and to punish with a word instead of a blow is still punishment'.[44] Punishment is the frustration of the will of a criminal whose 'choice runs counter to the choice of the society in which he lives. He is crushed because he is in the minority; it is a mere question of brute force'.[45] If punishment is force, then it is not a relation which holds among members of a society: 'Reward and punishment have no weight with free men, and the theory of them has no place in the theory of society. It belongs to the theory of the nonsocial community to which it is essential' (*NL*, 21.74). It is those people whose wills crack under the strain of the responsibility entailed in free and rational action who endanger the common life which the state upholds. In demonstrating their opposition to society by frustrating the common good, they at once commit a crime and render themselves ineligible for the benefits of the society they have rejected. In committing such acts they revert back to the nonsocial community (*NL*, 21.88). Essentially, then, where the criminal has never left the nonsocial community, or where the criminal has reverted to the nonsocial community, punishment is that force which is exercised by the social community in frustrating the harm inflicted upon it by its enemies. In Collingwood's view, the principle of retribution best defines punishment: Retribution is 'the infliction of deserved suffering on an offender'.[46]

Collingwood agrees with both Green and Bosanquet in believing that punishment is in part a self-inflicted penalty brought upon oneself by violating the law or a system of rights. Green and Bosanquet contend that punishment is the agent's 'own act returning on himself', in the sense that the person concerned shares in a system of rights and, in committing an offence against that system, also commits an offence against himself.[47] As far as Collingwood is concerned, punishment is the inevitable and necessary consequence of the violation of any kind of good. I violate the good of pleasure by inflicting pain on myself. The moral good is subverted by my immoral acts. And the political good is violated by a breach of rules in which I detach myself in certain respects from the way of life chosen and pursued by my society. The punishment as such is not inflicted upon me, but actually consists in 'that detachment from or forfeiture of the common life of society which I have myself deliberately brought about'.[48]

Punishment is of course inflicted upon the criminal by the community, but it is self-inflicted in that he brings it upon himself. In breaking the law he does not intend to reject or repudiate the common life and system of rights that his society has chosen and that it protects by punishing those who obstruct them, but the act defies the community whose common life the criminal shares, and in doing so he wills some form of punishment, namely, the deprivation of a public or political good. He does not necessarily will the actual punishment incurred, because its exact specification is a matter for the community itself. The criminal expresses his own will in bringing punishment upon himself, but the particular punishment he suffers is determined by the will of the community which made the law defining the offence and prescribing the penalty.[49]

Collingwood is suggesting, then, that punishment is the penalty incurred for a breach of law, and it is therefore administered to an offender for an offence which the community, of which he is a member, has itself defined. In this respect the community can only have its eye turned to the fact that a law has been broken. The person who has broken the law, from the point of view of punishment, is working against the society, whose goodness consists in members who live together under the auspices of good laws which are 'loyally obeyed' and 'well administered'.[50]

Punishment, Collingwood argues, is not vengeance. Vengeance differs from the idea of retribution in that the latter is limited by the principle of just desert, while the former is not. In his early writings Collingwood was able to distinguish punishment from vengeance by imputing a moral motive to the former. Punishment differs from vengeance, he claimed, in being 'a pronouncement of the moral consciousness'.[51] In the 1923 lectures on action he argued that 'the punishment meted out by law differs from the unreasoning revenge of conventional society precisely

in being moral, in being punishment which ought to be inflicted, as opposed to one which, human nature being what it is, actually is inflicted'.[52]
However, when Collingwood began to distinguish between right and duty,
that is, between politics and morality, he could no longer sustain the
distinction between punishment and vengeance on the same grounds.
Punishment, Collingwood later contended, is the injury done to a person,
inflicted by someone who is authorised by, or is consciously acting on
behalf of, the community, for the harm done to that community by the
person being punished. The same act, inflicted for personal interest and
without the sanction of the community, would be an act of vengeance.
Punishment, however, is not totally devoid of a vengeful element, but it
is a communal rather than a private vengeance.[53] Nor should punishment,
understood as the deserved infliction of hurt upon an offender, be confused with individual or communal anger. To hurt someone because he
deserves it is a different act from hurting someone because one is angry.
Indeed, until the anger has subsided and passed, one is hardly in a suitable
frame of mind for assessing what the offender deserves.[54]

If the order that the state seeks to maintain is violated, that is, if its
laws are broken, what right has the state to punish, and for what purpose?
In other words, what are the general justifying aims of punishment? The
right of the state to punish, according to T. H. Green, rests upon the right
of every individual as a social being to contribute freely to the common
good. This implies that the associated individuals have a corresponding
right to prevent actions which interfere with free actions designed to
contribute to the common good. This is the right of punishment.[55] In
The New Leviathan Collingwood assumes the right of the state to punish.
The very idea of the body politic involves the use of measures to maintain
its existence, and to pursue the joint enterprise for which it was instituted.
Elsewhere in his writings Collingwood declares that it is idle to ask what
right the state has to punish: 'If the state has a right to do anything, it
has a right to punish; ... the state is nothing but society itself as legislating
and executing its own laws'.[56] Indeed, a criminal sets himself against the
combined will of society, and his inability to overcome the opposition
is itself a form of punishment. If a society wishes to arrange its affairs in
a certain way, it simply cannot desist from punishing those wills that are
opposed to it. A breach of the law may inspire a society to ask itself
if a better law can be found, but in the absence of a worthy replacement
a society cannot tolerate wilful disregard of the existing law without
compromising the common good its members have chosen to promote
and protect.[57]

A society institutes such arrangements as it thinks necessary for preserving itself because of a recognition that freedom is always a matter of
degree, and that in some circumstances someone who in other circum-

stances is able to exercise free will may be overcome by desire or passion. Every society is subject to such strains and is in danger of breaking down into the nonsocial community out of which it arose (*NL,* 21.8). In order to prevent this, the members of a society may authorise certain people whom they believe to have the greatest strength of will to give such orders as are necessary to the maintenance of its existence. In order to supplement such a safeguard, certain machinery may be instituted forcibly to restrain those who endanger the existence of society. This machinery is the criminal law, which is invoked only when society exhibits signs of breaking down into the nonsocial community (*NL,* 21.84). The establishment of such procedures in the body politic is imperative. If no formal machinery exists, then informal measures will be implemented to deal with those people who violate the good of society. In the case of murder, for instance, if the law does not punish the murderer, then the mob will lynch him. Whether the mob ought to do so is not in question: It must do so, in the absence of law, to protect life.

The law when it hangs a murderer is not going out of its way to 'hang a man who but for the law would get off scot-free'; it is hanging a man who but for the law would be torn limb from limb together with many innocent victims of misguided violence by the mob. The law's right over the criminal is the right to take him out of the hands of an angry mob and deal with him as justly as it can.[58]

Collingwood is suggesting here that one of the justifying aims of punishment is to secure the criminal's right to be punished justly, and to rescue him from the anger and vengeance of the mob. The criminal not only deserves, but also has a right, to be punished.

Any justification of punishment must demonstrate the good or value it is designed to promote: Gratuitous punishment aimed at no good in particular would be unjustifiable and not punishment at all. Does punishment, then, fall within the categories of utilitarian, regularian, or dutiful action designed to promote the useful, right, or moral good? In *Religion and Philosophy* Collingwood, like Kant, did not distinguish between right and dutiful action. The good which punishment promotes would therefore be both political and moral. Not to punish a criminal 'would be a denial of social relations', because in the act of punishing we uphold the value of social relations and express to the criminal our 'moral attitude towards him'.[59] The crime is at once unlawful and immoral. The punishment is a moral condemnation of both.

When Collingwood came to distinguish between right and duty, he associated punishment with the political good, or regularian action, while not wishing at the same time to disassociate it entirely from utility and morality. To exclude either, of course, would be a denial of both the law of primitive survivals and the notion of a linked hierarchy of forms in which the latter is in some sense immanent in the former, and in which the latter includes within itself traces of that out of which it developed. A criminal act, Collingwood argues, is as a rule also an immoral act, but not invariably so, nor are all immoral acts illegal. Offenders are not punished because of the moral wrong that may be commensurate with breaking the law. The person is punished for having committed a 'politically bad', rather than a 'morally bad', act.[60] In other words, the moral objective of reforming the criminal is not central to the act of punishment. Collingwood agrees with Green in believing that it is no business of the state to assess the moral guilt of a criminal,[61] nor by means of punishment to promote moral goodness. Green argues that the state 'looks not to virtue and vice but to rights and wrongs'.[62] In Collingwood's view, the state through punishment certainly promotes the good life, but it is the political good of orderliness, and not that of the moral good of virtue, which it is capable of attaining. The moral goodness which is exemplified in an act of duty done by a person because it is his duty 'cannot be promoted or impeded, cannot be created or destroyed, cannot even be fostered or discouraged to however small an extent, by political means'.[63]

The attitude needed for administering punishment is different from that required for making moral judgements, but this separation is a convenient abstraction, because all actions have moral determinations. The action in its totality is understood better if we desist from making such abstractions. Collingwood argues that

the judge would be a better man, and the law he administers would be the expression of the will of a better community, if he took the view that the criminal's moral state was relevant to the way in which he was to be treated. But though he would be a better man, he would not be a better judge; and though the community whose laws tried to take moral considerations into account would be a better community its laws would not be better laws. The purpose of law as law, and of the judge as judge, is fulfilled when they have solved the purely legal problem of making and enforcing law.[64]

In essence, punishment is a political act, and the good it wishes to promote is the political good: It 'deals with political values and no others'.[65]

Collingwood distinguishes himself from Green in giving a different emphasis to the deterrent value of punishment. Green, while acknowledging that punishment must also have retributive and reformatory elements, emphasizes that its primary aim is not to cause the criminal pain for the sake of causing pain, nor necessarily to prevent him from committing the crime again, 'but to associate terror with the contemplation of the crime in the mind of others who might be tempted to commit it'.[66] In Collingwood's mind, the instrumental view of punishment — that of using the person as a means to an end to deter others from committing crimes —

is not the reason for which, nor the good towards which, punishment is directed. Punishment, Collingwood argues, is fundamentally retributive, and, because it is a concrete action, it may be other things as well, but these things are in addition to its character as punishment. The public nature of punishment ensures that it has an effect on others besides the recipient by highlighting the consequences of breaking the law. The punishment may also affect the attitude of the criminal himself towards his crime and its future repetition.[67] Indeed, society, or the ruling class, as I suggested earlier, has an educative function in preparing the members of the nonsocial community for membership in the social community. Punishment, too, in societies sufficiently confident of the stability of their gains and which are not in constant fear of breaking down into the condition from whence they arose, will have an educative role to play. When the activity of the criminal is viewed as a 'temporary aberration', punishment, in upholding the political good, will look to the future in educating the person to take a place, or resume a place, in society.[68] In *Religion and Philosophy* Collingwood recognised that in addition to being an expression of condemnation, punishment must also treat the criminal as 'capable of reformation'. Punishment should, he claimed, awaken the criminal's 'moral consciousness'.[69] We can infer from this, in view of the fact that Collingwood came to view punishment in relation to the political good, that similarly it should attempt to awaken the political consciousness.

Collingwood concedes that unless punishment actually produces deterrent and reformatory effects it has probably failed to discover just and equitable penalties. Collingwood appears to admit that just punishments should improve people and raise the general level of obedience to law in the community.[70] Neither deterrence nor reform, however, can be justifiable if the person punished has not done anything to deserve punishment, or if his habits are such that they do not deserve to be reformed.[71] Here, then, Collingwood is confusing the general justifying aim of punishment – that it should reform the criminal and deter others – with the question of who should be punished. In fact, the general justifying aims of punishment he gives are much closer to those of Green than Collingwood would admit, and with regard to distribution, too, both writers have similar views on who should be punished and by how much.

On the question of who should be punished, Green argues that only those who have transgressed the system of rights and who have therefore incurred public indignation deserve to be the recipients of punishment. Punishment cannot be just unless the person to be punished intentionally violated the rights of, or neglected his obligations to, the community, provided the acts could have been avoided by the agent.[72] Like Green, Collingwood gives a retributive justification of who should be punished.

Following the retributivists (such as Kant, for instance),[73] Collingwood argues that punishment can only be justifiably inflicted on the grounds of desert. In other words, only those guilty of a crime deserve to be punished. The determination of desert is not a moral question, but a matter of ascertaining whether the law has been broken, and if so, what law and by whom.[74] For Kant, of course, the determination is both moral and legal.

The person who deserves punishment, in Collingwood's view, is one whose will has broken and who has committed acts which violate the political good, and which society deems undesirable. By perpetrating such acts the criminal subverts the order of society.[75] In other words, he ceases to function as a member of society, but may very well 'continue to be a member of the non-social community from which it was derived' (NL, 21.87). He automatically puts himself in such a condition by disobeying not this or that law, but by violating the law in general, and unless the law is violated punishment cannot be deserved.[76] Collingwood agrees with Bradley that the essence of the retributive principle is 'the absolute restriction of punishment to crime'.[77]

Not all crime is perpetrated by people whose wills have cracked, and therefore criminals other than those who have reverted to the condition of the nonsocial community may be punished. People, for instance, who hold high political ideals which are at variance with those of the society in which they live may commit crimes to further their conceptions of the common good. Such crimes inspired by a conception of the social good are no less crimes than those that are committed from self-interest, 'but a crime of this kind, characteristic as it is of a person with a high degree of political intelligence, has redeeming features. In especial, its punishment may be endured wholly without resentment'.[78] Collingwood means that such people will be criminals of a special category: political criminals, who deserve punishment, but who retain the ability to act rationally and freely, and who, because of their heightened political intelligence, recognise that the ideals against which they fight must be credited with having some merit, and that their upholders therefore justifiably use the instrument of punishment in their defence. In such circumstances the criminal submits to punishment and accepts and respects its imposition. Collingwood specifically mentions Sir Thomas More in this context, but the category of civil disobedients in general may be more apposite. Their crimes are principled, designed to promote the common good, committed openly, and the perpetrators readily submit to punishment.

We now come to the second aspect of the distribution of punishment, that is, defining the principle which determines the severity of a sentence. Collingwood initially subscribed to the retributivist view in answering this question, but later moved much closer to Green's position. Kant, for example, argued that the punishment should, in principle, be equivalent to the crime. This would entail taking into consideration the different circumstances of offenders. For example, in a case of slander where a rich man does an injustice to a poor man, a fine may be insufficient to redress the grievance. In such circumstances a more humiliating sentence may be appropriate to satisfy the principle of equivalence.[79]

In *Religion and Philosophy* Collingwood argued that the degree of 'punishment is fixed by one standard only; what we suppose [the criminal] to deserve'.[80] Desert, then, is both the criterion of who should be punished and to what degree. Collingwood admits that the standard is difficult to define, but claims that in practice it serves as a rough guide to sentencing. In a later formulation Collingwood puts forward both the principles of equivalence and respect for human dignity as the limiting constraints upon punishment. The punishment, he argues, should fit the crime in that it must always be partial. A crime is never the complete denial of the political good, and therefore punishment should never be complete. The partial character of punishment is evident even in capital sentencing, because death, although final, is not the most horrendous treatment that could be devised. The murderer who awaits execution is still entitled to be treated in a humane and just manner.[81]

We should not assume from this that Collingwood was wholeheartedly in favour of capital punishment. He was not. He did think, however, that it was appropriate for some societies. Its necessity is relative to the degree of sophistication a society has reached in its political organization and intelligence. Politically backward societies in which the members are 'relatively unaccustomed to obeying laws' should not pretend that they are civilized enough to do without hanging murderers when really such measures are necessary for the preservation of society. It is much better, though, in a society which has a mature political organization, to work towards the institution of arrangements which would not lead to the destruction of 'an appreciable number of its members', but rather to a process of assimilation which would not be disastrous to the body politic as a whole.[82] Collingwood here appears to be conceding that the criterion of the degree of punishment to be administered is not desert at all, but the amount of punishment deemed necessary to sustain the common life of the body politic by upholding the principle of deterrence. In this respect Collingwood agrees with Green. Green contends that there can be 'no *a priori* criterion of just punishment'.[83] The necessary terror which needs to be associated with a crime in order to preserve the system of rights which belongs to the community can be worked out only through experience, and this has to do with trying to achieve an equality between the magnitude of the crime and the amount of punishment inflicted. For

Collingwood, the degree of punishment is largely determined by political necessity. Different societies, depending upon the degree of civilization they have attained, need to institute different punishments appropriate to the threat to which they believe society to be subjected: Such questions 'cannot be answered on general or abstract grounds, but only on concrete political grounds'.[84]

Crime, Collingwood argues, is a necessary and permanent feature of human life: It is the resistance of the individual to the social good, or the particular to the universal. Such resistance is the necessary negative moment in the dialectic of all action. This does not mean that crimes must necessarily be committed: only that the forces of society, such as law and order, education, and political acumen, are directed to circumventing them. Political action – that is, action according to rule – has as its opposite or negative element criminal behaviour, that is, the violation of law. As long as political activity is sustained and maintains itself, it is contributing to the minimalisation, and even negation, of crime.[85]

4. International relations

Having looked at the internal relations of a body politic, it remains in this section to identify its external relations. The international community of bodies politic is in some respects analogous to a single body politic. Even if some members of the community of bodies politic are capable of establishing social relations, there will nevertheless be others which have not reached sufficient maturity to do so. In such circumstances it may be appropriate for the former to impose the higher levels of civilization upon those that have not yet attained them. In other words, the body politic at a higher level of civilization may exercise transeunt rule over those of a lower form.[86]

Just as crime threatens to reverse the process of conversion from a nonsocial to a social condition, aggressive war, being in international relations the equivalent of crime, threatens and destroys the possibility of a harmonious society of states: 'War is the same thing as crime, in the sense that it represents the failure of man to devise a political system which shall be really political, really law-abiding or rationally organized'.[87] War differs from crime, however, in that the former involves a clash between more than one system of law which defines and promotes the common good for each of the communities in conflict.

Just as society needs law, so does the international community. Collingwood maintains that the international law of modern Europe is ancient in origin. It is the customary law which developed out of the international, nonsocial community. This law resembles that of 'the Iceland of the sagas' in that there were people who could articulate the law if one should

184   The social and political thought of R.G. Collingwood

enquire as to its content, but no class of persons existed to enforce the law if it was disregarded. Most people obeyed the law, and those who did not were frowned upon. The only way of maintaining the law was for those who wished to see it obeyed to join together to thwart the attempts of those who did not. In modern European relations between bodies politic, all the conditions were fulfilled with the exception of the last. Instead of crushing those bodies politic that offended against the law, we preferred to see it neglected (*NL*, 28.79).

War is the adoption of an eristical rather than a dialectical attitude in external politics, that is, a disposition towards adversarial politics rather than the politics of agreement. Nonagreements become hardened into disagreements because the eristical attitude can only conceive of victory and thus rejects the way of compromise, that is, the conversion of non-agreement into agreement. For Collingwood, '*War is a state of mind*' (*NL*, 29.63). War does not necessarily entail military force: It is a belief that differences can only be settled when one body politic triumphs over another by forcing it to give way. To put it in the current vernacular of studies of international politics, war is a state of mind which views relations between bodies politic in terms of a zero-sum game, in which if someone gains there must also be a corresponding loss suffered by one or more of the players. Collingwood's view of war is essentially that of Hobbes: 'The nature of War, consisteth not in actuall fighting; but in the known disposition thereto, during all the time there is no assurance to the contrary'.[88] War reverses the dialectical process which operates within the body politic, and upon which external politics is postulated. Indeed, people are used, in the context of their social lives, and in internal politics, to approach problems dialectically, but to make or acquiesce in war is a departure from the dialectical method, that is, from liberal politics, in the international sphere.

The blame for war cannot wholeheartedly be placed with one party. A country, or body politic, may be acting like 'a criminal lunatic' in attacking another out of fear, but the object of aggression must bear some of the blame for having provoked such fear. This does not mean that a partial acceptance of blame should lead one to desist from responding to aggression. Pacifism, Collingwood argues, far from contributing to peace, is a positive factor in the promotion and provocation of war:

29.97.   Not realizing that modern war is a neurotic thing, an effect of terror where there is nothing to fear and of hunger where the stomach is already full, [the pacifist] proposes to deal with it by throwing away his arms so that the war-makers shall not be afraid of him, and giving up what they would snatch (from him or others) so that their hunger shall be appeased.

Pacifism, Collingwood believes, is a pernicious and parasitic doctrine, espoused by people who would not be able to propound it if it were not

for the fact that centuries of conflict have gradually facilitated the evolution of a settled system of law indicative of a peaceful society in which
the views of nonresistance can be freely expressed. The pacifist forgets
that he can only articulate his views because other people 'are making
the world safe for him by doing precisely the work which he condemns
as wrong'.[89] Pacifism, Collingwood argues, has rarely been put into practice, even by those Protestant countries heavily influenced by Wycliffe
and Luther. Quakers who individually have refused to fight have justifiably
incurred the charge that they, in renouncing war, allow others to fight
in their defence. War is not waged by individuals, and therefore the refusal
of individuals to fight makes no difference to the state's perpetration of
war. The individual can influence policy through the appropriate channels,
but if he fails to attain the policy he wants, then he is obliged to follow
the course which others have succeeded in implementing. Noncompli-
ance itself, Collingwood maintains, is complicity in war. Let it be granted,
he suggests, that war is evil and that it comes about because states have
failed in their primary aim of seeking and maintaining a condition of peace.
Each party in war shares some degree of blame for its occurrence. War
is not evil in general, but is a specifically political kind of evil. War reflects
the failure of government to discharge its primary duty of keeping the
peace. If governments were able to do their work better, the number of
wars would greatly diminish. Anything which facilitates a better political
life therefore contributes 'towards the abolition of war; every impediment
of political life helps to make war more likely'.[90] Collingwood goes as far
as to suggest that refusal to obey the law, even by pacifists, reinforces
those evils which contribute to war: 'War is a symptom of misgovernment:
every enemy of government is a friend to war, however little he may
recognize it'.[91]

The idea of a society presupposes harmony, and the achievement of
such a condition is consciously dialectical. In a body politic, force becomes a more conspicuous element, and is evident in the relation between
the ruled and ruling classes. The act of ruling, however, establishes law
and order, and facilitates the progress of the ruled towards becoming
capable of sharing in the ruling process. To institute such conditions and
to set the dialectical processes in motion 'is the first article of any policy'
for the rulers of a body politic (*NL*, 30.26). The extension of such policy
into the international sphere constitutes the equivalent of harmony in
the internal sphere, namely, peace. War is the breakdown of this dialectical
policy. Why has such a breakdown occurred in the twentieth century?

Collingwood addressed himself to this question on a number of occasions. In 'Man Goes Mad', for instance, Collingwood attributes the militarism of his day to the collapse of liberalism. Collingwood, as we saw,
viewed liberalism in much the same way as de Ruggiero. A liberal society
is one in which free expression is fostered and political opinions freely

articulated. Liberalism seeks a unity in the multiplicity of views by means of a dialectical method in which opposing views are freely discussed until their exponents begin to uncover, beneath the opposition, some underlying common ground which will help them move forward.[92] In other words, there is a concept of the common good above and beyond the particular interests of those individuals who compose society.[93] The liberal transformation of the inner life of the state failed to transform the state in its external relations. Instead of seeing the body politic in an organic relation with other bodies politic, in which the good of one contributes to the good of all, 'the liberal government which "trusted the people" hated and feared peoples other than its own. It was this unnatural union of internal liberalism with external illiberalism that led by way of international anarchy to the militarism of today'.[94]

This failure to extend liberal principles to the external environment was something that liberals, in general, acknowledged. A few years earlier Croce, for example, had lamented the fact that political liberty, having 'been firmly established in the territorial divisions and in the internal order of almost all the European states', had failed to extend the 'principle to international relations'.[95]

Collingwood maintained that little had changed in international relations over the last three centuries, but what changes had transpired had been for the worse. Weapons had become more destructive than ever, and national hatreds, to a greater degree than in the past, were 'smouldering everywhere'.[96] Nations, possessed by the individualist mentality in internal relations, found themselves in the paradoxical position of spending ever-increasing amounts of money on arms in order to maintain peace. They were driven to this because it had by then become the test of nationhood that the nation possessed the ability to wage war. 'War', Collingwood argued, 'is the ultimate end of the modern state. All forces that go to make up the modern state combine to drive its activity in the direction of warfare'.[97] The origins of the modern belligerent state appeared during the nineteenth century, when people began to believe that the highest function of the state was to wage war.

During the First World War and the interwar years, many writers attempted to explain the belligerence of modern states. An aspect of this literature was devoted to the question of the extent to which Hegel could be blamed for the cult of state worship, and the degree to which he had justified the necessity of war.

Initially, as John Morrow has pointed out, such discussions appeared in the correspondence columns of the *London Times*, but the issue rapidly became contested in academic circles. Many of the British idealists themselves, feeling that their integrity was being questioned because they were associated in the public mind with Kant, Fichte, and Hegel, entered the arena and either exonerated Hegel or disassociated themselves from the more pernicious implications of his doctrines.[98] In what is now a very well-known contribution to this debate, L. T. Hobhouse charged Hegel with having formulated the 'false and wicked doctrine' that was eventually to lead to a tangible manifestation in the bombing of London during the First World War.[99] It is a mistake to think that German militarism is the product of Bismarckian politics, he argued. Hegel's identification of freedom with obedience to law, his merging of the personality of the individual with the state, and the elevation of the state to the highest form of association all led Hobhouse to conclude that there was a direct connection between the teaching of Hegel and the ethics of the Bismarckian state. Hobhouse was not only concerned to deprecate Hegel but also to expose and refute the Hegelian legacy in the English-speaking world, a legacy which viewed the state 'as an incarnation of the Absolute, a superior personality which absorbs the real living personality of men and women'.[100] Excluding Green from the more invidious aspects of Hegelianism, Hobhouse set out systematically to destroy the logical foundations of Bosanquet's theory of the state. Indeed, it became commonplace during the interwar years to associate Hegel, not only with German aggression, but with the rise of totalitarianism in Europe.[101] Joseph Kennedy, the American ambassador to Britain, for example, maintained that 'Hegelian theory made the state supreme mind and will, the dominant personality to which the total man – economic, political, family and religious – was absolutely subjected. Man had no rights or liberties save those which the dominant state gave him and which it could withdraw'.[102] Such views were sufficiently prevalent in the late 1930s to provoke T. M. Knox, Collingwood's former student, to come to Hegel's defence. Knox denied the claim that Hegel viewed individuals as 'mere means to the ends of the state', and rejected the claim that the *Philosophy of Right* was the theoretical foundation of the practice of fascism and National-Socialism.[103] Such indictments of Hegel, Knox claimed, could only be made by means of a highly selective reading of the texts, a reading which ignored the overall spirit and emphasis of the doctrines. Much of Knox's argument was directed at E. F. Carritt, Collingwood's former tutor. Carritt immediately replied by claiming that his own interpretation of Hegel was confirmed by H. von Treitschke, W. Wallace, T. H Green, F. H. Bradley, D. G. Ritchie, B. Bosanquet, and professors Lord, Reyburn, and Sabine. As far as Carritt was concerned, there could be no misconstruing such statements as this: 'The nation to whom such a mission is entrusted by the World-spirit is, for its epoch, supreme. Against this, its absolute right, the spirits of other nations have no rights whatever'.[104]

It is in the context of this debate about the extent of Hegel's culpability that Collingwood's own pronouncements on the matter have to be

viewed. Although Collingwood never mentions the discussion in his published work, nor directs his arguments towards any of the arguments of
the protagonists, there can be little doubt that he was fully aware of the
debate. In a letter dated 6 January 1940, Collingwood says that he had
read Knox's piece on Hegel with 'delighted approval'. Knox had, Collingwood suggests, done justice to Hegel against those such as Carritt
who tended to treat Hegel like a 'dead dog'.[105] Immediately after the First
World War Collingwood addressed himself to the question and was inclined to side with those who thought that Hegel must carry some of
the blame. In an essay delivered to a conference of Belgian students at
Fladbury in 1919, Collingwood attempted to analyse the reasons which
led to the First World War, and to formulate an answer as to the question
of how such a situation could be prevented from arising again. He made
a distinction between the right kind of imperialism, where a civilized
community rules over a less civilized community, and the wrong kind
of imperialism, in which one civilized state attempts to impose its will
upon another civilized state. It was Germany's attempt to impose its civilization upon other civilized states that constituted the immediate cause
of war. However, at a deeper level of analysis, the 'Prussian philosophy'
provided the justification for such aggression. Hegel, Collingwood maintains, was the first to articulate it, but 'it appears rather as an irrational
excrescence than as an integral part' of his philosophy.[106] The Prussian
doctrine claimed that all creative and innovative initiative was vested in
the power of the state. The state was viewed as equivalent to God, in
that it was answerable only to itself, possessed absolute rights, and exercised absolute power over all of its subjects. In its external relations
the state owed 'no duties, no obligations, no responsibilities towards any
other state'.[107] In Collingwood's view, the German philosophy is false in
that the very fact that there are other states, that is, a plurality of absolutes,
contradicts the primary axiom of this philosophy, namely, that the absolute
is indivisible; there is only one absolute.

This diseased and false philosophy breeds despair and pessimism, because the possibility of understanding the world in such terms is untenable. It is only by eradicating this theory, espoused in Prussian philosophy,
that peace can permanently be restored. The Prussian philosophy was in
error because it failed to realise that all power is limited. Even though
Germany had been defeated, the Prussian philosophy still survived, thus
rendering the possibility of its reemergence in an even more menacing
form. With the rise of fascism and nazism in Europe, and the reemergence
of militarism, Collingwood's fears were proved to be well founded. In
1936 Collingwood once again associated Hegel with the view that war
is the highest function of the state, and that it is a necessary corollary of
the external relations between states. War, Collingwood claimed, had

become a compulsion. The reason for this is the dual emphasis upon the state as an individual and as a sovereign body. Collingwood explains the rise of militarism by suggesting that it 'is sovereignty conceived in terms of individuality: the absolute and unlimited form of the state in all that affects its own concerns, combined with its merely external relation to all other states'.[108]

Collingwood later extends his analysis by suggesting that in the Prussian philosophy the state was equated with the body politic as a whole. This equation was given credence by T.H. Green and a number of 'other writers who thought a German book a sufficient authority and its author's nationality all the guarantee of which his words stood in need'.[109] In Collingwood's view, the state, as we saw, is not an individual or institution correlative with the body politic; it is instead the political activity of the ruling class. The primary aim of this ruling class, properly conceived, is not to subordinate the members of the body politic to the will of the state, but to engage in political education in order to facilitate the conversion of members to share in, and give expression to, the rational life of the body politic. In Germany this ideal was never realised, and the people were never conceived as the nursery towards which the rulers should look for potential converts to the society of rulers. It was, then, the absolutist political experience of Prussia that led many brilliant philosophers to misconceive the nature of the body politic (NL, 33.2–33.22). They simply did not understand the problems that Hobbes, Locke, and Rousseau posed, namely, how individuals could spontaneously create a social order with a view to secure their rights from the encroachment of princely power. Because of the 'social backwardness of German life', the problem of classical politics simply did not arise. It is no surprise, then, that German philosophers made nonsense of classical politics; what is surprising is that some of them, and in particular Hegel, nearly did make sense of it (NL, 33.29). The Germans were simply not able to comprehend society as an 'artificiall Man'. Both Hegel and Marx, Collingwood suggests, denied 'the existence, even the possibility, of free joint activity' (NL, 33.46). This was partly because they had no experience of it.

We see once again the relevance of Collingwood's theory of mind to his political philosophy as a whole. The German people had not attained full rational consciousness, that is, they lacked the ability to exercise freedom of will. This is not because they did not have the capacity to do so, but because the capacity had been repressed. The Germans still lived in the state of nature; their condition was similar to that of a non-social community. Freedom of the will was something alien, obedience to a superior almost divine. A people used to living in servility look in horror at freedom. As far as Collingwood is concerned, 'The Germans made nonsense of the classical politics because they feared and hated the freedom of social life' (*NL*, 33.52). This tendency to hate freedom did not render Germans incapable of thinking, but instead distorted their notion of what thinking rationally entails. Indeed, freedom to them was what we would describe as subservience. The problem was not that rational thinking could not occur – there was, for instance a healthy natural-scientific tradition – but that it could not emerge in the areas of history and politics in which the obsession with herd worship prevailed.

The German emphasis upon state worship is not, strictly speaking, 'a genuine state-worship, for it lacks the notion of a state' (*NL*, 33.75). Marx, for instance, in believing that the state would wither away, proved for Collingwood that he had no concept of a ruling class, and instead associated the state with the nonsocial community:

His socialism, based negatively on the traditional German hatred of freedom and hence of the 'capitalists' who are, for him, the chief representatives of freedom in European history, is based positively on the traditional German worship of the herd, and culminates in an act whereby the believer offers himself and everything he has in sacrifice to the adored object. The God of Marxism is a jealous God, and will have no rivals (*NL*, 33.79).

Similarly, Marx's dialectical materialism is seen to be a consequence of the German obsession with herd worship. Hegel had reintroduced the Platonic idea of dialectic into Germany, but in addition to seeing it as an amicable 'dialectic of words' saw it as a 'dialectic of things'. Each of these processes, Hegel believed, must proceed from the abstraction of opposites to a concrete synthesis. The dialectic of things was seen to conform to the pattern set down by the dialectic of words. Hegel's mistake was in not acknowledging that we must have a concrete to begin with; otherwise the abstractions of which it is composed become elusive (*NL*, 33.89).

Marx's inversion of the Hegelian dialectic does not, in Collingwood's view, escape the pretence of extracting 'a concrete rabbit from an abstract hat' (*NL*, 33.91). Why, then, did Marx subscribe to dialectical materialism? Collingwood answers that Marx, in upholding the idea of herd worship, wished to reject the idea of the freedom of the will. Such a denial was to be found already formulated in the doctrines of materialism. Marx's substitution of a materialist dialectic for that of Hegel, 'if it changed nothing else, did constitute a denial of freedom of the will and an act of submission to the great German god, the omnipotent herd' (*NL*, 33.99).

Essentially, then, Collingwood's contribution to the debate concerning Hegel's responsibility for the militarism of the twentieth century was that we cannot directly blame the German, or Prussian, philosophers as such, because being possessed of insufficient political experience, that is, living in conditions where the freedom of the will was repressed and perverted, it would have been an immense task for them to have risen above these conditions, recognised the difficulties that faced the classical theorists, and contributed a solution to the problem of the nonsocial community. What this means for external relations of the state is evident. Having no concept of a social community in internal matters in which problems are solved dialectically (that is, on the basis of liberal principles), they can hardly have conceived the external relations of the body politic other than they did, namely, as individual sovereign states in constant conflict with each other. Even Marx viewed this conflict as inevitable, but envisaged a time when class cohesion would triumph over nationalism.

Given his theory that political activity, in its internal and external relations, can exhibit the characteristics of utilitarian, regularian and dutiful action – that is, the levels on the ascending scale of rationality – did Collingwood believe that war could be abolished? A body politic that had reached the level of utilitarian action would view external differences as a conflict of interests; regularian action, as a conflict of rights; and, dutiful action, as a conflict of duties. At all of these levels a dialectical rather than an eristical solution is possible. Collingwood believed that conflict among nations was necessary and inevitable as long as complete systems of laws coexisted side by side, but that there was no necessity for the conflict to become manifest in military war.[110] War, then, can be averted but never entirely abolished. At one time, Collingwood did believe that the League of Nations could play a positive role in preventing racial, national, and class wars.[111] In addition, he believed that the more advanced Western states had a dual obligation: first, to prevent anyone of their number from imposing its ideals and values upon another; and second, 'to bring light to the dark places of the earth', in the hope of preventing conflicts of class, race, nation, and language, in 'the service of civilization'.[112] Such missionary zeal on the part of the advanced nations, as far as Collingwood was concerned, would certainly make the world a safer place in which to live.

By 1932, having witnessed the ineffectiveness of the League of Nations, Collingwood believed that war among European countries could be prevented by creating a Federation of Nations. Such a federation could include North and South America, as well as the constituent members of the British Empire. Its governing body would be stronger than that of the League of Nations, but weaker than that of the United States of America. Armed forces would still need to be maintained against races outside the frontiers of this federation, but within its boundaries, and among its members, war could be averted.[113] This, of course, is a reiteration of Kant's plan for perpetual peace in which republican nations voluntarily join a confederation pledged to maintaining peaceful relations, and, through example and by forceful responses to aggression from outside the confederation, more and more nations would come to see the benefits and rationality of peace.[114] Collingwood's optimism was soon to be diminished. The Spanish civil war between 'Fascist dictatorship and parliamentary democracy',[115] the Abyssinian and Czechoslovakian crises, all led Collingwood to lose faith in the sincerity of the British government, which he had now come to believe was pro-fascist, and confirmed his view that the League of Nations was too weak to be effective in containing the belligerence of a state intent on expansionist policies. The very idea of appeasement was abhorrent to him,[116] and, consistent with the view he had held in 1919, he believed it was the duty of the nations of Europe to prevent any one of its members from imposing its civilization on any other advanced nation. By the summer of 1939, in the light of the increased tension in Europe, Collingwood appears to have regained some of his faith in the British government and in democracy. He says, for example, that the prime minister's renunciation of the alliance with Hitler gave him hope that 'the Munich Policy has not come to stay'.[117] Furthermore, he affirmed that 'compared with a democracy, Fascism stands for incompetence, muddle, and waste'.[118]

It is not surprising that in *The New Leviathan,* when Collingwood theorized about these matters more systematically, he concluded that a universal body politic was impossible, and that 'hopes for the abolition of war are vain' (*NL*, 30.8). Why did Collingwood reach these conclusions?

He argued that social consciousness implies a distinction between a *particular society* and the *universal society.* A particular society is distinguished from others on account of having a different aim from them. The idea which informs a universal society is that it aims only to be a society. This idea of a universal society is implied in each particular society, because the latter always has a twofold function. It attempts to establish social relations, but at the same time promotes the devotion of that activity toward the pursuit of particular enterprises. In Collingwood's view, 'The universal society can never be realized as an actual society having its own membership, its own organization, its own executive, and so forth' (*NL*, 21.44). The League of Nations was one such futile attempt at establishing a universal society. The attempt was bound to fail, because no society could ever lose the elements of the nonsocial community out of which it emerged. Every society was also partly a nonsocial community, in that the conversion process from the one to the other was never finished. A society devoted to the study of mathematics, for instance, will be comprised of those who speak the language of mathematics. Those who are unable to speak this language have an impenetrable barrier to surmount. The restriction might not be intentional, but seems merely on practical grounds to be inevitable: 'The social will always aims at the universal society; what it produces is always some particular society which is half-way between the universal society and a non-social community'

(*NL*, 21.54). Such discrepancies exist because the aim of reforming society is never to abolish the nonsocial community, but to transform it. In the process of such a transformation, that which is transformed must retain a continuous identity. If there is no continuity between the beginning and the end of the process, 'nothing would have been transformed; no problem would have been solved' (*NL*, 21.55).

The traces of the nonsocial community which prevent the establishment of a successful supranational organization, or universal society, are exactly the same elements which prevent the abolition of war. It is the traces of the nonsocial elements in society, or the individuals whom Collingwood calls Yahoos, which 'vitiate the life of every ruling class; they vitiate the relation between rulers and ruled in every body politic; they vitiate the relation between every body politic and every other' (*NL*, 30.82). Such defects can never be cured, only modified as the defect itself undergoes innumerable changes. Wars will never be abolished, and will constantly change, according to the measures employed to alleviate them.[119] The manifestation of these nonsocial elements in societies is infinitely variable, and the ingenuity of mankind in responding to them needs to be equally flexible. Systems of relations among bodies politic must be adaptable. They can never be perfect, nor permanent. Societies 'must always be ready to use force, and always a new kind of force, against criminals within a body politic and enemies outside it who would forcibly destroy what has been already achieved without replacing it with anything better' (*NL*, 30.88).

Consistent with the view that he held in 1919, Collingwood maintains that a body politic is justified in waging war against another if it feels that advances that it has achieved are under threat or attack from the other. Where such a threat holds out the prospect of reducing the rest of mankind to the condition of Yahoos, that is, of those barely capable of rational choice, then any such body politic under threat is bound to destroy that which constitutes the threat, 'for the sake of the world at large' (*NL*, 30.92). War can be the promoter of peace and is therefore wholly justified if it is the only means by which the members of another so-called body politic, having succumbed to their irrational emotions, and who are subject to a popular ruler whose social inclinations are aggressive and belligerent rather than dialectical, can be stopped from extending the tyranny under which they live at home to the bodies politic they wish to subvert (*NL*, 30.99).[120] In these respects Collingwood's view on the right of nations to interfere in the affairs of nations which threaten the traditional values of European society are similar to the views of Edmund Burke. Burke argued that a country which blatantly cast off the wisdom of ages and threatened to undermine the common European heritage would indeed be inviting war by its actions. He thought it legitimate to interfere in the internal affairs of a state if its practices were so contrary to the practices of its neighbours as to constitute a threat. This he called the right of *vicinage*.[121]

Collingwood's analysis of the causes of war constitutes a partial explanation of the factors which he believed threatened European civilization. The decline in liberalism, for example, and its failure to transform the external relations between states, as well as precipitating war, also meant that liberal societies were a very weak defence against all those irrational forces that have threatened civilization. Indeed, liberal values are the values of civilization, and those of nazism and fascism of barbarism. It is to Collingwood's discussion of such matters that we must now turn.

7

The process of civilization

1. Introduction

The discussions of civilization and barbarism in *The New Leviathan* constitute the meeting places of all that Collingwood had to say about mind, society, and politics. Freedom of the will, that is, the highest stage of mental development, is a prerequisite of civilization. Freedom of the will, as we saw, necessarily entails mutual recognition and respect for other wills. Such recognition and respect have profound implications for conduct *inter homines* and for the existence of a civil life in which civility stands as the ideal of human conduct. Civilization, for Collingwood, is not a condition, nor an ideal, of society: It is the process of converting the nonsocial into the social community. In other words, civilization is the process of education which the social element in the body politic, and the parents or guardians in the family, promote in order to assist the mentally and socially immature members to attain their full potential. The process of civilization is conditional upon the exercise of free will and the achievement of a social life. Similarly, barbarism is the revolt against the conversion process. It is the attempt to retard or reverse the process of civilization and reduce the body politic to a nonsocial community. The ideal of civility, to which the process of civilization aims to achieve an approximation, presupposes a dialectical relationship among the members of a body politic, whereas the condition which barbarism realises presupposes and engenders an eristical relation.

Given that mind, society, and civilization are so integrally connected in the social and political philosophy of Collingwood, it is difficult to understand why so many commentators have chosen to ignore the very close theoretical connections. Ernest Barker set the trend by suggesting that he preferred 'to leave out of account the last two Parts' of *The New Leviathan;* the last in particular, because the Second World War and illness

195

appeared to have weighed rather 'heavily on the mind of a sick man, and the pen [was] beginning to slip from his fingers'.[1] Even Alan Donagan, who purported to be integrating 'the first three parts of *The New Leviathan*' into 'a coherent philosophy'[2] of the later writings of Collingwood, did not seriously attempt to incorporate part III into this philosophy and made only passing reference to part IV.[3]

Collingwood's theory of civilization and barbarism in *The New Leviathan* is at once the culmination of the argument of the book itself, and of the many investigations that he had conducted into the character of civilization and into the most appropriate methods to use for such investigations. In addition, if we cast our minds back to my original formulation of the long-term intellectual concerns of Collingwood, we are reminded that in Collingwood's view, history itself negated the dichotomy which traditionally existed between theory and practice. It overcomes this distinction because history enacts its object, thus rendering it no object at all, but instead unites the thought and its object in the activity of mind. Such a transcendence of theory and practice, Collingwood believed, would enable him to characterise both a historical morality and a historical civilization. We saw how the idea of duty fulfilled the first promise; it now remains to see how he went about fulfilling the second.

This chapter explores Collingwood's theory of civilization and barbarism with reference both to his own concerns and those of others who addressed themselves to problems similar to those confronted in *The New Leviathan*. This exercise, it is hoped, will serve to reveal the connections between mind, society, and civilization.

2. The vocabulary of the problem

The idea of civilization and its relation to other forms of human association attracted a great deal of attention during the latter part of the nineteenth and the first half of the twentieth centuries. The proliferation of 'ethnographic', or anthropological, literature disseminated a vocabulary in terms of which the relationship between past and present social groupings at different levels of culture could be conceptualized. This is not to say that the vocabulary came into existence with the appearance of this literature – merely that this vocabulary stabilized into a set stock of terms, each of which exhibited various degrees of laudatory and pejorative connotations as well as a diversity of descriptive referents. The terms *savagery, barbarism, civilization,* and their derivatives formed the basis of this vocabulary. Each term, with its associated derivatives, denoted a different stage in cultural development. Particularly important in establishing the terms of reference for discussion of the nature and character of cultural development were the books by Lewis H. Morgan (1877) and Edward

Tylor (1871).[4] Scott Nearing, writing in 1927, claimed that 'the familiar division of cultural history into savagery, barbarism and civilization', although arbitrary and 'intended to describe certain broad differences in economic and social relations', had after Morgan 'employed this division ... been quite generally accepted and followed by later writers'.[5] Morgan's reputation in Britain, however, was not great,[6] and Collingwood shows no evidence of having read *Ancient Society: or Researches in the Lines of Human Progress from Savagery through Barbarism to Civilization.* Marx and Engels had found Morgan's ideas particularly congenial. Engels, for instance, admired Morgan's criticism of the manner of production for profit in modern civilization and praised him for envisaging a future condition of mankind of which Karl Marx himself would have approved.[7] Edward Carpenter, writing in 1910, employed the familiar characterisation of savagery, barbarism, and civilization to depict human development, but like Morgan envisaged a stage beyond civilization. This new stage which he foretold was to come about by the 'balancing and correcting' of two complex human trends: that of communism, and that of the individual freedom associated with savagery.[8]

The theories of Morgan and Tylor represent a reaction against those explanations of savagery and barbarism which viewed them as the result of a regression from civilization. This view, deriving its legitimacy from the 'Mosaic cosmogony', Morgan argued, was untenable. It simply could not be supported with reference to the facts of human experience.[9] Tylor looked upon the degradation theory with similar incredulity. He thought that it was inconceivable, on the basis of the ethnographic evidence available, that people of different cultures began in a condition of civilization and regressed into conditions of barbarism and savagery. Both Morgan and Tylor subscribed to the progression theory of cultural development. Tylor argues that in this theory 'both advance and relapse have their acknowledged places. But so far as history is to be our criterion, progression is primary and degradation secondary'.[10] Collingwood's own view of cultural development, as we will see, is a version of the progression theory, but one which he wished to distinguish quite clearly from that of Tylor.

The relationship between different cultural stages could alternatively be conceptualized with reference to a cyclical framework. Such cyclical theories are familiar to us through the thought of the Greeks, Machiavelli, and Vico, but variations were also invoked during the latter part of the nineteenth and the early part of the twentieth centuries in order to explain the relationship between one cultural stage and another. Brooks Adams, for instance, in 1896, formulated a theory which postulated that human society, from the condition of being physically dispersed, gradually achieves a condition of concentration, that is, of civilization, only to decay and regress into dispersion, or barbarism, to begin the cycle once again.[11] Spengler's more elaborate and sophisticated version of the cyclical theory[12] aimed, by means of the 'analogical' method, to discern the logic in world history. He claimed that each culture had its own civilization towards which it inevitably progressed. It was the destiny of each culture to attain its civilization. The differentiae of culture from civilization were in the fact that the individual of the former directed his energy inward to the society in which he lived, whereas the energy of civilization-man was directed outwards. Every culture that attained its civilization had become imperialistic: 'Imperialism is Civilization unadulterated'.[13] The transition from culture to civilization was manifest in the emergence of the city as the victor over the town or country and in the subordination of politics to money. Having reached such a stage, each civilization inevitably declined. The cycle through which each culture went had analogous stages in every other culture.

The cyclical view of the rise and fall of civilizations, and in particular Spengler's articulation of it, inspired Collingwood to examine and criticize its claims and assumptions. In essence, Collingwood believed that the modern exponents of cyclical theories were infected with positivism.[14] Positivism converted history into nature, in that it posited a past independent of the historian and upon which the historian could gaze only as a spectator. Spengler, for all his protestations about understanding civilizations historically rather than as natural phenomena, isolated each culture into a self-contained entity whose stages were analogous to, but not identical with, the structural stages in every other culture. Such an approach ignored the continuities between cultures, that is, those elements which inspired cultures to take up and develop ideas from another. Spengler's guiding principle that one idea or tendency characterises a culture, is peculiar to it, and generates its whole intellectual, social, and economic heritage predisposed him to ignore internal tensions and external connections.[15] In Collingwood's view, if we are to understand other cultures at all it is only by rethinking their thoughts for ourselves, and in doing so those cultures live on within our own. Spengler's method did not involve historical research, but depended instead upon the researches of others, taking their histories as the 'facts' on the basis of which comparisons were to be made. In Collingwood's view, 'Spengler's morphology is simply the comparative anatomy of historical periods'.[16] The surest sign of a naturalistic science is its claim to predict the future on the basis of general laws, and this is exactly what Spengler claims for his morphological method,[17]

but his own claim to foretell the future is absolutely baseless. Just as his morphology does not work at history but only talks about it, does not *determine* the past but, assuming it as already determined, attaches labels to it, so this same method does not determine the future, but only provides a set of labels – the same old set – for a future that is undetermined.[18]

Although Spengler himself did not use the typology of savagery, barbarism, and civilization to denote the different stages in the development of cultural groupings, Collingwood did employ the conventional vocabulary, but went to some pains to divest the term *savage* of its pejorative connotations. He did not agree with the methods predominantly used for studying the lowest level of culture, nor with the characterisations of the relationships between the levels deduced from the use of such methods. In his writings on fairy tales and magic we get the clearest indication of what Collingwood thought the relationship was between savagery and civilization. This relationship is articulated in the context of an argument designed to show how fairy tales can be used as evidence in historical enquiries.

Hitherto, Collingwood argues, fairy tales and folktales, mythology and magic, have been studied by means of three defective methods. The first is the philological approach, predominant between 1810 and 1870 and exemplified by Grimm and Müller. The second is the functional approach, predominant between 1870 and 1910 and exemplified by Tylor and Frazer. The third is the psychological approach, fashionable between 1900 and 1920 and exemplified by Freud and Jung.

The first approach entailed the comparative study of language and myths and was pioneered by Jacob Grimm. Grimm's interest in fairy tales and German mythology, Collingwood argues, was inspired by the romantic nationalism prevalent in Germany early in the nineteenth century. Romantic nationalism awakened the curiosity of the German people about the ancient civilization from which their own had descended. Grimm's work passionately reflected the curiosity and projected an ambivalent emotional relation between the present and the long-lost civilization of the past. The rediscovery was at once of the beloved mother who had given birth to the German nation, and of the childhood of the German people, 'so that the emotion which in one aspect appeared as the child's love for its parent appeared in the other aspect as the yearning for a vanished youth'.[19]

Grimm attempted to demonstrate the unity of the German nation by undertaking a comparative grammatical study designed to detect constant phonetic equivalents in the various Germanic languages. Such comparisons were applied much more broadly by Grimm's successors and embraced the languages of Europe (with the exception of Basque) and many of the languages of India and western Asia. Whereas Grimm had romanticized the primitive Germanic people, Max Müller did the same in creating a primitive Aryan civilization with its own Indo-European, or Aryan, language. Müller, like Grimm, assumed that common language meant a common blood relation. On the basis of this assumption he maintained that from one original stock of people 'all the Aryan-speaking peoples were descended'.[20] Both Grimm and Müller used fairy tales as evidence of their romanticized ancient primitive cultures. Müller, for example, re-created the life and mind of the primitive Aryan people by comparing words and myths common in the cultures of their descendants. The common occurrence of the words and myths, he argued, was evidence of their common origin in the ancient primitive Aryan language.

Apart from the fact that no archaeological evidence had been found to support the existence of a primitive Aryan race, and that current anthropology showed that there was no constant relation between race, or human biology, and language, there were, in Collingwood's view, a number of serious flaws in the method. The nature poetry and nature philosophy of modern romanticism had influenced Müller and led him to over-emphasize the evidence of nature mythology in Sanskrit texts. Anything which could be connected, however tenuously, with solar mythology was first identified in Sanskrit and then sought in the other related languages. It was the preconceptions, rather than the evidence, which sustained the idea of this primitive culture. It was verified by scouring the whole body of Indo-European fairy tales with a view to finding themes which could be converted into the terms of a common solar mythology. Armed with the requisite formulae, followers of the school could easily come up with the comparative sun myths which verified the original theory.

It was not so much that every fairy tale became converted into a sun myth as the fact that the evidence was used dishonestly by the philologists which made the method inadequate. Only that evidence which could be manipulated into supporting the preconceptions was emphasized, and everything else was ignored. The savage was then accused of having irrational thought processes and an incoherent mythology – a conclusion which appears to be inevitable, if one ignores many of the details of the life of the people studied.

The crucial question in Collingwood's mind, however, was Why should a mythology have arisen at all? If the cycle of light and darkness played such an important part in the lives of these primitive people, why were they not able to convey their thoughts without reverting to mythology? Müller explains this oddity in savage thought by postulating an age which arose after the origin of language and before the emergence of religion, poetry, and political society. The Mythological Age, or Mythopoeic Age, was akin to the childhood of the race, in which the mind was temporarily irrational and insane, subject to sudden convulsions and revolutions in thought. Mythology, on this view, was a disease of the primitive Aryan language. When Aryan men and women spoke of solar and lunar changes from day to night and dawn to evening, they lacked a neuter gender in their language and were therefore compelled to personify the natural occurrences and embroider for themselves a solar mythology.

The implication of all this for philological studies, in Collingwood's view, was that the primitive Aryan race so completely misunderstood the nature of the language they had invented that the confusion could be accounted for only by suggesting that, once having invented the language, primitive Aryans went mad. 'And once more', Collingwood argues, 'the unpleasant question arises: if the pseudo history thus projected upon the blank screen of the past is a history of mental confusion, where does the confusion arise? Has not the modern myth-maker created in these huge and sinister imaginings a symbolic picture of the unreason at work in himself?'[21]

Edward Tylor was taken by Collingwood to be the 'great master' of the 'functional school'.[22] Tylor was of the opinion that savages who differ in time and in geographic location were remarkably similar in their habits and lines of development. Human nature had everywhere displayed the same lines of development.[23] Collingwood was impressed by Tylor's recognition that no condition of savagery is absolutely devoid of civilization. There are elements of civilization in the most rudimentary savages. The general tendency is for these elements to become more and more pronounced, and as civilization progresses it retains 'survivals' of that out of which it developed. Many of our manners and customs, although inexplicable in the context of modern civilization, can be understood as survivals from an earlier cultural stage. This, in Collingwood's view, was a useful suggestion. However, he was not entirely happy with Tylor's use of the principle of survival, nor with J.G. Frazer's more widespread popularization of it. Both Tylor and Frazer viewed these survivals as irrational throwbacks, human follies out of step with civilization. Tylor, for instance, argued, 'It seems scarcely too much to assert, once for all, that meaningless customs must be survivals, that they had a practical, or at least ceremonial intention when and where they first arose, but are now fallen into *absurdity* [my emphasis] from having been carried on into a new state of society, where their original sense has been discarded'.[24] Collingwood argued that the vestiges of past stages of culture cannot be regarded as mere anomalies, 'survivals' of savagery. In so far as they play a part in our social and personal lives they have to be understood as essential features of civilization.[25] Collingwood illustrates his argument with reference to magic in relation to both fairy tales and art.[26] For the anthropologists of the functionalist school, magic illustrates the irrational behaviour of savages and barbarians. Tylor's view of the belief in magic was that it was 'one of the most pernicious delusions that ever vexed mankind'.[27]

Collingwood argued that the anthropologists of the functionalist school, heavily influenced by the prevailing positivist philosophy, wrongly identified the magician and the scientist as belonging to the same genus. Both the magician and the scientist, the anthropologists believed, were trying to come to terms with nature by practically applying scientific knowledge to their problems. What differentiates the two is that the scientist does possess scientific knowledge and the magician does not. The anthropologists were therefore able to conclude that 'magic is at bottom simply a special kind of error: it is erroneous natural science'.[28] Such a view of magic was considered by most professional anthropologists during the 1930s to be mistaken, but the increased demand for anthropological literature from the educated public had unfortunately been satisfied by Frazer's *Golden Bough*. In Collingwood's view, that 'inexhaustible scrap-heap of good reading', propounding as it does the same erroneous identification of magic and natural science, 'has been a disaster to contemporary anthropology and all the studies connected with it'.[29]

Before going on to develop Collingwood's criticisms of the functionalist school, it is appropriate to introduce the ideas associated with the third method, because the psychological approach is in fact a development of the functionalist in so far as the assumption of the latter, namely that savage practices are largely irrational, is accepted by the former as the problem which stands in need of explanation. In the manuscripts on fairy tales Collingwood examines the arguments of Freud and Jung, and in *The Principles of Art* he focuses upon Freud and Lévy-Bruhl. The irrationality of savagery is attributed, by Lévy-Bruhl, to the peculiarity of the primitive mind. Collingwood argues that this mentality is knowable only through its manifestations, that is, through the ways in which it thinks and acts. Lévy-Bruhl's curious metaphysics leads him to explain the savage's odd ways of doing things by hypothesizing that they have 'an odd kind of "mentality" '. The hypothesis, in Collingwood's view, is unscientific, that is, unverifiable.[30]

Both Jung and Freud avowedly set out to solve a historical problem – that is, the problem of why savages act in the ways in which they do – by means of 'the application of psychoanalytic knowledge; that is to say, knowledge drawn from the activity of the modern unconscious mind'.[31] Jung, for example, argued that thinking directed 'along a definite track' (by which he meant the ability to comprehend the transformations of nature in a sufficiently scientific manner to be able to reproduce these natural occurrences) was almost unknown to savages and was in fact a modern acquisition of mind explicable in terms of the *'mobility of the libido'*.[32] Thinking which 'lacks the major idea, and the feeling of direction which emanates from that' is *'dream or phantasy thinking'*.[33] Savagery is typified by such thinking, and its modern 'survivals' or parallels in modern civilization are to be found in children and in dreaming: 'The state of infantile thinking in the child's psychic life, as well as in dreams, is nothing but a re-echo of the prehistoric and the ancient'.[34] Collingwood dismisses Jung's enterprise as 'a pseudo-history in which the writer's desires and fears are projected on the blank screen of a past which to him is absolutely unknown'.[35]

Freud proved a much more formidable opponent than either Lévy-Bruhl or Jung. Collingwood believed Freud to be the greatest psychologist of the age, and 'nothing if not scientific'.[36] It is Freud's *Totem and Taboo* that Collingwood takes as his specific target in both the manuscripts on fairy tales and *The Principles of Art*. Freud was concerned to explain the rather strange behaviour of savages by means of the modern findings of psychoanalysis. Totemism, Freud argued, had long been abandoned and replaced by different modes of institutional behaviour in our civilization, and therefore 'psychoanalytic study', while giving useful insights into totemism, is severely limited in what it can do.[37] Taboo, on the other hand, was still prevalent in civilization. The origin of taboo is in the unconscious, and in this respect differs from the religious and moral prohibitions associated with totemism. In Freud's view, 'taboo prohibitions lack all justification and are of unknown origin. Though incomprehensible to us they are taken as a matter of course by those who are under their dominance'.[38] We can understand savage taboos because psychoanalysis, that is, 'the study of the unconscious part of the individual's psychic life', is familiar with such phenomena in contemporary 'compulsion neurotics'.[39] The conclusions drawn from our experience of compulsion neurosis can be used to explain the life of the savage. The origins of both neurotic and taboo prohibitions are enigmatic and lacking in motive. Similarly, both prohibitions involve renunciations and restrictions of an extraordinary kind, and entail the performance of acts which must be enacted because they have become compulsive or obsessive: 'These acts are in the nature of penances, expiations, defence reactions, and purifications'.[40] The savage's own terms of reference and system of beliefs are of no use in coming to understand taboo. It is therefore useless to ask a savage about what really motivates him to observe the prohibitions, or about how and why the taboos came into existence. The motivation and origin is a product of the unconscious, and therefore the savage is, like the neurotic, incapable of giving us an intelligible answer.

Collingwood expresses his amazement that psychoanalytic experience of neurotic patients can be thought sufficient for explaining savage customs and practices. Are we really to believe, Collingwood exclaims, that we can subject the savage to psychoanalysis on the basis of the 'general impression gained from reading books about him?'[41] In Collingwood's view, the savage and the neurotic are not comparable at all:

The compulsion-neurotic, being rather cracked, thinks that his wishes immediately fulfil themselves. Having method in his madness, he proceeds to invent means of breaking this immediate connexion, and earthing the power of his thought harmlessly. The 'savage', being a sensible man, knows that wishes do not immediately fulfil themselves. He therefore invents means by which to fulfil them.[42]

To explain the differences between European civilization and the life-styles of other cultures as a difference between mental health and mental disease is really an instance of Eurocentric scientific conceit. Freud's method or mode of enquiry, Collingwood thought, might have some value if the beliefs and customs of savages were used to throw light upon his neurotic patients, but 'used, as he uses it, the other way round, it is profoundly misleading'.[43]

All three approaches – the philological, the functionalist, and the psychological – suffer from the same fundamental difficulty: They all attempt to answer historical questions by means of naturalistic methods. In Collingwood's view, anthropology is only 'a special case of the problem of self-knowledge; and history is the only way in which man can know himself'.[44] Hitherto anthropologists have treated their subject matter as something external to themselves. They have constructed the savage mind as something other than, and separate from, the mind that seeks to understand it. This separation of the subject and object sets up an artificial opposition which inhibits understanding. In *Speculum Mentis*, as we saw, history was convicted of making the same error. Subsequently, however, history was viewed as the means by which the separation of theory and practice, the mind and its object, could be overcome. Similarly, the opposition that anthropologists have set up between savagery and civilization can be resolved, or overcome, when looked at historically. History 'is man's knowledge of man, not man's knowledge of an external world, history demands, or rather brings about a peculiar intimacy between the knower and known'.[45] We cannot understand that which we cannot rethink in our own minds. To posit the savage as other, something alien to our minds, of which only irrational vestiges survive, is to deny the possibility of understanding ourselves, because in us the primitive mind from which our civilized mind developed lives on. Anthropology, conceived historically, is particularly important to civilized people because the 'savage is not outside us' – he is 'inside us'.[46] In Collingwood's view,

It is because the civilized man contains a savage within him, in the special sense in which any historical present contains within itself its own past, and must therefore study this savage – not savages in the abstract, but the savage that he himself in this sense is – for the same reason for which all history is studied, namely to make possible a rational human life in the present day.[47]

Bearing this in mind, magic, for example, is not something peculiarly associated with less civilized peoples than ourselves, but something pervading our own civilization.

Fairy tales, Collingwood argues, have a common magical character.[48] Magic is an expression of emotion, or, to be more precise, the arousal of emotion for practical purposes, through artistic activities such as dancing, singing, drawing, or modelling.[49] The war dances of warriors are designed to inspire warlike emotions, and the magical ceremonies which are embraced by agricultural peasant societies engender and express the emotions of those societies towards their flocks, herds, crops, and work tools. For each season the apposite magical practice evokes the appropriate emotion for the agricultural duties to be performed at that time of year; indeed, 'magical activity is a kind of dynamo supplying the mechanism of practical life with the emotional current that drives it. Hence magic is a necessity for every sort of condition of man, and is actually found in every healthy society'.[50] Collingwood goes to some pains to show that many practices associated with manners, eating, dress, sport, and the use of machinery, although justified in utilitarian terms, retain a large element of magical emotive expression. We even become emotionally attached to things that we own and feel a deep sense of hurt and loss when they are stolen, damaged, or misplaced. Merely replacing them does not adequately compensate for our hurt.[51] Magic must be seen, then, 'not as a mere survival of savagery but as an essential feature of civilization'.[52]

Modern civilized people tend to ridicule and condemn savages because being confronted with primitive practices arouses fears which are explicable in terms of 'a secret voice within us whispering "that art thou" '.[53] Our own civilization has dealt with its emotional vulnerability by first suppressing and then denying the existence of magic. The rationalistic and utilitarian character of European civilization leads us to value and judge things in terms of their usefulness. In consequence we treat 'emotion as a thing that must be repressed, a hostile force within us whose outbreaks are feared as destructive of civilized life'.[54] In Collingwood's view, the horror we have of savages is really a horror of something in ourselves that the savage symbolises, namely, magic, or the expression of emotion.

In summary, then, to understand civilization we have to understand savagery, not as something alien and standing outside us, but as an integral, vital, and living component, that is, as the 'heart and root of our own civilization'.[55] This is not to say that savagery is civilization; savagery is in fact what civilization grew out of, but it is not entirely devoid of civilization itself. Savagery, in Collingwood's opinion, is one of two ways of being uncivilized. It is a negative idea which means not being completely civilized. Savagery is never absolute; 'there is only relative savagery, that is, being civilized up to a certain point and no more' (NL, 41.11). In addition, 'savages have a civilization of sorts, a different kind of civilization according to what kind of savages they are'.[56] It is clear that Collingwood wished the term *savagery* to carry no pejorative connotations. *Barbarism*, on the other hand, he did wish to taint with unfavourable connotations. In *The New Leviathan* and those unpublished manuscripts which appear to be preliminary explorations for the arguments in the book,[57] Collingwood is less concerned about savagery, and much more preoccupied with barbarism, than he had been previously. Barbarism, for him, is not the next stage to savagery on an ascending scale to civilization. Like savagery, barbarism is a way of being uncivilized, but unlike savagery it is hostile towards civilization (NL, 41.12). As Collingwood says elsewhere, barbarism 'involves not the absence of civilization but a revolt against civilization'.[58] Consciously or unconsciously, it is the attempt to be less civilized than one actually is. No society is without elements of barbarism, but a society which actually turns the tide of civilization back is barbarous. Thus, if I understand Collingwood correctly, both savages and civilized people can be barbarous, depending upon whether they are actively hostile towards civilization.

Civilization has so far been assumed to be a condition, or stage of culture. Collingwood's understanding of the term, however, goes much deeper than this, and it is to his investigations into the generic and specific meanings of civilization that we must now turn in order to discern the complex refinements in his understanding of the concept.

3. The meaning of civilization

Civilization is a concept of relatively recent origin both in English and French. In both languages the verb *to civilize* and the participle *civilized* (*civiliser* and *civilisé*, in French) appeared before the substantive *civilization* (*civilisation*). The substantive appears to have been used first in a French text of 1771 and an English text of 1772.[59] It was used in a very general and imprecise way to denote a moral idea, a condition which Europeans had reached and were improving upon and which distinguished them from other races. It referred to such factors as technological progress, refinement of manners, scientific achievements, customs, and religious ideas. In the words of Norbert Elias, 'This concept expresses the self-consciousness of the West'.[60] Civilization is the concept that expresses the West's self-perception relative to non–western European peoples.

It is a universal ideal condition, or process, that bestows intrinsic worth and dignity upon those so described as civilized.

Alongside this concept arose the idea, not of civilization as a universal standard or ideal, but of civilization as the collective heritage and cultural and social practices of any group of people. Thus people who were described as uncivilized from the point of view of the conception of civilization as an ideal condition were accredited with having a civilization with reference to the conception of it as an accumulated collective heritage. Similarly, one could have a conception of a plurality of civilizations, while having an ideal of civilization in terms of which to judge them. In addition, it was not uncommon to find the term *civilization* being used to refer to a process through which individuals went in attaining the condition of civility. The concept of civilization had all these connotations during the time that Collingwood wrote.[61] This can be illustrated by means of a few selective examples. Albert Schweitzer and Harold Laski used the concept of civilization in the singular as an ideal. In the view of the former, 'The real essential nature of civilization ... is ultimately ethical',[62] and for Laski the existence of the independent national sovereign state, knowing 'no will higher than its own', constitutes a threat to peace, and 'so long as there is the danger of conflict there exists a menace to the continuance of civilization'.[63]

As for the plurality of civilizations, we saw that Oswald Spengler argued that each culture had a civilization appropriate to itself. Paul Valéry, when he said, 'We later civilizations ... we too now know that we are mortal',[64] used the term to denote the cultural, social, and political heritage of past and present societies. It was quite common for people to speak of 'ancient' and 'modern' civilizations, or to speak of the civilization of a particular people, or country, or continent. Lord Halifax, for instance, talked of 'our Western civilization' and 'this European civilization'.[65] Gordon Childe used the terms 'Oriental civilization', 'urban civilization', and the 'débris of earlier civilizations' in an article in the *Times*.[66] Finally, Viscount Samuel associated civilizations with religions. He argued that 'the character of a civilization was determined by its creed. It was a Christian civilization or Islamic, Buddhist or Hindu, Confucian or Shinto'.[67]

To acknowledge the plurality of civilizations did not, for the most part, entail a cultural relativism. There might be many civilizations, but implicit or explicit in this recognition one often finds a standard being employed in terms of which civilizations are ranked. In a letter to the *Times,* 26 April 1939, a number of religious leaders, while tacitly accepting the plurality of civilizations, enumerated a number of fundamental characteristics that 'any true civilization' should possess. Among these characteristics were 'the keeping of promises by individuals, associations, and states'; freedom of speech, action, and religious belief; equality before the law; 'and security against deprivation of life, liberty or property'.[68] In other words, the essentials of a true civilization were exactly those found and valued in European civilization. H. N. Spalding, writing in 1939, thought that for the first time in history not one civilization, but all civilizations, were under threat of extinction. Up to the present time rational civilizations had only recognised part of reality: 'A fully rational civilization would put the fragments together and see the whole'.[69] If the 'moral and spiritual ideal' of seeking to 'know and love and enjoy Reality as a Whole' were to be rigorously pursued, there would arise 'one civilization and not many; a civilization without barbarians or Gentiles or foreigners; a civilization in which that competition alone will be respected that serves, or at least does not injure, others'.[70]

None of the meanings or connotations enumerated so far excludes or prohibits the idea of civilization also being used to characterise a process. Both Freud and Elias understood civilization to be a process. Freud argued that civilization is a 'special process which mankind undergoes', and that 'civilization is a process in the service of Eros, whose purpose is to combine single human individuals, and after that families, then races, peoples and nations, into one great unity, the unity of mankind'.[71] Elias illustrates this use of the word when he says,

We see people at table, we see them going to bed or in hostile clashes. In these and other elementary activities the manner in which the individual behaves and feels slowly changes. This change is in the direction of a gradual 'civilization', but only historical experience makes clearer what this word actually means. It shows, for example, the decisive role played in this civilizing process by a very specific change in the feelings of shame and delicacy.[72]

In both 'What Civilization Means' and *The New Leviathan* Collingwood emphasizes the importance of enquiring into the actual use of a concept as a preliminary to discerning its meaning (*NL*, 34.13).[73] Etymological enquiries are a useful aid to, but can never be a substitute for, historical enquiries into the actual use of the word in language (*NL*, 34.25).[74] Dictionaries perform an invaluable service by classifying distinct definitions of each word, but further than this they provide illustrations which enable the student to discern the meanings as they were used in the language by specific people.[75] There are, Collingwood suggests, three senses in which the term *civilization* has been used. First, it is used to refer to a process which happens to a community, or which a community undergoes (*NL*, 34.4). The process is one of approximating an ideal state, that state being *civility*. When this process is in recession, the community approaches the contradictory of civility, that is, *barbarity* (*NL*, 34.51). In so far as the process of civilization occurs within a nonsocial community, it is transeunt, that is, imposed upon the nonsocial community by a social community. In contrast, civilization occurring within a social community is an immanent process. The more advanced the process, then the closer a community will be to the ideal towards which it is advancing, and the further it distances itself from the contradictory of civility, namely barbarism. Civility and barbarity are ideal states: Neither exists in isolation from the other. Every existing society is both civil and barbarous. Second, the term *civilization* is used to refer to the condition which is achieved as the result of undergoing the process of civilization; that is, we find the ideal of civility approximated in different ways. We may refer to these approximations as 'Bronze Age civilization', 'Neolithic civilization', 'Chinese civilization', and so on (*NL,* 34.92). Third, the ideal of civility itself, towards which the process of civilization aims, is often referred to as civilization.

Collingwood proposes to use the term *civilization* as he has found it used: to refer to a process; to refer to the result of the process; and, as an equivalent to the ideal to which the process is directed. For the sake of symmetry he believes that it is justifiable to use corresponding senses of the term *barbarism:*

34.79.   (i) as a name for the *process of barbarizing;* (ii) as a name for *the condition to which in a given case that process leads;* (iii) as *equivalent to 'barbarity'.*

In 'What Civilization Means' Collingwood addresses himself to the question of the relation between civilization and barbarism by exploring different characterisations of the relation. The simplest relation is that of conceiving them as two contradictory entities separated by a dichotomy. To put the relation in the terms used in *An Essay on Philosophical Method,* civilization and barbarism can be understood as two distinct, separate, and opposed concepts, neither of which includes nor implies the other. Thus each community is either civilized or barbarous, either having completed the civilizing process or being completely devoid of it. There are no intermediary positions. The process of civilization is telescoped into a vanishing point where communities stand either side of the dichotomy which separates civilization and barbarism. This understanding of the relation is outmoded and the result of obsolete conceptions of historical change which on this view remain essentially unintelligible.

A second view of the relation between civilization and barbarism arises out of late eighteenth-century historical thought, which viewed every period in history as one of transition. The relation which this concept postulates is more complex than the preceding view. On the one hand it takes barbarism and civilization as absolute contraries, each denoting the opposite end of a scale between which there are numerous intermediate positions. The ends of the scale are absolutes which have never actually existed. On the other hand, the terms are also taken to have a relative meaning. Each existing society stands on the scale somewhere between the two contraries, that is, between the absolute zero of barbarism and the infinity of civilization. Although no society can be barbarous or civilized in an absolute sense, it can, relative to others lower down the scale, claim to be civilized, and, relative to those above it, be considered barbarous. The absolute meanings are now the ideals or terms of reference in terms of which to ask, not whether a society is civilized or barbarous, but the degree to which it is civilized relative to the ideal. This idea of degrees of civilization presupposes that there is one universal civilizing process through which all communities go, to varying extents. To think of the civilizing process in these terms reflects the monism of the historical thought of the nineteenth century.[76] If we consider this view of the relation between barbarism and civilization in terms of *An Essay on Philosophical Method*, it is clearly deficient, in that, although the ideal of civility, as the generic essence, is recognised to be manifest in differing degrees, the manifestations are not acknowledged to be different in kind. There is a failure, then, to exhibit the concept of civilization as a fusion of differences of degree with differences of kind, in which each of the species embodies the generic essence of civility in a specific way, and in a specific degree.[77] Furthermore, the scale is divided into opposite species, with civilization representing the infinity, and barbarism the zero, end of the scale. Each of the intermediate forms is an embodiment of both opposites. All are unique fusions of opposites, distinct and mutually exclusive.[78] In other words, this view of the relation between barbarism and civilization denies the overlap of forms which Collingwood so forcefully contends is a distinguishing characteristic of the philosophical concept. This view recognizes the coexistence of opposites, while refusing to acknowledge the fusion of distincts. Opposition and distinction are thought to be mutually exclusive types of relation, whereas an adequate understanding of the concept of civilization must exhibit it as a fusion of opposites and distincts. To extend Collingwood's argument further: the minimal realisation of the generic essence of civility on a scale of civilization is a distinct embodiment which nevertheless is an opposite relative to the forms on the scale which stand above it. There is no point on the scale at which civility is absent. Absolute barbarism is not only nowhere to be found, but also inconceivable. Barbarism, then, cannot stand in the scale as zero, but instead represents unity.[79]

Twentieth-century historians, Collingwood claims, have rejected historical monism and embraced historical pluralism. They recognise that at various times different communities have followed their own ideals and instituted different processes to achieve them. All of the civilizations of which modern historians speak are different in kind, having realised, or attempted to realise, their own ideals, and they are therefore incapable of being characterised as embodiments of different degrees of one single ideal.[80]

Collingwood argues that the relation between civilization and barbarism is presently conceived as one in which each society has its own standard of civilization and believes itself to be civilized to the extent that it lives up to that standard. Other societies which fail to comply with the standard are deemed to be barbarous. Each civilization, then, attempts to live a different kind of civilized life. The question to be asked of each particular society is no longer what level it has attained on a single scale of civilization, 'but in what way it is civilized'.[81]

This view of civilization, Collingwood argues, may appear to imply historical relativism. It amounts to the denial of an ideal of civilized behaviour and appears to affirm that there are many ideals, each of which may be appropriate to one or other society at a particular time. If the ways in which people behave in different societies are viewed by each society as being civilized, then there is no ideal character to the meaning of the term *civilized,* and it is left merely with a factual content. If this is the case, then the verb *to civilize* has no meaning, because there can be no civilizing process unless there is an implication that 'the process has direction and the act purpose, and these imply a distinction between fact and ideal'.[82]

The implication of historical relativism in this view, Collingwood argues, is unfounded. It does not entail the substitution of social facts for social ideals. What it really implies is that the social facts, or civilizations, are not devoid of ideals, but are aiming at different ideals, and

though in one way divergent, are in another way convergent; for they are both called ideals of civilized conduct, and unless this purpose means that in some way they are the same ideal it means nothing. Thus the historical pluralism of the present day does not exclude a certain kind of historical monism. The plurality of civilizations does not exclude a sense in which civilization is one.[83]

Each civilization is both an ideal and a fact. In so far as each will have attained 'a certain kind and degree of civilization', it actually exists and is a fact. In so far as each civilization promotes the civilizing process, the degree and kind of fact achieved will have been conceived as something desirable and worth aiming for. Its continuing existence is dependent upon its continuing to be thought of as desirable, that is, as an ideal worth pursuing, and in this respect the 'fact of civilization actually existing in a certain kind and a certain degree is ... both fact and ideal'.[84] This attainment of a certain degree and kind of civilization implies the concept of a further ideal that is as yet unrealised. It is the realisation that in that particular civilization there still remain degrees of civilization to be achieved. Ideals which are attained by individuals – that is, those ideals that are facts – are ideals of the first order, and those that are recognised but not realised are ideals of the second order.[85]

The extent to which the second-order ideals differ from those of the first will vary considerably from person to person and from society to society, and 'only a very ignorant and very foolish person expects that everyone to whatever society he belongs, will agree with everyone else as to what kind of actions are civilized and what barbarous',[86] on particular kinds of occasions. Beyond the first- and second-order ideals, however, is a third order. This is an 'ideal of universal civility' – not civility on this or that occasion, but civility on each and every occasion. It is the logical rather than the temporal source of all other ideals: It is the ideal which is constantly referred to in Christian literature. To be civil on this or that particular occasion, to realise particular ideals of civility, and, to recognise those that are not yet realised is logically to presuppose the ideal of civility:

This is the sense, and the only sense, in which all civilizations, or ways of living in a civilized manner, are one. They are one in the sense that they all converge upon this ideal. It must be one ideal, there can be no other beyond it, because it is absolutely unqualified. . . . Every man must recognize it when he reflects on his own life as a member of a civilized society. He finds himself behaving civilly in certain limited ways. On reflection, he discovers that he is trying to behave civilly in other and more far-reaching, but still limited, ways. On further reflection, he discovers that he is trying to behave civilly without any limit whatever.[87]

Collingwood is not arguing that civilization is one long progression to-wards this ideal. The facts of civilization, that is, its achievements, are inherited by succeeding generations. There is progress in so far as each generation leaves better opportunities to its heirs than did the generation before it. These opportunities progress, but the will does not. The will is as capable as it always has been of using the opportunities well or ill, and 'the greater the opportunities it inherits, the greater the temptation to abuse them. This temptation, which no progress can abolish, is the origin of barbarism'.[88]

Collingwood's argument in 'What Civilization Means' could be used to discount the claim that after 1936–1937 he became a radical historicist and relativist,[89] and cited in support of those who claim 'that at no time did he subscribe to the doctrines of radical historicism'.[90] The problem is that those who line up on either side of this debate are left with the embarrassing task of having to explain away statements by Collingwood which appear to be saying exactly the opposite of what they contend. In a recent attempt to refute the radical-conversion hypothesis, for example, Tariq Modood admits that in some passages Collingwood does 'flirt with something like a "sociology of knowledge" ', but Modood quickly explains them away by saying that 'such "sociological" passages are the exception rather than the rule and ... run contrary to the main brunt of Collingwood's thesis'.[91]

I do not wish to enter this debate in any detail, but a few remarks are warranted. Certainly Collingwood denied historical relativism in 'What Civilization Means'. In *An Autobiography,* however, he had used arguments similar to those he employed in 'What Civilization Means' but had failed to reach the same conclusion. In asking whether Plato's *Republic* and Hobbes's *Leviathan* are two different theories of the same thing, namely the state, Collingwood answers no. The nature of the state in ancient Greece and in early modern England was 'genuinely different': 'I do not mean the empirical nature of the state; I mean the ideal nature of the State'.[92] The people in each state had different ideals about personal conduct, and these ideals are 'just as impermanent as ideals of social organization'.[93] One could argue that these ideals, on the logic of the later argument, would imply that beyond the first-order ideals (that is, the facts) and the second-order ideals (that is, the condition to which and beyond which those facts point, namely an ideal yet to be realised) is the third-order ideal of the universal state. The point is that Collingwood did not go on to argue this: Instead he suggested that there is no such 'unchanging, and eternal' ideal.[94] In *An Essay on Metaphysics* Collingwood again seems to employ historical relativism. He maintains that one does not ask whether absolute presuppositions are true or false; one asks only whether they were absolutely presupposed. People are 'ticklish' in their absolute presuppositions because the presuppositions are adhered to as a matter of faith. This does not preclude the possibility of criticizing absolute presuppositions. However, this activity is confined to special circumstances, when 'stresses and strain' necessitate such forms of enquiry. Even then, the question one asks is not whether they are right or wrong, but whether they are continuing to be useful and doing their job effectively. Similarly, in an unpublished manuscript written before *An Essay on Metaphysics,* Collingwood is quite clear about the role of the metaphysician. Collingwood contends that in relation to the 'pre-propositions' (that is, what he was later to call 'absolute presuppositions') presupposed by the thinking of the community in which the metaphysician lives, and in relation to those presupposed in other communities, the task of the metaphysician is not critical, but simply descriptive and historical. Even in comparing the different systems of presuppositions, the metaphysician is engaged in a historical rather than in a critical enquiry:

But in his relation to other metaphysicians his function is critical. If, for example, the science of his own day really does presuppose the law of universal causation, his business toward that presupposition is to detect it and state it. But if metaphysicians have got into the habit of thinking that this science presupposes the law of universal causation whereas really it does not, then his business is two fold: (a) to state the facts (b) to criticize the metaphysicians who have misrepresented them.[95]

Metaphysical presuppositions, Collingwood contends, are variables and not constraints. When one civilization is replaced by another, 'one set of Metaphysical presuppositions gives way to another set. People stop presupposing one set of things and begin presupposing others'.[96] The metaphysician does not ask which set is true and which false. It is 'impossible to decide' such matters. No one can compare them with an open mind. This is because 'no one is ever in this situation of open-mindedness'.[97] In his 'Notes on HISTORIOGRAPHY written on a voyage to the East Indies', Collingwood suggests that both logic and ethics are historical sciences,[98] and in this respect one can only assume that like the metaphysician, the logician and moral philosopher have tasks which are descriptive and historical rather than critical, with respect to the logic and ethics employed in their own and other people's societies, but critical in relation to other logicians and moral philosophers in so far as they may be wrong in their characterisations of the logic or ethics current in their societies.

It is clear that in 'What Civilization Means', 'Fascism and Nazism', 'The Three Laws of Politics', and the *New Leviathan* itself, Collingwood is much more inclined to reject relativism, perhaps because of the partially polemical purpose of these writings. *The New Leviathan,* in particular, being Collingwood's contribution to the war effort, was hardly likely to propound a relativism supporting the view that Nazi and fascist ideals were as good as those of the people whom these ideals threatened.

Collingwood was certainly a historicist in that he extolled the virtues of history as a form of knowledge over all other modes of thought and believed, like Hegel, that each person is a child of his, or her, times, but we should not assume that historicism entails relativism. This is a mistake which van der Dussen makes when he says, of a certain passage in Collingwood's 'Lectures on Philosophy of History II (T. T. 1929)', that it 'certainly expresses an historicist and thus relativistic view'.[99] Most of the philosophical idealists, including Green and Bradley, were historicists in that they subscribed to Hegel's view that every philosopher is a child of his times and could not have been other than he was. Hegel and Engels were historicists but certainly not relativists. They always argued that real progress is made in the development of society and philosophy. In 'What Civilization Means' this is the sort of historicism Collingwood espoused, whereas on other occasions he espoused a radical historicism that was avowedly relativist. I think that we have to accept, rather than try to explain away, inconsistencies, and that Collingwood was a historicist who could never work out a coherent position in relation to relativism.

He was never an out-and-out relativist and never an out-and-out realist, or absolutist. These were the poles between which he tended to waver; sometimes one was more dominant than the other, but neither was totally eclipsed.

After this brief digression we must return to Collingwood's discussion of civilization. Every existing society, Collingwood argues, is both civil and barbarous. At any given time neither of the absolute opposites exists in purity, nor can be conceived as such. If the elements of civility gradually come to predominate over those of barbarity, the 'process of civilization would thus be one *of asymptotic approximation to the ideal condition of civility*' (*NL,* 34.56). Why can the ideal of civilization only be approximated? Civilization is a thing of the mind, and must therefore conform to the character of thought in general. Reiterating in summary form the argument which he repeatedly made in *An Essay on Philosophical Method*,[100] Collingwood argues that 'a mental process from ignorance to knowledge or from fear to anger or from cowardice to courage never begins simply at the first term, but always at the first term with a mixture of the second; and never ends simply at the second term, but always at the second term qualified by the first' (*NL,* 34.58). All civilizations aim for the universal civility, but all, due to circumstances, fall short of it, just as those 'who create a particular society [aim] at creating a universal society but, owing to facts over which they have no control, find it turning under their hands into a particular society' (*NL,* 34.96). In a community there always remains a nonsocial element over which force is exercised, and the members of which are being prepared for induction into society. Similarly civilization includes within itself barbarous elements over which force is exercised. The reason, then, is essentially the same as that which prevents the attainment of a pure society devoid of crime, that is: 'Every particular society has about it a trace of the non-social community out of which it has emerged' (*NL,* 37.28). However much rules are formulated and enforced with the threat of punishment, civility can only be approximated. Indeed, a civility enforced by punishment has more than a hint of servility about it. Being civilized is always just an approximation to the ideal, and it 'means *living, so far as possible dialectically,* that is, in constant endeavour to convert every occasion of non-agreement into an occasion of agreement. A degree of force is inevitable in human life; but being civilized means cutting it down, and becoming more civilized means cutting it down still further' (*NL,* 39.15). Each civilization embodies the generic essence of civility in a distinct way, and in a certain degree. The distinct forms of civilization are not coordinate species of a genus. Instead they are overlapping forms which are both distincts, in that they embody the generic essence in different ways, but also opposed to each other, in that they embody the essence of civility in different degrees, that is, some embody it more adequately than others. Each form looked at in itself is civilized, but in relation to that distinct embodiment above it the former is barbarous in comparison to the latter, and both are barbarous in different degrees, and opposed to the succeeding form, and so on. In other words, the ideal of civilization whose variable, or generic essence, is civility is best characterised as a scale of overlapping forms which is a unity of differences of kind with differences of degree, and a fusion of opposites and distincts.

There is in Collingwood's writings an integral relation between mind, society, and civilization. Civilization presupposes society, and is in fact the collective equivalent of the process of socialisation. Socialisation itself presupposes practical reason, or rational consciousness, without which there could be neither society nor civilization. The relation between society and civilization becomes most evident in Collingwood's discussion of the specific content of the idea of civilization. He distinguishes between the internal relations of civilization, that is, the way that members of the same community behave towards each other, and its external relations. In external relations there are two dimensions – first, the ways in which a member of a community relates to nature, and second, the ways in which a member of a community treats a member of another.[101]

The process of civilization internal to a community is that of encouraging members to 'behave "civilly" to one another' (NL, 35.4). This is the point at which mind, society, and civilization become one, because acting civilly is nothing other than refraining from acting in a way that would arouse a passion or desire in another individual strong enough to diminish that person's self-respect – 'that is, threaten his consciousness of freedom by making him feel that his power of choice is in danger of breaking down and the passion or desire likely to take charge' (NL, 35.41). To arouse such passions and precipitate a breakdown of the will is to exercise force over a person. The ideal of civility, then, is social relations in which there is an absence of force. Similarly, as we saw, society entails joint social will as opposed to the exertion of force over its members. Civility, of course, is an ideal, and there will be occasions upon which force is both necessary and desirable in a civilization seeking to maintain itself. To be uncivil is to use force, as, for example, in our treatment of criminals. To be uncivilized is to use force where force is not needed.

In its external relations with nature, a community is civil when it gets from the natural world food, clothing, and other satisfactions, achieved by means of its own industry and efforts, that is, by intelligent labour 'directed and controlled by scientific understanding of that natural world' (NL, 35.5). It is this process of coming to understand nature, that is, mitigating sheer labour by the application of human intelligence, which leads 'to progress in this second constituent of civilization' (35.53). To be civilized, in this context, means getting what one needs from the natural world by means of coming to understand it better. Need, in this respect, is not a fixed entity. Needs change in accordance with expectations, and as these expectations are fulfilled by means of the intelligent exploitation of nature, new needs arise, along with new expectations.

The second aspect of external relations, that is, civility 'towards members of other communities' (*NL,* 35.6), is very much dependent upon whether foreigners are regarded as human. If the answer is yes, then the ideal of civility is applicable because it 'requires civil demeanour to whatever is recognized as possessing it' (*NL,* 35.63). If a community answers in the negative, foreigners are seen as part of nature and available for intelligent exploitation. The conviction that foreigners are human and entitled to be treated civilly arises when we have experience of common action, for instance, in the form of commerce. During the course of sustained common action, a social consciousness on the part of a member of one community may arise towards a member of another. The foreigner then becomes transformed from something we exploit into a person who is, in proportion to the degree the member of the other community is civilized, entitled to be treated civilly. This is something completely different from having a liking or an affection for someone, because such attitudes are capable of being adopted towards animals and slaves. Civility is something to which a person is entitled from another, whether he, or she, is liked or disliked.

In order to determine the essence of civilization, Collingwood argues, we must find a unifying connexion between the ways in which we treat fellow human beings, both within our community and outside it, and the way in which we treat nature. The differentiae of civilization must be reduced to one differentia, and from this all other properties of civilization should be logically derivable.

The development of natural science enables us to exploit the natural world intelligently. Such natural science need not be highly technical, nor particularly complex and sophisticated; it may be 'more akin to folklore than to mathematics, riddled with superstition, and from the point of view of a twentieth century "scientist" lamentably unscientific' (*NL,* 36.31). Thus, people who were normally referred to as savages could be credited with a certain degree of natural-scientific sophistication. Indeed, as we saw, Collingwood argued strongly against the anthropologists who, in their work, implied that savages were scientific imbeciles. People who could perform delicate 'operations in metallurgy, agriculture, stockbreeding, and so forth', as well as being sufficiently acquainted with the relation between cause and effect to construct a hoe from crude iron ore, could not by any stretch of the imagination be considered scientific imbeciles.[102] In so far, then, as savages have scientific knowledge and exploit nature intelligently, the civilizing process has begun. In Colling-wood's view, there could be no civilization without science, because 'science, the knowledge of nature which gives us power over nature, is the source of all wealth'.[103] What sort of natural science is indispensable to civilization?

In 'Man Goes Mad', Collingwood maintains that at bottom European civilization is agricultural in character, and that this 'civilization is a tra-ditional way of life acquired through an historical process in which the later developments are specialized outgrowths from the earlier'.[104] The view of the sort of natural science appropriate to a civilization put forward in *The New Leviathan* is consistent with his earlier thoughts.

36.32.   The sort of natural science which is inseparable from an intelligent ex-ploitation of the natural world means watching, and remembering, and handing down from father to son, things which it is useful for a hunter or a shepherd or a fisherman or a farmer or a sailor or a miner or the like to know: things about the seasons, the weather, the soil, the subsoil, the habits of game and fish and domestic animals and vermin; how to get materials for the implements needed in these various crafts, and how to work them up into finished articles and how to use and keep and mend these articles when made: the sort of 'natural science', if I may call it by that name, which was mostly discovered in what we call the Neolithic Age, and of which the chief masters among ourselves are what we call (I suppose for a joke) Unskilled Agricultural Labourers.

It is by acquiring, conserving, and developing a vast amount of this type of knowledge that a community undergoes the process of civilization in its relations with the natural world. The acquiring and passing on of such traditional knowledge entails a high degree of cooperation and agreement among individuals. It assumes a community in which someone who has a skill to impart is encouraged to teach it, and those who wish to learn this practical knowledge do so by listening and watching, 'confident by custom of a civil answer to a civil question' (*NL*, 36.46). In other words, the building up of knowledge which enables us to exploit nature intel-ligently is dependent upon harmonious relations among the members of the community.

The connection, then, between persons and persons, and persons and nature, is civility, and it is what constitutes a community's civilization relative to the human world and makes possible that community's civi-lization relative to nature (*NL*, 36.51). Civility is not something that has arisen in recent times: It is a primitive survival from ancient times, and, like magic, is an integral part of the present. We tend to ignore or suppress the magical elements and take for granted the 'ancestral, prehistoric ci-vility' of which we are the beneficiaries. It is the desire to impart and receive knowledge in a dialectical rather than in an eristical fashion –

that is, the tendency to make knowledge the outcome of agreement, co-operation, and sharing – that makes civilization possible:

36.7.   This is the origin and essence of civilization. Civilization, even in its crudest and most barbarous form, in part consists in civility and in part depends on civility: consists in it so far as it consists in relations of man to man; depends on it so far as it consists in relations of man to nature.

This is not to say, of course, that there is no tension between our natural inclinations to be both friends and enemies. In the course of the development of the mind, such tensions are manifest and first appear in our feelings of both pleasure and pain at having other human beings in close proximity. Such confusions reappear in appetite, with a strong inclination and a strong disinclination to associate with other human beings. We attempt to segregate these appetites by directing our affections to people we like and with whom we want to associate, and away from those whom we dislike and with whom we have no inclination to associate. But at the level of appetite the confusions are unabated, because we find ourselves liking those whom we think we dislike, and disliking those whom we think we like. At the level of desire, the self we have come to know becomes correlative with the not-self, and the question of disliking or liking other people becomes correlative to what we think about ourselves. We in fact both like and dislike ourselves. When we reach the level of will, 'it does not so terribly matter, that our feelings and appetites and passions and desires are inextricably confused and hopelessly contradictory; because, within limits, we can ignore them and make decisions' (*NL*, 36.81). We are in a position to make choices between behaving eristically towards our fellow human beings or acting dialectically, and it is here, 'with the appearance of free will in human life', that the process of civilization begins (*NL*, 36.84). The process is dependent upon each person, by means of the will, controlling his, or her, emotions (which capriciously bestow friendship upon and aversion to the same person at whim) in order to eliminate caprice in one's relations with others. 'Civilization', Collingwood argues, 'is the process in a community by which the various members assert themselves as will: severally as individual will, corporately as social will (the two being inseparable . . .)' (*NL*, 36.89). What this means, then, is that the process of conversion from the nonsocial to the social community is, in fact, the civilizing process: *'To civilize is to socialize'* (*NL*, 37.22). Civility, the ideal which civilization attempts to approximate, is in fact sociality: the respecting of oneself and of one's fellow members as free agents who are entitled to be treated as such – that is, entitled not to have their wills undermined by force. Similarly, these free agents are obliged to treat others accordingly.

In summary, then, civilization is the name for the process of converting the nonsocial into the social. Civility is the ideal towards which this process is directed. Savagery does not denote a complete absence of civilization; savagery is to be uncivilized relative to other societies, and to the ideal of civility. Nor does civilization denote a complete absence of savagery; indeed, the savage lives on within us. Barbarism, however, is similar to savagery in being uncivilized, but different from it in being hostile to civilization.

8

◁══════════════════════════════════▷

Conclusion: Civilization and its enemies

1. Introduction

In the preceding chapter we saw that Collingwood identified civilization as the socializing process which converts the nonsocial community into the social community. To have attained the level of free will is to have attained the will to civilization. The product of the socializing, or civilizing process – that is, the asymptotic approximation to the ideal of civility – is also identified by the term *civilization*. Civilization contains within itself primitive survivals of the condition out of which it grew, namely, savagery. Barbarism, on the other hand, is the active attempt to retard or reverse the civilizing process. In every civilization elements of barbarity and civility coexist, and the former can never be totally eradicated by the latter, because the conversion of the nonsocial into the social community is a process which has no end, and the transeunt rule exercised by the rulers over the nonsocial community in the body politic entails an element of force which is incompatible with the ideal of civility.

In this chapter we move on from the definition of civilization to the elements of civilization that can be deduced from it. These elements are the corollaries of civilization but may not be recognised in ordinary usage. The elements, or properties, are *education, wealth, law and order,* and *peace and plenty.* Further, this chapter explores those forces at work in civilization which attempt to undermine the asymptotic approximation to the ideal of civility.

2. The properties of civilization

Education, as we have seen, has a very prominent role in the formation of society. It is the function of the parent as well as of the politician to provide sufficient education to keep in perpetual motion the conversion

221

of nonsocial members into social members of the community. In so far as to civilize and to socialize are the same process, the process is equally dependent upon education. Education is the means 'by which a civilization keeps itself alive from one generation to the next' (*NL*, 39.18).[1]

The importance of education in relation to civilization had always been strongly emphasized by Collingwood. In 1919, for example, he argued that 'the rule of the more civilized over the less civilized ... is a necessary element in the education of mankind'.[2] In the context of *The New Leviathan,* this principle would be applicable both within a community, and to its external relations with other, less civilized communities. He justifies this role for civilization in its external relations with less civilized communities by suggesting that Europe could never have made the strides in civilization it did without 'the discipline of Roman rule and the legacy of Roman law'. Indeed, Collingwood asks rhetorically, what may Africa and Asia yet 'owe to the imperialistic rule of European nations'.[3]

What, then, is the general aim and purpose of education? It is not merely the teaching of such skills as reading, writing, and arithmetic. These are the external accomplishments of education. There is also an inner purpose of education, and that is to promote and facilitate self-control over one's 'own lower nature, ... which is the best gift that a good education can impart'.[4] This is particularly important in relation to the conversion process, because, as we saw, civilization cannot begin, nor be sustained, until the level of the freedom of the will has been achieved, that is, the level at which will dominates and controls emotions. Education, in Collingwood's view, has a strongly practical purpose: It 'does not mean stuffing a mind with information; it means helping a mind to create itself, to grow into an active and vigorous contributor to the life of the world'.[5] Education has 'to prepare the pupil for real life'[6] by 'inducing habits of orderly and systematic thinking'.[7] The importance of this can be emphasized with reference to *Speculum Mentis.* One of the guiding themes of that book was to impress upon the reader that mistaken thinking about an activity adversely influences its practice. In *An Autobiography* Collingwood praises the 'school of Green' for having educated its pupils, not to be 'professional scholars and philosophers', but for participation in practical public life.[8] Education is such a powerful instrument in the civilizing process that the differing attitudes in ancient Rome and modern England towards the capacity of women to enter into contracts is explained, not in terms of the chauvinism or arrogance of Roman men, but by the fact 'that the conditions of female education were different in the two places, and that the products of that education differed correspondingly' (*NL*, 23.39).

In Chapter 5 we saw how within the body politic those entrusted with the task of bringing about the conversion of the nonsocial into the social community, what we now know to be the socializing or civilizing process, were the rulers. Political activity and political education were seen to be correlative: 'In the case of the family, the agent in this process is the parental society, and the name of the process is education' (*NL*, 40.63). From the emphasis given to the parental role in the civilizing process, it is evident that Collingwood regarded parents as the principal trustees and prophets of civilization. Into their care the next generation of mentally mature adults is given. The responsibility is great, but it has been usurped by the state and its army of professional educators. Specialists, however, are disadvantaged in relation to parents. In the first place, parents have a greater power over the children. Children view their parents as omnipotent to a degree that they could never view the specialist. Dividing the civilizing process between the educator and the parent has vastly diminished the strength of both in relation to the child. In the second place, the parent has the versatility and resourcefulness of a nonspecialist. The specialist lacks the inspirational powers the parent has in stimulating a child to learn and explore. By professionalizing education, and even worse, making it a public service, society

has entrusted the conservation of its own traditions to a class of persons who, owing to their position, have not the power to conserve them. By doing this it has put itself as much at a disadvantage, as compared with peoples it calls barbarous, as if it were a tribe which threw away the paddles of its war-canoes, set sail and employed crews of professional medicinemen to whistle for a wind (*NL*, 37.42).

Parents must take responsibility for the education of their children themselves and overcome the deference they have felt toward the professional. Specialists have robbed us of the self-confidence to undertake, or perform, tasks in which we have no expertise. Collingwood is warning here of the dangers of what later theorists have called the technocratic society.[9] It is up to the parents to take the initiative and divest the specialists of their already diminished powers. If office and factory drudgeries appear to be a barrier to educating one's own children, then this, in Collingwood's view, is a good enough reason for smashing such soul-destroying activities. Professional educators are to be allowed to continue to teach if they so desire, but pupils will go to them only to acquire knowledge that their parents are not equipped to give them. Indeed, parents may wish to go along to learn such things with their children.

Collingwood's emphasis upon parental responsibility may appear to be rather naive. It was certainly influenced by his own educational experiences, and does to a certain degree demonstrate the extent to which Collingwood was divorced from some of the problems about which he theorized. He does not address, for instance, the plight of those children who are born to uneducated, ignorant, and uncaring parents. Earlier British idealists had turned their attention to this matter and concluded that there was a role for the state to play in education, in order to counteract the consequences of such conditions for the child. Both T. H. Green and Henry Jones, for example, while acknowledging the considerable short-comings of the educational system in Britain, had no illusions about the necessity of an improved system for overcoming the divisions in society caused by a rigid class system.[10] The condition of the poor and uneducated was hardly likely to improve without the provision of that greatest of social levellers, a liberal education. Green, writing over sixty years before Collingwood wrote *The New Leviathan,* was acutely aware of the in-creasing need for professional education. He says, for instance, that 'as the methods and material of knowledge become more complex with time, the possibility of acquiring it without the help of the schoolmaster be-comes less and less'.[11]

Given the importance of the role of education in Collingwood's social and political philosophy, what should the content of this education be, and why? Collingwood does not address himself directly to these questions in *The New Leviathan,* but answers are easily discernible in his writings. In *Speculum Mentis,* as we noted, Collingwood identified five forms of experience: art, religion, science, history, and philosophy. By the end of his career he had brought about the rapprochement between history and philosophy that he had long hoped to achieve. The philosophical sciences of metaphysics, logic, and ethics were not eradicated; instead they were converted into historical sciences.[12] Each of these forms of experience, including the his-torical sciences, at one time or another, was seen by Collingwood to be in-dispensable to the modern European civilizing process.

Art, 'the primary and fundamental activity of the mind, the original soil out of which all other activities grow',[13] is essential to the education of children. It is 'the absolute bedrock of all sane human life'.[14] Collingwood at first associates art with imagination,[15] which is the 'initial stage' in the 'formation of knowledge'.[16] 'Imagination is a fundamental mode of mind's activity, and the right training of imagination is therefore a fundamental part of education'.[17] We all have imaginative capacities, and in this respect we are all artists. Poetry, Collingwood contends, is 'pure imagination' and is ' "the mother-tongue of mankind", the universal form of primitive lit-erature, preceding it in historical evolution at every phase of the world's history'.[18] In poetry we create imaginery objects which we subject to the laws that imagination makes for itself. Such imaginative creativity is a prelude to prose, which 'is imagination as controlled by and consciously expressive of thought'.[19]

During the mid-1930s Collingwood developed a theory of art which laid greater emphasis upon art as the expression of emotion. In Chapter 4 we saw how Collingwood, in *The Principles of Art,* bridged the gap between feeling and intellect by arguing that consciousness converts sensa into imagination. Language, it was suggested, comes into existence with imagination. Language at the conscious, or imaginative, level has the function of expressing emotion. Collingwood's view of art is integrally connected with his theory of consciousness, because in language we have consciousness converting psychical emotion into 'a corresponding imaginative or aesthetic emotion'.[20] Art and language are identical and constitute an imaginative activity expressive of emotion.[21] We saw in the preceding chapter that Collingwood also viewed magic as expressing emotion. All magic uses art to evoke and express emotion, but not all art is magic.

Emotion is the dynamo that gives impetus to practical life,[22] and its faithful expression must be the aim of art education. This may be so, but why is it necessary to be able to express emotion? An inability to express one's emotions, as we have seen, has serious consequences for the development of consciousness. To express an emotion is to become conscious of its existence; it is to acknowledge to ourselves the feelings that we have. The failure to express an emotion is to disown it, an option made possible by selective attention, which divides emotional experiences into those to which we do not attend and those to which we do and recognise as our own. To disown an emotion is to repress it. This is what Collingwood calls the 'corruption of consciousness'.[23] In other words, consciousness, in converting psychical emotions into the imaginative expression of emotion, fails to do its job faithfully. Thus the facts passed on by consciousness for the intellect to work upon in building its fabric of thought are false: 'A truthful consciousness gives intellect a firm foundation upon which to build; a corrupt consciousness forces intellect to build on a quicksand'.[24] While art is an indispensable and integral component of every person's education, the artist has a vital role to play in the life of civilization. The artist, Collingwood claims, must be prophetic, not in the sense of foretelling the future, but in that he reveals, or lays bare, the very heart of civilization. The artist, contrary to the common view, is not merely discovering himself or expressing himself as an individual, but is instead the spokesman of the community whose secrets he reveals. His services are vital in that the community does not know itself as well as it might. If it deceives itself as to its essential character, the community itself precipitates its own demise. 'Art', Collingwood contends, 'is the community's medicine for the worst disease of mind, the corruption of consciousness'.[25] The denial of emotion which a corrupt consciousness entails is essentially the condition of barbarism which threatens to transform society back 'into the condition of the human brute'.[26] Two types of emotion are essential to a healthy civilization. First, there are those which are at the root of emotional life: emotions regarding our own bodies and personalities, our relation to our mothers, and our relation to our mates, as well as to other human beings. Second, there are those emotions which are fundamental to the particular type of civilization to which a person belongs. These include such things as the love of God and the love of nature. Collingwood sums up the importance of both these types of emotion when he says that 'the sanity of man, as man, depends on the health of his fundamentally human emotions. The sanity of man as civilised depends upon the health in him of the emotions fundamental to his type of civilization'.[27]

Art is no mere luxury; it is the way in which we express our emotions, and by expressing them we come to know them. Art, then, is a mode of self-knowledge, and, for Collingwood, the general aim of art education must be 'that the child should become able to speak its mind, to utter itself clearly and accurately in every medium that it handles. . . . A child so trained will need no dope, for it will be able to do something better with its emotions than to stimulate them artificially'.[28]

The second component of a comprehensive education is religion. The Christian religion lies at the heart of European civilization and stands as the foundation upon which European morality is built. Religion is an element in our nature which gives us the strength of character to conquer and overcome unhappiness. Religion is an inward flame burning in our minds, making us conscious of our 'personal relation to the infinite mystery of the universe'.[29] It is the source of an inner contentedness; of being at peace with oneself and with the world. To achieve this form of happiness is to be civilized, and in order to sustain such an achievement 'the inward flame of religion . . . must always be kept burning in the heart of civilization'.[30] Religion, then, is the 'vital warmth at the heart of a civilization'.[31] A people possessed of 'religious energy can overcome all obstacles and attain any height in the scale of civilization'.[32] In our own civilization, Collingwood argues, we have an affinity with, and a love of, the soil. The love we have of nature and of our country 'is an experience neither aesthetic nor political, but in the deepest sense religious. : . . And upon the vitality of this religious feeling depends the vitality of our civilization as a whole'.[33] We can infer from this, then, that parents have a responsibility to kindle and keep burning this religious flame in their children.

We have already seen the importance of natural science to civilization. Natural science is what facilitates the intelligent exploitation of nature. Any society will accumulate a vast amount of traditional scientific knowledge relating to the seasons, the soil, irrigation, the raising of animals, the tying of knots, and other useful information. It is the passing on of this vital scientific knowledge, born of 'that religious sense of loving union with the soil',[34] that keeps a civilization alive. It is not the mere conservation of such knowledge that is important, but its development and adaptation to match growing needs and expectations. Natural science should not be taken to be scientific thinking itself. Science, in the context of European civilization, 'means a body of systematic or orderly thinking about a determinate subject-matter'.[35] In so far as the understanding of a determinate subject matter assumes such a scientific approach, education has to 'be predominantly a method for inducing habits of orderly and systematic thinking'.[36] This applies not only to the natural sciences, but also to the historical sciences, namely, metaphysics, logic, ethics, and history itself. Scientific thinking, then, in the broad sense in which Collingwood uses the term, is an exhibition of intelligence: the manifestation of rational consciousness in the life of civilization.

The importance of history in the education of society goes without saying. Historical knowledge is the means by which we achieve self-knowledge of the mind. European civilization is a creation of the mind, and in order to understand that creation we must understand the mind whose creation it is. *The New Leviathan* itself, as we have seen, constitutes such an undertaking. The attainment of historical knowledge is not the mere satisfaction of an inquisitive mind; it enables us to understand the present. Indeed, the 'ultimate aim of history is not to know the past but to understand the present'.[37] To know the present is to prepare ourselves for future action. The process of civilization cannot even begin until mind has reached the level of reason, or rational consciousness. Reason exists only in the historical process,

and it is only in so far as this process is known for a process of thoughts that it is one. The self-knowledge of reason is not an accident; it belongs to its essence. This is why historical knowledge is no luxury, or mere amusement of a mind at leisure from more pressing occupations, but a prime duty, whose discharge is essential to the maintenance, not only of any particular form or type of reason, but of reason itself.[38]

Given that civilization presupposes reason, there can be no civilization without historical knowledge.

In Chapter 2 we saw that metaphysical analysis entails asking questions about the status of presuppositions. 'Relative presuppositions' are those to which the concepts of truth and falsity can be applied, whereas to 'absolute presuppositions' such considerations are inapplicable or meaningless. Relative presuppositions are 'relative' because they are both answers to logically prior questions and the immediate presuppositions of logically subsequent questions. These logically subsequent questions are the answers to the questions which the logically antecedent presuppositions pose. To determine the relative or absolute character of presuppositions, one works backwards from a certain point, asking what presupposition is presupposed in each statement, until a presupposition is reached to which no question stands in logical priority.

The modus operandi of detecting absolute and relative presuppositions is not peculiar to metaphysical analysis. To know whether a presupposition is relative or absolute is an integral part of all methodical analysis, because it enables us to determine which presuppositions are susceptible to questions about their truth or falsity. To ask such questions of absolute presuppositions, in whatever form of analysis, is logically absurd.

As regards its *modus operandi,* then, all analysis is metaphysical analysis; and, since analysis is what gives its scientific character to science, science and metaphysics are inextricably united, and stand or fall together.... As long as either lives the other lives; if either dies the other must die with it.[39]

In other words, the identification of presuppositions which need justification, and must be justified, and those which need no justification and for which no justification can be given, is both a metaphysical and a scientific enquiry: 'No metaphysician, no scientist'[40]; and no scientist, we may add, means no civilization. Metaphysics and civilization are inextricably connected, not, as some commentators seem to think, because the former merely detects the absolute presuppositions upon which the latter is built,[41] but because the modus operandi of metaphysics is that of all scientific enquiry, and without it the civilizing process cannot get very far. The metaphysician detects absolute presuppositions, but also exposes the logical fallacies entailed in the thought of those thinkers who call for proofs, refutations, or justifications of absolute presuppositions.[42]

Logic, as a historical science, is important in the civilizing or educational process in that it aims to expound the principles of valid thought applicable to contemporary society.[43] In this respect Collingwood's own logic of question and answer can be understood as an attempt to articulate the principles of valid thinking in the historical civilization emerging in modern Europe. Logicians such as Mill and Jevons, for example, gave the best account they could of the inductive logic employed by the positivist scientists of their day in determining the validity of a piece of scientific thinking. The logic applicable in the nineteenth century was superseded in the historical civilization of the twentieth. Indeed, Collingwood's criticism of Bradley's and Croce's attempts to articulate modern logic is that he thought that they had inadvertently slipped back into assuming the principles which governed the positivist logic of the natural sciences.

Ethics, as a historical science, attempts to articulate the principles of action applicable to particular societies. It expounds a theory of the type of life valued by a society and towards which it aims. The ethical sciences of economics and politics 'describe the political and economic principles accepted at [a particular] time and place'.[44] *The New Leviathan,* as we have seen, was such an attempt to formulate the principles of action which lay at the heart of European civilization, with a view to reminding Europeans of the values for which they were fighting in World War II.

Education, then, is the first, and one might contend the primary, property of civilization. A second property of civilization is wealth. Wealth, Collingwood argues, is a comparative term and implies a standard in terms of which a community is adjudged wealthy. The term *rich* is a relative term which implies no standard. To be rich is to be rich in relation to someone who is poor, where the terms *rich* and *poor* are not adjudged in terms of a standard:

38.6   To be rich is to stand in a certain relation to another party with whom one is connected by economic relations, this other person being poor in proportion as you are rich; but what relation?

The relation is in fact one of power. Riches and economic force are the same thing. An absence of force in economic relations entails a transaction or exchange freely entered into and viewed as mutually beneficial. The exercise of force in the same transaction introduces an element of compulsion which undermines the free will of the individual. In other words, a person is forced to sell something for less than he, or she, regards as a fair price, a fair price being that for which I am willing to exchange something when I am not forced to do so. Thus to take advantage of one's economic power by paying low wages to a labourer is to exploit the latter's economic weakness. To refrain from the use of force in one's relations with other people is to live up to the ideal of civility. Where a contrast between rich and poor in a community exists, the ideal of civility has been departed from. Such a departure, however, may be in keeping with the values of a particular civilization if the contribution to the wealth of the community is enhanced by the continuing discrepancy between the riches of individuals. If the contrast can be diminished (and, like all types of force in the community, it can never be totally abolished) without significantly detracting from the overall wealth of the community, then the ideal of civility demands that it should be done. The motive for the accumulation of wealth is to pursue the good life, or civilization. Where the motive is to create a contrast between rich and poor, civilization is actively being revolted against, and barbarism is being pursued. To become a civilized community means to become a wealthy community in which wealth is diffused throughout the population. The corollary of this is that poverty is abolished, which itself entails the abolition of riches.

A third property of civilization is that of law and order, that is, what we commonly call the rule of law. Civilization may exist without the rule of law, but it would be of such a low sort that modern Europeans would hardly recognise it as such. The principle of the rule of law entails a number of features. First, there must be law of some kind, whether it be customary or the pronouncement of a despot, as long as it remains law until he abrogates it (*NL,* 39.31). Second, those people who are subject to the laws should be able to find out what the laws are: In other words, the laws should be public. Third, the laws must be applied, and this entails the existence of a judicial system. Fourth, the rule of law implies equality before the law. In answer to the question Why is the rule of law essential to the European standard of civilization?, Collingwood answers, 'Because that is the standard to which it is accustomed' (*NL,* 39.42). It became accustomed to this standard by the example of the Greco-Roman city-state and the Roman Empire.

The rule of law means substituting for the eristical settlement of disputes, by vendettas or blood feuds, a dialectical method (*NL,* 39.5–39.6). Respect for the rule of law develops and strengthens the will by means of daily exercise. People become more and more capable of controlling their desires and passions and less and less likely to succumb to the threats of those who would cajole and frighten them into doing things that they would not do of their own free will. In Collingwood's view, '*Law and order mean strength*' (*NL,* 39.92). Peoples who honour law and order can stand against the greatest of adversities. Indeed, it is at times when the rule of law has been observed most scrupulously that peoples have gained their finest victories: 'It has always been so in the past ... [and] it will always be so in the future' (*NL,* 39.94).

The fourth, and final element that Collingwood discusses is that of peace and plenty. It is, essentially, the name for the fruits, or benefits, of civilization. Peace and plenty may be had without law and order, but law and order ensure them, and in more abundance. Peace in the community is the promotion and pursuit of the dialectical resolution of disputes: It is the attempt to convert occasions of nonagreement into occasions of agreement. A community whose political life is flourishing vigorously, that is, a community in which the Third Law of Politics is operating effectively, will encourage means by which the ruled class can aspire to the status of the ruling class, or at least foster a cooperative relation between the classes, in order to facilitate the expression and resolution of grievances. In the case of the family, it is the responsibility of the parents to promote the peaceful resolution of conflicts. A community in which the peace is kept by means of converting nonagreements into agreements is one which can be said to be '*wellmannered*' (*NL,* 40.71). The development of good manners is an outcome of the promotion of peace. A community which keeps itself polite and honest is a peace-loving community. It has become civilized up to a point and prides itself on the exercise of the free will that maintains the standard it recognises.

Plenty, in relation to the community, means the ability to balance the economic elements in its life in a way that will enable it to sustain the civilization that economic activity exists to support. In other words, it will devote some of its wealth to armaments in order to protect itself against potential enemies: 'Unless it met that expense it would not be providing the indispensable conditions of its own civilized existence' (NL, 40.87). The procurement of plenty entails the partial control of distribution and consumption, 'canalizing these in such a way as to promote the civilized life of the community' (NL, 40.9). This is primarily the responsibility of the individual, exercising his, or her, free will.

Having looked briefly at the properties of civilization and their importance for the civilizing process, we now turn to those palpable threats to civilization about which Collingwood expressed the gravest concern.

3. What is wrong with European civilization?

Just as Collingwood wrote extensively on the idea of civilization, he was also prolific in formulating theories about what ailed civilization. His diagnoses, prognoses, and remedies are best viewed as explorations into various aspects of the disease, constituting complementary, rather than alternative, theories.

The period between the two world wars in Europe saw a veritable explosion and proliferation of what may be termed 'crisis' literature, and it was almost invariably civilization that was described as being in a state of severe crisis, or even experiencing its final death throe.[45] E. H. Carr, for instance, described the whole period as 'the Twenty Years' Crisis'.[46] Some typical descriptions mentioned a 'crisis of the mind'; a 'crisis in our intellectual life'; 'a collapse of civilization'; a 'cracking in its very foundations'; a 'revolution which threatens every concept on which European civilization has been based'; and, an 'intensified manifestation of Disease – physical, social, intellectual and moral'.[47] The bishop of Chelmsford, Dr. Wilson, claimed that a 'panic closely resembling insanity is running like an epidemic over the whole world, crushing out all chivalry, decency, and humanity in human nature'.[48] For G. G. Coulton, European civilization faced 'one of the greatest crises ever recorded, especially for the educated classes'.[49] (Why the uneducated classes faced less of a crisis is left unexplained.)

The remedies for the crisis of civilization were many and varied, ranging from the novel to the bizarre. There were those who believed that too much science had brought civilization to the edge of a precipice. C. E. M. Joad, for example, argued that 'science was taking a man who from the ethical and political point of view was still an underdeveloped baby, and giving him a box of matches'.[50] It was only by putting our trust in people's reason that we could look forward to future improvement in modern civilization. Lord Horder and Viscount Samuel, on the other hand, thought that it was too little science, not too much, that was troubling civilization. Lord Horder had great faith in the sciences, 'especially sciences directed towards the study and development of the mind and spirit of man',[51] and looked forward to a revival in liberalism to bring civilization back to its senses, whereas Viscount Samuel thought that an intimate union 'of philosophy, science, and religion'[52] would turn the tide.

It is not surprising to find church leaders, such as the archbishop of Canterbury, suggesting that it might be possible 'to rediscover in the Christian faith new sources of spiritual strength to regenerate an imperilled civilization'.[53] The archbishop of York had a more idiosyncratic remedy for alleviating the pressures of our 'absurdly complicated civilization'. He recommended that 'everyone should spend a certain amount of time every year in quite disreputable clothes'.[54]

The amount of time and energy devoted to analysing the condition of modern civilization was already sufficiently great by 1930 to prompt Collingwood to declare that 'the flood of literature concerned with the unhappy state of the modern world is becoming a positive nuisance'.[55] He had contributed, and would continue to contribute, a great deal to this 'flood of literature' himself. Indeed, he always felt the need to return to the question of modern civilization and its discontents. The time he devoted at the end of his life to such matters was, therefore, no aberration or sudden whim.

We saw in Chapter 7 that Collingwood viewed the decline of liberalism, and liberalism's failure to extend its principles to international relations, as one of the most visible features of the crisis in civilization. There were, however, in his view more fundamental forces at work undermining the very foundations of modern civilization. These forces were associated with the natural-scientific, or positivist, tendency to undervalue or deny the efficacy and importance of the other forms of knowledge in civilization. Indeed, the civilization generated by an excessive deference to natural science is a utilitarian one in which emotion is denied or suppressed; art is perverted into an artificial stimulant to the senses; the mystical content of religion is eliminated, leaving only a rationalistic code of morals, devoid of the substance from which it emerged; and psychology claims to be a science of mind, leaving its legitimate realm of the psyche, or the science of feeling, and claiming instead the entire workings of mind as its province. In doing so psychology asks only why a certain thought arises, not whether that thought has any validity. Psychology is one of the main contributors to irrationalism in modern civilization. Psychology has prepared the way for fascism, the newest kind of barbarism to threaten civilization.

In *Speculum Mentis,* as we have already seen, Collingwood identified the crisis of civilization, or 'the nature of our disease',[56] as being the detachment of the forms of experience – art, religion, science, history, and philosophy – from one another. This fragmentation of the unity of the mind has diminished our ability to be able to see life as it is, in its unity, and achieve the happiness we so sadly lack. The 'sick' and 'morbid' condition[57] could be cured by a reunion of the forms of experience 'in a complete and undivided life'. The activity that emerges from this unification integrates and combines art, religion, science, history, and philosophy.[58] Each form is necessary, then, and none is noncontributory to the unity of life.

Collingwood gradually came to identify the problem of civilization more specifically. It was not only the separation of the forms of experience from one another, but the emergence of one which threatened to obliterate the rest. Natural science, although invaluable in the civilizing process, threatened to destroy civilization because of its denial of any form of knowledge that was not its own. Our civilization, Collingwood contends, is a scientific one[59] in which we have deliberately cultivated an insensitivity towards emotion. The rationalistic or thick-skinned attitude to life, formulated in the seventeenth century, developed and refined in the eighteenth, and applied to all aspects of life in the nineteenth, had become the dominant feature of civilization. It was now a utilitarian civilization in which everything had to be justified in terms of its usefulness or utility. Collingwood maintains, 'The doctrine that utility is the only kind of value that a thing can have is called utilitarianism; and it is obvious to anyone who reflects on the general character of our civilization that it is, characteristically, a utilitarian civilization'.[60] Civilization, then, predominately exhibited the first level of rational consciousness and was threatening to revert back into a form of irrationalism, or was at least showing signs of a perverse consciousness. Indeed, the utilitarian obsession, in its tendency to suppress emotion and ridicule magic, art, and religion, was precipitating a corruption of consciousness. It is only by expressing our emotions that we know what they are. The utilitarian obsession interferes, then, with the process whereby consciousness offers facts to the intellect. As we saw earlier, in so far as these emotional facts are disowned, the foundation upon which intellect builds its fabric of thought is false.[61] Indeed, our utilitarian obsession leads us to conceive civilization not as it is, but as we would like it to be. We like to think that our rationalism has superseded magic.[62] Magic, however, is an essential mode of emotional expression, and 'a society which thinks, as our own thinks, that it has outlived the need of magic, is either mistaken in that opinion, or else it is a dying society perishing for lack of interest in its own maintenance'.[63]

A good training in art, as we saw, was, in Collingwood's view, a prerequisite to being able to express our emotions. Modern civilization, however, has failed to live up to its responsibility in this respect. In both 'Art and the Machine' and *The Principles of Art,* he contended that art is increasingly being seen as an amusement, an emotional stimulant, rather than the expression of emotion. In 'Art and the Machine' Collingwood was particularly concerned about the mechanical reproduction of art. The subtleties of the original, both in fine art and music, were being mutilated by artificial means of reproduction. The masses who had not seen, or heard, the originals, unlike the expert, could not discern in the reproductions what was lost from the originals. Thus they infer that because the reproduction is visibly, or audibly, worthless, the same must be true of the original. Failure to educate the public in the appreciation of original art will eventually prove to be a disaster to civilization.

People are now fed pseudoart, with the intention of artificially stimulating the emotions. Civilization has become so dull and drab that we crave emotional excitement, and such cravings can be satisfied quite easily by stimulating 'crude emotional responses, especially those concerned with the simple and primitive emotions of sexual desire and bodily fear'.[64] We have become a civilization that lacks artistic appreciation and consequently have become unable to produce art. We produce only pseudoart designed to stimulate the emotions. Without an artistic basis to its rationality, that is, a healthy emotional life, no mind can be completely sane. For Collingwood, 'An inartistic civilization is, to that extent, an insane civilization, melancholy mad. The very drabness of its life drives it in search of relief, to the more furious madness of addiction to drugs'.[65] The solution to the problem rests with the education of the young with the intention that the child becomes articulate, that is, self-expressive, in the media of the arts. The development of the facility of self-expression will obviate the need to stimulate the emotions artificially.

These themes are pursued further in *The Principles of Art.* In that book Collingwood distinguished between magical art, art as amusement, and art proper. Magical art is designed to arouse emotions which are channelled into a practical activity with the intention of having practical effects. It is utilitarian in character. Art as amusement, or pseudoart, is designed to stimulate emotions, not in the context of a practical activity, but in a fantasy or make-believe situation. The emotion is stimulated and earthed – that is, harmlessly discharged. Amusement in itself is hedonistic and not utilitarian, but the so-called works of art which provide the amusement are 'strictly utilitarian'.[66] Art proper is the expression of one's emotions, 'and that which expresses them is the total imaginative activity called indifferently language or art'.[67] It has value in itself. Amusement art, on the other hand, has no value in itself and is merely a means to an end. Amusement entails dividing life into reality and make-believe. In discharging emotions in a make-believe world, people begin to think that they can excite and enjoy emotions for their own sake. In deflecting emotions from practical life, our everyday existence becomes a drudgery and a bore, alleviated only by more and more artificial stimulants to the emotions. Amusement becomes the only thing that makes life worth living: 'A society in which the disease is endemic is one in which most people feel some such conviction most of the time'.[68]

A society whose way of life is no longer valued by its members is one which is dying, or has died, because it is no longer considered worth preserving. Modern civilization has become devoid of its practical emotional energy and has instead become obsessed with amusement. This is evidenced by

the unprecedented growth of the amusement trade, to meet what has become an insatiable craving; an almost universal agreement that the kinds of work on which the existence of a civilization like ours most obviously depends (notably the work of industrial operatives and the clerical staff in business of every kind, and even that of the agricultural labourers and the other food-winners who are the prime agents in the maintenance of every civilization hitherto existing) is an intolerable drudgery; the discovery that what makes this intolerable is not the pinch of poverty or bad housing or disease but the nature of the work itself in the conditions our civilization has created.[69]

The traditional means by which we discharged our emotions into practical activities, namely through magic and religion, have been severely undermined in modern civilization. The traditional folklore and folk arts of the countryside have been almost entirely eradicated by the town dwellers' mentality. The emotional life of the country dweller has become empty as more and more of the traditional practices are abandoned, or suppressed, or destroyed by modern technology. In 'Man Goes Mad', Collingwood complains that the very fact that the country people could not resist the encroachment of the values of the town is a sign that the vitality of the countryside had already been sapped of its energy.

European civilization is an essentially agricultural civilization, and we no longer feel the necessary emotional commitment to the soil that would enable us to sustain our traditional way of life. Modern industry, although dependent upon and consciously nourished by modern agriculture, has nevertheless been severed from it. This is a kind of madness 'which may endure for a time in a feverish and restless consciousness, but can have no lasting vitality.... There is a cure, if only we could get it: the deep primitive, almost unconscious emotion of the man who, wrestling with the earth, sees the labour of his hands and is satisfied'.[70]

Religion, as we saw, lies at the very heart of civilization. The existence of God is an absolute presupposition for Christians. His existence is not susceptible to proof, and to question his existence is to bring into doubt the civilization at whose heart he stands. There has, however, been an increasing tendency to question religion and ask for proofs of its assertions. If no such proofs are forthcoming, we reject religion as superstition, but we still wish to retain the code of morality and forms of association to which religion gave rise. The intellectual sceptics and moral dogmatists of Victorian England suggested 'that the doctrines of Christian belief should be given up as being incapable of proof, while the Christian ethics should be preserved, as the best ethical system in existence'.[71] Collingwood elaborates upon this point in 'Fascism and Nazism'. Modern philosophy and science, with the best of intentions, have attempted to distil from Christianity principles which relate to activities such as politics and scientific method. The residue of superstition and ritual has been discarded, with the curious effect of at once clarifying the principles upon which civilization is based, and at the same time undermining 'religious emotion, passion, faith', labelling them 'superstition and magic'.[72] It was eighteenth-century Illuminism which accentuated this tendency, and by the nineteenth century it had become openly hostile towards religion. Thus the principles of free speech and freedom of thought, distilled from Christianity, became severed from their foundation, and the foundation was explained in other terms, such as Mill's Utilitarianism or Kant's notion of the categorical imperative.

. Belief in such democratic ideals as freedom of speech and enquiry, Collingwood argues, are based upon faith, not upon empirical verification. The ideals of freedom were derived from Christianity, but Christianity as dogma was abjured, while its principles of morality remained. Those who practiced the principles did so habitually, and without the passion of the love of God who authored them. Fascism and nazism have been able to conduct a successful attack on civilization because they are 'specialists in arousing the emotions'.[73] If we link this up to Collingwood's earlier arguments, we can infer that a people severed from its traditional roots, and fed on mechanical reproductions of art, seeking stimulation in a world in which it feels disoriented, is obviously particularly susceptible to the emotional stimulus aroused by fascism and nazism.

Fascism and nazism have been able to overwhelm liberalism, or democracy, in such countries as Italy, Germany, and Spain, because of the ability to arouse in their followers an intense emotional attachment to their beliefs. Liberalism, or democracy, having been purged of its emotional aspects, is overwhelmed by the emotional energy of its opponents. In consequence, Collingwood sounds this ominous warning: 'People rich in religious energy can overcome all obstacles and attain any height in the scale of civilization. Peoples that have reached the top of the hill by the wise use of religious energy may then decide to do without it; they can still move, but they can only move downhill, and when they come to the bottom of the hill they stop'.[74] Rejection of religion has still other consequences. Science, far from severing itself from religion, depends upon it for its continuing existence. Absolute presuppositions are not a consequence of experience: The mind creates them in order to experience. Absolute presuppositions enable us to manipulate experience and convert it 'into science and civilization'.[75] In order for science and civilization to flourish, there must be institutions for preserving and perpetuating absolute presuppositions. In Europe it is religious institutions which perform this function, and, in fact, in every civilization it is religious institutions which reinvigorate the will to preserve the presuppositions which convert experience into science. The conversion into science occurs in the light of our general convictions about the world, and it is religion that expresses these convictions 'for their own sake and hands them on from generation to generation'.[76] Whenever and wherever the habit first arose among peoples of categorizing and classifying the natural world in terms of resemblances and differences, 'we may be sure that this new habit of mind had its expression in their religious practices'.[77] If it is true, then, that we have become disillusioned with the church and have 'come to think of the religious ideas we once cherished as delusions',[78] the very institutions which preserve and perpetuate our absolute presuppositions are in grave danger, and in consequence civilization itself is under threat of death, if nothing remains to generate the will to preserve the absolute presuppositions upon which it rests.

In an age which prides itself on having ousted superstitions and on having abolished magic, we suppress their existence and fail to acknowledge that such things are as prevalent as ever. In failing to recognise them, we have lost the art of conquering them. Collingwood maintains that it is a characteristic of European civilization that we frown upon metaphysics and deny the existence of absolute presuppositions: 'This habit is neurotic. It is an attempt to overcome superstitious dread by denying that there is any cause for it. If this neurosis ever achieves its ostensible object, the eradication of metaphysics from the European mind, the eradication of science and civilization will be accomplished at the same time.'[79] The reason is, as we have already seen, that metaphysics and scientific enquiry have an identical modus operandi.

The various attacks upon civilization, and the emotional poverty that has beset it and drained it of its vital energies, are the manifestations of what Collingwood terms *irrationalism*. Irrationalism in philosophy has resulted from a move towards, and a preoccupation with, psychology. The great philosophers have tended, since the seventeenth century, to offer reductionist explanations of human activity, culminating in the eighteenth century in aspirations of formulating a science of thought, rather than a science of feelings, on the theory that 'intellectual activities, or operations of thought, were nothing but aggregations of feelings and thus special cases of sensation and emotion'.[80] Collingwood was always of the opinion that psychology could be of tremendous value to civilization as long as it restricted itself to its proper sphere or place, namely, the human psyche.[81] Unfortunately psychology had not kept to its proper sphere and had thus become a threat and a danger to scientific activity.

Collingwood's principal argument against psychology is that it is non-criteriological. It cannot determine whether the imagination is morbid or healthy, whether the feelings we have are good or bad, and our thoughts true or false. As early as 1913 Collingwood was already beginning to formulate his criticisms of psychology. Ethics, he argues, asks what the difference is between a good and a bad act, whereas psychology asks, for instance, whether people commit crimes more frequently in the morning than they do in the afternoon.[82] In *Religion and Philosophy* Collingwood once again emphasizes the noncriteriological nature of psychology. Using a realist argument, which he was later to abandon without abandoning the conclusion, he claims that psychology treats mental activity as a mere event unrelated to the reality of an external object. In omitting reference to the object to which the judgement is related, the question of whether the judgement is true or false is not raised.[83] Similarly, psychology claims that imagination is a morbid activity, and in this claim it 'possesses no criterion for distinguishing the healthy from the unhealthy imagination; it has only a pathology of the imagination, and does not recognize that there is such a thing as the healthy imagination'.[84]

In addition, Collingwood believed that psychology exempted itself from the conclusions of its own investigations. When psychological conclusions were turned back on the theory, they became self-condemned. Psychology, then, could not escape the implications of its own theories. Jung, for instance, in explaining scientific doctrines as the result of peculiarities in temperament, 'discredits all theory', including his own.[85] Behaviourists who have revealed a tendency in psychology to treat thought, not as an act of thinking, but as a mechanism, have exposed psychology to be 'nothing more nor less than a *reductio ad absurdum*'. Mind has been 'de-mentalized' and 'materialized' by the psychologist. The psychologist's own mind, as applied to the materialized object of his thought, remains untouched by the analysis. Psychology is self-condemned because it describes a 'wholly fictitious entity'. In ignoring in thought something that is intrinsic to it, namely the distinction between truth and falsity, the psychologist simply ignores thought, 'for thought is nothing whatever but the drawing of this distinction. And yet, in ignoring the distinction, he has asserted it implicitly in his own person, and is thus the living refutation of his own principles. Psychology is refuted by the psychology of psychology'.[86] It was criticisms such as these, and those formulated in the manuscripts on cosmology and fairy tales and in *The Principles of Art*, that provided the basis for Collingwood's most scathing and sustained attack on psychology and psychologists.

In *An Essay on Metaphysics*, Collingwood argues that psychology differentiates itself from logic in self-consciously ignoring the aspect of thought that is self-critical. Logic attempts to give an account of the criteria of self-criticism and their role in human thought, whereas psychology ignores this aspect of human activity, preferring instead to be content with offering crude epistemological materialist explanations of human thought. In Collingwood's view, psychology cannot live up to its claim of being a science of thought, because in jettisoning discussion of the criteria of self-criticism it precludes all questions of truth and falsity in human thought. As a science of feeling, that is, the study of sensation and emotion, psychology has a valuable role to play in furthering knowledge, and it is none of its business to discuss the truth or falsity of thought, but as a purported science of thought the exclusion of such questions has serious implications. Psychology in the guise of a science of thought is implicitly teaching that 'there is no difference between the pursuit of truth, or science, and the pursuit of falsehood, or sophistry; no difference between scientific teaching or the inculcation of error'.[87] Psychology as a science of thought thus exposes itself as a pseudoscience whose own theories are rendered suspect by its indifference to truth and falsity. This irrationalism, however, is an erosion of the fundamental principles upon which European civilization is built. The pursuit of truth, and freedom of thought to pursue systematic scientific enquiry, that is, orderly theorizing, have been the most cherished values of civilization, the pursuit of which it has been considered to be the duty of every person. Irrationalism, if it is allowed to take hold, will destroy European civilization, because it strikes at the very principles upon which that civilization is based. In addition, in claiming to be the science of mind, psychology is denying history its rightful domain. History, and not psychology, is the science of mind.

Modern philosophy has been unable to prevent the increasing swell of irrationalism. Such philosophies as positivism and realism, while standing opposed to irrationalism and venerating the principle of orderly and systematic theory, elevate natural-scientific knowledge to a status which reduces all knowledge of ethics and morality to the level of mere beliefs and superstitions, matters of opinion, rather than objects of knowledge. The realists, for instance, in believing that knowledge makes no difference to the object and in treating moral philosophy as a 'purely theoretical' activity which viewed the 'workings of the moral consciousness ... as if they were the movements of the planets',[88] ill equipped the young for practical life, and to a certain extent, by providing no effective moral opposition to irrationalism, helped to facilitate its growth. This abnegation of moral responsibility explains the passion with which Collingwood opposes realist philosophy, a passion so intense that one reviewer commented that the author of *An Autobiography* was 'in the dire state of one who sees a "realist" under every bed'.[89]

In essence, then, Collingwood believed nearly all those elements in education essential to the civilizing process to be under attack. All these trends towards the destruction of civilization become incorporated into one all-encompassing concept, namely, that of barbarism. In *The New Leviathan* and a number of related unpublished manuscripts, all the trends that Collingwood had previously identified as working against civilization become manifest in the idea of barbarism. Barbarism, unlike savagery, is not a primitive survival in modern civilization:

Thus the barbarisms against which the civilizing process has to contend are not residuary elements of a barbarism against which that process has been contending from the first; they are products of that process itself. The greater its achievements, the more power it puts into the hands of men for evil as well as good.... The achievements of civilization as inherited in the form of fact by any given man, are always opportunities out of which it is for him to build either a new civilization or a new barbarism.[90]

To will civilization is simply to will, but to will barbarism is to '*will to do nothing*' (*NL,* 36.94). Willing barbarism is the will to succumb to emotion. Barbarism asserts itself as will in overcoming emotion and then denies it in acquiescing to emotion. To will barbarism is to will servility, that is, to produce in others a servile spirit in relation to oneself.[91]

The identification of acts which can be characterised as civilized and uncivilized depends upon what Collingwood calls 'the sentiment of approval or disapproval' (*NL,* 41.3), by which he means something which is at once emotional and intellectual, that is, beginning as an impulse and developing into a rationalization of that impulse. My sentiment of approval, then, of someone's actions begins as a pleasurable feeling in contemplating the activity and develops into a rationalization, or moral theory, about that action (*NL,* 41.34). A sentiment, as opposed to a theory devoid of emotion, has vigour and liveliness. A moral and social sentiment values freedom of the will and joint social action. Such sentiments are directed towards making free and moral activities of all common action, that is, to make these actions civil. Sentiments to civilize are not necessarily consciously held, especially when those sentiments are near to the emotional end of the scale. The same sentiment nearer to the intellectual end of the scale may be consciously held and promoted. Civilized, or relatively civilized, people can work unconsciously at the civilizing process.

Barbarism, however, can never be promoted unconsciously, because it entails a clear conception of what it is revolting against in order to flourish. Its successes, nevertheless, are only temporary and last only so long as its enemy is in a state of unpreparedness for an attack. Barbarism can never win in its revolt against civilization, because there is 'no such thing as civilization' (NL, 41.68). All we have are various approximations to the ideal, with infinite capacities for modifying their civilizations and inventing new channels of development as soon as barbarism attacks. The artifacts of a civilization are not the civilization itself, and what created these artifacts can create them once again if they are destroyed by barbarism (NL, 41.71). There will always be partisans of civilization who will keep the civilizing process alive until it is victorious over barbarism. The very attainment of freedom of the will is the achievement of the will of civilization. German barbarism is only one in a long line of barbarisms to threaten civilization, and like its predecessors, Collingwood concludes on the inductive method (that is, on the grounds that all barbarisms have failed in the past), German barbarism is doomed to failure (NL, 45.94). Of all Collingwood's writings on civilization, *The New Leviathan* contains his most optimistic prognosis for the future.

We have seen in this last chapter how the apparently diverse concerns which occupied Collingwood's attention were integrally related to his view of the components of civilization and the revolt against the civilizing process. All those aspects of education which were essential to the promotion and healthy existence of civilization were being undermined in various ways, not merely from without, by the threat of fascism, but also from within, by all the negative tendencies he associated with a utilitarian civilization. By devaluing and perverting art, divesting religion of its mystical and emotional strength, worshipping the power and force of scientific technology, and, misconceiving the character of the historical science of metaphysics, utilitarianism works against civilization. Although fascism has failed in its revolt against civilization, all those other elements which Collingwood identified as insidiously eroding the foundations of modern European civilization have become, on the whole, accentuated rather than alleviated. The realisation of a historical civilization characterised by duty, rather than by utility, is as remote a possibility now as it was in Collingwood's own day, and his assessment of the crisis seems equally apposite: 'The gravity of the peril lies especially in the fact that so few recognize any peril to exist'.[92]

I have shown in this book that the questions which Collingwood addressed in *The New Leviathan* were not aberrations occasioned by the events of the late 1930s, but instead reiterations of questions that had troubled him since early in his career. The tone of the answers is perhaps more shrill in *The New Leviathan* than, for example, in the lectures on moral philosophy, but that is perfectly understandable, given that Collingwood's previous warnings and fears were now proving to be correct. The principles which had guided his work, especially the ideas of a scale of forms analysis; a rapprochement between philosophy and history; and, a rapprochement between theory and practice, are all manifest in his later work. In addition, much of the substantive content of earlier conclusions reappeared in modified form, when reconsidered in the light of the new circumstances to which, in Collingwood's view, they were peculiarly pertinent. In other words, the threat to civilization occasioned by nazism, the new barbarism, could be explained in terms of the theory of mind which Collingwood had previously developed, articulated, and constantly revised. His equation of freedom with rational consciousness was not, of course, novel, but of particular importance for him, and indeed for the future direction of ethical theory,[93] was the need to distinguish clearly between utility, right, and duty (the three forms of practical reason) and to identify their respective goods. In this project he saw himself firmly placed in the immanent tradition in ethics, going beyond subjectivism and intellectualism by rethinking and extending the ideas of Kant and his intellectual heirs. Kant, like the modern realists, Collingwood believed, had failed to differentiate clearly between right and duty and had ended up equating the two. The ethical theories of the modern realists, such as G. E. Moore, H. A. Pritchard, E. F. Carritt, and W. D. Ross,[94] Collingwood considered hopelessly confused because they persisted in identifying right and duty and attempted to consider ethics in terms of traditional classificatory logic, that is, analysing actions into coordinate species of a genus, instead of in terms of an overlapping series of forms which allows the theorist to view all actions as the embodiment, in differing degrees, of the universals of utility, right, and duty rather than as the distinct and opposed embodiments of the essence of only one, to the exclusion of the others. Ross, in Collingwood's view, although guilty of these sins, was less so than Moore, Pritchard, or Carritt. The importance of distinguishing duty from right, in the context of Collingwood's concerns, is that he was, after doing so, able to identify duty and history as the practical and theoretical counterparts of the highest form of reason, since both eliminate caprice, as far as it is possible, and are as perfectly rational as the European mind can presently be.

Society, and as a consequence civilization, cannot develop before mind has reached the level of practical reason. Collingwood saw his own contribution to the theory of society as rectifying an omission which the classical theorists had made. Such theorists as Hobbes, Locke, and Rousseau had failed to formulate theories of the nonsocial community and therefore were unable to account for the perpetual process of conversion to the social sphere within the community. The role of the ruling class, in Collingwood's view, was, through political education and by example, to prepare the members of the nonsocial community, on reaching mental maturity, to take up their places in, and the responsibilities of, social life. Society entails the recognition of free will in oneself and in others. Sociality implies the progressive elimination of force from social relations, an ideal which can never be fully accomplished in the body politic because of the existence of a nonsocial element over which the social element rules by force, that is, by the exercise of a superior will. Civilization is the name of the process which promotes progress in social relations. The ideal that it aims to approximate is civility, which becomes manifest in one's relations with the members of one's own community, and in the relations among members of different communities. Furthermore, civility is expressed in one's relations with nature, that is, in its intelligent exploitation.

When compared with such British idealists as T. H. Green, Bernard Bosanquet, Henry Jones, and J. H. Muirhead, Collingwood's involvement in and commitment to the practical political issues of his day was insignificant. Whereas these other idealists became deeply embroiled in the political controversies of their day and concerned themselves with the minutiae of social and educational reforms, as well as with the details of legislation, Collingwood tended to steer clear of public involvement in politics. He tells us himself that the man of action in him found sufficient 'release' in addressing the local antiquarian society in the county of his birth. He was inspired and rejuvenated by the enthusiasm for historical studies that he was able to engender in his audience. Collingwood even likened this experience to that of a political speaker who is able to arouse enthusiasm for himself and his policies.[95] The fact that he was not as actively involved in practical politics as, say, A. D. Lindsay, the master of Balliol, who stood as an anti-appeasement candidate in the 1938 Oxford by-election, does not detract from Collingwood's contribution to our understanding of the problems and predicaments integrally associated with European civilization. There are many academics who continue to 'cackle'[96] in warning of the dangers which confront modern civilization, but none so eloquently, and few so passionately and incisively, as R. G. Collingwood.

Notes

Note on Collingwood's manuscripts: The vast majority of Collingwood's manuscripts are held in the Bodleian Library, Oxford University. In the first citation for each such manuscript in the notes, the title is followed by the Bodleian Library box number (e.g., *DEP 27*) and page reference. Subsequent citations of the same manuscript give only the page reference, unless similarity of titles necessitates deviation from this practice. For other Collingwood manuscripts not in the Bodleian, the first citation in the notes is indicated by the words 'Collingwood ms.', followed by the name of the depository and the page number.

Chapter 1

1. Agnes Heller, *A Theory of History* (London, Routledge and Kegan Paul, 1982), preface.
2. Letter from R. G. Collingwood to H. T. Hopkinson, 7 May 1941. In the possession of the addressee.
3. 14 April 1941, Crawford mss., Box 4, Bodleian Library, Oxford University.
4. This point will be substantiated in section 5 of this chapter.
5. See, for example, *The Return of Grand Theory,* ed. Q. Skinner (Cambridge, Cambridge University Press, 1985).
6. See Francis Thomas Ficarra, 'Collingwood's *New Leviathan*' (Ph.D. diss., University of Illinois, 1961); D. E. Williams, 'The Metaphysical and Political Theories of R. G. Collingwood' (Ph.D. diss., London School of Economics, 1960); Peter Johnson, 'R. G. Collingwood: The Politics of Order' (Ph.D. diss., University College, Swansea, 1971); Robert Maurice Godbout, 'R. G. Collingwood's Theory of Action and Duty: A Systematic Restatement' (Ph.D. diss., University of Kansas, 1974); James Mark Connelly, 'Metaphysics, Method and Politics, Unity in the Political Philosophy of R. G. Collingwood' (Ph.D. diss., University of Southampton, 1984). Connelly's thesis gives a good descriptive guide to the unpublished manuscripts on politics. Connelly's bibliography of Collingwood's writings is a very useful guide to the unpublished manuscripts. For articles which give a sympathetic account of Collingwood's politics, see N. K. O'Sullivan, 'Irrationalism in Politics: A Critique of R. G.

Collingwood's *New Leviathan', Political Studies,* 20 (1972); and A. Milne, 'Collingwood's Ethics and Political Theory', in *Critical Essays on the Philosophy of R. G. Collingwood,* ed. Michael Krausz (Oxford, Oxford University Press, 1972). Alan Donagan, in his *Later Philosophy of Collingwood,* deals extensively with *The New Leviathan,* ignoring for the most part its political philosophy and focusing instead upon Collingwood's ethics and philosophy of mind. For a bibliography of Collingwood's writings, see Donald S. Taylor, 'A Bibliography of the Publications and Manuscripts of R. G. Collingwood, with selective annotation', *History and Theory, Beiheft* 24 (1985). Taylor's bibliography is an excellent source of information on Collingwood's writings.

7. Maurice Cowling, *Religion and Public Doctrine in Modern England* (Cambridge, Cambridge University Press, 1980), p. 184. Cf. the view of J. W. N. Watkins: 'Collingwood's *The New Leviathan* was an attempt to repair a gap he deplored, but it was the unhappy work of an ill man'. J. W. N. Watkins, 'Political Tradition and Political Theory: An Examination of Professor Oakeshott's Political Philosophy', *Philosophical Quarterly,* 2 (1952), p. 323.

8. R. G. Collingwood, *The New Leviathan; or Man, Society, Civilization and Barbarism* (Oxford, Clarendon Press, 1942), p. v. Henceforth cited in the text as *NL,* followed by the paragraph reference. Where confusion with other sources may arise, however, this work will be cited in the notes.

9. R. G. Collingwood and R. P. Wright, *The Roman Inscriptions of Britain,* vol. 1: *Inscriptions on Stone* (Oxford, Oxford University Press [Clarendon Press], 1965). W. van der Dussen has pointed out to me that Collingwood wrote to R. P. Wright on 21 October 1938, entrusting the completion of the work to him. In a series of six letters to Wright dated between 21 October 1938 and 13 June 1939, Collingwood gives him advice on completing the project. Collingwood continued to give assistance until April 1941. See Peter Johnson, 'The Letters of R. G. Collingwood: An Initial Descriptive Checklist', unpublished, p. 39.

10. 'Dr. Collingwood, Oxford Professor: Noted Authority on Life in Britain under Romans Dies at Age of 53', *New York Times,* 12 January 1943, p. 23, col. 2.

11. See, for example, R. G. Collingwood, 'Log of a Journey in the East Indies: 1938–1939', DEP 22.

12. 'Lifeboat Rescues', *London Times,* 3 June 1938, p. 14, col. d. In a letter to H. T. Hopkinson, 9 May 1939, Collingwood disputes the report in the *Times.* See Johnson, 'Checklist', p. 19.

13. R. G. Collingwood, *The First Mate's Log of a Voyage to Greece in the Schooner Yacht 'Fleur-de-Lys' in 1939* (London, Oxford University Press [Milford], 1940).

14. R. G. Collingwood, *An Autobiography* (London, Oxford University Press, 1970 reprint: first published 1939), pp. 2–4.

15. William M. Johnston, *The Formative Years of R. G. Collingwood* (The Hague, Nijhoff, 1967), p. vii.

16. Henry Jones and John Henry Muirhead, *The Life and Philosophy of Edward Caird* (Glasgow, Maclehose, Jackson, 1921), p. 36.

17. R. G. Collingwood, *Ruskin's Philosophy* (Chichester, Nelson, 1971 reprint: first published 1922), pp. 16 and 20. Collingwood claimed elsewhere that

'primarily and centrally [Ruskin] . . . was a mountain-lover: and he was interested in other things either because they were connected with mountains or because he was able to persuade himself that they were so connected'. R. G. Collingwood, 'Ruskin and the Mountains', *Oxford and Cambridge Mountaineering Journal* (1921), p. 21. James Connelly supplied me with a copy of this article.

18. Collingwood, *Autobiography,* p. 8.
19. Tom Hopkinson, *Of This Our Time: A Journalist's Story, 1905–1950* (London, Hutchinson, 1982), p. 86.
20. Collingwood, *Autobiography,* p. 10.
21. *Pembroke College Record* (Oxford, Pembroke, 1983).
22. Collingwood, *Autobiography,* p. 116.
23. Among Collingwood's papers remaining in the possession of his daughter, Mrs. Teresa Smith, is a copy of a letter that he wrote to the appointments committee for the Waynflete Chair. In this letter Collingwood said that he was giving up his historical research and devoting his time to articulating the philosophical principles derived from his researches. He also said that he had approached Oxford University Press with a view to publishing a series of ten to twelve volumes of essays, by different authors, on the history of philosophy. The letter ends with a testimonial written by S. Alexander in support of the application.
24. Knox, as well as editing Collingwood's posthumously published volumes *The Idea of History* (Oxford, Oxford University Press [Clarendon Press], 1945) and *The Idea of Nature* (Oxford, Oxford University Press [Clarendon Press], 1946), also made something of an industry of writing short biographical sketches of Collingwood. See 'Notes on Collingwood's Philosophical Work', *Proceedings of the British Academy,* 29 (1943), pp. 469–475; 'Collingwood, Robin George', *Dictionary of National Biography, 1941–1950,* pp. 168–170; 'Professor R. G. Collingwood, F. B. A.', *Nature,* 6 February 1943, pp. 163–164; 'R. G. Collingwood', *Hamburger Akademische Rundschau,* 2 (1947–1948), pp. 491–496; 'Collingwood, Robin George', *Encyclopaedia Britannica,* 14th ed. (1959), p. 19. Knox's review of William M. Johnston, *The Formative Years of R. G. Collingwood,* in *Philosophical Quarterly,* 19 (1969), pp. 165–166, also includes a good deal of biographical material. Circumstantial similarities between the article in the *DNB* and one of the three tributes published by the *London Times* on Collingwood's death indicate that Knox also penned 'Metaphysics at Oxford', *London Times,* 11 January, p. 6, col. f. Knox also wrote the obituary which appeared anonymously in the *Times Literary Supplement* (1943), p. 31. This is substantiated in a letter to Knox from Ethel W. Collingwood, 24 February 1943, Knox papers, St. Andrews University Library, ms. 375/435 (a).
25. 'Distinguished Scholars Honoured by St. Andrews University', *St. Andrews Citizen,* Saturday, 15 October 1938. I would like to thank Robert N. Smart, Keeper of the Muniments, University of St. Andrews, for sending me a copy of this article. *London Times,* October 11 1938, p. 11, col. b, also reported the conferment of the degree upon Collingwood.
26. In a letter to Kenneth Sisam, Collingwood refers to the lecture stage of his

books as 'being tried out on the dog'. Letter dated 19 October 1939, Clarendon Press Archives, file 824121 4662/KS.

27. For a list of the lectures delivered by Collingwood, see appendix II in W. J. van der Dussen, *History as a Science: The Philosophy of R. G. Collingwood* (The Hague, Nijhoff, 1981), pp. 433–434.

28. Johnston, *Formative Years*, p. 13. Cf. R. G. Collingwood, 'The Place of Art in Education', *Hibbert Journal*, 24 (1926): 'The best preparation for speaking is to be had by learning to sing', p. 446.

29. Hopkinson, *Of This Our Time*, p. 85. This is confirmed by a number of respondents to a Pembroke College survey of former students conducted in 1983. In answer to the question 'Can you recall names, characters, dominant personalities or incidents connected with dons?' one exstudent suggested that Collingwood 'was at that time the only Pembroke don with a University reputation who could entice outsiders to his lectures' (m.1921), and another claimed that Collingwood's 'lectures on Philosophy and Roman history were the only ones, so far as I discovered, where the attendance grew as the term went on' (m.1927). I am indebted to Mrs. M. van Loo, deputy librarian of the McGowin Library, Pembroke College, for sending me a transcript of the responses which make reference to Collingwood. The names of the authors are confidential; alumni are identified only by year of matriculation.

30. E. W. F. Tomlin, *R. G. Collingwood* (London, Longmans, Green, 1961, revised edition), p. 12; and C. V. Wedgwood, review of *The Idea of History, Observer*, 8 September 1946.

31. R. B. McCallum, 'Robin George Collingwood, 1889–1943', *Proceedings of the British Academy*, 29 (1943), p. 4; R. B. McCallum, 'Obituary', *Oxford Magazine*, 61 (1942–1943), p. 160; I. A. Richmond 'Appreciation of R. G. Collingwood as an Archaeologist', *Proceedings of the British Academy*, 29, (1943), p. 479; I. A. Richmond, 'Obituary Notice: Robin George Collingwood', *Antiquaries Journal*, 30 (1943), p. 84; C. H. L. Bouch, 'In Memoriam', *Transactions of the Cumberland and Westmorland Antiquarian and Archaelogical Society*, 43 (1943), p. 212. For Knox's praise of Collingwood as a teacher, see the article in *Nature*, p. 164, and *DNB*, p. 70, cited in note 24.

32. Hopkinson, *Of This Our Time*, p. 85. Collingwood's reputation as a tutor was well enough known for Isaiah Berlin to recommend students to choose Collingwood as their philosophy tutor. See Sheila Grant Duff, *The Parting of Ways* (London, Owen, 1982), p. 46. The survey cited in note 29 gives added weight to this view: 'R. G. Collingwood, one sensed, was an intellectual giant, but was very gentle in moulding the clay that came to him' (m.1920); 'The great, the revered, the charming Robin Collingwood. How lucky one was to have him as a philosophy tutor' (m.1924); 'I had a weekly tutorial for philosophy with Collingwood; he was brilliant but so far above one's head that the would-be learner emerged only conscious of his own inferiority' (m.1928); 'Collingwood was a great tutor, given to saying much that was unforgettable – and usually right' (m.1930); 'I have never met anyone since those days who could "grill" a person so kindly' (m.1930).

33. R. G. Collingwood, 'Report on quinquennium as University Lecturer, from

Summer 1927 to time of writing in January 1932', concluding paragraph, Oxford University Archives, Reports of the Board of the faculty of *Literae Humaniores*, 1912–1942, LH/R/1/5, 83. Also see the subsequent report for 1932–1935, LH/R/1/6, 76. Both of these reports are reprinted in van der Dussen, *History as a Science*, appendix III, pp. 435–441.

34. R. G. Collingwood, letter to E. B. Birley, 10 November 1930. Reprinted in van der Dussen, *History as a Science*, appendix IV, p. 444.

35. R. G. Collingwood, letter to de Ruggiero, 20 March 1921, DEP 27, and letter to B. Croce, 5 January 1928, reprinted in Alan Donagan, *The Later Philosophy of R. G. Collingwood* (Oxford, Oxford University Press [Clarendon Press], 1962), p. 315.

36. See R. H. S. Crossman, *The Charm of Politics* (London, Hamilton, 1958), p. 105.

37. Collingwood, *Autobiography*, p. 120.

38. Letter to de Ruggiero, 16 September 1924, DEP 27.

39. Ibid., 20 March 1921.

40. Collingwood, *Autobiography*, pp. 74–75.

41. Ibid., chapters 3 and 6.

42. Ibid., p. 14.

43. J. H. Muirhead, *The Platonic Tradition in Anglo-Saxon Philosophy: Studies in the History of Idealism in England and America* (London, Allen and Unwin, 1931).

44. See the letters to de Ruggiero dated 29 May 1921 and 22 November 1921. In the latter one Collingwood reveals the extent of his researches: 'The most interesting person whom I have discovered is a man who in about 1830–40 travelled over Europe studying philosophy and finally settled at Capri: I can't find him referred to in the ordinary histories, and think there must be others like him and men who were studying Kant and Hegel 30 years before Stirling wrote'. Collingwood does not name the traveller.

45. Anthony Quinton, 'Absolute Idealism', in *Thoughts and Thinkers* (London, Duckworth, 1982), p. 187.

46. R. G. Collingwood, *Speculum Mentis: Or the Map of Knowledge* (Oxford, Oxford University Press, [Clarendon Press], 1924), p. 74.

47. See my 'Creation of the Past: British Idealism and Michael Oakeshott's Philosophy of History', *History and Theory*, 23 (1984), esp. pp. 195–202; and *Texts in Context: Revisionist Methods for Studying the History of Ideas* (Dordrecht, Nijhoff, 1985), pp. 39–47. It should be emphasized that for all of the British idealists the idea of the historical development of societies, and in particular of moral ideals, is crucial to their political philosophies.

48. Letter to de Ruggiero, 20 March 1921. Cf. letter to Gilbert Ryle, 9 May 1935, DEP 22, p. 2.

49. Collingwood, *Autobiography*, p. 1.

50. G. W. F. Hegel, *Lectures on the History of Philosophy*, vol. 1, trans. E. S. Haldane (London, Kegan Paul, 1892), p. 38.

51. Benedetto Croce, *The Philosophy of Giambattista Vico* (London, Macmillan, 1913).

52. Giambattista Vico, *The New Science of Giambattista Vico*, trans. Thomas

Goddard Bergin and Max Harold Fisch (Ithaca, Cornell University Press, 1970), par. 331.

53. Malcolm Knox, preface to *The Idea of History* by R. G. Collingwood (Oxford, Oxford University Press [Clarendon Press], 1946), p. viii.

54. W. Dilthey, *Selected Writings,* trans. H. P. Rickman (Cambridge, Cambridge University Press, 1976), p. 191.

55. Collingwood makes brief reference to him in *Idea of History,* pp. 142–143.

56. His first choice was Hobbes and his second Butler.

57. Robert Flint, *The Philosophy of History in Europe,* vol. 1: *France and Germany* (Edinburgh, Blackwood, 1874); *Vico* (Edinburgh, Blackwood, 1884); *The Philosophy of History: Historical Philosophy in France and French Belgium and Switzerland* (Edinburgh, Blackwood, 1893). Also see Donald Macmillan, *The Life of Robert Flint* (London, Hodder and Stoughton, 1914).

58. F. H. Bradley, *The Presuppositions of Critical History* (1874), reprinted in *Collected Essays,* vol. 1 (Oxford, Oxford University Press [Clarendon Press], 1935). For Collingwood's comment, see *Idea of History,* p. 240.

59. Flint, *Philosophy of History in Europe,* vol. 1, p. 8.

60. Flint, *Vico,* pp. 9 and 17.

61. Robert Flint, *Agnosticism* (Edinburgh, Blackwood, 1903: Coral Lectures, 1887–1888), p. 322; *Philosophy of History* (1893), p. 124.

62. Cf. with Collingwood's later more sympathetic view in 'Lectures on the Philosophy of History: 16th Lecture – 16 June, 1940', DEP 15, p. 44a. He says, 'They were all interested in history. Green lectured in 17th Century English history. Bradley's first work published was a remarkable essay called The Presuppositions of Critical History. Bosanquet taught history for Greats. The main doctrines of the school can only be understood (e.g. the doctrines of Bradley's *Logic*) by conceiving them as an attempt on the part of a few philosophers to take history seriously and to grapple with the philosophical problems to which it gave rise'.

63. Bernard Bosanquet, *The Principles of Individuality and Value* (London, Macmillan, 1912), p. 78; R. G. Collingwood, *Essays in the Philosophy of History,* ed. W. Debbins (Austin, University of Texas Press, 1965), p. 90.

64. Henry Jones, letter to A. C. Bradley, 7 May 1920, reprinted in H. J. W. Hetherington, *The Life and Letters of Sir Henry Jones* (London, Hodder and Stoughton, 1924), p. 264.

65. Bernard Bosanquet, 'Life and Philosophy', in J. H. Muirhead, *Contemporary British Philosophy,* first series (London, Allen and Unwin, 1924), p. 60. See also pp. 68–69. Bosanquet was also extremely critical of Croce and questioned the actual idealism of Gentile in *The Meeting of Extremes in Contemporary Philosophy* (London, Macmillan, 1924).

66. Letters to de Ruggerio, dated 20 March 1921 and 2 September 1926, respectively, DEP 27.

67. Vico, *New Science,* par. 338.

68. Bradley, *Collected Essays* (New York, Books for Libraries Press, 1968), p. 43. Also see p. 28.

69. Collingwood, *Idea of History,* p. 139. For a criticism of Bosanquet's elevated view of science, see Collingwood, *Essays in the Philosophy of History,* p.

95. Also see Collingwood's claim that Bradley is 'the father of modern Realism. . . . Modern realism is supposed to be a revolt against Bradley, led by people like Cook Wilson here and Moore at Cambridge who had begun their philosophical careers as his followers. I venture to say that this is a misunderstanding of the position'. R. G. Collingwood, 'The Nature of Metaphysical Study' (1934), DEP 12, p. 27.

70. Benedetto Croce, *Logic as the Science of the Pure Concept,* trans. Douglas Ainslie (London, Macmillan, 1917), p. 324.

71. Benedetto Croce, *Teoria e Storia della Storiografia* (Bari, Laterza, 1917). Translated by Douglas Ainslie as *The Theory and History of Historiography* (London, Harrap, 1921).

72. R. G. Collingwood, 'Croce's Philosophy of History' (1921), reprinted in *Essays in the Philosophy of History,* pp. 3–22.

73. B. Croce, 'In Commemorazione di un amico inglese, Compagno di pensiero e di fede, R. G. Collingwood', *Quaderni Della 'Critica',* pp. 63–64. Translated as 'Appendix A: In Commemoration of An English Friend, a Companion in Thought and Faith, R. G. Collingwood', in *Thought, Action and Intuition,* ed. L. M. Palmer and H. S. Harris (New York, Olms, 1975), pp. 52–53.

74. Croce, *Logic,* p. 170.

75. J. A. Smith, 'Philosophy as the Development of the Notion and Reality of Self-Consciousness', in *Contemporary British Philosophy,* second series, ed. J. H. Muirhead (London, Allen and Unwin, 1925), p. 231; J. A. Smith, 'Knowing and Acting', in *Oxford Lectures in Philosophy, 1910–1923* (Oxford, 1910–1923).

76. H. S. Harris, introduction to *Genesis and Structure of Society* by Giovanni Gentile (Urbana, University of Illinois Press, 1960), p. 8.

77. J. A. Smith, 'The Philosophy of Giovanni Gentile', *Proceedings of the Aristotelian Society,* 20 (1919–1920).

78. H. Wildon Carr, translator's introduction to *The Theory of Mind as Pure Act* by Giovanni Gentile (London, Macmillan, 1922), p. xviii.

79. Smith, 'Philosophy as the Development of the Notion . . . of Self-Consciousness', p. 233.

80. John Passmore, *A Hundred Years of Philosophy* (Harmondsworth, Penguin, 1980: 2nd ed.), p. 300. Collingwood and Hannay make a similar point: 'The primary characteristic, the very backbone of Italian idealism, is a historical training of the most thoroughgoing kind. Idealism for these Italians, as it was for Hegel, is a philosophy deeply rooted in history'. R. G. Collingwood and A. Howard Hannay, translator's preface to *Modern Philosophy* by Guido de Ruggiero (London, Allen and Unwin, 1921), p. 6. De Ruggiero expresses a similar view in his 'Science, History and Philosophy', *Journal of Philosophical Studies,* 6 (1931), p. 166.

81. Smith, 'Philosophy of Gentile', pp. 64–67.

82. Collingwood, *Autobiography,* p. 14.

83. Smith, 'Philosophy as the Development of the Notion . . . of Self-Consciousness', p. 231.

84. Johnston, *Formative Years,* p. 79, puts forward a good case for Carritt's influence upon Collingwood.

85. B. Croce, *The Philosophy of Giambattista Vico* (London, Allen and Unwin, 1913); B. Croce, *An Autobiography* (Oxford, Oxford University Press [Clarendon Press], 1927); B. Croce, 'Aesthetic', *Encyclopaedia Britannica*, 14th ed. (1929); de Ruggiero, *Modern Philosophy*; G. de Ruggiero, *The History of European Liberalism* (London, Oxford University Press, 1927). Collingwood had unwittingly infringed Ainslie's exclusive right to translate Croce when he published the translation of Croce's *Vico*. In order to make amends Collingwood translated substantial parts of Croce's *Aesthetic* and revised the rest of Ainslie's translation, which appeared as the second edition (London, Macmillan, 1922). Ainslie's name remained on the title page as the translator. The evidence for this is contained in sixteen letters to the Macmillan Press concerning the translation, written between 15 March 1920 and 19 January 1922. Peter Johnson gives an account of the negotiations between Macmillan and Collingwood in 'Checklist', pp. 25–28. See T. M. Knox, review of W. M. Johnston's *Formative Years*, *Philosophical Quarterly* 19 (1969), p. 165. Also see R. G. Collingwood, 'List of Work Done', DEP 22, pp. 61 and 83. Collingwood was paid one hundred pounds for the translation of Croce's *Estetica*. Another translation by Collingwood which I have not seen cited in any bibliography of his works is G. de Ruggiero, 'Science, History and Philosophy', *Journal of Philosophical Studies*, 6 (1931). There is, I think, sufficient evidence for attributing the translation to Collingwood. In a letter to de Ruggiero dated 9 January 1931 Collingwood mentions a manuscript of de Ruggiero's which he had just translated and 'sent to Hooper, proposing that he should publish it in the Journal'. Indeed, Collingwood cites the translation in 'Report on quinquennium as University Lecturer, from summer 1927 to time of writing in January 1932', van der Dussen, *History as a Science*, appendix III, p. 437. Collingwood was also responsible for choosing the translator of Croce's *History as the Story of Liberty*, trans. S. Sprigge (London, Allen and Unwin, 1941). See Croce, 'In Commemoration of an English Friend', p. 50.
86. Harris, introduction to *Genesis and Structure*, pp. 14–20.
87. Gentile, *Theory of Mind as Pure Act*, p. 33.
88. R. W. Holmes, *The Idealism of Giovanni Gentile* (New York, Macmillan, 1937), p. 3.
89. Gentile, *Theory of Mind as Pure Act*, pp. 6 and 37.
90. Ibid., p. 40.
91. Harris, introduction to *Genesis and Structure*, p. 18.
92. Gentile, *Theory of Mind as Pure Act*, p. 215.
93. Harris, introduction to *Genesis and Structure*, pp. 18–19. In a letter to the Clarendon Press, dated 9 March 1933, Collingwood gives a brief indication of what he thought the relation between *Speculum Mentis* and *An Essay on Philosophical Method* was. He says of his manuscript of the latter book, 'It is in fact my first genuine technical, philosophical work. I have written it in a much chaster and less exuberant style than *Speculum Mentis*, which was an introduction to a philosophy: here the philosophy itself is beginning to take shape, and the style aims at elegance and economy'. Clarendon Press Archives, file 824123.

94. Bernard Bosanquet, *The Philosophical Theory of the State* (London, Macmillan, 1965, 4th ed), p. 2; Bosanquet, *Principles of Individuality and Value,* p. 268.
95. Bosanquet, 'Life and Philosophy', p. 60.
96. Gentile, *Theory of Mind as Pure Act,* p. 211.
97. R. G. Collingwood, 'Can the New Idealism Dispense with Mysticism?', in *Faith and Reason: Essays in the Philosophy of Religion* by R. G. Collingwood, ed. Lionel Rubinoff (Chicago, University of Chicago Press [Quadrangle Books], 1968), p. 274.
98. Collingwood, *New Leviathan,* pp. 60, 7, and 61, respectively. The view that mind is what it is because of what it does is expressed in his first book: 'This idea of the mind as a thing distinguishable from its own activities does not seem to be really tenable; the mind *is* what it *does;* it is not a thing that thinks, but a consciousness; not a thing that wills, but an activity'. R. G. Collingwood, *Religion and Philosophy* (London, Macmillan, 1916), p. 34. In 'Notes on History of HISTORIOGRAPHY and Philosophy of History', DEP 13, pp. 10–11, he once again expresses this Gentilian view: '*Mind is Pure Act.* Mind *is* not anything apart from what it *does*'.
99. Collingwood, 'Can the New Idealism Dispense with Mysticism?', p. 276.
100. Collingwood, translator's preface to de Ruggiero's *History of European Liberalism,* p. vii. Connelly, in his *Metaphysics, Method and Politics,* also detects the similarity between Collingwood's description of de Ruggiero's project and the aims and conclusion of *The New Leviathan,* p. 399. The observation, however, is not pursued in any detail.
101. R. G. Collingwood, 'Political Action', *Proceedings of the Aristotelian Society,* n.s. 29 (1928–1929); R. G. Collingwood, 'Stray Notes on Ethical Questions', DEP 6. The letter to de Ruggiero is in DEP 27.
102. De Ruggiero, *History of European Liberalism,* p. 156; and Guido de Ruggiero, 'Liberalism', *Encyclopaedia of the Social Sciences* (London, Macmillan, 1933), vol. 9, p. 441.
103. Richard Bellamy, *Modern Italian Social Theory* (Cambridge, Polity Press, 1987), pp. 91–92.
104. Richard Bellamy, 'Liberalism and Historicism: Benedetto Croce and the Political Role of Idealism in Modern Italy, 1890–1952', in *The Promise of History,* ed. Athanasios Moulakis (Berlin, de Gruyter, 1986), p. 91.
105. Harris, introduction to *Genesis and Structure,* pp. 14–15.
106. Collingwood, *Autobiography,* p. 158.
107. See 'Can the New Idealism Dispense with Mysticism?'; and 'Croce's Philosophy of History', in *Essays in the Philosophy of History,* ed. Debbins, p. 22.
108. Collingwood, *Autobiography,* p. 99.
109. J. H. Muirhead, review of *An Autobiography, Philosophy,* 15 (1940), p. 90.
110. J. Laird, review of *Speculum Mentis, Mind,* 34 (1925), p. 236.
111. Review of *Speculum Mentis, Times Literary Supplement,* 23, 30 October 1924, p. 676.
112. C. E. M. Joad, review of *Speculum Mentis, Spectator Literary Supplement,* 18 October 1924, p. 550.
113. L. J. Russell, review of *Essay on Philosophical Method, Philosophy,* 9 (1934), p. 350.

114. E. F. Carritt, review of *Principles of Art, Philosophy,* 12 (1938), p. 492.

115. E. W. F. Tomlin, review of *Principles of Art, Criterion,* 18 (1938–1939), p. 118.

116. R. G. Collingwood, review of *Plato, the Man and his Work* by A. E. Taylor, and *Etude sur le Parménide de Platon* by Jean Wahl, *Monthly Criterion,* 6 (1927), p. 67.

117. R. G. Collingwood, *An Essay on Philosophical Method* (Oxford, Oxford University Press [Clarendon Press], 1933), p. 192.

118. R. G. Collingwood, *The Principles of Art* (London, Oxford University Press, 1977: First published 1938), p. 319.

119. Gilbert Ryle, 'Mr. Collingwood and the Ontological Argument', *Mind,* 44 (1935); L. S. Hearnshaw, 'A Reply to Professor Collingwood's Attack on Psychology', *Mind,* n.s. 51 (1942); and, Gilbert Ryle, 'Back to the Ontological Argument; Rejoinder', *Mind,* 45 (1937); G. de Ruggiero, *Filosofia del Novecento* (Baria, Laterza, 1934).

120. G. Galloway, review of *Philosophy and Religion, Mind,* 28 (1919), p. 365.

121. Collingwood, *Autobiography,* pp. 56–57. Also see the letter to de Ruggiero dated 4 October 1927, DEP 27, in which he says, 'No reviewer has treated it as a serious philosophical statement to be criticized seriously; Croce's review in *Critica* is the only one written by a man who grasped the meaning of the book'.

122. Reviews of *Speculum Mentis* by C. Delisle Burns, *International Journal of Ethics,* 35 (1925), p. 323, and L. Susan Stebbing, *Hibbert Journal,* 23 (1924–1925), p. 568.

123. Reviews of *Speculum Mentis* by F. S. Martin, *Nature,* (17 January (1925), p. 79; C. E. M. Joad, *Spectator Literary Supplement* (18 October 1924), p. 550; and anonymous, *Revue de Métaphysique et de Morale,* 33 (1926), p. 8.

124. Quotations from reviews of Collingwood's *Essay on Philosophical Method* by C. Hartshorne, *International Journal of Ethics,* 44 (1934), p. 357, and anonymous review, *Times Literary Supplement* (1 March 1934), p. 136, respectively.

125. Quotations from reviews of *The Principles of Art* by G. Price-Jones, *Burlington Magazine,* 73 (1938), p. 185; and E. W. F. Tomlin, *Criterion,* 18 (1938–1939), p. 124, respectively.

126. Quotations from reviews of *The New Leviathan* by Willoughby Dewar, *Time and Tide,* 15 August 1942, p. 659; Ivor Thomas, *Observer,* 12 July 1942; and John Laird, *Philosophy,* 18 (1943), p. 75, respectively.

127. Letter to Kenneth Sisam, 6 August 1941. Clarendon Press Archives, file 824122 4766. By this time Collingwood was seriously ill and unable to write legibly.

128. For an assessment of Collingwood as an archaeologist, see van der Dussen, *History as a Science,* chapter 5. Also the *Times,* 16 September 1926, col. 9c; 19 May 1928, col. 11e; 15 March 1930, col. 9d; 12 March 1931, col. 9c; 1 September 1936, col. 6b; 22 May 1936, col. 15c. The last article describes the content of a letter sent to the *Times* by Collingwood and published in the same issue, col. 15e. Collingwood's letter calls for private collectors to bring to his attention any Roman inscriptions found in Britain which they may hold in their collections.

Chapter 2

1. See Lionel Rubinoff, *Collingwood and the Reform of Metaphysics: A Study in the Philosophy of Mind* (Toronto, University of Toronto Press, 1970), pp. 168–176. The implications Rubinoff reads into the relation will be criticized in the next chapter. Also see Louis O. Mink, *Mind, History and Dialectic: The Philosophy of R. G. Collingwood* (Bloomington, Indiana University Press, 1969), p. 81; Alan Donagan, 'Collingwood and Philosophical Method', in *Critical Essays on the Philosophy of R. G. Collingwood*, ed. Michael Krausz (Oxford, Oxford University Press [Clarendon Press], 1972), p. 17; and Rex Martin, 'Collingwood's *Essay on Philosophical Method*', *Idealistic Studies,* 4 (1974), p. 242.
2. Collingwood, *Essay on Philosophical Method,* pp. 27–31.
3. R. G. Collingwood, 'Action: A Course of Lectures (16 lectures) on Moral Philosophy', 1923. DEP 3, p. 39. The theory is also worked out in 'Utility Right and Duty', DEP 6, pp. 21–50. The manuscript is undated but is written, for the most part, on the back of Admiralty War Staff Intelligence Division notepaper. Van der Dussen dates it about 1920. The tentative way in which Collingwood makes the distinctions among utility, right, and duty indicate that this was an early attempt to explicate his moral theory. The mention of E. F. Carritt's and W. D. Ross's moral theories suggests that parts of the original essay were later revised.
4. Collingwood, 'Action', p. 42
5. Collingwood, *Speculum Mentis,* p. 46.
6. Ibid., p. 55.
7. R. G. Collingwood, *Outlines of a Philosophy of Art* (London, Oxford University Press, 1925), reprinted in *Essays in the Philosophy of Art* (Bloomington, Indiana University Press, 1964), ed. Alan Donagan, pp. 144–145.
8. Ibid., p. 146.
9. For a version of this characterisation see R. G. Collingwood, 'Moral Philosophy Lectures' [fragments found in a binder marked 'Moral Philosophy Lectures, New Ms., 1932'], DEP 7. These lectures discuss the forms of goodness which also constitute the serial form that appears in *The New Leviathan.* The preceding lectures experiment with variations of the characterisation. Collingwood argues that 'different forms of action aim at realising different forms of good. The specific good realised by adopting means to an end is utility; that which is realised by conforming to rule is rightness'. Collingwood, 'Moral Philosophy Lectures' [1932?], p. 104. He goes on to argue that moral goodness is good in itself. Ibid., pp. 105–106.

The date of the manuscript is difficult to determine. A note attached to it suggests that pp. 1–34 were found in a binder unclearly marked 1920 or 1928. The pages which follow, i.e., 35 fol., were found in a binder marked 'Moral Philosophy Lectures, New Ms., 1932'. This fragment, it is claimed, 'begins with the third division of part VI as designated in the contents of the above mentioned "1928" Ms. J. W. R.' (The manuscripts of the lectures on moral philosophy were lent by Kate Collingwood to J. W. Rush, one of Collingwood's former students, who arranged them in their present form and commented upon their dates of composition.) The fragment cannot be dated 1928, because Collingwood makes reference to the argument of the provost of Oriel, whose book *The Right and the Good* was not published by Oxford until 1930. See 'Moral Philosophy Lectures', [1932?], p. 93. The provost, W. David Ross, is not mentioned in the 1929 lectures, which would seem to indicate that 1930–1932 would be an appropriate date. Ross is also discussed in the 1933 lectures.

10. Collingwood, *Essay on Philosophical Method,* p. 88.
11. Collingwood, 'Utility, Right and Duty', [1920?], p. 2.
12. Ibid., pp. 21–50.
13. Collingwood, 'Moral Philosophy Lectures' [1932?], p. 106.
14. R. G. Collingwood, 'Moral Philosophy Lectures' [1929], DEP 10, p. 95. The cover of the folder which housed these lectures is in the possession of Mrs. Teresa Smith. Donald Taylor dates these lectures 1932, but he is mistaken. They are the remains of the 1929 lectures which were superseded by 'Moral Philosophy Lectures' [1932?]. Taylor, *A Bibliography,* item 154, p. 10.
15. Ibid., p. 135.
16. Collingwood, 'Moral Philosophy Lectures' [1932?], p. 108.
17. Collingwood, 'Moral Philosophy Lectures' [1929], p. 142. For similar views expressed in relation to a different content, see Collingwood, 'Economics as a Philosophical Science', *International Journal of Ethics,* 35 (1925), p. 166. Also see the earlier draft of the article 'Economics as a Philosophical Science', DEP 24, p. 3, and 'Economics as a Philosophical Science: For a section of a comprehensive ethical treatise: or alternatively as a small book under the above title', DEP 24, p. 3. The thesis of the last-cited work is 'that the concept of utility or the economic good is an *a priori* ethical category, and that therefore the science of utility is a branch of philosophical ethics i.e. an integral part of the philosophy of the spirit', p. 1. Many of the examples used to illustrate the points made in the *Essay on Philosophical Method* are taken from the field of ethics. It is odd, however, that he does not talk of the serial form of utility, right, and duty with which he was exemplifying the idea of a linked series of overlapping forms in his moral philosophy lectures after 1928. The reason for this, I think, is that he was not yet confident enough about how to distinguish duty clearly from the idea of right.
18. R. G. Collingwood, 'Lectures on Moral Philosophy' [1933], DEP 8; and R. G. Collingwood, 'Goodness, Rightness, Utility: Lectures delivered in HT 1940 and written as delivered', DEP 9.
19. Letter to Chapman of the Clarendon Press, dated 9 March 1933. Clarendon Press Archives, file 824123, P. 10.383.
20. Mink, *Mind, History and Dialectic,* p. 60.
21. Donagan, 'Collingwood and Philosophical Method', p. 7.
22. Collingwood, *Speculum Mentis,* p. 256.
23. Ibid., p. 263.
24. Collingwood, *Essay on Philosophical Method,* p. 190.
25. Ibid., p. 221.
26. Ibid., p. 49.
27. Ibid., p. 48.
28. Ibid., p. 49.
29. Ibid., p. 57.
30. Ibid., p. 60.

31. Ibid., p. 73.
32. Ibid., p. 74.
33. Ibid., p. 81.
34. Ibid., p. 82.
35. Ibid., p. 83.
36. Ibid., p. 87.
37. Ibid., p. 91. Rex Martin makes the important point that 'there is a perfect congruence of coextension of all the species concepts with one another and with the genus concept itself'. 'Collingwood's *Essay on Philosophical Method*', p. 5.
38. Collingwood, *Essay on Philosophical Method*, p. 173.
39. Ibid., p. 89.
40. Ibid., pp. 11, 100, 161, 163, 164, 168, and 205. Cf. Nathan Rotenstreich, 'An Essay on the System', *Scripta Hierosolymitana*, 20 (1968), p. 201.
41. Collingwood, 'Moral Philosophy Lectures' [1929], p. 10.
42. Collingwood, *Essay on Philosophical Method*, p. 3.
43. Letter from R. G. Collingwood to T. M. Knox, 11 November 1936, Knox Papers, St. Andrews University Library, Ms. 37524/420. This could be the documentary evidence to which Knox refers when he says that in 1936 Collingwood still held that metaphysics was a separate discipline from history. Preface, *Idea of History*, p. x.
44. Ibid.
45. Collingwood, 'Notes on HISTORIOGRAPHY', p. 10.
46. Margit Hurup Nielson, 'Re-enactment and Reconstruction in Collingwood's Philosophy of History', *History and Theory*, 20 (1981), p. 1.
47. Knox, preface, *Idea of History*, p. xxi.
48. T. M. Knox, 'Collingwood, Robin George (1889–1943)', *Encyclopaedia Britannica* (1959), 10th ed. p. 19. For Knox's previous view, see preface, *Idea of History*, p. vi; and 'Notes on Collingwood's Philosophical Work', p. 473.
49. Even on this point there is a notable exception in Collingwood's writings, 'Are History and Science Different Kinds of Knowledge?', in Collingwood, *Essays in the Philosophy of History*, ed. Debbins, pp. 23–33. The essay was first published in *Mind* (1922). In this article he argues, 'The analysis of science in epistemological terms is thus identical with the analysis of history, and the distinction between them as separate kinds of knowledge is an illusion', p. 32. A year later, in 'Science and History', Collingwood argued that science and history are different forms of knowledge. Both the historian and the scientist are doing the same thing, in that they are 'trying to understand the facts'; the former, however, differs from the latter 'in realizing what he is doing'. R. G. Collingwood, 'Science and History', *Vasculum*, 9 (1923), p. 58.
50. Collingwood, *Autobiography*, p. 19; Collingwood, 'Ruskin's Philosophy', p. 21. For this reason I am sceptical of those studies which attempt to establish a consistency in Collingwood's writings and explain away or ignore those aspects of his thought which appear to detract from the consistency.
51. Collingwood, *Religion and Philosophy*, p. 49.
52. Ibid. and p. 54.

53. Ibid., p. 49.
54. Ibid., pp. 46–47. It should be noted that the view that what can and cannot happen in history is ultimately based on scientific knowledge of natural phenomena was regarded as unfounded by Collingwood in his discusion of Bradley. See *The Idea of History,* pp. 139–140. Also see R. G. Collingwood, 'Croce's Philosophy of History', in *Essays in the Philosophy of History,* ed. Debbins, pp. 17–22. The essay was first published in *Hibbert Journal* (1921).
55. Collingwood, *Religion and Philosophy,* p. 51.
56. B. Croce, *Logic as the Science of the Pure Concept,* trans. Douglas Ainslie (London, Macmillan, 1917), p. 173.
57. Ibid., p. 258.
58. Collingwood, *Speculum Mentis,* p. 34. Cf. Gentile's concern with the unity of the mind: 'The unity of mind is itself a multiplicity, a concrete multiplicity unfolded in the unity of the spiritual process'. Gentile, *Theory of Mind as Pure Act,* p. 111.
59. R. G. Collingwood, 'The Nature and Aims of a Philosophy of History', in *Essays in the Philosophy of History,* ed. Debbins, p. 44. Essay first published in *Proceedings of the Aristotelian Society* 25 (1924–1925).
60. Collingwood, *Speculum Mentis,* pp. 39, 45, 87, and 291, illustrate my contention.
61. Van der Dussen, *History as a Science,* p. 25. The pages in *Speculum Mentis* that he cites are 208, 210–211, 216, and 231.
62. Collingwood, *Speculum Mentis,* pp. 208 and 214.
63. Ibid., p. 217.
64. Van der Dussen, *History as a Science,* p. 27.
65. Collingwood suggests, for instance, that he has articulated the 'claims of historical thought ... without favour or exaggeration', *Speculum Mentis,* p. 231.
66. Letter to de Ruggiero, 24 August 1923, DEP 27. In a summary of the argument of *Speculum Mentis* sent to the Clarendon Press, August 20 1923, Collingwood says, 'History sets itself a task it cannot accomplish'. Clarendon Press Archives, file 824124, P.6100.
67. Letters to de Ruggiero, dated 24 August 1923 and 2 October 1920. DEP 27.
68. Letter to de Ruggiero, 16 November 1924, DEP 27. For the comments in *An Autobiography,* see pp. 56–57.
69. Van der Dussen, *History as a Science,* p. 24.
70. Collingwood, *Speculum Mentis,* p. 231.
71. Ibid., p. 234.
72. Ibid., p. 241.
73. Ibid.
74. Gentile, *Theory of Mind as Pure Act,* p. 215.
75. Ibid., p. 208.
76. Ibid., p. 202. Collingwood uses similar terminology in reference to that state of mind he calls 'barbarism'. He says that barbarism is 'not something that "is" but something that "becomes" '. See *The New Leviathan,* p. 376.
77. Gentile, *Theory of Mind as Pure Act,* p. 213.
78. Ibid., p. 216.

79. Collingwood, 'Croce's Philosophy of History', in *Essays in the Philosophy of History*, ed. Debbins, p. 20.

80. Ibid., p. 21.

81. Collingwood, *Speculum Mentis*, p. 244.

82. Ibid., p. 249.

83. Gentile, *Theory of Mind as Pure Act*, p. 240.

84. Collingwood, *Speculum Mentis*, p. 291.

85. Croce, *Logic*, p. 258; Gentile, *Theory of Mind as Pure Act*, pp. 230–231.

86. Collingwood, *Essay On Philosophical Method*, pp. 1–2.

87. Ibid., p. 26.

88. Collingwood, *Philosophy and Religion*, p. 34.

89. This is made explicit on p. 226 of Collingwood, *Essay On Philosophical Method*.

90. Ibid., p. 10.

91. Letter to Knox, 11 November 1936, Knox papers, St. Andrews University Library.

92. Collingwood, *Idea of History*, pp. 215–216.

93. Letter to Knox, 11 November 1936.

94. Collingwood, *Idea of History*, pp. 142, 202, 174, 175, respectively.

95. Ibid., p. 218. Collingwood claimed in his *Autobiography* that he had made the important step in bringing about the rapprochement between philosophy and history in 1928, when he wrote down the results of his previous nine years' work. Collingwood, *Autobiography*, p. 107. In the 1928 'Outlines of a Philosophy of History' the idea of reenactment is presented as the means by which history overcomes the dichotomy of positing an object outside itself. See van der Dussen for a description of the contents of this manuscript. *History as a Science*, pp. 143–157. Rex Martin has argued that when Collingwood talks of history as self-knowledge of the mind, what is conceived as mind, in this context, is rational thought which is capable of being reenacted. Such thought (as opposed to feelings, or psyche, which are the province of psychology and susceptible to being classified and subsumed under general laws) is understood and explained without recourse to generalisations by means of reenactment. History does not preclude restricted, or historical generalisations, which characterise certain epochs, but the generalisations themselves are the summaries of historical facts already achieved by means of reenactment. Rex Martin, *Historical Explanation: Re-enactment and Practical Inference* (Ithaca, Cornell University Press, 1977), chapter 2.

96. Croce, *Logic*, pp. 208–210. Cf. Collingwood, *Autobiography*, chapter 5. For an elaboration and substantiation of this point, see my *Texts in Context*, pp. 57–59.

97. R. G. Collingwood, *An Essay On Metaphysics* (Oxford, Oxford University Press [Clarendon Press], 1940), pp. 23, 29–32, and 44–45.

98. Ibid., pp. 48, 74, and 76.

99. Collingwood, *Autobiography*, pp. 65–66; Collingwood, *Essay on Metaphysics*, pp. 21–77.

100. W. H. Walsh, 'Collingwood and Metaphysical Neutralism', in *Critical Essays on the Philosophy of R. G. Collingwood*, ed. Krausz, p. 145.

101. R. G. Collingwood, 'Function of Metaphysics in Civilization' (1937–1938), DEP 19, p. 47.

102. Collingwood, 'Notes on HISTORIOGRAPHY', p. 10.

103. Ibid., p. 17.

104. Ibid., p. 10.

105. Collingwood, letter to de Ruggiero, 12 June 1937, DEP 27.

106. Letter to Kenneth Sisam, 19 October 1939, Clarendon Press Archives, file 824121 4662/KS. In this letter Collingwood speaks of *The Principles of History* as being vol. 2 in a series entitled *Philosophical Principles,* of which *Principles of Art* was to be vol. 1.

107. This scheme is reprinted in van der Dussen, *History as a Science,* pp. 431–432.

108. R. G. Collingwood, 'Log of a Journey in the East Indies 1938–1939', DEP 22.

109. Letter reproduced in van der Dussen, *History as a Science,* pp. 443–444.

110. Letter to O. G. S. Crawford, 14 April 1941. Crawford Mss., Box 4, Bodleian Library, Oxford University. In a letter to Knox, Collingwood contends that the war with Germany may lead to 'intellectual bankruptcy' in Britain and that 'people like you and me have a clear duty to prevent this if it can be prevented; and to diminish the evil effects if it can't'. Letter dated 6th January 1940. Knox papers., Ms. 37524/430, St. Andrews University Library.

111. Letter to E. R. Hughes, dated 8 December, 1939. Ms. Eng. Misc. C516, fols. 38–39, Bodleian Library, Oxford University.

112. Benedetto Croce, *Philosophy of the Practical: Economic and Ethic,* trans. Douglas Ainslie (New York, Biblo and Tannen, 1967), p. 6.

113. Ibid., p. 31.

114. Ibid., p. 88.

115. Benedetto Croce, *My Philosophy and Other Essays on the Moral and Political Problems of Our Time,* ed. R. Klibansky, trans. E. F. Carritt (London, Allen and Unwin, 1949), p. 198. Cf. Benedetto Croce, *Theory and History of Historiography: Philosophy of the Spirit,* vol. 4, trans. Douglas Ainslie (London, Harrap, 1921), p. 12. Gentile's actualism united theory and practice. Knowing the world is at the same time making it. See Bellamy, *Modern Italian Social Theory,* p. 103.

116. Benedetto Croce, 'In Commemoration of an English Friend', p. 63. Also see Collingwood, *Autobiography,* chapter 12, and *Essay on Metaphysics,* p. 343.

117. Croce, *History as the Story of Liberty,* p. 187.

118. Collingwood, *Speculum Mentis,* p. 36.

119. Collingwood, *Principles of Art,* pp. vi–viii.

120. R. G. Collingwood, 'Aesthetic Theory and Artistic Practice' (1931), DEP 25, p. 38 (reverse of page).

121. Ibid., p. 40.

122. R. G. Collingwood, 'Can Historians Be Impartial?', Paper read to the Stubbs Historical Society, 27 Jan. 1936, DEP 12, pp. 9 and 13. In attempting to bring about a rapprochement between theory and practice Collingwood was, of course, following in the footsteps of many British idealists. Indeed, Collingwood praises the school of Green for providing its pupils with practical

ideals. See *An Autobiography*, pp. 17 and 48. In a recent study of British idealism Andrew Vincent and Raymond Plant concur with Una Cormack's view that idealism was strongly practical in intent. Vincent and Plant argue that 'for Cormack, the peculiar character of the work of the Idealists was their attempt to show the unity of theory and practice, and also the relevance they tried to bring to philosophy'. *Philosophy, Politics and Citizenship: The Life and Thought of the British Idealists* (Oxford, Blackwell Publishers, 1984), p. 116.

123. Letter to T. M. Knox, dated 2 November 1937. Knox papers, Ms. 37524/ 421, St. Andrews University Library.

124. Collingwood, 'Notes on HISTORIOGRAPHY', p. 21.

125. Collingwood, *Speculum Mentis*, p. 15. Cf. p. 35.

126. R. G. Collingwood, 'The Present Need of a Philosophy', *Philosophy*, 9 (1934), p. 262.

127. Collingwood, 'Political Action', p. 158.

128. Collingwood, 'Present Need of a Philosophy', p. 263.

129. Collingwood, *Autobiography*, p. 47.

130. Collingwood, 'Lectures on Moral Philosophy' [1933], pp. 127–130. In the 1929 lectures Collingwood suggests that 'it is not the business of moral philosophy to give a list of rules which the philosopher advises his disciples to follow', 'Moral Philosophy Lectures' [1929], p. 111. In the 1940 lectures he argues that moral philosophy makes explicit things we already knew, but without knowing that we knew them. It 'has as its only aim the improvement of our moral life'. 'Goodness, Rightness, Utility', p. 3.

131. Collingwood, *Speculum Mentis*, p. 250.

132. Collingwood, ' "Action" ', p. 77.

133. Cf. Rubinoff, *Collingwood and the Reform of Metaphysics*, p. 7. Collingwood makes this point in *An Autobiography*, p. 147.

134. R. G. Collingwood, 'Draft of Human Nature and Human History', DEP 12, p. 22.

135. Collingwood, *Autobiography*, p. 150.

136. Ibid, p. 114. Cf. Collingwood's statement that history stands 'in the closest possible relation to practical life', ibid., p. 106.

137. Ibid., p. 147.

138. Ibid., pp. 146–167.

139. T. M. Knox, 'R. G. Collingwood', *Dictionary of National Biography, 1941– 1950*, p. 170; R. H. S. Crossman, 'When Lightning Struck the Ivory Tower', in *The Charm of Politics* (London, Hamilton, 1958), p. 108; H. Laski, review of *The New Leviathan*, *New Statesman and Nation*, 24 (1942), p. 98; Tomlin, 'R. G. Collingwood', p. 32.

140. Joseph Needham, letter to the *New Statesman*, 19 (1940), pp. 174–175. Cf. Collingwood, *Autobiography*, pp. 152–153.

141. See Collingwood, *New Leviathan*, p. v.

142. Collingwood, *Autobiography*, pp. 158–159.

143. R. G. Collingwood, 'Art and the Machine', DEP 25, p. 13. Undated, but probably written about 1934 or 1935.

144. R. G. Collingwood, 'The Spiritual Basis of Reconstruction', 10 May 1919, DEP 24, p. 14.

145. Collingwood, *Autobiography,* 160–167.

146. R. G. Collingwood, 'Man Goes Mad: rough ms. begun 30 Aug. 36', DEP 24, p. 7.

147. Ibid., p. 16. cf. de Ruggiero, *History of European Liberalism,* esp. pp. 362 and 442. In the latter of the two references, de Ruggiero says of liberalism, 'Its nature, a nature strictly dialectical, draws nourishment from all oppositions, from discord no less than concord, dissent no less than consent'.

148. Collingwood, 'Man Goes Mad', p. 36.

149. R. G. Collingwood, 'Fascism and Nazism', *Philosophy,* 15 (1940), p. 176, fn. 1. It is also clear that chapter 12 of *An Autobiography* is inspired by the same problem.

150. Collingwood, *Autobiography,* p. 159. Cf. Collingwood, 'Fascism and Nazism', p. 172.

151. Collingwood, *Autobiography,* pp. 165–166.

152. Letters to T. M. Knox, dated 3 September 1939, Knox papers, Ms. 37524/429 and 6 January 1940, Ms. 37524/430. Cf. 'Fascism and Nazism', pp. 170–172.

153. Knox, review of Johnston, *Formative Years,* p. 166. It is often argued that Collingwood never actually participated in practical politics. Mrs. Teresa Smith, Collingwood's daughter, says that this conflicts with the view that Kate Collingwood, her mother, had of Collingwood. Mrs. Smith suggested to me in conversation that both her mother and father were strongly active in an Oxford anti-Nazi society.

154. Letter to A. D. Lindsay, dated 20 October 1938. A. D. Lindsay papers, University of Keele Library. Partially reproduced in Drusilla Scott, *A. D. Lindsay: A Biography* (Oxford, Blackwell Publishers, 1971), p. 251. Both sources are cited in Johnson, 'Checklist', p. 23.

155. The letter from Hughes to Collingwood is in the possession of Mrs. Teresa Smith. Mrs. Smith also has a copy of the minutes of one of the meetings of the 'Standing Committee for Intellectual Cooperation with China', which lists as present professors Collingwood, Dodds, Price, Zimmern, and Hughes, as well as the master of Balliol and the provost of Oriel. Dated 9 February 1940.

156. Letter to E. R. Hughes, 8 December 1939.

157. C. E. M. Joad, 'Appeal to Philosophers', *Philosophy,* 15 (1940), p. 410.

158. Ibid., p. 415. Joad himself was inspired by Collingwood's *Autobiography* and makes reference to it on pp. 407 and 416. The inspiration, then, was reciprocal. Joad's article was read to the Aristotelian Society at Cambridge in February 1940, and Collingwood must have read it before it was published.

159. H. D. Lewis, 'Is There a Social Contract?', pt. 1, *Philosophy,* 15 (1940), p. 65.

160. H. D. Lewis, 'Is There a Social Contract?' pt. 2, *Philosophy,* 15 (1940), p. 189.

161. Ibid.

162. J. H. Muirhead, 'With Whom Are We at War?', *Philosophy,* 15 (1940), p. 3.
163. Ibid.

Chapter 3

1. R. G. Collingwood, 'N. L. Fasc. 1.1 = preliminary matter' and 'N. L. Fasc. 1.2 = preface', Collingwood ms., DEP 24, p. 8.
2. R. G. Collingwood, *Speculum Mentis,* pp. 307 and 194; Collingwood, 'Economics as a Philosophical Science', p. 163; Collingwood, *Principles of Art,* pp. 175–176, 177, 194, and 226; R. G. Collingwood, 'The Limits of Historical Knowledge', in *Essays in the Philosophy of History,* ed. Debbins, p. 95; 'Fascism and Nazism', p. 173.
3. Collingwood, *Autobiography,* pp. 61–63.
4. Collingwood, *Idea of History,* pp. 100, 107, and 229.
5. R. G. Collingwood, 'Lectures on Moral Philosophy for M-T 1921', DEP 4. The quotation is taken from 'Action', p. 16.
6. In 'Man Goes Mad' Collingwood quotes p. 63 of the *Leviathan* (pp. 97–98 of the Clarendon Press reprint of 1909), p. 26. Also see p. 29. In 'Rough Sketch of the Problem of Freedom', Hobbes is described as 'the chief materialist determinist. Will is appetite and fear'. DEP 19, p. 3. Also see p. 4. There is also a very brief reference to Hobbes in 'Notes on HISTORIOGRAPHY', p. 10.
7. M. Oakeshott, 'Thomas Hobbes', *Scrutiny,* 4 (1935–1936).
8. T. Hobbes, *Leviathan* (London, Routledge, n.d.). The strong clear handwriting of Collingwood in this copy is without doubt that of his early period as an academic. The flyleaf facing the front cover is inscribed in Collingwood's handwriting with the following lines from Joseph Jacobson, *More English Fairy Tales* (London, Nutt, 1894), pp. 118–124 (the quotation appears on all of these pages):

> The next night the Hobyahs came again and said:
> Hobyah! Hobyah! Hobyah!
> Tear down the Hempstalks!
> Eat up the old man and woman!
> and carry off the little girl!
> See page 121.

The reference to page 121 directs the reader to a passage in the Routledge edition of the *Leviathan* which reminded Collingwood of the fairy tale quoted on the flyleaf: 'But a man may here object, that the Condition of Subjects is very miserable; as being obnoxious to the lusts, and other irregular passions of him, or them that have so unlimited a Power in their hands ... not considering that the estate of Man can never be without some incommodity or other; and that the greatest, that in any forme of Government can possibly happen to the people in general, is scarce sensible, in respect of the miseries, and horrible calamities, that accompany a Civil Warre; or that dissolute condition of masterlesse men, without subjection to Lawes, and a coercive Power to tye their hands from rapine, and revenge' (p. 94 in the original). Both the Routledge copy of the *Leviathan* and Collingwood's copy of *More English Fairy Tales* are in the possession of Mrs. T. Smith. The edition of Hobbes's *Leviathan* cited in Collingwood's *New Leviathan* is that of Oxford University Press (1909) which includes an introduction by W. G. Pogson Smith. References to Hobbes's *Leviathan* given later in these notes are from the Oxford edition, unless otherwise stated.

9. Collingwood, 'Lectures on Moral Philosophy for M-T 1921', pp. 31–33; 'Action', pp. 15–16.

10. Collingwood, 'Lectures On Moral Philosophy for M-T 1921', p. 34.

11. Ibid., p. 6. In the following section of the present chapter, Collingwood's self-perception of his relationship with Hobbes will form the basis of a comparison between the two *Leviathan*s.

12. Collingwood, *New Leviathan*, p. 1; Hobbes, *Leviathan*, p. 94.

13. R. G. Collingwood, letter to H. T. Hopkinson, dated 7 May 1941, in the possession of the addressee. The quotation is reproduced in J. Connelly, 'Appendix Three; A Collingwood Chronology', in *Metaphysics, Method and Politics*, p. 460.

14. See, for example, the reviews by John Laird, *Philosophy*, 18 (1943), p. 75; George Catlin, *Political Science Quarterly*, 58 (1943), p. 435; John MacCormac, *Sunday New York Times*, 1 August 1943, p. 16; Ernest Barker, 'Man and Society', *Oxford Magazine*, 4 February 1943, p. 162; Ivor Thomas, 'Hobbes Redivivus', *Observer*, 12 July 1942.

15. Collingwood, *New Leviathan*, p. iv.

16. Mink, *Mind, History and Dialectic*, p. 80.

17. Collingwood, 'N. L. Fasc. 1.2 = preface', pp. 6 and 8. The answer, however, is implicit in the four parts which Collingwood did write.

18. Collingwood, *New Leviathan*, p. v.

19. Anonymous review of *The New Leviathan*, *Scotsman*, 20 August 1942.

20. Laird, review of *The New Leviathan*, p. 75.

21. Thomas, review of *The New Leviathan*.

22. Mortimer Taube, review of *The New Leviathan, Journal of Politics*, 5 (1943), p. 435.

23. See, Collingwood, *Religion and Philosophy*; R. G. Collingwood, 'The Devil', in B. F. Streeter et al., *Concerning Prayer: Its Nature, Its Difficulties and Its Value* (London, Macmillan, 1916); and Collingwood, *Speculum Mentis*, chapter 4. Also see 'Science, Religion and Civilization' and 'War in Its Relation to Christian Ethics', DEP 1.

24. See the reviews cited in notes 14 and 22.

25. Collingwood, *Essay on Philosophical Method*, p. 25.

26. Ibid., pp. 22–23.

27. Collingwood, *Essay on Metaphysics*, pp. 67–68. This discussion of Collingwood's supposed use of a deductive method owes much to F. T. Ficarra's discussion in 'Collingwood's *New Leviathan*', pp. 17 and 18. Ficarra does not address the question of the source of Collingwood's numbering system.

28. Hobbes, *Leviathan*, p. 209.

29. G. W. F. Hegel, *Lectures On the History of Philosophy,* vol. 1, trans. E. S. Haldane (London: Kegan Paul, Trench, Trübner, 1892), pp. 5–6.
30. Ibid., p. 92.
31. Ibid.
32. Ibid.
33. This is also true of Italian idealism. Bellamy contends that Croce wished to 'exclude from philosophy both the empirical and transcendent – only for spirit immanent within history is the universe fully concrete'. Richard Bellamy, 'Croce, Gentile and Hegel and the Doctrine of the Ethical State', *Revista di Studi Crociani,* 20 (1983), p. 269. Also see Bellamy, *Modern Italian Social Theory,* p. 73. We will see in section 5 of this chapter that Collingwood followed Croce's dialectic of concepts, rather than Hegel's dialectic of opposites. W. H. Greenleaf has been the leading figure in articulating the characteristics of this triadic conception of the history of political thought. See W. H. Greenleaf, 'Hume, Burke and the General Will', *Political Studies,* 20 (1972); W. H. Greenleaf, 'Burke and State Necessity: The Case of Warren Hastings', in *Staaträson,* ed. R. Schnur (Berlin, Dunker and Humblot, 1975). Also see my 'W. H. Greenleaf, Idealism and the Triadic Conception of the History of Political Thought', *Idealistic Studies,* 16 (1986).
34. F. H. Bradley, *Ethical Studies* (Indianapolis, Bobbs-Merrill, 1951: first published 1876), p. 51. This edition reprints only five of the original eight essays.
35. Ibid., p. 97.
36. Ibid., p. 110. It is beyond the scope of this study to enter into a discussion of the qualifications that Bradley makes in the subsequent essays in *Ethical Studies,* but an excellent interpretation is offered by P. Nicholson, 'Bradley as a Political Philosopher', in *The Philosophy of F. H. Bradley,* ed. A. Manser and G. Stock (Oxford, Oxford University Press [Clarendon Press], 1984), pp. 117–130.
37. Bernard Bosanquet, *The Philosophical Theory of the State* (London, Macmillan, 1965: first published 1899), pp. 98 and 99.
38. T. H. Green, *Works,* vol. 3 (London, Longmans, Green, 1888), p. 98.
39. Ibid.
40. T. H. Green, *Lectures on the Principles of Political Obligation* (London, Longmans, Green, 1917), pp. 60–67; and *Works,* vol. 2 (London, Longmans, Green, 1890: 2nd ed.), pp. 366–373.
41. Collingwood, 'Lectures on Moral Philosophy for M-T 1921'; and Collingwood 'Action'.
42. Collingwood, 'Lectures on Moral Philosophy for M-T 1921', p. 8. In the lectures entitled 'Action', p. 6, Collingwood names this tendency in ethical theory the 'Intellectualist theory of the Good'.
43. Collingwood, 'Lectures on Moral Philosophy for M-T 1921', p. 8.
44. Collingwood, 'Action', p. 8.
45. Collingwood, 'Lectures on Moral Philosophy for M-T 1921', p. 23.
46. Collingwood, 'Action', p. 8.
47. Collingwood, 'Lectures on Moral Philosophy for M-T 1921', p. 8.
48. Collingwood, 'Action', p. 8.

49. Collingwood, 'Lectures on Moral Philosophy for M-T 1921', p. 25.
50. Collingwood, 'Action', p. 9.
51. Ibid., p. 10.
52. Ibid., p. 11.
53. Ibid.
54. The tendency with which these theories are associated is named, by Collingwood, 'abstract subjectivism' or the 'Sensationalist theory of the Good', in 'Lectures on Moral Philosophy for M-T 1921', p. 25, and 'Action', p. 12, respectively.
55. Collingwood, 'Lectures on Moral Philosophy for M-T 1921', p. 30.
56. Collingwood, 'Action', p. 15.
57. Collingwood, ibid., and 'Lectures on Moral Philosophy for M-T 1921', p. 23.
58. Ibid., pp. 32–33. It is beyond the scope of the present work to enter into the question of the validity of Collingwood's interpretation of Hobbes.
59. Collingwood, 'Action', p. 16, and 'Lectures on Moral Philosophy for M-T 1921', p. 35.
60. Ibid., p. 35.
61. Ibid., p. 37. The significance of this criticism of Hobbes in relation to Collingwood's theory of mind will become more apparent in the next chapter.
62. Collingwood, 'Action', p. 20a.
63. Ibid., p. 22.
64. Collingwood, 'Lectures on Moral Philosophy for M-T 1921', p. 33.
65. Collingwood, 'Action', p. 23.
66. Ibid., p. 25.
67. Ibid. Cf. 'Lectures on Moral Philosophy for M-T 1921', p. 44.
68. Collingwood, 'Action', p. 25.
69. Collingwood, 'Lectures on Moral Philosophy for M-T 1921', p. 104.
70. Ibid.
71. Ibid.
72. Ibid., p. 103.
73. Ibid., p. 105.
74. The 1923 lectures incorporate various revisions inserted in 1926 and 1927, but were completely rewritten in about 1928 for delivery in 1929. Essentially, then, the historical survey would have been delivered up to and including 1927.
75. Although, it must be added, not all three always appear together. In addition to the lectures on moral philosophy, see, for example, 'The Good, the Right, and the Useful', lecture delivered to Exeter College Dialectical Society, 3 March 1930; and 'Utility, Right and Duty' (1920?). Both are in DEP 6. Also see Collingwood, 'Economics as a Philosophical Science', pp. 162–185; Collingwood, 'Political Action', pp. 155–176. 'Economics as a Philosophical Science' (draft), DEP 24, and 'Economics as a Philosophical Science: For a section of a comprehensive ethical treatise: or alternatively as a small book under the above title', DEP 24.
76. Collingwood, 'Lectures on Moral Philosophy for M-T 1921', p. 36.
77. Bradley, for example, is criticized for putting forward a realist, or intellec-

tualist, theory of ethics: 'for his theory, with its emphasis on an objective social world which dictates his duties to the subject, *is* realistic'. Collingwood, 'Lectures on Moral Philosophy for M-T 1921', p. 24.

78. Collingwood, *New Leviathan*, pp. 181–182. Cf. Collingwood, *Essay on Philosophical Method*, pp. 10–11.

79. Collingwood, *Autobiography*, p. 148.

80. Ibid., pp. 148–149.

81. Collingwood, 'Utility, Right and Duty', p. 21. In 1919 Collingwood wrote a lecture entitled 'Money and Morals' which he delivered to the London Branch of the Student Movement on 27 May 1919 and to the Indian Students' Hostel in London in June 1919. In the lecture he argues that economics should be supplemented by ethics and politics, but he does not distinguish between them in terms of duty and rightness. DEP 1, p. 10.

82. Collingwood, 'The Good, and Right and the Useful', 1930. DEP 6, p. 18. In his 'Stray Notes on Ethical Questions', Collingwood makes a concerted effort to distinguish political goodness and moral goodness in relation to punishment. DEP 6, pp. 16–46.

83. See W. D. Ross, *The Right and the Good* (Oxford, Oxford University Press [Clarendon Press], 1930), pp. 3–4.

84. In *An Essay on Philosophical Method*, Collingwood is concerned to articulate the differentia of the philosophical concept and illustrates his argument with reference to ethics, but he indicates that the distinctions he uses are not his own by referring to goods which are 'traditionally divided' into 'the pleasant, the expedient, and the right' (p. 41). The corresponding series of actions on this scale would be those motivated by 'desire, self-interest, duty' (p. 42). In *The First Mate's Log*, Collingwood talks of how to assess the worth of the monks of the Prophet Elijah, Santorin. Here the discussion revolves around utility and intrinsic worth, or moral goodness (p. 151).

85. Benedetto Croce, *What Is Living and What Is Dead of the Philosophy of Hegel*, trans. Douglas Ainslie (New York, Russell and Russell, 1969: English translation first published 1915), p. 9.

86. Croce, *Logic*, p. 77.

87. See Giacomo Rinaldi, 'A Few Critical Remarks on Croce's Historicism', *Idealistic Studies*, 18 (1987), p. 51.

88. Cf. Croce, *What Is Living and What Is Dead*, pp. 9–10.

89. Benedetto Croce, *Aesthetic as Science of Expression and General Linguistic*, trans. Douglas Ainslie (New York, Macmillan, revised edition, 1953), p. 61.

90. Croce, *Logic*, p. 93.

91. Croce, *What Is Living and What Is Dead*, p. 19.

92. Croce, *Logic*, p. 93.

93. Cf. M. E. Moss, 'The Crocean Concept of the Pure Concept', *Idealistic Studies*, 17 (1987), p. 45.

94. Collingwood, *Essay on Philosophical Method*, p. 84.

95. Croce, *Logic*, p. 99.

96. Collingwood, *Essay on Philosophical Method*, p. 106.

97. Ibid., p. 108.

98. In the 1923 lectures he also discusses mechanical action, reflex action, and instinct, prior to discussing play and convention. See Collingwood, 'Action', pp. 43–58. In the revisions of 1927 the new conclusion passes from instinct to the life of reason, in which he incorporates caprice. Convention now becomes incorporated in his discussion of caprice. The rational will succeeds reason and is manifest in utility and duty. Here the discussion of absolute action, or absolute ethics, is dropped from the lectures.
99. Collingwood, 'Action', original conclusion, p. 54.
100. Ibid., 1927 conclusion, p. 71.
101. Ibid., original conclusion, p. 55.
102. Collingwood, *Speculum Mentis,* p. 102; and Collingwood, 'Action', original conclusion, p. 55.
103. Collingwood, 'Action', original conclusion, p. 56.
104. Collingwood, *Speculum Mentis,* p. 102.
105. Collingwood, 'Action', original conclusion, p. 58.
106. Ibid., p. 59.
107. Collingwood, *Speculum Mentis,* p. 135.
108. Ibid, p. 137.
109. Collingwood, 'Action', original conclusion, p. 61.
110. Ibid., 1927 conclusion, p. 82.
111. Collingwood, *Speculum Mentis,* p. 169.
112. Ibid., p. 171.
113. Collingwood, 'Economics as a Philosophical Science: For a section of a comprehensive ethical treatise', ms., p. 1.
114. Collingwood, 'Economics as a Philosophical Science', published version, p. 162.
115. Benedetto Croce, *Philosophy of the Practical: Economic and Ethic,* trans. Douglas Ainslie (New York, Biblo and Tannen, 1967). See especially the first section of the second part of chapter 5, entitled 'The Philosophy of Economy and the So-called Science of Economy', pp. 364–381.
116. Collingwood, 'Economics as a Philosophical Science', draft ms., p. ii. This recognition does not appear in the published version.
117. Collingwood, 'Economics as a Philosophical Science: For a section of a comprehensive ethical treatise', ms., p. 1.
118. Collingwood, 'Economics as a Philosophical Science', p. 167.
119. Ibid., p. 168.
120. Collingwood, 'Action', 1927 conclusion, p. 82.
121. Ibid., original conclusion, p. 63.
122. Ibid., p. 66.
123. Collingwood, *Speculum Mentis,* p. 172.
124. Ibid., p. 174.
125. Ibid., p. 175.
126. Collingwood, 'Action', original conclusion, p. 64.
127. Ibid., 1927 conclusion, p. 85.
128. Ibid., original conclusion, p. 58.
129. Croce, *Philosophy of the Practical,* p. 362.

130. Collingwood, *Speculum Mentis,* p. 222.
131. Ibid., pp. 223–224.
132. Collingwood, 'Action', 1927 conclusion, p. 85.
133. Collingwood, 'Action', original conclusion, p. 69.
134. Collingwood, *Speculum Mentis,* p. 224.
135. Collingwood, 'Action', original conclusion, unrevised section on law, p. 70.
136. Ibid., original conclusion, revised section on law, pp. 69–70 (reverse of sheets).
137. Ibid., original conclusion, unrevised section on law, p. 73.
138. Ibid., 1927 conclusion, p. 85.
139. Croce, *Philosophy of the Practical,* p. 481.
140. Ibid., p. 506.
141. Ibid., p. 530.
142. Ibid., p. 531. The state as a finite and particular institution is economic activity. The state as idea, in so far as each state contributes to the universal end of the good will, is an ethical institution. See Bellamy, 'Croce, Gentile and Hegel and the Doctrine of the Ethical State', p. 269. Cf. Benedetto Croce, *The Conduct of Life,* trans. Arthur Livingston (Freeport, N.Y.; Books for Libraries Press, 1967: first published 1924), chapter 36.
143. Benedetto Croce, *Politics and Morals,* trans. Salvatore J. Castiglone (London, Allen and Unwin, 1945: translation of *Etica e Politica,* Bari, 1931), p. 9. Also see Angelo A. de Gennaro, *The Philosophy of Benedetto Croce* (New York, Citadel Press, 1961), pp. 56–57.
144. Collingwood, *Speculum Mentis,* p. 225.
145. Collingwood, 'Action', original conclusion, revised section on law, p. 71.
146. Collingwood, *Speculum Mentis,* p. 230.
147. Collingwood, 'Action', 1927 conclusion, p. 86.
148. Ibid., p. 87.
149. Collingwood, *Speculum Mentis,* p. 305.
150. Collingwood, 'Action', 1927 conclusion, p. 88.
151. Collingwood, 'Action', original conclusion, revised section on 'absolute action', p. 78.
152. Ibid., p. 79.
153. Rubinoff, *Collingwood and the Reform of Metaphysics,* p. 171.
154. Ibid., p. 172.
155. Collingwood, 'Moral Philosophy Lectures' [1929], p. 95.
156. Ibid., p. 129.
157. Ibid.
158. Ibid., p. 149. Louis Mink says of Collingwood's ethical scheme, as it found expression in *Speculum Mentis,* 'He returned again and again to his classification of types of ethical theories, but in every later recapitulation the scheme culminates not with "Absolute, Ethics" but with Duty. One must assume that in *Speculum Mentis* Collingwood felt that Hegel had spoken the last word; later he decided that Hegel had had one word too many'. Mink, *Mind, History and Dialectic,* p. 55. It is quite conclusive that Collingwood's later schemes did, for the most part, end in 'absolute ethics', but it was now the province of duty.

159. Collingwood, 'Moral Philosophy Lectures' [1929], p. 149. It should be noted here that Collingwood does not link up the three forms of practical reason with the three forms of theoretical reason.

160. Ibid., p. 95. Cf. Collingwood, 'Moral Philosophy Lectures' [1932?], p. 105; Collingwood, 'Lectures on Moral Philosophy' [1933], pp. 88 and 115–116; Collingwood, 'Goodness, Rightness, Utility: Lectures delivered in H. T. 1940', p. 62.

161. Edward B. Tylor, *Primitive Culture: Researches into the Development of Mythology, Philosophy, Religion, Art and Custom* (New York, Gordon Press, 1974: first published 1871), pp. 6 and 14.

162. R. G. Collingwood, [Folk Tales] 'B II. Three Methods of Approach: Philogical, Functional, Psychological', DEP 21, pp. 11–20. Also see Collingwood, *Principles of Art,* pp. 58–69.

163. Collingwood, *Essay on Philosophical Method,* p. 48.

164. Collingwood, 'Goodness, Rightness, Utility', p. 14.

165. Ibid., p. 35.

166. Ibid., p. 36.

167. Ibid., p. 38.

168. Ibid., p. 39.

169. Collingwood, 'Moral Philosophy Lectures' [1929], p. 95. He also calls them three 'different forms of good'. Collingwood, 'Moral Philosophy Lectures' [1932?], p. 104. Similarly, in the 'Lectures on Moral Philosophy' [1933], they are called 'the Three Forms of Goodness', p. 73.

170. Collingwood, 'Moral Philosophy Lectures' [1929], p. 96.

171. Ibid., p. 98.

172. Collingwood expresses this differently in the 1940 lectures. He says, 'The agent whose reason for choosing something because it is useful must, when he thus chooses it, already have in mind some end which he serves by choosing it. In the temporal order he proceeds from means to end; in the logical order he proceeds from end to means'. Collingwood, 'Goodness, Rightness, Utility', p. 41.

173. Cf. this passage from the moral philosophy lectures: 'This analysis of action into means and end is applicable not only to certain acts but to every act of whatever kind. It is a universal and necessary characteristic of action, that we can distinguish within it a consequent, namely that which we have reason for doing, from a ground namely the reason which we have for doing it'. Collingwood, 'Moral Philosophy Lectures' [1929], p. 96.

174. Ibid., p. 97.

175. Collingwood, 'Lectures on Moral Philosophy' [1933], p. 89.

176. Ibid.

177. In the 1940 lectures, for example, a much more extensive discussion of the etymology of the word 'right' appears than in the published formulation. Bradley is also quoted at length as having given the definitive definition of right as action according to rule. See Collingwood, 'Goodness, Rightness, Utility', pp. 45–48. Collingwood says, 'I conclude that Bradley's statement is true, and that in actual English usage as organized by O.E.D the word right does in fact mean conformable with rule. I agree with him that in actual usage the word invariably means this'. Ibid., p. 47.

178. Collingwood, 'Moral Philosophy Lectures' [1929], p. 125.
179. Collingwood, 'Goodness, Rightness, Utility', p. 49.
180. Ibid., p. 54.
181. Cf. ibid., p. 59.
182. Collingwood, 'Political Action', pp. 155–159.
183. Collingwood, 'Moral Philosophy Lectures' [1929], p. 108.
184. Collingwood, 'Moral Philosophy Lectures' [1932?], p. 105.
185. Ibid., p. 106.
186. Collingwood, 'Lectures on Moral Philosophy' [1933], p. 106.
187. Ibid., p. 107.
188. Ibid.
189. Ibid., p. 108; cf. p. 114.
190. Collingwood, 'Moral Philosophy Lectures' [1929], p. 146.
191. Collingwood, 'Lectures on Moral Philosophy' [1933], p. 116.
192. Collingwood, 'Moral Philosophy Lectures' [1929], p. 138.
193. Collingwood, 'Moral Philosophy Lectures' [1932?], p. 98.
194. Ibid., p. 99. Cf. 104.
195. Collingwood, 'Lectures on Moral Philosophy' [1933], p. 116.
196. Collingwood, 'Goodness, Rightness, Utility,' p. 71.
197. Cf. de Ruggiero, 'The really free man is not the man who can choose any line of conduct indifferently – this being rather a frivolous and weak-willed man – but the man who has the energy to choose that which is most conformable to his moral destiny ... the man who acts according to duty'. *European Liberalism,* pp. 351–352.
198. Milne, 'Collingwood's Ethics and Political Theory', p. 303.
199. Collingwood, 'Moral Philosophy Lectures' [1932?], p. 106.
200. Ibid., p. 108.
201. Collingwood, 'Moral Philosophy Lectures' [1929], p. 137.
202. Ross, *The Right and the Good,* p. 4.
203. Ibid., pp. 46–47.
204. Ibid., p. 156. Cf. W. David Ross, *Foundations of Ethics* (Oxford, Oxford University Press [Clarendon Press], 1939), pp. 308–309.
205. Collingwood, *Essay on Philosophical Method,* p. 78, fn. 1. Ross in fact suggests that pleasures differ in degree of intensity, and that if one pleasure is more intense than another, it must have a 'definite amount of extra intensity'. Ross, *The Right and the Good,* p. 143. This, of course, is at variance with Collingwood's idea of a philosophical scale of forms, in which the degrees are not measurable. Collingwood discusses this aspect of Ross's argument in the 1940 lectures on moral philosophy and shows that Ross actually reaches a position, after a number of qualifications, which agrees with his own. Collingwood, 'Goodness, Rightness, Utility', pp. 17–26.
206. Collingwood, 'Lectures on Moral Philosophy' [1933], p. 107; and Collingwood, 'Goodness, Rightness, Utility', pp. 46 and 64.
207. Collingwood, 'Moral Philosophy Lectures' [1932?], p. 93.
208. Ibid., and 'Lectures on Moral Philosophy' [1933[, p. 111.
209. Collingwood, 'Lectures on Moral Philosophy' [1933], p. 111. For further ref-

erences to Ross, see pp. 108, 110, and 117; and Collingwood, 'Goodness, Rightness, Utility', pp. 32, 35, and 65.

210. Collingwood, 'Goodness, Rightness, Utility', p. 75.

211. Ibid., p. 76.

212. Ibid.

213. For an interesting discussion of the a priori imagination, see W. H. Dray, 'R. G. Collingwood on the A Priori of History', *Clio,* 12 (1983), pp. 169–181.

214. Collingwood, *Idea of History,* pp. 244–245.

215. See Paul Ricoeur, *The Reality of the Historical Past* (Milwaukee, Marquette University Press, 1984), p. 9.

216. Collingwood, *Idea of History,* p. 243. Cf. p. 245. He argues that those elements which go into a historian's construction go 'into it not because his imagination passively accepts it, but because it actively demands it'.

217. Collingwood, 'Lectures on Moral Philosophy for M-T 1921', p. 7. Cf. Collingwood, 'Goodness, Rightness, Utility', p. 68.

Chapter 4

1. Cf. Collingwood, 'Lectures on Moral Philosophy' [1933], p. 115. He says 'In order to have, or rather to be, a good will, I must be a will'.

2. Collingwood, *Idea of History,* p. 218.

3. Ibid., p. 221.

4. Ibid., p. 209.

5. Collingwood, *NL.,* 9.1 and 9.6; *Idea of History,* p. 209.

6. Locke, quoted by Collingwood, *Idea of History,* p. 71.

7. Ibid., pp. 206 and 209.

8. Gentile, *Theory of Mind as Pure Act,* p. 20. Cf. p. 37.

9. Collingwood, 'Can the New Idealism Dispense with Mysticism?', p. 276.

10. Gentile, *Theory of Mind as Pure Act,* p. 213.

11. Ibid., p. 275.

12. De Ruggiero, *Modern Philosophy,* p. 358.

13. See, for example, John Grier Hibben, *Hegel's Logic: An Essay in Interpretation* (New York, Scribner's, 1902), pp. 151–152 and p. 299; Green, *Works,* vol. 3, p. 225; F. H. Bradley, *Appearance and Reality* (Oxford, Oxford University Press [Clarendon Press], 1930, 2nd ed.), pp. 107 and 307. An outline of the doctrine of identity in difference appears in my *Texts in Context,* pp. 108–109.

14. Gentile, *Theory of Mind as Pure Act,* p. 216.

15. Lionel Rubinoff believes that the immanence and transcendence doctrine lies at the heart of Collingwood's philosophy. See his *Collingwood and the Reform of Metaphysics,* p. 316. Rubinoff appears to be arguing that it was de Ruggiero's interpretation of Gentile in de Ruggiero's *Modern Philosophy,* the book which Collingwood co-translated, that inspired the questions which Collingwood attempted to resolve in his own philosophy (Rubinoff, *Collingwood and the Reform of Metaphysics,* pp. 315–322). De Ruggiero's summary of Italian idealism is short and incisive, but can hardly carry the weight Rubinoff attributes to it. Indeed, Rubinoff relies entirely on de Rug-

giero's and Collingwood's accounts of Gentile without attempting to relate *The Theory of the Mind as Pure Act* itself to Collingwood's ideas.

16. Collingwood, *Idea of History,* p. 229.

17. Ibid., p. 216.

18. Cf. Martin, *Historical Explanation,* pp. 34–35.

19. Gentile, *Theory of Mind as Pure Act,* p. 256.

20. Collingwood, *Essay on Metaphysics,* p. 294.

21. Ibid., pp. 294–295.

22. Collingwood, *The Idea of Nature* (Oxford, Oxford University Press [Clarendon Press], 1965: first published 1945), pp. 9–10.

23. Ibid., p. 177. A number of reviewers found Collingwood's understanding of modern cosmology seriously deficient. See, for example, Edmund Whittaker's review of *The Idea of Nature* in *Philosophy,* 20 (1945), pp. 260–261; John Laird's review, in *Mind,* 54 (1945), pp. 274–279; and Arthur E. Murphy's review, in *Philosophical Review,* 55–56 (1946–1947), pp. 198–202. Nevertheless, all the reviewers found *The Idea of Nature* stimulating and enlightening, especially the part which Collingwood had actually revised for publication.

24. R. G. Collingwood, 'On the So-called Idea of Causation', *Proceedings of the Aristotelian Society,* n.s. 38 (1938), p. 85; Collingwood, *Essay on Metaphysics,* p. 289. In *The Idea of History* Collingwood says that 'words like "cause" ' are used in history 'in a special sense'. *Idea of History,* p. 214. Collingwood had previously argued that the concept of cause had no place in the vocabulary of explaining human actions. See R. G. Collingwood, 'The Devil', in *Faith and Reason,* ed. Rubinoff, pp. 218–219, and the draft version of 'Outlines of a Philosophy of History', dated Le Martouret, Die, Drome, April 1928, DEP 12, p. 42.

25. Collingwood, 'On the So-called Idea of Causation', pp. 86–87; Collingwood, *Essay on Metaphysics,* pp. 290–293.

26. Collingwood, 'On the So-called Idea of Causation', p. 88; Collingwood, *Essay on Metaphysics,* p. 294.

27. Van der Dussen, *History as a Science,* p. 332.

28. Collingwood, *Idea of History,* p. 316.

29. This illustration is based upon an example which Collingwood gives in *The Idea of History,* p. 317.

30. Ibid, p. 205.

31. Ibid., p. 231.

32. Ibid., p. 302.

33. Ibid., p. 308.

34. Ibid., p. 302.

35. Ibid., p. 305.

36. Ibid., p. 311. Cf. p. 330.

37. Collingwood, *Principles of Art,* p. 164; Collingwood, *Essay on Metaphysics,* p. 110.

38. Collingwood, *Essay on Metaphysics,* chapter 11. Whether Collingwood's understanding of psychology is mistaken is not of concern here. Professor L. S. Hearnshaw has argued that Collingwood (1) misrepresents the psy-

chologists he criticizes; (2) misunderstands the subject matter of psychology; and (3) from time to time attempts to explain thought himself in terms of psychology. See L. S. Hearnshaw, 'A Reply to Professor Collingwood's Attack on Psychology', *Mind,* n.s. 51 (1942), pp. 160–169.

39. Collingwood, *Idea of History,* p. 231. For the contextual character of understanding, see p. 299.

40. Collingwood, *Idea of History,* pp. 216, 231, 287–288, 294–296. I am sustained in my interpretation by the argument of Margit Hurup Nielson. She maintains, against those who suggest that Collingwood's doctrine of reenactment was put forward as a condition of historical understanding, that he in fact intended it as a methodology. On the basis of a thorough knowledge of the published and unpublished works, Nielson concludes that one aspect of this methodology was the principle that 'the "object" of knowledge must be "re-enactable": it must be of such a kind that it is possible to know it by re-enacting it. This means that it must be an expression of mind in a reflective act, as only such acts leave traces which are convertible to evidence and permit reasoning backwards'. Nielson, 'Re-enactment and Reconstruction in Collingwood's Philosophy of History', p. 30. Reenactment may be both a methodology and a condition of historical knowledge.

41. See Collingwood, 'Notes on HISTORIOGRAPHY', pp. 10–17.

42. Collingwood, *Essay on Philosophical Method,* p. 11.

43. Collingwood, *Idea of History,* p. 29.

44. G. W. F. Hegel, *Reason in History,* trans. Robert S. Hartman (Indianapolis, Bobbs-Merrill, 1953), pp. 68–69.

45. Ibid., pp. 69–70.

46. See Chapter 3 of this study for a discussion of how this conception of philosophical method is applicable to the specification of action in the forms of utility, right, and duty.

47. R. G. Collingwood, 'Notes toward a Metaphysic', 'D', DEP 18, p. 16. Written 6–22 April 1934. Cited in van der Dussen, *History as a Science,* pp. 260–261. Cf. Collingwood, 'Action', pp. 42–43.

48. Collingwood, *Principles of Art,* p. 164.

49. Collingwood takes Occam's (Ockham's) principle to be 'Entia non sunt multiplicanda praeter necessitatem', that is, 'Entities are not to be multiplied without necessity', *NL,* 5.39.

50. Collingwood, 'Lectures on Moral Philosophy for M-T 1921', p. 37.

51. Collingwood, *Principles of Art,* p. 175.

52. Quoting from Hobbes's *Leviathan,* p. 4.

53. Hobbes, *Leviathan,* p. 25. Collingwood cites page 35, but this is obviously a misprint, *NL,* 10.21.

54. See Hobbes, *Leviathan,* p. 25., and Spinoza, *Ethics,* trans. Andrew Boyle (London, Dent [Heron Books], 1934), 'Definitions of Emotions', propositions VI and XXXVI.

55. Hobbes, *Leviathan,* p. 24, and Spinoza, *Ethics,* book III, proposition IX.

56. R. G. Collingwood, 'Fragment on Epistemology and Action', DEP 16, p. 1. Undated.

57. Collingwood, 'Action', 1927 conclusion, pp. 62–66.

58. Collingwood, 'Economics as a Philosophical Science', pp. 165–166.
59. Collingwood, *Principles of Art*, p. 161.
60. Ibid., pp. 228–231. In *The New Leviathan* Collingwood refers to the psychical level of experience as that of bodily feelings, where body is used in its psychological rather than physical, chemical, or physiological senses. See *NL*, 3.13–3.2.
61. Collingwood, *Principles of Art*, p. 215.
62. Collingwood, *Speculum Mentis*, p. 61.
63. Ibid., p. 61.
64. Ibid., p. 58.
65. Ibid., p. 65.
66. Ibid., p. 107.
67. Collingwood, *Outlines of a Philosophy of Art*, reprinted in *Essays in the Philosophy of Art*, ed. Donagan, p. 55.
68. R. G. Collingwood, 'Aesthetic' in *The Mind*, ed. R. J. S. McDowall (London, Longmans, 1927), p. 240.
69. Collingwood, *Principles of Art*, pp. 217–220, 251, 282, 285, and 336.
70. R. G. Collingwood, [Fairy Tales] D, 'IV Magic', DEP 21, p. 16.
71. Collingwood, *Principles of Art*, p. 65.
72. Ibid., p. 69.
73. Collingwood, [Fairy Tales] D, 'IV Magic', p. 21.
74. Collingwood, *Principles of Art*, p. 76.
75. Collingwood, 'Lectures on Moral Philosophy' [1933], p. 125.
76. Ibid.
77. Ibid., p. 126.
78. Ibid.
79. Collingwood, *Speculum Mentis*, chapter 3; Collingwood, *Outlines of a Philosophy of Art*; R. G. Collingwood, 'Plato's Philosophy of Art', *Mind*, 34 (1925); R. G. Collingwood, 'The Place of Art in Education', *Hibbert Journal*, 24 (1926); Collingwood, 'Aesthetic', in *The Mind*, ed. McDowall; R. G. Collingwood, 'Form and Content in Art', *Journal of Philosophical Studies*, 4 (1929); Collingwood, *Principles of Art*. In addition, Collingwood wrote many reviews of books on aesthetics, as well as lectures and unpublished papers on many aspects of the philosophy of art.
80. Collingwood, *Principles of Art*, p. 225.
81. Ibid., p. 231.
82. Ibid., p. 247. The account I have given of Collingwood's theory is based upon pp. 225–247.
83. Ibid., p. 252.
84. Donagan, *Later Philosophy of Collingwood*, p. 14.
85. Collingwood, *Principles of Art*, pp. 266–267.
86. See W. Dilthey, *Selected Writings*, ed. H. P. Rickman (Cambridge, Cambridge University Press, 1976), p. 231; Vico, *The New Science*, especially book III, 'The Discovery of the True Homer', pp. 245–282. Also see B. A. Haddock, 'Vico's "Discovery of the True Homer": A Case Study in Historical Reconstruction', *Journal of the History of Ideas*, 40 (1979).

87. Croce, *Logic,* pp. 112–113. The contextual understanding of language was also strongly emphasized in the writings of the British idealists.

88. Ludwig Wittgenstein, *Philosophical Investigations,* trans. G. E. M. Anscombe (Oxford, Blackwell Publisher, 1978), p. 20e, par. 43.

89. Collingwood, *Principles of Art,* p. 250.

90. My reason for identifying the manuscript as a draft for *The New Leviathan* is that the manuscript consists of numbered paragraphs – numbered in a way similar to, but not identical with, the numerical system used in *NL.*

91. R. G. Collingwood, 'Observations on Language', DEP 16, pp. 1–2.

92. Collingwood, 'Goodness, Rightness, Utility', pp. 8 and 12, respectively.

93. Collingwood, *Principles of Art,* p. 269.

94. This theory of art is closely allied to those of Gentile and Croce. For an extensive, but irritatingly carping, comparison see Merle E. Brown, *Neo-Idealistic Aesthetics: Croce-Gentile-Collingwood* (Detroit, Wayne State University, 1966).

95. Collingwood, *Principles of Art,* p. 226.

96. R. M. Martin, 'On the Semantics of Hobbes', in *Hobbes's Leviathan: Interpretation and Criticism,* ed. B. H. Baumrin (California, Wadsworth, 1969), pp. 127–134. First published in *Philosophy and Phenomenological Research,* 14, 2 (1953).

97. Terence Ball, 'Hobbes' Linguistic Turn', *Polity,* 17 (1985), p. 758. Also see Geraint Parry, 'Performance Utterances and Obligation in Hobbes', *Philosophical Quarterly,* 17 (1967); and David R. Bell, 'What Hobbes Does with Words', *Philosophical Quarterly,* 19 (1969).

98. Hobbes, *Leviathan,* p. 27.

99. Collingwood, although presumably familiar with *The Elements of Law,* did not point out Hobbes's sensitivity to the problems of interpreting meaning. Indeed, Hobbes, like Collingwood, was a contextualist. Hobbes says, for example, 'Though words be the signs we have of one another's opinions and intentions; yet, because the equivocation of them is so frequent according to the diversity of contexture, and of the company wherewith they go (which the presence of him that speaketh, our insight of his actions, and conjecture of his intentions, must help to discharge us of): it must be extreme hard to find out the opinions and meanings of those men that are gone from us long ago, and have left us no other signification thereof but their books; which cannot possibly be understood without history enough to discover those aforementioned circumstances, and also without great prudence to observe them'. T. Hobbes, *The Elements of Law,* ed. M. M. Goldsmith (New York, Barnes and Noble, 1969: 2nd ed.), p. 68, sec. 8. I am indebted to W. H. Greenleaf's article 'Hobbes: The Problem of Interpretation', in *Hobbes and Rousseau,* ed. M. Cranston and R. Peters (New York, Doubleday, 1972), p. 29, for directing me to this passage.

Chapter 5

1. Joad, 'Appeal to Philosophers', pp. 401–417.
2. Lewis, 'Is There a Social Contract? – II', p. 181.

3. It is interesting that Green also believed that the same thinkers, with the addition of Spinoza, provide the starting point for new developments in political theory. T. H. Green, *Lectures on the Principles of Political Obligation*, chapters B, C, D, and E. Collingwood's list of thinkers would have been exactly the same as Green's had not the former omitted Spinoza on the grounds that the *Tractatus Politicus* was only a fragment. See *NL,* p. 247, fn. 1. Lewis himself discusses Green's lectures and may have been in sympathy with Green's implicit endorsement of Hobbes, Locke, and Rousseau as the thinkers to whom to return in any attempt to formulate a new political theory.

4. Ernest Barker was quick to point out that this was not a common view of Hobbes. Clarendon, Barker points out, took the opposite view: Hobbes 'spent too much time in thinking, and too little in exercising those thoughts in the company of other Men of the same or of as good faculties'. 'Man and Society', p. 162. See *NL,* 31.55 and 32.71.

5. Collingwood, *NL,* 31.61, 31.8–31.93, 32.16, and 32.2.

6. Collingwood always viewed the social contract as a mythological device for explaining how society arises out of the condition of nonsociality. See, for example, 'Lectures on Moral Philosophy for M-T 1921', pp. 102–103, and 'Notes on HISTORIOGRAPHY', p. 10. 'The desire for an account of absolute beginnings is a desire not for history but for *myth.* Examples: Livy and the origin of Rome. Hobbes and the origin of Civil Society'. Collingwood wrote this on 17 January 1939.

7. R. G. Collingwood, letter to de Ruggiero, dated 2 September 1926, DEP 27. In a letter dated 4 October 1927, Collingwood warns de Ruggiero, 'Your conception of an idealistic liberalism will find, I think, very few favourable readers. It will remind people of Green, and Green is out of fashion – today the fashionable colour is red'.

8. De Ruggiero, *History of European Liberalism,* p. 32. Cf. p. 354, where he says, 'We . . . are profoundly convinced that men are not born free but become free. This applies both to the life of the individual and to the historical life of humanity'.

9. Hobbes's warning of the danger of regression was something that struck a chord in Collingwood's mind quite early in his career. At the top of page 79 in his copy of the Routledge edition of the *Leviathan,* Collingwood noted that ' "natural condition" is for H – less a *past state* than a *present danger'.* On the following page Collingwood marked the passage which refers to the three principal causes of quarrels in the state of nature, namely, competition, diffidence, and glory. In *The New Leviathan* Collingwood gives special significance to this passage because it at once gives an account of the hindrances to the achievement of a social life, and the reasons why the conversion process may be reversed (*NL,* 32.57–32.69).

10. R. G. Collingwood, 'The Three Laws of Politics', L. T. Hobhouse Memorial Trust Lectures, no. 11 (London, Oxford University Press, [Milford], 1942), p. 3.

11. Collingwood, *NL,* 20.1–20.22, 20.61–20.62, and 20.9–20.94.

12. R. G. Collingwood, 'Rule-making and Rule-Breaking', sermon preached in St. Mary's the Virgin's Church, Oxford, 5 May 1935. DEP 1, p. 10. Andrew Vincent has suggested to me that this view is similar to that of Hegel in *Encyclopaedia*

of the Philosophical Sciences and the introduction to *The Philosophy of Right.*

13. Bellamy, *Modern Italian Social Theory,* p. 104.
14. Croce, *Politics and Morals,* p. 100.
15. Ibid., p. 104.
16. Ibid., pp. 105–106. Essentially Croce feared communism and the authoritarian brands of socialism. Socialism, as it had arisen within a democratic context, was for the most part compatible with liberalism, and, indeed, was being converted into liberalism. Take, for example, his view of English socialism: 'No attempt was ever made in England to persecute or to suppress socialism, nor were grave efforts and much trouble needed to gather it into liberalism, because from the very beginning the problems pertaining to labour were spontaneously incorporated into the framework of English society and politics, and liberals and conservatives busied themselves about them; and left little field to specific socialist activity. Liberal in spirit was also the socialism of the Fabians (1883), as the name itself implies'. Benedetto Croce, *History of Europe in the Nineteenth Century,* trans. Henry Furst (London, Allen and Unwin, 1934), p. 309. Cf. pp. 297, 298, 302, 306, 307, 310, 313.
17. Ibid., p. 313.
18. De Ruggiero, *History of European Liberalism,* p. 351. Croce is, of course, famous for his conception of the 'concept of history as the history of liberty'. See Croce, *History of Europe in the Nineteenth Century,* p. 10. Cf. his view that 'we always tend toward liberty and work for it even when we seem to be working for something else; liberty is realized in every thought and in every action that has the character of truth, poetry and goodness'. Croce, *History as the Story of Liberty,* p. 232.
19. Ibid., pp. 356–359.
20. Guido de Ruggiero, 'Liberalism', *Encyclopaedia of the Social Sciences',* (London, Macmillan, 1933), vol. 9, p. 435.
21. De Ruggiero, *History of European Liberalism,* p. 156.
22. Ibid., p. 369.
23. There are some notable exceptions. Bradley is often believed to be a conservative, but there is very little evidence upon which to base any attribution of political belief. Bosanquet's views are difficult to classify, although he was an active Liberal. On some issues, such as poor law relief, he appears to have been reactionary, but on others his inclinations were more towards socialism. Bosanquet's opposition to too much government interference in poor relief was based upon the idea that such action might impede the development of the freedom of the will. D. G. Ritchie's inclinations were later redirected towards socialism. It should be noted that many of the idealists who were liberals, or should I say New Liberals, could accept and sympathise with much that socialists argued. The former tended to oppose the socialist emphasis upon class struggle, and the tendencies which could lead to authoritarianism.
24. Green, *Lectures on the Principles of Political Obligation,* p. 123.
25. Henry Jones, *The Principles of Citizenship* (London, Macmillan, 1919), pp. 130–131.
26. Henry Jones, *A Faith That Enquires* (London, Macmillan, 1922), p. 290.

27. Henry Jones, *Idealism as a Practical Creed* (Glasgow, Maclehose, 1909), p. 115.
28. L. T. Hobhouse, *The Metaphysical Theory of the State: A Criticism* (London, Allen and Unwin, 1951: first published 1918).
29. L. T. Hobhouse, *Liberalism* (London, Oxford University Press, 1977: first published 1911), p. 71.
30. Hobhouse, *Metaphysical Theory of the State*, p. 60.
31. Ibid., p. 61. It was these aspects of Hobhouse's thought which de Ruggiero admired and sought to make his own. See de Ruggiero, *History of European Liberalism*, pp. 154–155; de Ruggiero, 'Liberalism', p. 441. For a discussion of de Ruggiero and Hobhouse, see Richard Bellamy, 'Idealism and Liberalism in an Italian "New Liberal Theorist": Guido de Ruggiero's *History of European Liberalism*', *Historical Journal*, 30 (1987), pp. 194–199.
32. Cited by Vincent and Plant, *Philosophy, Politics and Citizenship*, p. 74. Hobhouse's idealist elements are highlighted with care and sympathy by Stefan Collini, *Liberalism and Sociology: L. T. Hobhouse and Political Argument in England, 1880–1914* (Cambridge, Cambridge University Press, 1979), esp. chapter 4.
33. Ibid., p. 76.
34. Gerald C. MacCallum, Jr., 'Negative and Positive Freedom', *Philosophical Review*, 76 (1967), pp. 314, 319, 320, and 334.
35. Ibid., p. 320. For a discussion and extension of MacCallum's argument, see William E. Connolly, *The Terms of Political Discourse* (Oxford, Robertson, 1983: 2nd ed.), pp. 143–173.
36. MacCallum, 'Negative and Positive Freedom', p. 328.
37. Collingwood, *Autobiography*, p. 153.
38. De Ruggiero, *History of European Liberalism*, p. 394. Croce, similarly, thought that socialism had made a positive contribution to the advancement of liberalism, particularly in enabling liberalism to escape from its identification in the public mind with economic freedom. Croce, *History of Europe in the Nineteenth Century*, p. 313.
39. Ibid., pp. 156–157. Croce, it is well known, was an admirer of Marx's work, while at the same time maintaining a highly critical stance.
40. Ramsay MacDonald, 'The "Corruption" of the Citizenship of the Working Man: A Reply', *Hibbert Journal*, 10 (1911–1912), p. 361. The reply is in response to Henry Jones, 'The Corruption of the Citizenship of the Working Man', *Hibbert Journal*, 10 (1911–1912). This example was suggested to me by reading Vincent and Plant, *Philosophy, Politics and Citizenship*, p. 79. Cf. Francis Anderson, 'Liberalism and Socialism' (Adelaide, University of Adelaide, 1907), pp. 1–10. 'True and False Socialism' was the subject of a number of Henry Jones's public lectures during his Australian tour of 1908. In Wollongong he argued: 'False socialism tends to weaken the individual ... but true socialism extends his mind and brings out his powers'. Reported in the *Illawara Mercury*, 24 July 1908. In Newcastle Jones contended that 'every true socialistic movement was in itself a deepening of the individual's personality'. Reported in *Newcastle Morning Herald*, 6 August 1908.

41. R. G. Collingwood, 'The Nature and Aims of a Philosophy of History', in *Essays in the Philosophy of History,* ed. Debbins, p. 40. Collingwood consistently held to the view that Marx was a brilliant economic historian, but as a philosopher had made considerable mistakes. See, for instances, Collingwood, *Idea of History,* pp. 122, 126 and 264; and Collingwood, *Essay on Metaphysics,* p. 75. We will examine Collingwood's philosophical criticism of Marx in more detail in the next chapter of this book.

42. Collingwood, *Autobiography,* pp. 152–153.

43. Collingwood, 'Spiritual Basis of Reconstruction', p. 14.

44. Collingwood, 'Political Action', p. 165.

45. Collingwood, 'Spiritual Basis of Reconstruction', p. 14. Also see Collingwood, 'Man Goes Mad', pp. 17–26; and 'Money and Morals', DEP 1, p. 10.

46. R. G. Collingwood, 'Lectures on the History of Philosophy – 1929', DEP 12, p. 20.

47. See, for example, T. M. Knox, 'Collingwood, Robin George', *Dictionary of National Biography: 1941–1950,* p. 170.

48. Collingwood, 'Man goes Mad', p. 27. The effect of liberalism on international politics will be examined in the next chapter.

49. Collingwood, *Autobiography,* chapter 12.

50. Collingwood, 'Fascism and Nazism', pp. 170–171.

51. Ibid., pp. 172 and 173.

52. Collingwood, 'Three Laws of Politics', p. 13.

53. De Ruggiero, *History of European Liberalism,* p. 358.

54. R. G. Collingwood, [Fairy Tales] C, III, 'The Historical Method', DEP 21, p. 3.

55. Collingwood, 'Three Laws of Politics', p. 10.

56. Ibid., p. 5.

57. Ibid., p. 9.

58. Ibid., p. 8, and Collingwood, *NL,* 25.8.

59. Collingwood, 'Three Laws of Politics', pp. 16–17.

60. Ibid., p. 22.

61. Ibid., p. 21.

62. Collingwood, *NL,* 25.83–25.85. Cf. 27.74–27.75.

63. Cf. Ibid., 21.62–21.72.

64. Croce, *Philosophy of the Practical,* p. 132.

65. Croce, *Politics and Morals,* p. 83.

66. For a very interesting and perceptive examination of Green's criteria for invoking the state in promoting legislation in removing hindrances to making the best of one's life, see Peter P. Nicholson, 'T. H. Green and State Action: Liquor Legislation', *History of Political Thought,* 6 (1985), pp. 517–550.

67. It is unnecessary to trace Collingwood's historical substantiation of this point. He finds the Greeks, the Romans, the Roman Empire, feudal governments, and even French revolutionaries subscribing to aristocratic and democratic principles. The Latin term *populus,* the Greek *demos,* and the English *people,* Collingwood suggests, when used correctly, always had aristocratic undertones. *NL,* 26.5.

68. Collingwood, 'Man Goes Mad', pp. 16 and 25.
69. De Ruggiero, *History of European Liberalism,* p. 361.
70. Ibid.
71. Croce, *History of Europe in the Nineteenth Century,* p. 320; Collingwood, *NL,* 28.2; de Ruggiero, *History of European Liberalism,* p. 365.
72. Collingwood, translator's preface to de Ruggiero, *History of European Liberalism,* pp. vii–viii.

Chapter 6

1. Collingwood, 'Political Action', p. 153.
2. Croce, *Politics and Morals,* pp. 9–10.
3. R. G. Collingwood, 'Outlines of a Concept of the State', DEP 24, p. 1.
4. Collingwood, 'Lectures on Moral Philosophy' [1933], p. 99.
5. Ibid. Cf. Collingwood, 'Moral Philosophy Lectures' [1929], p. 107.
6. Ibid., p. 108.
7. Collingwood, 'Lectures on Moral Philosophy' [1933], p. 99.
8. Collingwood, 'Political Action', p. 156.
9. Collingwood, 'Moral Philosophy Lectures' [1929], p. 107.
10. Collingwood, 'Three Laws of Politics', pp. 14–15; and Collingwood, 'Political Action', p. 157.
11. Collingwood, 'Moral Philosophy Lectures', [1929], p. 128. Elsewhere he suggests that the state is 'pure-act'. 'Outlines of a Concept of the State', p. 1.
12. Collingwood, 'Rule-Making and Rule-Breaking', p. 10.
13. Collingwood, 'Moral Philosophy Lectures' [1929], p. 128.
14. R. G. Collingwood, 'Stray Notes on Ethical Questions', 1928. DEP 6, p. 30. Cf. Collingwood's statement that 'the business of rules is to make action regular, orderly, law-abiding. . . . The relation of rules to their instances lies at the base of the science of politics, which, as a philosophical and not an empirical science is the pure theory of law and order, that is, the theory of the relation between the universal element in action, the rule, and the particular element, obedience to the rule'. Collingwood, 'The Good, the Right, and the Useful', p. 17.
      It needs to be reemphasized at this point that the different forms of goodness are not coordinate species of a genus. Goodness is 'a whole consisting of these (and perhaps other) parts. Hence none of the parts can exist without the rest'. 'Moral Philosophy Lectures' [1932?], p. 64.
15. Collingwood, 'Political Action', p. 163.
16. Collingwood, 'Lectures on Moral Philosophy' [1933], p. 100.
17. Collingwood, 'Stray Notes on Ethical Questions', p. 30.
18. R. G. Collingwood, 'Notes towards a Theory of Politics as a Philosophical Science', DEP 24, par. 7.
19. Collingwood, 'Stray Notes on Ethical Questions', p. 32.
20. Collingwood, 'Lectures on Moral Philosophy' [1933], p. 100. This argument was probably inserted later, about 1939.
21. Collingwood, 'Political Action', p. 159.
22. Collingwood, 'Economics as a Philosophical Science', p. 175.
23. Collingwood, 'The Good, the Right, and the Useful', p. 18.

24. Collingwood, 'Moral Philosophy Lectures' [1932?], p. 105; Collingwood, 'Moral Philosophy Lectures'[1929], pp. 95 and 142; and Collingwood, 'Goodness, Rightness, Utility', p. 34.

25. Collingwood, 'Stray Notes on Ethical Questions', p. 28.

26. Collingwood, 'Lectures on Moral Philosophy' [1933], p. 99.

27. Collingwood, 'Political Action', p. 162.

28. Collingwood, 'Economics as a Philosophical Science', p. 176.

29. C. F. G. Masterman, *The New Liberalism* (London, Parsons, 1920), p. 131.

30. I will explore this ideal of civilization in detail in the following chapters.

31. In an early manuscript Collingwood contends that state action may be justified, in some instances, on both moral and political grounds. The practice which is common in finance and business, he argues, of buying up all of a commodity in one market and charging what price one likes in another is an indication that economics alone is not a very good guide to practical life. It is ethically wrong because payment is being received for services not rendered. It is politically wrong because such malpractices diminish the wealth of the state: 'and therefore if anyone chooses to say "my conscience does not object to my making profits of this kind" the state ought to reply "if your conscience doesn't prevent you, I shall prevent you by putting you in prison" '. Collingwood 'Money and Morals', p. 10. Such considerations were later replaced by the principle of orderliness. If such economic practices are not conducive to good order in the state, they should be regulated.

32. Collingwood, 'Moral Philosophy Lectures' [1929], p. 107.

33. Ibid.

34. Ibid., p. 111.

35. Ibid., p. 107.

36. Collingwood, *Principles of Art,* pp. 78 and 85.

37. R. G. Collingwood, manuscript notes on MacIver, *The Modern State.* Unnumbered pages (pp. 17), with references to the pages of MacIver's book. The quotation appears in a discussion of p. 149. DEP 20. Cf. Collingwood, 'Political Action', p. 174.

38. H. L. A. Hart, *Punishment and Responsibility: Essays in the Philosophy of Law* (Oxford, Oxford University Press [Clarendon Press], 1973), pp. 2–3.

39. Green, *Lectures on the Principles of Political Obligation,* pp. 181, 189, and 204; F. H. Bradley, 'Some Remarks on Punishment', in *Collected Essays* (New York, Books for Libraries Press, 1968), pp. 149–164; and, Bosanquet, *Philosophical Theory of the State,* p. 205. Bosanquet, for example, suggests that punishment is the reaction of a community against an act which has offended it. To attempt to characterise the 'collective sentiment' of the reaction in terms of one principle would be idle. He argues that 'an Aggression is *ipso facto* a sign of character, an injury, and a menace; and the reaction against it is equally *ipso facto* an attempt to affect character, a retaliation against an injury, and a deterrent or preventive against a menace.... A consideration of each of these aspects is necessary to do justice both to the theories and to the facts'. Ibid. Cf. p. 212.

40. Collingwood, 'Lectures on Moral Philosophy' [1929], p. 114.

41. Hart, *Punishment and Responsibility,* p. 4.

42. Collingwood, 'Lectures on Moral Philosophy' [1929], p. 115.
43. Collingwood, 'Stray Notes on Ethical Questions', p. 42.
44. Collingwood, *Religion and Philosophy,* p. 178.
45. Collingwood, 'Lectures on Moral Philosophy' [1929], p. 121.
46. Collingwood, *Philosophy and Religion,* p. 172. Cf. Collingwood, 'Lectures on Moral Philosophy' [1929], pp. 113–114.
47. Green, *Lectures on the Principles of Political Obligation,* p. 186; and, Bosanquet, *Philosophical Theory of the State,* pp. 207 and 212.
48. Collingwood, 'Stray Notes on Ethical Questions', p. 38.
49. Ibid., p. 40.
50. Ibid., p. 30.
51. Collingwood, *Religion and Philosophy,* p. 171.
52. Collingwood, 'Action', p. 71.
53. Collingwood, 'Stray Notes on Ethical Questions', pp. 8, 19, and 24. Cf. Collingwood, *Religion and Philosophy,* p. 172. Also see Bosanquet, who suggests that 'the general or social indignation is not the same as the selfish desire for revenge', *Philosophical Theory of the State,* p. 211; and Green, *Lectures on the Principles of Political Obligation,* pp. 181–184.
54. Collingwood, 'Moral Philosophy Lectures' [1929], p. 113.
55. Green, *Lectures on the Principles of Political Obligation,* p. 180.
56. Collingwood, 'Stray Notes on Ethical Questions', p. 24.
57. Collingwood, 'Moral Philosophy Lectures' [1929], p. 120.
58. Collingwood, 'Stray Notes on Ethical Questions', p. 28.
59. Collingwood, *Religion and Philosophy,* p. 177.
60. Collingwood, 'Stray Notes on Ethical Questions', p. 33.
61. Green, *Lectures on the Principles of Political Obligation,* p. 202; Collingwood, 'Moral Philosophy Lectures' [1929], p. 116. Collingwood says, 'Moral guilt as such slips between the fingers of the law-courts'.
62. Green, *Lectures on the Principles of Political Obligation,* p. 202.
63. Collingwood, 'Stray Notes on Ethical Questions', p. 30.
64. Collingwood, 'Moral Philosophy Lectures' [1929], pp. 117–118.
65. Collingwood, 'Stray Notes on Ethical Questions', p. 33.
66. Green, *Lectures on the Principles of Political Obligation,* p. 192.
67. Collingwood, 'Moral Philosophy Lectures' [1929], p. 116.
68. Ibid., p. 123.
69. Collingwood, *Religion and Philosophy,* p. 179.
70. Collingwood, 'Moral Philosophy Lectures' [1929], p. 114.
71. Ibid., p. 112.
72. Green, *Lectures on the Principles of Political Obligation,* pp. 185 and 187.
73. Immanuel Kant, 'The Right to Punish', in *Punishment and Rehabilitation,* ed. Jeffrie G. Murphy (Belmont, Calif., Wadsworth, 1973), p. 35. Kant says, 'Judicial punishment can never be used merely as a means to promote some other good for the criminal himself or for civil society, but instead it must in all cases be imposed on him only on the grounds that he has committed a crime'. Also see Howard Williams, *Kant's Political Philosophy* (Oxford, Blackwell Publisher, 1983), pp. 97–109.
74. Collingwood, 'Moral Philosophy Lectures' [1929], p. 114.

75. Collingwood, 'Stray Notes on Ethical Questions', p. 38.
76. Collingwood, *Speculum Mentis,* p. 226.
77. Bradley, *Collected Essays,* p. 153.
78. Collingwood, 'Stray Notes on Ethical Questions', p. 45.
79. Kant, 'Right to Punish', pp. 35–39.
80. Collingwood, *Religion and Philosophy,* p. 174.
81. Collingwood, 'Stray Notes on Ethical Questions', p. 37.
82. Collingwood, 'Moral Philosophy Lectures' [1929], p. 123. Cf. the idea that to punish with a word 'is, perhaps, a better and more civilized form of punishment; it indicates a higher degree of intelligence and a more delicate social organisation'. Collingwood, *Religion and Philosophy,* p. 178.
83. Green, *Lectures on the Principles of Political Obligation,* p. 189. The system of rights itself acts as a constraint on the degree of punishment.
84. Collingwood, 'Stray Notes on Ethical Questions', p. 37.
85. Collingwood, 'Moral Philosophy Lectures' [1929], p. 124.
86. This is a view which Collingwood promotes in 'The Spiritual Basis of Reconstruction', p. 8.
87. Collingwood, 'Moral Philosophy Lectures' [1929], p. 123.
88. Hobbes, *Leviathan,* p. 96.
89. Collingwood, 'Action', p. 71.
90. R. G. Collingwood, 'War in Its Relation to Christian Ethics with Special Reference to the Lambeth Report, 1930', written 1932. DEP 1, p. 4.
91. Ibid.
92. Collingwood, 'Man Goes Mad, p. 16. Cf. de Ruggiero, *History of European Liberalism,* pp. 362 and 442. In the latter of the two references de Ruggiero says of liberalism, 'Its nature, a nature strictly dialectical, draws nourishment from all oppositions, from discord no less than concord, dissent no less than consent'.
93. R. G. Collingwood, 'The Breakdown of Liberalism', DEP 24, p. 2
94. Collingwood, 'Man Goes Mad', p. 27.
95. Croce, *History of Europe in the Nineteenth Century,* p. 325.
96. Collingwood, 'Man Goes Mad', p. 26.
97. Ibid., p. 7.
98. See John Morrow, 'British Idealism, "German Philosophy" and the First World War', *Australian Journal of Politics and History,* 28 (1982), pp. 380–390.
99. Hobhouse, *Metaphysical Theory of the State,* p. 6.
100. Ibid., p. 24.
101. Ibid., pp. 24, 83, 96, 116, 118, 119–125.
102. Joseph Kennedy, in an address celebrating Thanksgiving Day. Reported in the *London Times,* 25 November 1938, p. 16, col. c.
103. T. M. Knox, 'Hegel and Prussianism', *Philosophy,* 15 (1940), pp. 62–63.
104. E. F. Carritt, 'Hegel and Prussianism', *Philosophy,* 15 (1940), p. 194. Also see the responses and replies, pp. 219–220 and 313–317. Another interesting article written during this period was D. A. Routh, 'The Philosophy of International Relations: T. H. Green versus Hegel', *Politica,* 3 (1938).
105. Knox papers, Ms. 37524/430.
106. Collingwood, 'Spiritual Basis of Reconstruction', p. 10. Cf. Collingwood's

view that, 'Hegel, the greatest philosophical exponent of the protestant mind, wrote of war as the great restorer of a nation's moral health, the wind which blowing over the waters of humanity prevents them from rotting in stagnation'. Collingwood, 'War in Its Relation to Christian Ethics', p. 5.

107. Ibid., p. 9.
108. Collingwood, 'Man Goes Mad', p. 14. Cf. Collingwood, 'Moral Philosophy Lectures' [1929], p. 128.
109. Collingwood, 'Three Laws of Politics', p. 15.
110. Collingwood, 'Moral Philosophy Lectures' [1929], p. 124.
111. Collingwood shared his enthusiasm for the league with many prominent liberals. See Masterman, *New Liberalism,* p. 53. Masterman says, 'The League, and again the League, and always the League; in this may be summed up the foreign policy of the New Liberalism'.
112. Collingwood, 'Spiritual Basis of Reconstruction', pp. 13, 14, and 15. Also see Collingwood, 'Political Action', p. 175: 'There is no more reason why the state should resist inclusion in a League of Nations without, than why it should suppress associations within'.
113. Collingwood, 'War in Its relation to Christian Ethics', p. 10.
114. Immanuel Kant, *Perpetual Peace: A Philosophical Essay,* reprinted in *The Theory of International Relations,* ed. M. G. Forsyth, H. M. A. Keens-Soper, and P. Savigear (London, Allen and Unwin, 1970), pp. 200–258.
115. Collingwood, *Autobiography,* p. 163.
116. Knox says that Collingwood 'felt so strongly about the policy of appeasement that he went to the headquarters of the Labour Party and begged its leaders to oppose that policy with all their strength'. Knox, review of W. M. Johnston, *Formative Years of R. G. Collingwood,* p. 166. Furthermore, Collingwood sent a letter of support to A. D. Lindsay, who stood as a nonpartisan anti-appeasement candidate against Quentin Hogg in the Oxford by-election of 1938. Drusilla Scott, *A. D. Lindsay: A Biography* (Oxford, Blackwell Publisher, 1971), p. 251.
117. Collingwood, *First Mate's Log,* p. 74.
118. Ibid., p. 173. Cf. Collingwood, 'Fascism and Nazism', p. 173. He did, however, doubt whether democracy had the energy and enthusiasm to defeat fascism and nazism. This issue will be discussed in the following chapter.
119. These later ideas of Collingwood are at variance with what Peter Nicholson has called the 'cosmopolitan' tendency in idealism. Idealists like Green, Bradley, and Bosanquet appear to acknowledge the possibility of a more rational organization of states, or even of their supersession in a world society with a single common morality. On the principle that nothing can be denied its place in the whole, they had to theorize the place of war, as a given fact, in experience as a whole, but this did not commit them to the view that war could not be abolished. See Peter P. Nicholson, 'Philosophical Idealism and International Politics: A Reply to Dr. Savigear', *British Journal of International Studies,* 2 (1976), pp. 76–83.
120. The idea of a just war is a principle which Collingwood always condoned. In agreement with Saint Thomas Aquinas, Collingwood says, 'The ideas of just cause and right intention throw the onus of justifying every war on the

conscience of the parties concerned: and it is a far more effective appeal than the distinction between offensive and defensive war, which is fatally popular nowadays – fatally because every belligerent can always claim with some show of justice, that he is acting in self-defense'. Collingwood, 'War in Its Relation to Christian Ethics', p. 3.

121. Edmund Burke, *Works: Letters on a Regicide Peace,* vol. 6 (London, Oxford University Press, [Henry Frowde], 1907), pp. 159–160.

Chapter 7

1. Barker, 'Man and Society', p. 162.
2. Donagan, *Later Philosophy of R. G. Collingwood,* p. vii.
3. Ibid., pp. 298 and 305. In addition, the influential books by Mink and Rubinoff fail to incorporate Collingwood's theory of civilization, as expounded in *The New Leviathan,* into their interpretations. The omission is all the more surprising in Mink's case in view of the fact that he devotes a chapter to 'The Rhetoric of Civilization: Art'. In the volume of essays edited by Krausz, only A. J. M. Milne gives brief consideration to part III of *The New Leviathan.* See Mink, *Mind, History and Dialectic;* Rubinoff, *Collingwood and the Reform of Metaphysics;* Krausz, *Critical Essays on the Philosophy of R. G. Collingwood.*
4. Lewis H. Morgan, *Ancient Society* (Cambridge, Mass. Harvard University Press [Belknap Press], 1964: originally published 1877), and Edward B. Tylor, *Primitive Culture: Researches into the Development of Mythology, Philosophy, Religion, Art, and Custom* (New York, Gordon, 1974: First published 1871), vols. 1 and 2. Also see F. C. Müller-Lyer, *History of Social Development* (New York, Knopf, 1921).
5. Scott Nearing, *Where Is Civilization Going?* (New York, Vanguard Press, 1927), pp. 4 and 6. Such a categorization of stages of culture was also prevalent in France. Even before the substantive noun *civilization* appeared in the French vocabulary, French writers classified societies in terms of a hierarchical scale. At the bottom of the scale came *sauvages;* a little above them came *barbares,* followed by peoples who were in possession of *civilité, politesse,* and good *police,* that is, good government, administration, and laws. Subsequently, with the invention of the substantive noun 'at the top of the great ladder whose bottom rungs were occupied by savagery and whose middle rungs were occupied by barbarity, *"civilisation"* took its place quite naturally at the same point where *"police"* had reigned supreme before it'. Lucien Febvre, '*Civilisation:* Evolution of a Word and a Group of Ideas', in *A New Kind of History from the Writings of Febvre,* ed. Peter Burke, trans. K. Folca (London, Routledge, 1973), p. 232. The essay was first published in French in 1930.
6. See Leslie A. White's introduction to *Ancient Society* by Lewis H. Morgan, pp. xxxii, xxxix, and xl.
7. F. Engels, *Origin of the Family,* p. 26. Quoted in Morgan, *Ancient Society,* p. xxxv.
8. Edward Carpenter, *Civilization: Its Causes and Cure, and Other Essays* (London, Swann Sonnenschein, 1910), p. 49. Morgan is quoted and discussed

on pages 30–31. Both Scott Nearing and F. C. Müller–Lyer discuss a new social order, or fourth stage of human development, occurring after that of civilization.

9. Morgan, *Ancient Society*, p. 14.

10. Tylor, *Primitive Culture*, p. 34. Morgan maintains that 'as it is undeniable that portions of the human family have existed in a state of savagery, other portions in a state of barbarism, and still other portions in a state of civilization, it seems equally so that these three distinct conditions are connected with each other in a natural as well as necessary sequence of progress', *Ancient Society*, p. 12.

11. Brooks Adams, *The Law of Civilization and Decay: An Essay on History* (New York, Knopf, 1943: first published 1896). For an excellent summary of Adams's theory and its reception, see Charles A. Beard's introduction, pp. 30–53.

12. Oswald Spengler, *The Decline of the West*, vol. 1: *Form and Actuality*, and vol. 2: *Perspectives on World History* (London, Allen and Unwin, 1918 and 1922, respectively).

13. Ibid., vol. 1, p. 36.

14. R. G. Collingwood, 'Oswald Spengler and the Theory of Historical Cycles' (first published 1927) and 'The Theory of Historical Cycles' (first published 1927), in *Essays in the Philosophy of History*, ed. Debbins, pp. 57–75 and 76–89; Collingwood, 'Toynbee' and 'Spengler' in *Idea of History*, pp. 159–165 and 181–183.

15. Collingwood, 'Oswald Spengler', p. 71. In *An Essay on Metaphysics*, Collingwood contemptuously dismisses Spengler in the following manner: 'If Oswald Spengler, who was so much talked about a few years ago, is today deservedly forgotten, it is because whenever he set himself to describe a constellation of historical facts (what he called a 'culture') he deliberately ironed all the strains out of it and presented a picture in which every detail fitted into every other as placidly as the pieces of a jig-saw puzzle lying at rest on a table', p. 75.

16. Collingwood, 'Oswald Spengler', p. 67.

17. Collingwood, *Idea of History*, pp. 181–182.

18. Collingwood, 'Oswald Spengler,' pp. 68–69.

19. R. G. Collingwood, [Fairy Tales] 'B, II, Three Methods of Approach: Philological, Functional, Psychological', *DEP* 21, p. 2.

20. Ibid., p. 4.

21. Ibid., p. 10.

22. Ibid., p. 11. The manuscripts in which Collingwood deals with magic, fairy tales, folklore, and folktales are titled 'Folklore 1–8' by van der Dussen, *History as a Science*, pp. 450–451. The content of these manuscripts is described in both van der Dussen, pp. 183–191, and Donald S. Taylor, 'A Bibliography of the Publications and Manuscripts of R. G. Collingwood, with Selective Annotation', pp. 17–21. Both van der Dussen and Taylor, however, give no details of Collingwood's views on the philological approach, and very little of his argument in general.

23. Tylor, *Primitive Culture*, vol. 1, pp. 28 and 143.
24. Ibid., p. 85.
25. Collingwood, [Fairy Tales] 'A', DEP 21, p. 19.
26. Collingwood's criticisms of Tylor and Frazer in *The Principles of Art*, pp. 58–62, are developed from those formulated in the manuscripts on fairy tales.
27. Tylor, *Primitive Culture*, vol. 1, p. 101.
28. Collingwood, *Principles of Art*, p. 58.
29. Ibid., pp. 61 and 58, fn. 1.
30. Ibid., p. 62. Collingwood comments upon the first edition of Lévy-Bruhl's *La Mentalité Primitive: Les Fonctions Mentales dans les Sociétés Inférierures* (1913).
31. C. G. Jung, *Psychology of the Unconscious: A Study of the Transformations and Symbolisms of the Libido. A Contribution to the History of the Evolution of Thought*, trans. Beatrice M. Hinkle (New York, Dodd, Mead, 1965: translation first published 1916), p. 6; cf. Sigmund Freud, *Totem and Taboo: Resemblances between the Psychic Lives of Savages and Neurotics*, trans. A. A. Brill (London, Penguin, 1942: translation first published 1919), p. 36.
32. Jung, *Psychology of the Unconscious*, p. 20.
33. Ibid., p. 22.
34. Ibid., p. 28.
35. Collingwood [Fairy Tales] 'B, II, Three Methods of Approach', p. 48.
36. Collingwood, *Principles of Art*, pp. 62 and 64. In *An Essay on Metaphysics* he says that 'Freud is by common consent the greatest psychologist of the last half-century', p. 118. In 'Aesthetic' Collingwood says, 'Frankly, I regard Freud as one of the greatest men of our age, and his works as almost perfect examples of scientific method and dispassionate analysis', in *The Mind*, ed. McDowall, pp., 236–237.
37. Freud, *Totem and Taboo*, pp. 5–6.
38. Ibid., p. 29.
39. Ibid., p. 36.
40. Ibid., p. 38.
41. Collingwood, [Fairy Tales] 'B, II, Three Methods of Approach', p. 38.
42. Collingwood, *Principles of Art*, p. 64.
43. Collingwood, [Fairy Tales] 'C, III, The Historical Method', p. 3. It should be remarked here that Collingwood tended to ignore Freud's subsidiary concerns in psychoanalysing savages. Every psychological problem, Freud claims, is intrinsically interesting and therefore worthy 'of investigation for its own sake'. The study of the taboos of savages, however, does have a contemporary practical value in so far as 'the moral and customary prohibitions which we ourselves obey may have some essential relation to this primitive taboo, the explanation of which may in the end throw light upon the dark origin of our own "categorical imperative" ', *Totem and Taboo*, p. 33. Freud did, of course, subsequently address himself to the problems of modern civilization *(Kultur)* and explained them in terms of an unresolved tension between our primeval instincts, especially the instinct of aggression, and the constraints

of civilized life. This aggressiveness becomes inhibited by becoming internalized and directed towards one's own ego, where a portion of the ego takes over the aggressive tendency and sets it over, as superego, the remainder of the ego. The superego, as conscience, exerts the same degree of aggression towards the ego as the ego would like to have done in its external relations with other individuals. This tension between the ego and the superego is our sense of guilt, and 'the price we pay for our advance in civilization is a loss of happiness through the heightening of the sense of guilt'. Sigmund Freud, *Civilization and Its Discontents,* trans. James Strachey (New York, Norton, 1961), p. 81. The first German edition was published in 1930 and the second in 1931. The book was published in translation by the Hogarth Press (London) in 1930. For some reason best known to himself Collingwood ignores this book in his examination of Freud.

44. Collingwood, [Fairy Tales] 'C, III, The Historical Method', p. 4.

45. Ibid., p. 20.

46. Ibid., p. 7.

47. Ibid., pp. 3–4.

48. Collingwood, [Fairy Tales] 'A', p. 19.

49. Collingwood, *Principles of Art,* p. 65.

50. Ibid., pp. 68–69.

51. Collingwood, [Fairy Tales] 'D, IV, Magic'.

52. Collingwood, [Fairy Tales] 'A', p. 19.

53. Collingwood, [Fairy Tales] 'C, III, The Historical Method', p. 11.

54. Collingwood, [Fairy Tales] 'D, IV, Magic', p. 15–16. Collingwood's views on our utilitarian civilization will be elaborated in due course, when we come to discuss those factors which are inimical to civilization.

55. Collingwood, [Fairy Tales] 'C, III, The Historical Method', p. 11.

56. R. G. Collingwood, untitled and undated notes on barbarism, DEP 24, p. 3. This fragment was probably written in 1939 or 1940 as a preliminary to the discussion in *The New Leviathan.*

57. Ibid., and R. G. Collingwood, 'What "Civilization" Means', DEP 24. Written about 1939 or 1940.

58. Collingwood, notes on barbarism, p. 1.

59. Febvre, *'Civilisation',* p. 223.

60. Norbert Elias, *The Civilizing Process,* vol. 1: *The Development of Manners,* trans. Edmund Jephcott (New York, Urizen, 1978: first published 1936), p. 4. For a discussion of the development of the idea of civilization across the Atlantic, see Charles and Mary Beard, *The American Spirit: A Study of the Idea of Civilization in the United States* (New York, Macmillan [Collier], 1962: first published 1942).

61. It also had more. Lord Cranborne, for instance, as reported in the *London Times,* 'said that the word civilization had come to have some new and strange meanings in certain other lands. We were told that Italy marched against the Abyssinians purely to civilize them. When they were battered into submission they were dragooned and drilled into a slave army to serve the interests of their conquerors'. 'The Livingstone Spirit', *London Times,* 12 December 1940, p. 6, col. a.

62. Albert Schweitzer, *The Decay and Restoration of Civilization* (London, Black, 1955: first published 1923), p. v.
63. Harold J. Laski, *Nationalism and the Future of Civilization* (London, Watts, 1932), pp. 22 and 25. R. B. Bennet, to give a further illustration, thought that the British Empire was both the custodian and disseminator of civilization. It was the sense of justice in the empire that had enabled it 'to bring civilization to the remotest parts of the world'. Reported in 'Justice and Civilization', *London Times,* 25 May 1939, p. 18, col. d.
64. Paul Valéry, 'The Crisis of the Mind', in *History and Politics,* trans. Denise Folliot and Jackson Mathews (New York, Bollingen Foundation, 1962: essay first published 1919), p. 23.
65. Lord Halifax, reported in the *London Times,* 28 February 1940, p. 9, col. f.
66. Gordon Childe, reported in 'Criticism of B. B. C. Talks: "Heresy" instead of Scientific views', *London Times,* 23 August 1938, p. 12, col. c. The title of Sidney and Beatrice Webb's *Soviet Communism: A New Civilization?* (London, Longmans Green, 1935) also falls into this category of usage (the question mark was omitted in later editions), as does Jacob Burckhardt's *The Civilization of the Renaissance in Italy* (London, Allen and Unwin, 1944; first published 1860).
67. Viscount Samuel, 'Civilization', *Philosophy,* 13 (1938), p. 4.
68. William Ebor, Archbishop of York, et. al., 'Essentials of True Civilization', *London Times,* 26 April 1939, p. 10, col. g.
69. H. N. Spalding, *Civilization in East and West: An Introduction to the Study of Human Progress* (Oxford, Oxford University Press [Milford], 1939), pp. 297–298. Collingwood mentions this book, along with Lord Raglan, *How Came Civilization* (London, Methuen, 1939), in 'What Civilization Means', p. 6. He was not impressed by either book, although he thought the former was marginally better than the latter.
70. Spalding, *Civilization in East and West,* pp. 259–295.
71. Freud, *Civilization and Its Discontents,* p. 69. It is sometimes argued that the German word *Kultur* has slightly different referents to the French *civilisation* and the English *civilization,* but such considerations need not detain us here.
72. Elias, *Development of Manners,* pp. xii–xiii.
73. Collingwood, 'What Civilization Means', pp. 1–2.
74. This is consistent with what he says in 'Observations on Language', p. 1.: 'Words are never used except in a context, and have no meaning except as used'.
75. Collingwood, 'What Civilization Means', p. 1.
76. Ibid., pp. 2–12.
77. Collingwood, *Essay on Philosophical Method,* p. 57.
78. Ibid., p. 64.
79. See ibid., p. 82, for the application of this argument to goodness and wickedness. Cf. *NL,* 34.51.
80. Collingwood, 'What Civilization Means', p. 12.
81. Ibid., p. 14.
82. Ibid.

83. Ibid., p. 15.

84. Ibid., p. 16.

85. Ibid., pp. 15–18.

86. Ibid., p. 18.

87. Ibid., p. 21.

88. Ibid., p. 25.

89. The most notorious exponent of what Rubinoff calls the 'radical conversion hypothesis' is Knox, Collingwood's literary executor. Rubinoff, *Collingwood and the Reform of Metaphysics,* p. 23. For Knox's argument see his preface to *The Idea of History,* pp. x–xiii.

90. Rubinoff, *Collingwood and the Reform of Metaphysics,* p. 23.

91. Tariq Modood, 'The Later Collingwood's Alleged Historicism and Relativism', *Journal of the History of Philosophy,* forthcoming. I would like to thank Dr. Modood for letting me see the manuscript of this article. The quotation can also be found in his Ph.D. thesis (Swansea, 1985), p. 376.

92. Collingwood, *Autobiography,* pp. 62–63.

93. Ibid., p. 65.

94. Ibid.

95. R. G. Collingwood, 'The Function of Metaphysics in Civilization', DEP 19, p. 47. Written 1937–1938.

96. Ibid., p. 81.

97. Ibid., p. 48.

98. Collingwood, 'Notes on HISTORIOGRAPHY', pp. 16–17.

99. Van der Dussen, *History as a Science,* p. 360. For the various meanings of the term *historicism,* see my *Texts in Context,* pp. 6–19.

100. Collingwood, *Essay on Philosophical Method,* pp. 11, 100, 161, 163, 164, 168, and 205.

101. Schweitzer expressed a similar view differently when he said, 'Civilization is then twofold in nature: it realizes itself in the supremacy of reason, first, over the forces of nature, and, secondly, over the dispositions of men'. *Philosophy of Civilization,* vol. 1, p. 36.

102. Collingwood, *Principles of Art,* p. 59.

103. R. G. Collingwood, 'Science, Religion and Civilization; the third in a series of lectures under that title delivered in Coventry Cathedral, Oct. Dec. 1930, by Joseph Needham, B. H. Streeter, and R. G. C.', Collingwood ms., DEP 1, p. 6.

104. Collingwood, 'Man Goes Mad', p. 30.

Chapter 8

1. Cf. Diderot, who said, 'Instructing a nation is the same as civilizing it; stifling learning in it means leading it back to the primitive state of barbarity.... Ignorance is the lot of the slave and the savage'. Quoted in Febvre, *'Civilisation:* Evolution of a Word and a Group of Ideas', p. 233.

2. Collingwood, 'Spiritual Basis of Reconstruction', p. 8.

3. Ibid.

4. Collingwood, 'Science, Religion and Civilization', p. 1.

5. Collingwood, *Speculum Mentis,* p. 316.

6. Collingwood, 'Place of Art in Education', p. 443.

7. Collingwood, *Essay on Metaphysics,* p. 135.
8. Collingwood, *Autobiography,* pp. 17 and 48.
9. See Ronald Beiner, *Political Judgment* (London, Methuen, 1983); Hans-Georg Gadamer, *Reason in the Age of Science* (Cambridge, Mass., MIT Press, 1982).
10. See, for instance, T. H. Green, 'Lecture on the Work to be Done by the New Oxford High School for Boys', in *Works,* vol. 3, pp. 456–458. Henry Jones, 'The Education of the Citizen', in *Essays on Literature and Education* (London, Hodder and Stoughton, n.d.: essay first published 1917), pp. 225–281; and *The Principles of Citizenship* (London, Macmillan, 1919), pp. 133–137.
11. T. H. Green, 'Lecture on the Grading of Secondary Schools', in *Works,* vol. 3, p. 390.
12. See Collingwood, 'Notes on HISTORIOGRAPHY'.
13. Collingwood, *Outlines of a Philosophy of Art,* p. 55.
14. Collingwood, 'Place of Art in Education', p. 448. Cf. 'Art and the Machine', p. 14.
15. See Collingwood, *Speculum Mentis,* pp. 58–63; 'Place of Art in Education', pp. 439–443; *Outlines of a Philosophy of Art,* pp. 52–55 and 125–128; and 'Aesthetic', pp. 234–244.
16. Collingwood, 'Aesthetic', p. 238.
17. Collingwood, 'Place of Art in Education', p. 442.
18. Ibid.
19. Ibid.
20. Collingwood, *Principles of Art,* p. 274.
21. Ibid., p. 275.
22. Ibid., pp. 68–69.
23. Ibid., pp. 217–220, 251, 282–285, 336.
24. Ibid., p. 284.
25. Ibid., p. 336.
26. Collingwood, 'Man Goes Mad', p. 31.
27. Ibid., p. 32.
28. Collingwood, 'Art and the Machine', p. 14.
29. Collingwood, 'Science, Religion and Civilization', p. 15.
30. Ibid., p. 16.
31. Collingwood, 'Fascism and Nazism', p. 168.
32. Ibid., p. 176.
33. Collingwood, 'Man Goes Mad', p. 33.
34. Ibid., p. 36.
35. Collingwood, *Essay on Metaphysics,* p. 4.
36. Ibid., p. 134.
37. R. G. Collingwood, 'History as the Understanding of the Present', DEP 16, p. 1.
38. Collingwood, *Idea of History,* pp. 227–228.
39. Collingwood, *Essay on Metaphysics,* p. 41.
40. Ibid., p. 233.
41. See, for example, Julian N. Hartt, 'Metaphysics, History and Civilization: Collingwood's Account of Their Interrelationships', *Journal of Religion,* 33 (1953), p. 206.
42. Collingwood, 'Function of Metaphysics in Civilization', p. 47.

43. Collingwood, 'Notes on HISTORIOGRAPHY' p. 16.
44. Ibid., p. 17.
45. Cf. Louis Wirth, preface to *Ideology and Utopia* by Karl Mannheim (London, Routledge, 1976: first published in English 1936). Wirth argues that those intellectual problems once thought to be the peculiar preoccupation of German thinkers have now engendered 'an extensive literature which speaks of the "end", the "decline", the "crisis", the "decay", or the "death" of Western civilization', p. xiii. Randolph Starn talks of 'the self-styled crisis literature that grew up around the Second World War', 'Historians and "Crisis" ', *Past and Present,* 52 (1971), p. 11.
46. E. H. Carr, *The Twenty Years' Crisis: 1919–1939* (London, Macmillan, 1978: first published 1939).
47. Valéry, 'Crisis of the Mind', p. 23; Mannheim, *Ideology and Utopia,* p. 89; Schweitzer, *Decay and Restoration of Civilization,* p. 1; 'Modern Threat to Civilization', *London Times,* 12 October 1936, p. 9, col. b; Peter F. Drucker, *The End of Economic Man: A Study of the New Totalitarianism* (London, Heinemann, 1939), p. 5. Collingwood, in 'Nazism and Fascism', speaks highly of Drucker's books. See p. 172. Carpenter, *Civilization Its Causes and Cure,* p. 11.
48. Dr. Wilson, quoted in the *London Times,* 'Europe More Savage than for 1,000 Years', 22 March 1938, p. 12, col. f.
49. G. G. Coulton, *Studies in Medieval Thought* (London, Nelson, 1940), p. 9.
50. C. E. M. Joad, quoted in the *London Times,* 'The Perils of Modern Civilization', 17 April 1936, p. 14, col. c.
51. Lord Horder, 'Strain of Modern Civilization', *London Times,* 16 September 1936, p. 6, col. a.
52. Samuel, 'Civilization', p. 16.
53. Archbishop of Canterbury, quoted in the *London Times,* 'Idols of Race and Power', 19 January 1939, p. 17, col. a.
54. Archbishop Temple, quoted in the *London Times,* 27 March 1939, p. 19, col. b. Professor Hilton, at a Foyle's luncheon at Grosvenor House in 1939 devoted to 'a *post-mortem* examination on our civilization', recommended 'a Five-Power Conference in favour of dictators wearing carpet-slippers instead of top-boots'. Quoted in the *London Times,* 'The Shape of Things to Come', 1 February 1939, p. 19, col. c.
55. Collingwood, 'Science, Religion and Civilization', p. 8.
56. Collingwood, *Speculum Mentis,* p. 36.
57. Ibid., p. 22.
58. Ibid., p. 36.
59. Collingwood, 'Notes on HISTORIOGRAPHY', p. 21.
60. Collingwood, [Fairy Tales] 'IV. Magic', p. 15.
61. Collingwood, *Principles of Art,* p. 284.
62. Collingwood, [Fairy Tales] 'IV. Magic', p. 18.
63. Collingwood, *Principles of Art,* p. 69.
64. Collingwood, 'Art and the Machine', p. 9.
65. Ibid., p. 13. Van der Dussen gives no date for this manuscript. Taylor dates it circa 1926, because he claims that 'much of this essay is a version of "The

Place of Art in Education" ', 'A Bibliography', p. 4. James Connelly, in a note attached to the manuscript, dates it 1935 or slightly before. Connelly's dating is, I think, nearer the mark. 'Art and the Machine' is best seen as taking up themes from 'The Place of Art in Education' rather than anticipating them. Indeed, its themes are more closely related to those that appear in *The Principles of Art.*

66. Collingwood, *Principles of Art,* p. 81.
67. Ibid., p. 275.
68. Ibid., p. 95.
69. Ibid., p. 96.
70. Collingwood, 'Man Goes Mad', p. 38. Cf. *The Principles of Art,* pp. 101–104.
71. Collingwood, 'Ruskin's Philosophy', p. 27.
72. Collingwood, 'Fascism and Nazism', p. 169.
73. Collingwood, *Autobiography,* p. 159. Cf. 'Fascism and Nazism', p. 172.
74. Collingwood, 'Fascism and Nazism, p. 176.
75. Collingwood, *Essay on Metaphysics,* p. 197.
76. Ibid., p. 198.
77. Ibid., p. 199.
78. Collingwood, 'Science, Religion and Civilization', p. 13.
79. Collingwood, *Essay on Metaphysics,* p. 46.
80. Ibid., p. 113.
81. See, for example, Collingwood, 'Aesthetic', in *The Mind,* ed. McDowall, pp. 236–237. Collingwood says, 'I hope it will not be thought that I am laughing at, or in any way disparaging, the immensely important fruits of psychological inquiry in the last two generations. On the contrary, I take these results very seriously indeed, and believe that they constitute an infinitely more important series of discoveries than wireless telegraphy, the aeroplane and the internal combustion engine'. In 'Science, Religion and Civilization' he says, 'I fully believe that psychology will learn to minister to diseased minds no less successfully than medicine already ministers to sick bodies', p. 9. Also see Collingwood, *An Autobiography,* p. 95, and R. G. Collingwood, 'Notes towards a Metaphysic' (1933), introduction, A, DEP 8, p. 24. J. D. Mabbott testifies to how seriously Collingwood adhered to the view that it was imperative to have firsthand experience about an activity before subjecting it to theoretical analysis. Mabbott says that Collingwood's 'attitude to psychology was . . . typical of him. Many of my friends were all agog about Freud and his obvious relevance to problems concerning free will and morals. We were content to read "The Interpretation of Dreams" but Collingwood went off and was psychoanalysed – the full fifty-session process – so that he could reflect on something first-hand. I fear it did him serious harm'. John Mabbott, *Oxford Memories* (Oxford, Thornton's, 1986), p. 76.
82. R. G. Collingwood, *'Aristotelis de Anima',* DEP 11, p. 1.
83. Collingwood, *Religion and Philosophy,* p. 39. He is also critical of psychology in 'The Devil', in *Faith and Reason: Essays in the Philosophy of Religion,* ed. Rubinoff (Chicago, University of Chicago Press [Quadrangle Books], 1968), p. 215. Essay first published 1916.
84. Collingwood, 'Aesthetic', pp. 238–239. Cf. *Speculum Mentis:* 'Thought now

294 Notes to pp. 238–243

becomes something that happens and nothing more. It is a mere event, whose claim to be an act of knowledge is ignored. This abstraction of thought from its own truth or falsity is the characteristic mark of the psychology of knowledge', p. 274.

85. R. G. Collingwood, review of *Psychological Types, or the Psychology of Individuation,* by C. G. Jung, *Oxford Magazine,* 41 (1922–1923), p. 426. I am indebted to van der Dussen for this reference, *History as a Science,* p. 428.
86. Collingwood, *Speculum Mentis,* pp. 275–276.
87. Collingwood, *Essay on Metaphysics,* p. 120. Cf. *Autobiography,* pp. 94–95.
88. Collingwood, *Autobiography,* p. 47.
89. S. P. L., review of *Autobiography, Journal of Philosophy,* 35 (1939), pp. 717–718.
90. Collingwood, 'What Civilization Means', pp. 24–25.
91. Cf. Collingwood, 'Three Laws of Politics', pp. 18–20.
92. Collingwood, *Essay on Metaphysics,* p. 343.
93. Alasdair MacIntyre's *After Virtue: A Study in Moral Theory* (London, Duckworth, 1981) may be read as a contribution towards directing ethical theory in the same direction as Collingwood envisaged.
94. See Collingwood, 'Utility, Right and Duty', p. 24.
95. Collingwood, *Autobiography,* pp. 151–152.
96. Collingwood, *Essay on Metaphysics,* p. 343.

Index

absolute action, 55, 92, 93, 104
absolute immanence, 17, 112, 113, 114
act and fact, 112, 113
Adams, B., 197–198
aesthetics, 2–3, 14, 18, 19, 20, 22, 23, 52–53, 132
  and practical life, 52–53
anthropology, 68, 95, 196, 217
  functional, 95, 199, 200–201
  and history, 204–205
  philological, 199–201
  psychological, 199
appeasement, 60, 192, 243
archaeology, 2, 5, 6, 8, 23
aristocracy, *see* democracy
Aristotle, 70, 75, 128, 142
art, 16, 20, 29, 45, 53, 58–59, 84–85, 102, 132, 173, 201, 232, 233, 234–235, 241
  education, 224–226
  and language, 135, 138, 225
  and magic, 133, 225
Austin, J.L., 139
authority, 62, 77, 90–91, 93, 148, 154–155, 158, 162, 178

Ball, T., 139
barbarism, 25, 61, 67, 68, 194, 195, 196, 208–211, 215, 216, 221, 225–226, 233, 240, 242, 257n76
  and civilization, 208–210, 220, 240
  revolt against civilization, 195, 206, 211, 220, 221, 229, 241
Barker, E., 195–196, 276n4
Bellamy, 146, 264n33
Bergson, H., 12, 115
Bernard, C., 53

body politic, 25, 79, 99, 102, 107, 144, 154, 158–165, 167, 168, 178, 183, 186, 189, 191, 192, 193, 195, 221, 222, 243
Bosanquet, B., 9, 10, 12, 16–17, 53, 73–74, 80, 174, 176, 187, 243, 277n23
Boutroux, H.L., 53
Bradley, F.H., 9, 10, 11, 12–13, 20, 53, 73, 80, 100, 106, 174, 181, 187, 214, 228, 277n23
Burke, E., 193

Caird, E., 4, 8, 12, 53
Canterbury, archbishop of, 232
capital punishment, 182–183
caprice, *see* choice
career, 5–6
Carpenter, E., 197
Carr, E.H., 231
Carritt, E.F., 8, 14, 187–188, 242
causa quod (efficient cause), 115, 116
causa sui (self-causing), 112–113, 114, 115
causa ut (final cause), 115, 116
causality, 52, 112–116, 120
  historical sense, 115–116, 272n24
Chamberlain, N., 60
Chelmsford, bishop of, 231
choice, 24, 82, 85, 93, 97–109, 124, 129
  capricious, 82, 85, 86–87, 89, 96, 97, 98, 99, 101, 102, 103, 105, 108, 114, 130, 141, 148, 152, 169, 219, 242
  and freedom, 24, 62, 96, 104–105, 114, 129, 146–147, 154, 159, 164
  and goodness, 89
  rational, 85, 93–94, 96–97, 104, 146, 193, 216, 233

295

and sensation, 130–131
  suppression of, 111, 132, 133, 205,
    225, 232, 233
Engels, F., 197, 214
eristic, 80, 164–165, 191, 195, 230
ethics, 67, 72, 74, 79, 80, 82, 87, 89, 92–
    93, 119, 147, 214, 228–229, 232,
    238, 242
  absolute, 82, 92–93, 94, 95
experience, forms of, 16, 24, 32, 41, 42,
    43, 44, 52, 58, 132, 233
expression, 137
  linguistic, 131–132, 135
  psychic, 131–132, 135, 138

fairy tales, 66, 199, 200, 205
fallacies, 43
  disjunctive, 32
  identified coincidents, 33
  precarious margins, 32, 34, 96
fascism, 24, 56, 58, 60, 142, 147, 153,
    187, 188, 192, 233, 236, 241
feeling, 66, 110, 114, 117, 118, 121, 122–
    124, 135, 140, 225, 238, 240
  and intellect, 131–132, 225, 238
  and language, 138
Fichte, G., 186
Flint, R., 11–12
force, 26, 147, 155, 158, 159, 161, 162–
    163, 175, 215, 216, 219, 221, 229,
    243
forms, scale of, 16, 27, 28–37, 39, 41, 45,
    57, 80, 82, 83–84, 87, 92, 93, 95,
    96, 106, 109, 110–111, 120–121,
    178–179, 215–216, 242
  and civilization, 209–212
Frazer, J.G., 199, 201–202
free will, 25, 95, 96, 103–114, 115, 142,
    144, 145–146, 147, 148, 155, 156–
    157, 159, 160–162, 163, 167, 169,
    178, 189, 190, 195, 219, 221, 222,
    231, 241, 243
freedom, 41, 90, 104, 114, 149, 150–152,
    153, 157, 163, 170, 177–178, 189–
    190, 236, 239
  and choice, 24, 62, 96, 114, 129, 242
  and liberalism, 18, 147, 148, 165
  and society, 25, 91, 146, 148, 149,
    150, 154
Freud, S., 199, 202–203, 208, 287n36,
    n43

Gentile, G., 16, 19, 20, 41, 42, 47, 142
  Collingwood's understanding of, 17
  historical–mindedness, 13, 17, 39
  on history and philosophy, 16, 38, 43–
    45, 112, 114
  and Smith, J.A., 14

theory and practice, 53
theory of mind as pure act, 15–17,
    112, 146
unity of mind, 15, 53
Gladstone, W.E., 163
good, forms of, 30–31, 33, 36, 66, 81, 83–
    84, 85, 88, 95–109, 127, 170, 177,
    242, 254n9
  economic, 30, 55, 88, 95, 97, 99, 103,
    171, 178
  moral, 30, 55, 95, 99, 103, 170, 171,
    176, 178, 179
  political, 30, 55, 95, 99, 100–102, 103,
    170, 171–174, 176, 178, 179, 180,
    182
Gough, W.J., 61
grand theory, 1
Green, T.H., 9, 10, 12, 42, 53, 61, 74, 144,
    148, 149, 150, 163, 174, 176, 177,
    179, 180, 182, 187, 189, 214, 222,
    224, 243, 276n3
Greenleaf, W.H., 264n33
Grimm, J., 199–200

Haldane, J.S., 123
Halifax, Lord, 207
Harris, H.S., 14, 16, 17, 19
Hart, H.L.A., 174–175
Hearnshaw, L.S., 21
Hegel, G.W.F., 3–4, 16, 20, 22, 41, 42, 72,
    80, 82, 83, 84, 91, 109, 120, 186–
    188, 189–191, 214
Heller, A., 1
herd worship, 62, 190
hermeneutics, 2
historical civilization, 54, 196, 227, 228,
    241
historical morality, 54, 90, 91, 107, 196
historical plain method, 11–14, 118, 120
historical relativism, 211–213
historical sciences, 38, 48–49, 214, 227–
    229, 241
history, 29, 38, 68, 94, 111, 114, 141,
    227, 233
  and anthropology, 204–205
  and causation, 115–116, 273n24
  Gentile's view of, 16, 38, 43–45
  highest form of theoretical reason, 56,
    94, 107–108
  and the liquidation of philosophy, 49,
    94
  and mind, 46, 51, 56, 111, 112, 132,
    202–204, 227, 239
  and natural science, 13, 39, 198
  overcoming the dichotomy between
    theory and practice, 51, 196, 204
  as a philosophical mistake, 42, 43
  and philosophy, 16, 21, 24, 27, 37–51,